CHRONOLOGICAL ENCYCLOPÆDIA OF

SOVIET

SINGLE-ENGINED

FIGHTERS

1939-1951

Piston-engines or mixed power-plants
(Studies, projects, prototypes series and variants)

Herbert LÉONARD

Translated from the French by Alan McKay

The three-view line drawings and the detailed cutaway are by the author.
The colour aircraft profiles are by Nicolas Gohin.

HISTOIRE & COLLECTIONS

PREFACE

This book deals only with Soviet single-seat, single-engined fighters and interceptors powered by piston engines, conceived and produced from the beginning of 1939 according to the specifications called 'K' (or 'Kh'). They were ordered by Stalin himself during a conference held in January in the Kremlin which gathered together all high-ranking politicians, soldiers and scientists concerned with the Air Force. Included with the usual 'front-line' fighters are all the projects and studies which were never developed; experimental prototypes and extrapolations of these fighters, such as the models fitted with one (or several) strato-jet, pulse-jet, turbo-compressor (VRDK), rocket-motor; and the projects powered by turbo-jet (s); the sub-variants of these fighters - reconnaissance, light bombing, ground attack, two-seat trainers, and liaison – are also described. At the date of going to press however, the author cannot guarantee that this encyclopaedia is completely exhaustive, since the archives of the former Soviet Union regularly reveal 'surprises' or new discoveries which up to now have remained concealed.

The plans, profiles, partial views and other representations have all been made by the author (except where indicated). To simplify matters, they have not been cluttered up with all sorts of rivets and 'nuts and bolts' where metal parts are shown. Some views (front, above and below) have lost a portion of wing, or aileron; this is for the needs of the page lay-out. In this case the parts which have been removed are identical to those shown on the other side. Sometimes it is the structure of the parts which is shown. In other cases it is the fabric covering which is shown (for example, the topside view of a machine will be shown with the ailerons and the rudder all 'bare' whereas the underside view shows them covered, or vice versa.) Often several different designations were given to the same model of some of the machines described in this book.

This is because these different designations were used in the original documents drawn up by the various producing, testing or administrative organisations before a final designation was officially adopted. As far as Yakovlev fighters were concerned, the type of engine was also added to the version's designation in order to differentiate between them (e.g. Yak-1/M-105P and Yak-1/M-105PA). Finally in some cases, the same official designation was given to several fighter programmes. Thus the 'MiG-7' was used several times because the same designation was attributed to successive programmes when the preceding ones failed or was abandoned.

All the Russian names have been anglicised (where possible) but the author would have the reader know that transliterating or transcribing the sounds of the Russian words is not always easy, especially with the Russian 'e', for example, which is often preceded by the 'y' sound. For instance Gurevich is pronounced Guryevich. But transliterating proper names has to be done with caution. Faced with the problem of transliterating sounds from the written texts, the author has preferred to ignore the sounds which are only suggested and not identified by a letter: several translators and linguists were consulted on this point and all gave the author different opinions. The endings of the patronymics in -ski and – in pose no problems however. On the other hand the Cyrillic 'y' is normally represented by 'u' in English, e.g. Tupolev. (. x. x.) Finally the Russian 'v' is pronounced 'f' in English, but no translator advised the author to use an 'f'; all recommended using the 'v', thus leaving it as it was. It was only the first wave of White Russian *émigrés in France* and sometimes elsewhere following on the Revolution who replaced the 'v' by 'f' and sometimes 'ff'. Finally, the author has made two exceptions when transcribing patronymics in this book: he has kept the names Mikoyan-Gurevich and Yakovlev with their 'y's, without changing them to Mikoian and Iakovlev. This was simply so as not to confuse readers accustomed to the now-accepted international spelling of these two well-known names.

In the text when the author mentions a 'factory', it goes without saying that it is a factory which turns out aircraft (experimental or series), unless otherwise specified, when referring to other items (engines, equipment, etc.).

TRANSLATOR'S NOTE
In order to save space in such a densely-packed volume the term "axial canon" has been used to designate any canon firing through the propeller hub. Likewise "rear decking" is used to express the part of the fuselage between the cockpit and the tail which was often cut away to give the pilot rear and all-round visibility

USUAL ABBREVIATIONS

W: *Wingspan*	**Mw.:** *Max. Take-off Weight*
L: *Length*	**Ms:** *Max. Speed*
Wa: *Wing Area*	**Sc:** *Service Ceiling*
We: *Weight Empty*	**R:** *Range*

Studies, Prototypes and front line Fighters (colour code).

 Preliminary Design or Study

 Flying prototype

 Unfinished prototype

Front Line fighter

Cover drawing by Bruno PAUTIGNY (photographs © RR).

Editing by Denis GANDILHON and Dominique BREFFORT
Design and lay-out by Yann-Erwin ROBERT and Jean-Marie MONGIN,
© Histoire & Collections 2005

ISBN: 2-915239-60-6

Publisher's number: 2-915239

© Histoire & Collections 2005

A book from
HISTOIRE & COLLECTIONS
SA au capital de 182 938, 82 €
5, avenue de la République
F-75541 Paris Cédex 11, France
Telephone (33-1) 40 21 18 20
Fax (33-1) 47 00 51 11
www.histoireetcollections.fr

This book has been designed, typed, laid-out and processed by *Histoire & Collections* an *'le Studio Graphique A & C'* on fully integrated computer equipment. Color separation by the *Studio A & C*

Printed by ZURE, Spain, European Union
June 2005

Lieutenant P.P. Osipov in front of his brand-new LaGG-3 in August 1941. When Operation Barbarossa was launched the units equipped with this fighter were on the eastern border of the USSR and were only transferred to the west during the summer.
(RR)

CONTENTS

FOREWORD
"HOW DID THE SECOND WORLD WAR START"

Lieutenant V.N. Yakovlev, with a tally of 9 kills in one month, poses in front of his LaGG-3 in August 1941.
(RR)

Major Matveyev and several pilots from his squadron in front of a MiG-3 camouflaged with branches, a few miles from the front.
(RR)

The events which caused the world to tear itself apart again in 1939, after a First World War which in the main covered the European Continent, Russia and the Balkans from 1914 to 1918, have been popularised in the history books and all too often hide *"historical details"* which were extremely important in the development of political tension in Europe, reaching a point where they started this second confrontation which this time was truly worldwide.

The Versailles Treaty imposed by the winners on the losers effectively tried to remove Germany from the map of industrialised countries, reducing it to the *"Weimar Republic"*, without any rights to anything and without any heavy industry, either for developing armaments or rebuilding an army over one hundred thousand men which was restricted anyway to the role of «internal policeman».

It was another treaty however which one scarcely comes across in the history books that was the first step in the fateful progression towards WWII: the Treaty of Rapallo. This little port on the Mediterranean, near Genoa, became famous in 1923 because of its "treaty" which was signed under the nose of the rest of the world by two countries which had been repudiated by the rest of Europe: Russia which in the meantime had become the Soviet Union, and which had succeeded in having its revolution and assassinating its Imperial family to which most of the ruling houses of Europe were related by blood; and Germany for «having started a war which it then went and lost». Moreover these two countries had «dared to call for peace» unilaterally, to the detriment of the other belligerent, a year before the war finally ended really.

In 1923, this international conference at Genoa tried to reintegrate the Soviet Union and Germany into the world economic order. But the war reparations were so incredibly high and the political restrictions so severe that the Soviet Union and Germany at the instigation of Chicherin, leading the Russian delegation, ended up by coming up with a bilateral *'modus vivendi'* which did not please the Western Powers. The resulting economic treaty included secret military clauses which allowed Germany to have access to facilities in the USSR to train officers and soldiers, to develop and test combat vectors «which it had no right to dispose of», and for the USSR to benefit from German technological systems «which it needed desperately».

Why, therefore, go back to Rapallo to convince oneself that the hostilities triggered off in 1939 against Poland in theory protected by both France and Great Britain had their roots in this little port? Because the USSR's permission given to Germany «to come to the USSR to recover its military health» galvanised the thirst for revenge of a lot of lost officers and generals whose pride was only equalled by their notion that they had not really lost the war out there on the battlefield which was probably not exactly false when one comes to think about it. But also because at the same time, Adolf Hitler «little Austrian corporal from out of the trenches and failed activist», wrote a book *Mein Kampf* in his prison which marked the spirits of these revenge seekers and breathed into them a renewal of political interest in order to recreate a grand Germany, confident in itself and dominating.

When Europe (and then rest of the world) was only thinking of reducing its strength and arsenals of weapons so as «not to have to go through again what it had just suffered», when the Soviet Union had nothing else to worry about and affirm except its political, social and economic credibility in the eyes of the rest of the world, Germany was looking for ways of getting rid of the shackles imposed by the Ver-

Lavochkin La-5FN piloted by Captain Petr J. Likholetov, from the 159th Fighter Regiment. The plane belonging to this ace (he finished the war with 24 confirmed kills and 6 probables) who was a Hero of the Soviet Union, bears the inscription *"for Vazek and Zhora"*.

sailles Treaty. And the best of them all after many internal political jolts was Adolf Hitler who after many setbacks ended up by imposing his National-Socialist party and his points of view which were themselves very "revolutionary", on a German population which was being crushed under the crushing economic inflation and a catastrophic unemployment rate.

At the same time, the USSR allowed the German military and certain industries to "prepare" the necessary initial programmes, to test them in all impunity and thus to put them into use when the time came. Hitler became Chancellor of the Weimar Republic in 1933 whereas the Soviets benefited from German technology. A year later thanks to the death of the president, Field Marshall Hindenburg, and to an overwhelming plebiscite Hitler was able to make himself *«Führer of the Thousand Year Reich»* coupling the responsibilities of both President and Chancellor. War was no longer far off since nobody among all the politicians of the planet could ignore the premonitory writings of the new master of a consolidated Germany.

The Western Powers let things be and did not intervene in German internal affairs, neither inn those of the USSR whose political regime was considered just as dangerous as the one Hitler was setting up. Nobody budged when the Führer decided to rearm Germany in 1935. Nobody had the courage to counter his desire to reoccupy the Rhineland occupied by the French since the end of WWI (and yet, Hitler had given his officers instructions to turn back *«at the first shot fired by either the Belgians or the French»*). Nobody intervened when the government of the Third Reich annexed Austria in 1937. Nobody interfered when German territorial claims concerning the Sudetenland in Czechoslovakia in 1938 led to that country's break-up and

occupation. And nobody undertook anything "physically" when German troops invaded Poland in 1939 to reduce it within three weeks, thus triggering the Second World War.

So why claim that all that goes back to Rapallo and the Germano-Soviet agreement? Because to get rid of Poland, Germany signed a new Treaty in August 1939 with the USSR which, in accordance with related secret clauses took part in the invasion of Poland attacking its troops from behind.

Moreover, like the rest of the world, the USSR did nothing to counter Hitler's ambitions. Stalin tried to open the USSR's political borders thanks to a new constitution voted in 1936 which «at last» gave him full powers which actually he already possessed. But negotiations with France and Greta Britain regarding military cooperation to contain and isolate Germany exasperated the Soviet Government, the *"bad faith"* of the Western powers was so obvious, pushing *«Stalin into Hitler's arms»* thanks to new common interests: to Hitler the bigger portion of the "Polish cake"; to Stalin, a portion of Finland which up until then had always been supported by Germany. And for both of them, sharing the world, which thank God never took place.

Some may think that this "idea" is daring that the link with Rapallo and the 1939 Treaty is not at all proven, that WWII was nothing but the result of egocentric will of a "madman" in whom his people had complete faith. But *«Western neutrality and its laisser-aller»*, as much towards Germany as the terrifying regime of Stalin, following in Lenin's footsteps in his desire to overwhelm the world with the Communist ideal, the effective cooperation first then underlying between the two countries well and truly had its origins in 1923...

And what if nothing had happened at Rapallo?

5

"FOR A BETTER UNDERSTANDING OF THE REVIVAL OF SOVIET FIGHTERS"

In the spring of 1938, Stalin presided over a meeting of the Central Committee of the Communist Party which gave its findings on the state of the Soviet aircraft industry. He was assisted by members of the Presidium, the Narkomavprom, the Glavaviaprom, the NII VVs, the UVVS and the TsIAM. Russian "fighters" were on the agenda seeing that the aircraft sent to Spain in support of the Republican cause against the Nationalists were being given a hammering by their German counterparts in the *Condor Legion*. Up until then, the Polikarpov I-15 (sesquiplane) and I-16 (monoplane) fighters had won air superiority over anything that was flying around in the Spanish skies; they had also got themselves a serious reputation, as much for their speed and manoeuvrability, as for their firepower. But the advent of new German fighters on the scene in 1937 upset all this. The Soviet planes were outclassed, and Polikarpov's I-16 and Willy Messerschmitt's Bf 109B were compared at length during this meeting. A team from the NII VVS had the opportunity of examining a Messerschmitt captured intact in Spain and shipped to Russia at the end of 1937. The results of the trials showed that in general the I-16 handled and climbed better. But the Bf 109 outclassed it in speed at all altitudes, climbed higher and lost it easily in a dive. In the USSR, nobody was able to give a serious enough analysis of the reasons why the Soviet air force equipment which had been sent to Spain had been so easily outmatched, or to explain how the German aircraft industry had obtained so apparent and "sudden" an ascendancy.

As a general rule, the VVS bosses seemed to be satisfied with the new Type 10 I-16 developed by Polikarpov and with the different variants being finalised for the near future. Moreover the Polikarpov OKB was also working on the development of the new I-180 monoplane fighter which was due to come out in the autumn of 1938. But like other personalities present, Stalin was not taken in. He knew that Messerschmitt would not be happy with just the «B» version of the Bf 109 and would go to a great deal of trouble to perfect his plane. As a result, he decided on a new five-year plan (the third since 1928), once again to stimulate industrial expansion and the building of airframes, engines and aircraft equipment. He had the meeting approve a forward-looking two-phase plan for the development of fighter programmes:

The first was short-term, relatively conservative in outlook and consisted of adapting existing airframes to more powerful 14-cylinder double row radial engines; and the second longer-term one concerning the development of a generation of more modern fighters, powered by 18-cylinder double row radial engines.

Considering his great experience and his reputation as "Fighter King", N.N. Polikarpov was given priority for carrying out the two phases successfully. He sped up finalisation of the I-153 (the sesquiplane with retractable undercarriage based on the original I-15) and started studies on the I-185 monoplane with a fourteen-cylinder engine. At the same time he launched programmes for the I-190 and I-195 sesquiplanes with 18 cylinder engines, derived from the I-153. Unfortunately none of these programmes came to anything and there were no production series; the I-180 under development turned out to be particularly disastrous and deadly, so much so that Polikarpov was sent packing in "semi"-disgrace. Only Stalin's esteem for him prevented him from suffering a worse fate,

allowing him to pursue his work (at the time the USSR had embarked upon a sinister series of purges which lasted from 1937 to 1941).

Polikarpov and a few other builders like Yatsenko and the Borovkov and Florov duo (who were also committed to developing a modern fighter) very quickly felt that there would be difficulties and they were very deeply affected by this. In December 1938, another very secret meeting was held at the Party Headquarters/PCUS; it attempted to review the situation. The comparison between the Bf 109B and the I-16 was brought up again and Stalin had the meeting approve specifications drawn up recently (exactly when remains a «mystery») by the GU VVS, concerning the development of a "front" ("front-line") fighter which was quite obviously modern and which no longer had anything to do with any of the previous programmes. It was based on in-line engines (liquid-cooled Vees), just like the Germans with the Bf 109, the French with the Dewoitine D-520, the British with the Hawker Hurricane and Supermarine *Spitfire* and the Americans with the Bell-P39 and Curtiss P-40.

With the deteriorating politico-military situation in Europe and the end of the Spanish Civil War, Stalin held another meeting in the Kremlin in January 1939. The following were invited to attend:
- V.M. Molotov, Foreign Minister,
- K.E. Voroshilov, Field-Marshall and Defence Minister,
- A.D. Loktyonov, General and Head of the GU VVS,
- M.M. Kaganovich, Head of the NKAP,
- M.N. Shuljenko, Head of the TsAGI,
- A.I. Filine, Head of the NII VVS,
and the heads of:
- the various OKB who were not interned by the purges,
- the various experimental teams,
- the TsIAM,
- the aircraft production and industry factories, etc.

Stalin asked them to give him an in-depth study of the state of the Soviet aircraft industry, to define the new directions and priorities for future combat aircraft, and to define the characteristics of all military types without exception; all this was to be done with the briefest possible delay, given the situation in Europe. In the context of the third Five-Year Plan, he ordered 18 new factories to be built for airframes and engines (the plan was effective from September 1939 only), and decided to take the destiny of Soviet aviation into his own hands. He also approved the NKAP's 1938 recommendation for «another study and production contract attribution policy», allowing autonomous and semi-autonomous brigades (KB) to be created to foster a spirit of competition and emulation for the given programmes, but also to motivate and give more responsibility to all the new young talent, to examine their ideas so as to perfect the specifications or define new ones.

On 11 January, a short while before this meeting, the Ministry of the Defence Industry had been divided up and the *Galavaviaprom* had become the NKAP (*Narodnoi Komissariat Aviatsionnoy Promyshlennosti* or *Narkomaviaprom* - the People's Ministry of Aircraft Industry) under the aegis of Kaganovich, who

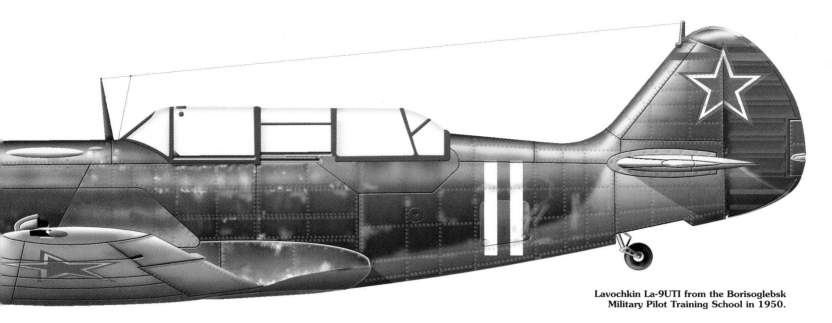

**Lavochkin La-9UTI from the Borisoglebsk
Military Pilot Training School in 1950.**

had been Commissar for the Defence Industry with Ilyushin as his deputy. This restructuring was intended to improve the organisation, management and volume of aircraft production so as to prepare the USSR and the VVSs for possible major conflicts with Germany and Japan, but also with Great Britain whose naval power Stalin greatly feared.

Following the launch of this new Five-Year Plan in September 1939, and after the Defence Committee had given directives to the NKAP on 17 September for the construction or modernisation of the 18 aircraft and engine factories he had ordered (nine of which were set up deep within Russian territory) so that production would increase to 17 000 aircraft per year by 1 July 1941, Stalin sacked Kaganovich and replaced him with A.I. Shakhurin, one of the Party bosses who actually did have experience of the aircraft industry. Shakhurin immediately decided to use seven other factories, which until then had been building civilian aircraft, for military aircraft production with the result that in 1941 there were 24 factories producing aircraft (15 for fighters, nine for bombers) and seven making engines, all working full out to supply the VVS.

These factories were huge industrial complexes at Irkutsk, Kazan, Ulan-Ude, Ufa, Perm, Novosibirsk, Komsomol on Amur (all of them out reach of a potential attack) and Moscow and Leningrad, Kiev, Kharkov and Taganrog (which were the most vulnerable). This production programme was organised very wisely by Shakurin where his immediate entourage was concerned. Experienced and well-tried men became his assistants, people like P.V. Dementyev (Chief-Assistant, ex-manager of Factory N°1); P.A. Voronin for fighter production (ex-works manager of Factory N°1); A.I. Kuznetzov for bomber production; A.A. Zavitayev for aircraft engine production; V.P. Kuznetzov for experimental engine development; A. S Yakovlev, head of the experimental department for aeronautical development; M.V. Khrunochev, responsible for building the factories and supplying them with raw materials and equipment.

The original specifications for the «front» fighters, issued at the end of 1938 and referred to as *K* (often *Kh* in the period documents) specified the use of Klimov M-103 or M-103A liquid-cooled V-12 in-line engines. The specifications were brought up to date after the January 1939 conference and recommended using Klimov M-105 engines (with two TK superchargers) or M-106s.

The specifications required speeds of 385 to 405 mph at 19 800 feet, a range of 500 miles (later increased to 625 miles), a service ceiling of 36 300 to 39 600 feet, a climb to 33 000 feet in 11 minutes maximum and armament comprising one heavy axial BS 12.7-mm machine gun (here Stalin wanted a 20-mm canon) and two light 7.62-mm ShKAS machine guns). After they had submitted their preliminary studies to the government the programme, classified as «urgent», was entrusted to the following builders in particular:
- N.N. Polikarpov who studied the «K», alias I-200 preliminary project from the summer of 1939 onwards: a high altitude fighter.
- the *Lavochkin-Gorbunov-Gudkov* trio who presented their I-301 project in the spring of 1939: a low and medium altitude fighter.
- A.S. Yakovlev who only entered the competition in June 1939, designing the I-26 project: a low and medium altitude fighter.

- the *Mikoyan-Gurevich* duo whom the government entrusted with Polikarpov's I-200 preliminary study while he was absent at the end of 1939, taking part in the delegation sent to Germany to visit the Third Reich's aircraft plants.
- *P.O. Sukhoi* who designed the I-135 (aka Su-1): another high altitude fighter programme starting March 1939.
- *M.M. Pashinin* who developed the I-21 project «during 1939»: a low and medium altitude fighter.

Only the model developed by Sukhoi had a supercharger, the others kept the M-105P without the TK-2 (the P meant that it was possible to install an axial canon between the two banks of cylinders) because the development of the M-106 was causing so many problems. Other builders were invited to take part in the programme but they were not considered as being a «priority», or they were given contracts concerning "experimental" development work, like Moskaliev (SAM-13), Kozlov and Belayev (EOI and "370"), Borovkov-Florov (N°10 and N°11, D), Bisnovat (SK-2) and one or two others.

In fact, the I-26 programme was the one which attracted Stalin's attention most because A.S. Yakovlev was, for him, a «*typical young builder*», exactly what the Soviet aircraft industry needed in those troubled times. The man was "bold", had "dared" to impose his point of view and above all had succeeded in winning Stalin over by developing two types of light aircraft for fighter training (the single-seat U-1 and the two-seat UT-3). Yakovlev took part in the January 1939 Kremlin meeting as a training aircraft builder and when in June he suggested developing the I-26 to Stalin, Stalin pressed him to finish it «*for the end of the year*» and made his programme a priority.

While working on the *K* (or *Kh*) programme, the builders came across two particular difficulties: the lack of a really powerful and reliable engine, and the insufficiently developed non-ferrous metal processes which prevented widespread use of Duralumin to lighten the airframes.

With the fighters, the engine-makers were only able to get two air-cooled in-line engines approved (the Klimov M-105 and the Mikulin AM-35) and one double row radial air-cooled engine (Shvetsov M-62 and its variant, the M-63). Others were in the process of being brought up to standard (AM-37, M-106, M-17, M-71 and M-82); but, except for the M-82 which was approved shortly before war started between Germany and the USSR, none of the others was really ready before the second half of WWII, and even then…

As for the availability of light alloys and special steel, it was with the help of the USSR's allies that the situation improved and only then towards the end of the war, when the lighter airframes indispensable to the Soviet air force could be designed, enabling it to compete with foreign products. It was for these two reasons that the fighters designed according to the *K* (or *Kh*) programme turned out to be so heavy, because they were built of wood ("densified" for some of them). Lightening the airframe was only possible to the detriment of other features: technological efficiency, resistance to bullets and shell splinters, on-board equipment reduced to the strictest minimum, etc….

But the Soviets won, not without a lot of trouble however, because they chose "quantity" rather "quality", when Germany invaded Russia on 22 June 1941.

1939

Yakovlev Yak-1b flown by Major Yeriomin, commanding the 31st Guards Fighter Regiment (GvIAP). Aboard this aircraft from 24 December 1942 until 2 September 1943, this officer carried out 75 missions and obtained eight kills. The career of this aircraft continued with other pilots and its final tally was 14 kills. The camouflage worn is that used at the beginning of the war: dark green and black on the upper surfaces and pale blue on the lower ones. The inscription on the sides indicates that the plane was supplied thanks to donations from the Ferapont Golovaty Kolkhoz.

GLOSSARY

8

KOSLOV

Unfinished prototype, «EI» or «EOI»
(Project in 1939, built in 1940)

The «EI» (Eksperimenalni Istrebityel - experimental fighter) or «EOI» (Eksperimenalni Odnomyestni Istrebityel - experimental single-seat fighter) programme was developed by Sergei Grigorevich Kozlov and a team of engineers from the «Jukovski» Academy in Moscow in 1939: M.M. Shishmariev for the undercarriage, S.N. Kan and I.A. Sverdlov for the general calculations, D.O. Gurayev and V.S. Chulkov for the low cantilever wing. This was a variable-geometry wing built around a metal structure with two spars covered with 'chpon', having a span of 31 ft 9 in. The right aileron was trimmed and the flaps on the underside took up two-thirds of the trailing edge of each wing surface. The tail was classic with a trimmed rudder. The monocoque fuselage was entirely made of metal. It had an oval cross-section and it was powered by the 1 650 bhp (1214 kW) M-107 Klimov engine which was still under development, or Klimov M-106P with axial canon. The engine was cooled by means of two large rectangular air intakes on both leading edges. The oil radiator was positioned under the nose. The undercarriage consisted of two main legs which retracted towards the fuselage into wells incorporated into the central section of the wing. The tail wheel was fixed or retracted into the end part of the fuselage. Apart from the axial canon, two synchronised guns were to be fitted over the engine which had two rows of four pipes for the exhaust.

The prototype was under construction in 1940 (the documents available reveal that it was built in a 'factory in the neighbourhood of Moscow', without specifying which or when), but development work took a long time because of the aircraft's technological complexity and the need to make a lot of modifications during the development stage. The plane was still not finished when the factory used by the Kozlov team was evacuated on 16 October 1941 because of the approaching German troops who had invaded the USSR at the beginning of the summer. The incomplete prototype was simply destroyed on the spot together with bundles of technical papers and documents. It is not known which guns were to be fitted and no other details survived the war.

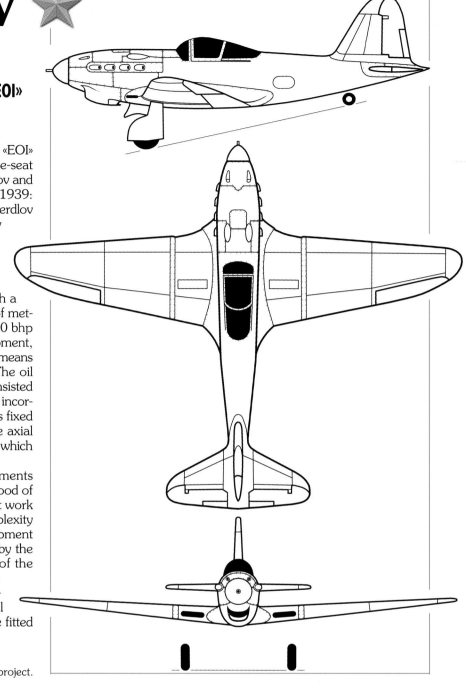

Kozlov's «EI» fighter project.

RYJKOV - LAVOCHKIN - GORBOUNOV - GOUDKOV

Preliminary design (I-22)
(Spring 1939)

In 1939, Vladimir Gorbunov was the head of a department of the GUAP and was thus very well placed to be informed of decisions taken in high places concerning developments in the aircraft industry. In the spring he was the first to offer M. Kaganovich a preliminary design for a «front» fighter based on the 'K' or 'Kh' specifications which had been defined at the end of 1938 and approved by the Kremlin in January 1939. Studies were carried out by Semyon Lavochkin at the request and under

the leadership of Gorbunov, joined by Mikhail Gudkov, an engineer with the NKAP. The lack of light alloys and special steel in the USSR led Lavochkin and Gudkov to choose a structure made of 'dense wood'. This technique, which had already been used in making German propellers, was totally unknown in the USSR. However, a year earlier, Leonti Rujkov, chief-engineer of a factory making propellers and skis at Kuntsevo (Moscow District) developed a similar process, called 'Kapliurite', or 'delta-dreviesina', a mixture of tar, whale-glue (balenite) and bakelite which soaked into the wood, increased its density and gave it a 'plastic' look. Treated in this manner, it was harder to break and burnt very slowly in the case of fire, essential advantages for structural parts of planes, like wing flanges and fuselage spars. But its mass was double that of good quality natural wood.

At the time, Lavochkin spent a lot of time with Rujkov who had built up a small team within the factory to test his process by creating a fighter made entirely of wood. With Rujkov's agreement, Lavochkin decided to apply his process to the «front» fighter which he wanted to design according to the 'K' (or 'Kh') programme specifications. After studying the preliminary design put to him by Gorbunov and in spite of the fact that only the position of the centre of gravity and the maximum speed had been worked out, Kaganovich approved and asked the three men to join Rujkov's team at Kuntsevo, enriching it by bringing with them almost all the Sylvanski OKB personnel who had been dismissed recently after the failure of the I-220 fighter programme (this was a fighter based upon the Polikarpov I-16, more modern but a total failure nevertheless). At the end of 1939, the preliminary design was completed and on the whole approved. At the same time the government issued a

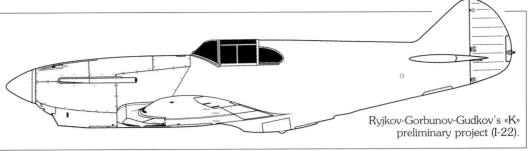

Ryjkov-Gorbunov-Gudkov's «K»
preliminary project (I-22).

decree highlighting the need to develop new combat aircraft urgently. The Kuntsevo factory being totally unsuitable for aircraft production, Gorbonov, Lavochkin and Gudkov were transferred to Factory N°301 at Khimki (Moscow) which housed A.A. Dubrovin's OKB and which was to make French Caudron airplanes under licence. Dubrovin was transferred to Kharkov and nearly all his team was absorbed by the new OKB set up for Lavochkin, Gorbunov and Gudkov. No figures or estimations are known to be available for this type.

N.B. Until recently, a lot of documents written about this programme designated it as the I-22. But there is no Soviet document of the period which mentions this designation and it no doubt never existed. But for clarity's sake, this same reference is used in this book to designate the preliminary design of the projects designated I-301 (see below).

KOCHERIGIN

OKB-3 or OBCh-3/M-81-2TK2 project (Summer 1939)

In May 1939, following decisions taken at the beginning of the year concerning the new combat aircraft programmes which had to be got under way urgently, the VVS presented the government with a series of specifications in order to renew equipment for their operational units. One section was intended for Kocherigin so that he would create a ground attack plane (a Sturmovik), to be presented on 1 September 1939. The machine had to be fitted with an engine which performed well at low altitudes and armour to protect the vital parts of the aircraft. It had to be able to fly at least at 280 mph and have a range of 625 miles. It was to be armed with two 12.7 mm and two 7.62 mm machine guns.

Like Polikarpov, Kocherigin was a supporter of the notion of 'versatility'. He studied plans for a single-engined monoplane which could be produced in different variants: two for ground attack, three for light bombing; all had to be fighters, too. From the beginning, Kocherigin was a keen supporter of the fighter bomber and the bomber which «could support ground troops» concepts.

When he was given the specifications, Kocherigin was one of the chief designers at experimental prototype factory N°156 (manager: Lenkin) where he headed OKB-3. His preliminary design bore the factory designation then that of OBCh-3. In order to go beyond the performances of the ground-attack BCh-2 designed by Ilyushin and to be able to fulfil the secondary fighter role properly, Kocherigin chose the M-81 engine with two TK-2 (M-81/2TK-2) superchargers which suggests that the machine would have been used at higher altitudes as an interceptor. Its design also suggests that it had better performances than those demanded by the

VVS, thanks to conclusive research on aerodynamic refinements on the airframe and the M-81's compactness.

The M-81/2TK-2 engine was indeed very well built. Its NACA-type cowling was extended by a ring of flaps round its trailing edge, regulating the flow of cooling air. The two TK-2s were installed on either side of the engine cowling. A big exhaust extension pipe took away the exhaust gases from each supercharger. The low cantilever wing had two sections with a slight dihedral angle and elliptical wing tips. The single-seat cockpit was enclosed under a hood consisting off a windshield and one-piece canopy (swing-over, no details available). Rear visibility was possible through low elliptical glazing in the sides of the rear decking which extended to the base of the fin. The tail was classic and the undercarriage retracted completely. The four machine guns recommended by the VVS were fitted into the fuselage and the ports were located in the lower part of the engine cowling (the two 12.7-mm machine guns could be replaced by two 23-mm cannon). The armour was incorporated into the structure and covered the vital parts of the aircraft. It weighed about 675 lb.

The rare figures given for this model are estimates:

Max. Speed: 304 mph at sea-level and 380 mph at 29 700 ft.
Range: 540 miles (normally-laden) or 653 miles (loaded).

Unfortunately Yakovlev decided very early on to abandon the M-81 engine. As a replacement, only the M-82 (in different versions) could be used, giving an estimated top speed of 387 mph at 19 800 ft, in spite of an increase in the estimated mass from 924 lb to 946 lb. But although the NII VVS approved it when the aircraft was presented to it and then included it in the experimental plans for 1940, the OKB-3/OBCh-3 was never built.

The Kocherigin OKB-3 project, or OBSh-3/-81TK, fighter or ground attack aircraft.

BELIAYEV

Unfinished «EOI»/»PBI» prototype
(Project in August 1939, model in April 1940)

V.N. Beliayev's «EOI» experimental fighter project can be put into the same category of 'avant-garde' concepts as Kozlov's. But this was a completely different aircraft design: a twin tail boom with a central engine/fuselage nacelle powered by an M-106 Klimov engine driving a three-blade pusher propeller. In August 1939 the preliminary design was approved by Stalin himself. The aircraft was made entirely of metal with stressed skin surfaces.

The single-seat cockpit was very well-designed, incorporated into the nose of the nacelle together with the planned armament: two 23-mm VYa-23 cannon installed in the nose. The whole of this section could be ejected downwards if necessary and slowed down by parachutes.

Thus the pilot did not have to bale out and risk getting caught up in the propeller. Cooling was by means of two air intakes in the wing roots (wingspan: 37 ft 7 in. Wing area: 204.497 sq. ft.) As the M-106 engine was not ready, Beliayev thought of using an M-105 so as to be able to carry out the trials, but these never happened because of the German invasion at the end of June 1941.

A drawing of the "PBI". It has a pusher engine and the two guns fire out from under the cockpit. Normally the tricycle landing gear was retractable. (RART)

Reconstitution of a model of the experimental "EOI" fighter. The nose had much less glazing than its "PBI" variant, but the two nose-mounted guns were the same. (RR)

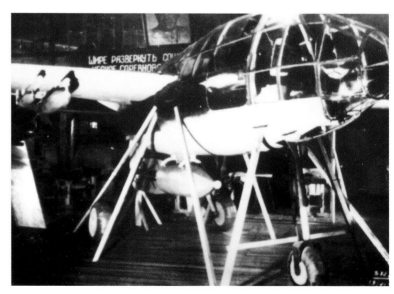

Full-size model of the Beliayev «PBI» with mock bombs underwing and the wing built into the fuselage at mid-height. The whole of the front part of the fuselage was amply glazed. (RART)

Artist's impression of a formation of three "PBIs" diving on an imaginary ground target. (RR)

A full-size model was built in April 1940 but it was destroyed during the evacuation in the autumn of 1941 together with all the plans and technical documents. Fortunately, some photographs classified as «secret» (Sekretno) escaped the chaos caused by the evacuation and now enable the work of Beliayev and his team (which included L.L. Seliakov) to be properly appreciated.

They are dated 19 November 1941, one month after the workshop moved which suggests that the model was abandoned or stored away «somewhere» before being destroyed. They were published recently in specialised Russian journals and they clearly show this «so-called fighter and dive-bomber» «EOI»/ «PBI» model. The whole of the front part of the smooth fuselage was glazed (PBI). This mid-wing aircraft had tricycle undercarriage.

A large-sized bomb could be attached under the fuselage (no doubt an FAB-500) and four more of various sizes (FAB-100 or FAB-50) could also be carried underwing.

The «EOI» fighter variant had a nose with less glazing but the remainder of the characteristics were the same as those for the «PBI».

BISNOVAT (TsAGI)

The IS-TsAGI projects
(September 1939 and January 1940)

At the beginning of October 1939, Matus Ruvimovich Bisnovat completed a low-wing single-seat monoplane fighter project within the framework of the experimental part of the new 'front' fighter programme started in January of the same year. At the time, he was already working on completing the SK-2 fighter (see below) which was derived from the experimental SK-1 prototype which had produced excellent results as far as design, performance and in-flight behaviour were concerned. The new project was designated «IS-TsAGI» because it followed both the «IS» and the «TsAGI» specifications. It bore the latter designation however, so as not to be confused with another «IS» prototype, designed by V. V Nikitin and V.V. Shevchenko. Studies got under way in the summer of 1939 and a first model was presented on 2 September. The engine must have been an M-105 or an M-106 with two- or three-stage superchargers. But the type of structure initially proposed was based on the use of spars made of bamboo to save weight (for the fuselage, wings and other structural elements) but this was not taken seriously: it was quite unrealisable because it was impossible to find this particular commodity anywhere in the USSR!

Bisnovat went back to the drawing board on 15 September 1939, designing a more classic metal structure including the skin (with sunken rivet heads). It is not easy to describe the IS-TsAGI as elements are missing. However it was known to have been a monoplane with very tapered wings, with a fuselage housing an M-105 engine fitted with Type E-42A, two- or three-stage centrifugal superchargers developed by the TsIAM and driving a metal three-blade VICh-52 propeller. The central section of the wing and the tail were built with the fuselage. The intended armament included four machine guns mounted under the lower part of the engine cowling: two Ramjet and two UBS, all synchronised. Their ammunition cases were fitted between the spars of the central wing section for the UBSs (360 rounds each) and in the sides of the fuselage for the Ramjet (825 rounds per gun). A self-sealing tank contained 80 gallons of fuel. The cooling radiator for the M-105 was incorporated into the fuselage, fed by a ventral tunnel with hot air escaping through the dorsal part of the air frame (there was an S-shaped conduit). A hydraulic system activated the Fowler

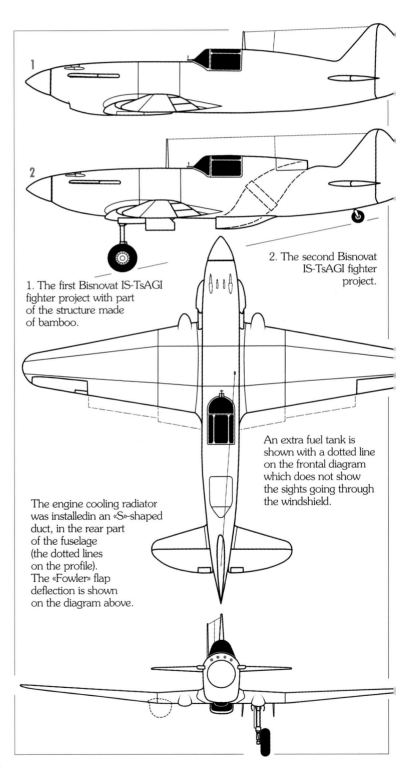

1. The first Bisnovat IS-TsAGI fighter project with part of the structure made of bamboo.

2. The second Bisnovat IS-TsAGI fighter project.

An extra fuel tank is shown with a dotted line on the frontal diagram which does not show the sights going through the windshield.

The engine cooling radiator was installed in an «S»-shaped duct, in the rear part of the fuselage (the dotted lines on the profile). The «Fowler» flap deflection is shown on the diagram above.

NB: Nikitin and Shevchenko's «IS» programme concerned an experimental sesquiplane fighter equipped with «polymorphous wings», i.e. the lower wing folded up in flight thus transforming the plane into a high wing monoplane. Although this programme was started in 1939 and tested from 1940 onwards (prototype IS-1 and IS-2) it was the result of a design based on specifications dating back to 1938 and not on those for the new generation of combat planes, among which the «front» fighters, which had been approved in the Kremlin in January 1939.

flaps on the training edges of each wing, and the landing gear; this retracted backwards flat into the thickness of the wing, each member turning through 90° (the main wheels had 300 x 125 tyres).

The new project was submitted to the NKAP aediles on 25 January 1940. Beforehand, the TsAGI N°3 laboratory had recommended eliminating the ventral intake and replacing it with a special «reactor» system made up of a heat exchanger fed with air by means of gills. Air expelled by the cooling and oil radiators was mixed with the exhaust gases and compressed, then propelled at great speed through the special conduit. At an estimated speed of 406 mph, it was hoped to increase power by a further 300 bhp with this technology.

The plane could carry a 220-lb load of various projectiles under the wings: four 22-lb AO bombs or four 55-lb AO-25 bombs or two 110-lb FAB bombs. These could be replaced by two extra tanks of fuel placed under the wing outer sections, increasing the range over 625 miles, as recommended by an amendment to the specifications for «front» fighters. But at the time, several new fighter prototypes had been accepted by the authorities and were already in the process of being developed. Others had been refused as was, in this case, the IS-TsAGI. Although the dimensions of this project are not known the performance estimates are.

Technical specifications

Wingspan: 28 ft. 6 in.
Length: 29 ft. 7 in.
Wing Area: 145.300 sq. ft.
Max. Take-off Weight: 5 940 lb.
Max. Speed: 387 (412) mph at 16 500 ft with M-105 and two-stage supercharger; 447 (468) mph

with three-stage supercharger; 412 mph with an M-106.
Service Ceiling: 31 020 ft (*) to 38 280 ft (**).
Range: ?

(two-stage supercharger, ** three-stage supercharger). The figures in brackets refer to the speed using the reactor system.*

POLIKARPOV

«K»/ I-200 preliminary designs
(Objects 61 and 63) (Summer/Autumn 1939)

In the summer of 1939, after a stormy discussion with Stalin, Polikarpov started to study the design of a «front» monoplane fighter with a liquid-cooled Vee engine according to the new criteria for «modernity» set out at the January 1939 Kremlin meeting - the preliminary design called «K». He used two of his previous fighter programmes as a basis for the design: the I-17 of which he kept the wing (without dihedral) and the fuselage characteristics, and the abandoned I-173 programme; both of these went back to the I-16. The most modern building techniques were planned to build the machine. The engine was to be the Mikulin AM-37K with two TK-1 superchargers, then still under development. The plane was given the unofficial designation I-200 by the NKAP (Object 63 for Polikarpov). An AM-35A was also held in reserve («Object 61»). His assistants on this programme were Selietski, Andrianov, Matiuk, Gurevich, Kariev Tetivkin and Romodin.

Polikarpov was selected to take part in an official delegation sent to visit some installations in Germany in the autumn of 1939, so he put the project aside until he came back, because he wanted to refashion its wing design by shortening the length and reducing the surface before submitting the design to the authorities. During his absence however, Kariev and Romodin showed it to the authorities who, taking note of the theoretical performances, decided to go ahead and develop it, but with a new team led by Mikoyan and Gurevich. When he returned from Germany, Polikarpov was faced with a *fait accompli*: 40% of his team had followed the project over to Mikoyan and Gurevich where the project was designated «Kh» and gave rise first to the MiG-1 high altitude fighter, then to the MiG-3. When the plan was taken up by the new team, the theoretical «K» specifications were:

Technical specifications

Wingspan: 33 ft. 7 in.
Length: 26 ft. 9 in.
Wing Area: 184.155 sq. ft.
Max. Take-off Weight: 5 821 lb.

Max. Speed: 418 mph at 23 100 ft and 448 mph at 38 280 ft.
Service Ceiling: 42 900 ft.
Range: unknown

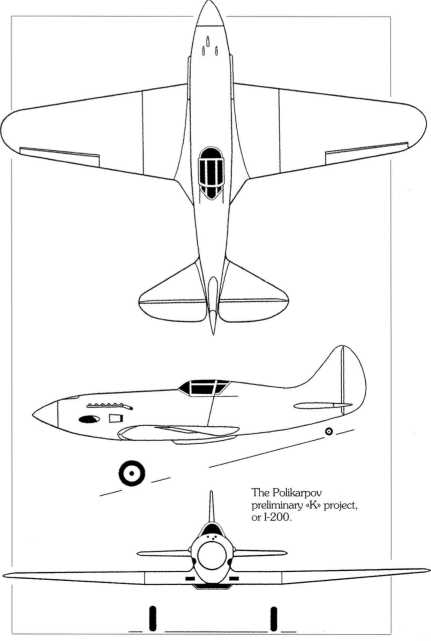

The Polikarpov preliminary «K» project, or I-200.

BELIAYEV

Preliminary design and incomplete «370» prototype
(Project in summer 1939, worked on until 1941)

The January 1939 meeting did not order only «front» fighters. Several design teams were authorised to carry out experimental research, including that of Victor Nikolaevich Belayev. He based his design on the specifications asking for a fighter powered by an M-105 engine armed with two 23-mm VYa cannon and able to reach the 435 mph. Belayev had worked for a long time at the OMOS, the AGOS, the KOSOS, and with Tupolev. He had started to specialise in tail-less plane and flying wing designs.

He chose a radical solution: preliminary design «370» whose engine was housed in the centre of a laminar profiled fuselage was made up of two elements. The front housed the single-seat cockpit incorporated in the cone-shaped nose, access being through a car-type «door» on the left-hand side; the two recommended 23-mm cannon were installed under the cockpit floor with the tubes protruding from the ports. This part could be dismantled for easy maintenance of all on-board equipment and weapons, and was ejected downwards in flight, as with the «EOI/PBI» programme (see above), in emergencies.

The engine was housed in a compartment at the end of this portion. The rear thinned out progressively towards cruciform tail assemblies. Between the two booms there was a three-blade pusher propeller. It had a hollow shaft through which passed the controls for the tail surfaces.

The aircraft had a laminar mid-wing with a sharply swept leading edge. Because of the shape of the tail/s and the position of the propeller, it also had tricycle undercarriage; the nose wheel retracted up between the two cannon and the main members folded up towards the fuselage into the wing wells. The «370»

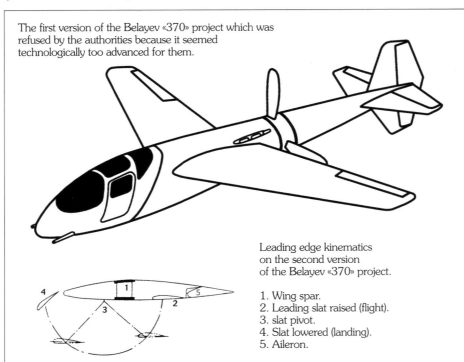

The first version of the Belayev «370» project which was refused by the authorities because it seemed technologically too advanced for them.

Leading edge kinematics on the second version of the Belayev «370» project.

1. Wing spar.
2. Leading slat raised (flight).
3. slat pivot.
4. slat lowered (landing).
5. Aileron.

preliminary project however was turned down by the military because the aircraft's technical aspects and configuration were too complex.

Belayev made another version of his «370» at Factory N° 156 by choosing a twin tail, twin boom with central fuselage, laminar wing and pusher engine. On the recommendation of G.P. Svishchiev who advised against there being any protuberances or intakes on the leading edges, Belayev invented slats pivoting on an axis on the underside of the trailing edges towards the leading edges and controlled by the pilot. The validity of the invention was confirmed by tests carried out in the TsAGI wind tunnel.

It was to be powered by an M-105 with two TK-2 (M-105/2TK-2) superchargers installed in the tail of the fuselage, whose whole nose section resembled the first «370»; the armament and the landing gear were the same. This new version gave rise to a prototype which was build at Factory N° 156 «between 1939 and 1941». But it was left unfinished because of the German invasion which, by threatening the areas close to Moscow, caused the factory to be evacuated in October 1941. «Everything which was not being experimented on or tested» was irretrievably destroyed on the spot, including documents… as was the case with the «370».

NB: There was a similarity between the second version of the «370» and the «EOI/PBI» programme (which was both a fighter and a dive-bomber) of which a model was made. It was destroyed or lost shortly after the evacuation, as were the documents concerning it. It is not possible therefore for the «EOI/PBI» and «370» (second version) to be the «same programme» or that the latter was the «office» designation for the programme. For the memoirs of L.L. Seliakov, one of Belayev's assistants, are the only source mentioning the existence of the twin boom, twin tail «370».

SUKHOI

Two «Bell P-39»-type preliminary designs without designation (October 1939)

In October 1939, P.O. Sukhoi's design team submitted a preliminary design for a low-wing cantilever high altitude fighter to the NII VVS; it was influenced by the American Bell P-39. It was made entirely of metal, except for the rudder and ailerons which were fabric-covered. It was powered by an M-120UV Klimov engine rated at 1 800 bhp with supercharger installed in the centre of the monocoque fuselage (hence the suffix UV added to the engine designation) which enabled it to reach

437 mph, at least in theory. Cooling was by means of a radiator installed behind the engine, air entering by means of a ventral intake. It had retracting tricycle undercarriage. Its armament included an axial 23-mm canon (with 100 rounds) and two BS (400 rounds) or ShKAS (200 rounds) synchronised machine guns housed in the nose. Two tanks were incorporated in the central section of the wing (1 430 lb of fuel) and two underwing drop tanks (330 lb each). The preliminary design, which had no designation or design team reference, was approved by the authorities and included in the experimental production programme for 1939-1940. But in the end it was never developed as the engine was just not available. A pressurised version was also «buried».

Technical specifications

Wing surface: 215.26 sq. ft.	**Max. Speed** 437 mph to 462 mph
Take-off weight: 7 249 lb	at 33 000 ft.
(8 580 lb fully-laden).	**Range:** 406 miles.
Service ceiling: 42 900 ft	*These figures are estimates.*

The Yakovlev I-26 prototype painted entirely cherry red except for the rudder which had white stripes. The carburization intake was installed on the engine cowling. *(J. Marmain)*

YAKOVLEV

I-26.1, I-26.2 and I-26.3 Prototypes
(December 1939, April and September 1940)

It was only in the spring of 1939, during a meeting with aircraft manufacturers that A.S. Yakovlev announced to Stalin that his team was working on the development of a «front» fighter project following the «K» (or «Kh») programme issued by GU VVS. In fact, Yakovlev had only conceived the general outline of the project, designated I-26, and his OKB had been working on it since 9 May. Its development, but also that of the subsidiary I-27, I-28 and I-30 variants included in the same project, fell to K.V. Sinelshchikov and K.A. Vigant at Factory N°115 under the supervision of Yakovlev whose role was that of coordinator. In October when the plans for the models were ready, he took part in the Soviet delegation which went to Germany (like Polikarpov) and then, upon his return, became one of Shakurin's assistants who gave him responsibility for the experimental programmes.

Sinelshchikov and Vigant designed an airframe of mixed construction: a fuselage with an ovoid cross-section, whose structure was made of welded steel and chrome tube, with dorsal decking and wooden underside; the wing was monobloc, built around two spars which formed a box with a secondary construction; the tail was classic and made of wood. Except for the engine compartment, the skin was made of plywood, itself covered with smooth glued canvas. The structure of the movable surfaces (Frise ailerons, elevators and rudder) was made of metal with fabric covering (all of them were trimmed except for the right aileron). The «Schrenk» split flaps were completely made of metal. The undercarriage comprised two single legs with shock absorbers ending in a semi-fork, braked wheels and 600 x 180-mm tyres. The legs retracted up towards the fuselage into wells which were closed by doors attached to the legs (half of the wheel remained uncovered when retracted). The tail wheel could be steered or left in a free position.

The aircraft was powered by an M-105P (the M-106 which was originally recommended was not yet ready) driving a 10-foot diameter VISh-52P variable pitch propeller with a conic boss. The glycol radiator (or heat exchanger) was housed in a tunnel under the belly. The oil radiator was cooled by a fairing under the rear of the engine, between the undercarriage legs. A long air intake for the carburiza-

The I-26.2 prototype painted like the I-26.1. The carburization intake has been moved and the wingtips are more rounded than on the first prototype. Note how well the red paint of the skin has been polished. *(J. Marmain)*

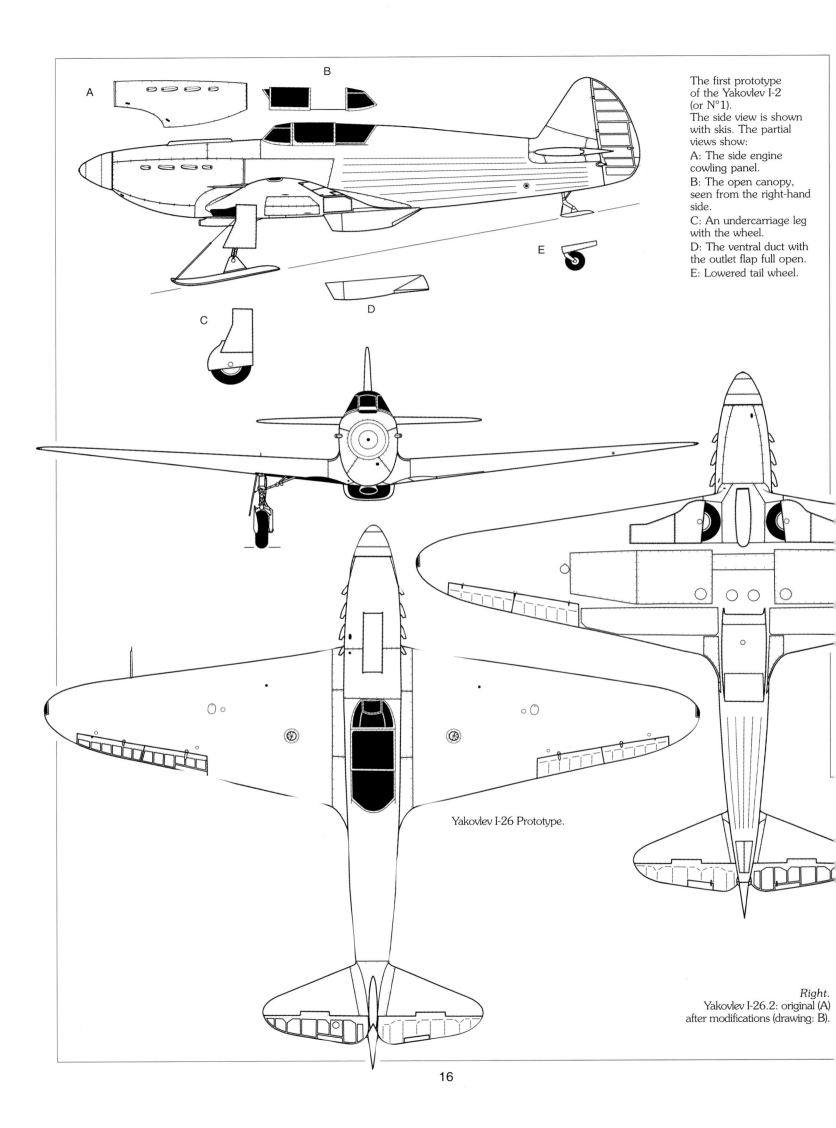

The first prototype
of the Yakovlev I-2
(or N°1).
The side view is shown
with skis. The partial
views show:
A: The side engine
cowling panel.
B: The open canopy,
seen from the right-hand
side.
C: An undercarriage leg
with the wheel.
D: The ventral duct with
the outlet flap full open.
E: Lowered tail wheel.

Yakovlev I-26 Prototype.

Right.
Yakovlev I-26.2: original (A)
after modifications (drawing: B).

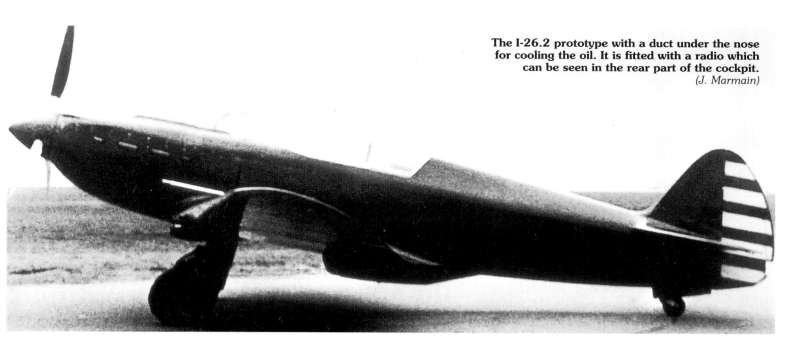

The I-26.2 prototype with a duct under the nose for cooling the oil. It is fitted with a radio which can be seen in the rear part of the cockpit.
(J. Marmain)

tion was located on the engine cowling and made of movable plates. Four AMT welded steel tanks protected by strips of self-sealing vulcanised rubber, holding a total of 90 gallons were housed between the wing spars.

Armament consisted of an axial ShVAK canon (Yakovlev thus respected Stalin's wishes rather than the specification) with 130 rounds, two ShKAS with 420 rounds above the engine, plus two others in the sides with 650 rounds. The PAN-23 sights were optical. The cockpit was installed above the wing. It was covered by a rearwards-sliding canopy. The on-board equipment was very Spartan, reduced to the strict minimum: controls for power plant, firing, piloting, navigation, KAP-3 oxygen system, 12-A-5 accumulator, cockpit lighting and position lights.

The presentation of the I-26 to the VVS remains a grey area. Some say that the first prototype was shown; others that it was only a model. Nevertheless, the I-26.1 was finished by 27 December 1939. Three days later, it was delivered to the Moscow Central Airfield to do its factory tests at the hands of the pilot, Yu. I. Piontkovski. It took off for the first time on 13 January 1940 with skis instead of wheels; the flight lasted less than twenty minutes because the oil started to overheat. It was tested with its wheels on 19 March but on the 43rd flight, the prototype crashed, killing Piontkovski. The inquest was unable to determine the exact causes of the crash but presumed that it was the landing gear which locked up badly and came down during the flight. Under the effect of aerodynamic turbulence, the legs damaged the skin on the lower surface of the wing, tearing it and causing the aircraft to become very unstable and then uncontrollable.

Before I-26.1 was lost a host of defects had been noted, the main ones being: the general structure was not thought strong enough (the calculation of the resistance was based on a MTOW of 5 060 lb when it was actually more like 5 720 lb); the skin was of bad quality; the design of the undercarriage was defective (kinematics, fragile locking system, etc.); the radiators were ineffective with glycol and oil overheating and spraying onto the windshield; there were carburization failures (ignition breakdowns, spark plugs burning out too quickly); vibrations caused piping to break; the propeller was inadequate and tended to race; etc. During these trials, the power plant was changed five times and the propeller replaced by a VISh-61. Quite a few of the tests were carried out with partly filled tanks to reduce take-off weight; the armament was not fitted either. The lack of airframe strength precluded aerobatic tests, spins and dives.

The second prototype came out before the first crashed but for a short while the factory test programme was carried out using both machines. Designated I-26.2, it was built between 9 January and 14 April 1940 (some sources say it flew for the first time on 23 March). It was modified following what was learnt from the I-26.1: generally reinforced wing structure (tested in the wind tunnel at the TsAGI) and wing-

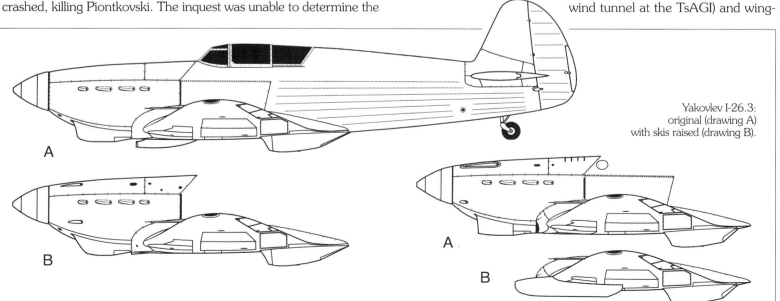

Yakovlev I-26.3: original (drawing A) with skis raised (drawing B).

A

B

A

B

fuselage and tail-fuselage joints; the skin was thicker; the half-moon (previously round) oil radiator was repositioned under the nose of the engine; the carburization air intake on the cowling was removed and reinstalled under the centre section of the wing: a VISh-61P propeller was fitted; the ventral tunnel was redesigned; the surface area of the tailfin was increased and its tip rounded; etc.

For centring reasons, the Yakovlev OKB only fitted the machine with the ShVAK axial canon (120 shells) and the two ShKAS above the engine (380 rounds each).

With the loss of the I-26.1, the I-26.2 had to undergo all the finalisation and flight parameter testing before being transferred on 26 May 1940 for its State trials. But the NII VVS turned the machine down considering it had only finished 65% of its factory test programme and because most of the defects noted on the I-26.1 had not been corrected. At the hands of the pilot, S. A Korzintsikov, the I-26.2 displayed good flight qualities, did a few aerobatics (loops, Immelmanns, figures of eight, tight bends, etc.) at reduced speeds but the armament was not tested nor was the aircraft put into spins; fuel consumption was not calculated either. But already the decision had been taken to prepare the production of a batch of pre-series machines at Factory N°301. In this context,

where urgency was more important than quality, an NKAP commission made up of Yakovlev, Korzintsikov and M.M. Gromov decided on 29 May that the model was «very close to government demands» and that it could be submitted to State trials without delay even though it lacked overall airframe strength and did not have any radio, landing light, generator, sealing or electro-static insulation.

The NII VVS evaluated the I-26.2 from 1st to 15th June 1940 at the hands of P.M. Stefanovski, A.S. Nicolayev and several other experienced pilots. The machine was weighed; its centring, its fuel capacity and its consumption were determined; its weapons were tested at the firing range; the radio and the other missing equipment were installed which increased the plane's mass by about 200 extra pounds. During the 52 test flights which were made, all the flight parameters were established. Some corrections were made by the engineers on the spot but once again the spin, aerobatic and diving trials were compromised. There were still a lot of defects: insufficient stability and inadequate manoeuvrability in the horizontal and vertical planes; overheating glycol and oil (with leaks and sprays) preventing the engine being revved to its limits; long take-off and landing distances; incorrect anti-nose-over angle with risk of nose- and roll-over; brakes to be used with care; weak wing leading edge; windshield not very transparent and canopy impossible to open at high speeds; undercarriage kinematics, locking system and strength of undercarriage door fixations to be reviewed; excessive vibration of weapon mountings with empty shells thrown out onto the tail surfaces; high temperature inside the cockpit (lack of ventilation), etc. In fact, 123 defects were noted of which 38 concerned the wing, 25 the power plant and 24 the equipment. But none of them were considered to be major; all the

pilots praised the new fighter's flight qualities and its ease of piloting. Nobody had any doubts that once the more important faults were ironed out, the plane would be an excellent fighter. The only really big defect of the I-26 was its monobloc wing made of wood which was impossible to repair without being taken apart completely. This had to be done more often than not «on the spot» because in the case of an accident the whole airframe could not be transported except if this occurred on flat ground. Following trials at the NII VVS, the I-26.2 was returned to Factory N°301 to be used as a standard for mass-production.

Built after 25 January 1940, the I-26.3 was delivered for its State trials on 17 September after various modifications dictated by the I-26.2 tests: all-metal wing; redesigned undercarriage retraction and lowering system and shock-absorbers; ventilation system installed in the cockpit; increased ammunition load (135 shells for the canon, 750 rounds for each ShKAS) with empty canon shells ejected under the fuselage and empty machine gun cartridge cases recovered in collectors; improved sliding section of canopy and access to cockpit; revised tabs on moving surfaces; transfer of the carburization air intake to the left wing root and a few other minor modifications. On board equipment was the same as that of the I-26.2, but overall weight had risen to 6 162 lb and the centre of gravity had slipped back towards the rear (24.4% of the MAC instead of 23.85% on the I-26.2).

The factory trials took place from 18 September to 12 October 1940. This time, during the 27 test flights, all the acrobatic figures, spinning, diving (up to 406 mph) and firing tests were carried out. The State trials were carried out at the NII VVS from 13 October to 12 November by Stefanovski, Nicolayev and a few other pilots. They confirmed the good handling qualities of the plane in flight, its improved stability, its satisfactory armament, but they complained about the inadequate cooling for the engine and its bad carburization, the absence of indispensable on-board equipment (radio, reliable fuel gauges, variometer, night landing instruments, etc.) and tyres capable of taking the extra weight of the machine, all preventing the I-26.3 from being used to its utmost capabilities. The test report caused the technical council to demand that all essential problems be solved when mass-production started and the rest in the course of production. After a long stay with the NII VVS - until 14 February 1941 - during which it carried out a number of diving tests, the I-26.3 was delivered to the 12.IAP based at Moscow Central Airfield for operational evaluation.

Technical specifications

Wingspan: 33 ft.
Length: 27 ft. 11 1/2 in.
Wing Area: 184.585 sq. ft.
Weight Empty: 4 853 lb. (1), 5 099 lb. (2), 5,282lb. (3).
Max. Take-off Weight: 5 720 lb. (1), 6,166lb. (2)*, 6 162 lb. (3).

Max. Speed: 362 mph at 16 500 ft. (1), 365 mph at 15 840 ft. (2).
Service Ceiling: 36 795 ft. (1), 33 660 ft. (2).
Range: 437 miles (3).
* The I-26.2 trials were carried out with MTOW of 5 940 lb.

The I-26 prototype during its trials, here with skis. Two coloured stripes have been painted on each propeller blade. *(J. Marmain)*

1940

LaGG-3 Type 35, flown by Captain Sergei Lvov, 3rd Guards Fighter
Regiment (GvIAP), Baltic Fleet Air Force, Order of the Red Flag.
As is clearly visible, the rudder on this plane has been replaced,
which explains why there is only one half of the star.

GLOSSARY

POLIKARPOV

Unfinished Prototype I-185/M90 («Object 62») (First airframe of the I-185 programme) (January-March 1940)

Unfinished Polikarpov I-185/M-90 Prototype.

At the same time as studying «K»/I-200 programme, Polikarpov developed that of the I-185, or «Object 62», a low wing cantilever monoplane extrapolated from the «unfortunate» I-180 programme. It used the most modern technology of the time as required by the NKAP and the VVS in accordance with the «K» or («Kh») specifications issued at the end of 1938 for the new generation of «front» fighters and with the go-ahead given following the January 1939 conference. Five airframes were ordered in 1940 of which one as for static tests. Their role was two-fold: to prepare a model that was easy to build and maintain (as always with Polikarpov), fast and powerfully armed with cannon; to be used as flying test beds for the new radial engines which were being developed and tested (M-71, M-81, M-82 and M-90). The first airframe was designated I-185/M-90 as it was intended for the most promising engine as far as power was concerned: the M-90 by the engine designer E.V. Urmin.

The monocoque fuselage was of mixed construction: metal at the front and wood covered with chpon at the rear. The wing was made entirely of metal with a NACA-230 profile and was designed around two spars which formed a caisson. The leading edges had automatic slats. The ailerons and the split flaps were on the trailing edge. The M-90 engine was mounted on a frame held to the front of the fuselage by only four nuts. The NACA engine cowling had a half ring of flaps on the trailing edge. The exhaust gases were collected by an annular manifold and were ejected through two thrust pipes on either side of the fuselage. The carburization air intake was faired on the cowling and the oil radiator was fed air through a ventral tunnel. The cockpit was covered with a sliding canopy and part of the rear decking was glazed and bevelled. Although the tail had a fabric-covered metal structure, the rudder and the elevators were made entirely of metal. A fuel tank was installed in the fuselage and two others were built into the wings between the two spars. The undercarriage comprised two single members with shock-absorbers to which the doors were attached, and a tail wheel. The retraction mechanism was pneumatic.

The planned armament rested on a common mounting which originating from experiments carried out with I-16s modified for the I-180 and comprised two BS heavy machine guns and two ShKAS, all synchronised and regrouped around the engine. Two bomb launchers could be installed underwing, on each outer section; a normal load of 440 lb (1 100 lb in overload mode) could be carried. Eight RS-82 rockets could be carried in place of the bombs.

This first airframe was not equipped with its M-90 engine which had the particularity of having a propeller boss with an incorporated fan for cooling it and the reduction gearing for the AV5-119 propeller. Urmin was only able to deliver two non-approved examples of his engine which were tested in the wind tunnel at the TsGAI on the airframe intended for the static tests, equipped first with cut back wing sections, then with complete wings. These tests were not satisfactory since the engine was clearly not ready. As a result the first airframe remained in an incomplete state waiting for another engine.

The first airframe in the I-185 programme with its M-90 engine (not approved) being tested in the TsAGI wind tunnel with cut down wings (subsequently it had complete wings). Note the fan incorporated into the propeller boss. *(J. Marmain)*

Below. **The same airframe, this time with the whole wing, still in the TsAGI wind tunnel.** *(J. Marmain)*

An artist's impression of I-185/M-90 as it might have been if it had been finished. The first airframe was then re-fitted first with an M-81 then with an M-71 engine. *(RR)*

Technical specifications

Wingspan: 32 ft. 4 in.
Length: 24 ft. 11 in. (23 ft. 11 in. depending on the sources).
Wing Area: 167.472 sq. ft.
Weight Empty: 4 549 lb.

Max. Take-off Weight: 7 090 lb. (overload mode)
Max. Speed: 441 mph at 23 100 ft.
Service Ceiling: 33 825 ft.
Range: 500 miles

POLIKARPOV

DIT-185 Project
(January - March 1940)

In order to enable the VVS to facilitate pilot conversion on the new I-185 programme, Polikarpov envisaged a two-seat version designated DIT-185 (Dvukhmestni Istrebityel Trenirovochy or two-seat fighter trainer). The project incorporated a second cockpit for the pupil in front of the instructor's which was the original. The two cockpits were covered by the same canopy. Each man had a rear-wards sliding section. The windshield on the pupil's cockpit started just behind the ring of engine cowling flaps. For the rest, the DIT-185 was identical to the single-seat I-185/M-90, including propeller boss with incorporated fan, and ejector effect exhaust pipes. The armament comprised only a ShKAS and a BS. But the project never got beyond the drawing board.

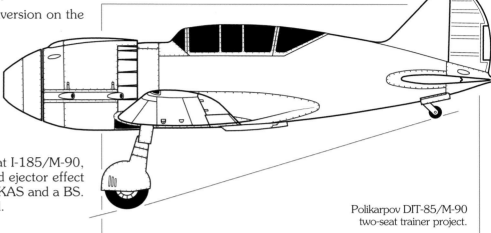

Polikarpov DIT-85/M-90
two-seat trainer project.

Artist's impression of the DIT-185 as it might have been if it had been built.
(RR)

Technical specifications

Wingspan: 32 ft. 4 in.
Length: 24 ft. 11 in. (23 ft. 11 in. depending on the sources).
Wing Area: 167.472 sq. ft.
Weight Empty: ?
Max. Take-off Weight: 6 380 lb
Max. Speed: 438 mph at 19 800 ft.
Service Ceiling: ?
Range: 450 miles.

These figures are estimates.

LAVOCHKIN
GORBUNOV - GUDKOV

I-301 N°1 and N°2 prototypes, or LaGG-1
(March and November 1940)

In spite of a warm welcome on the part of the manager of Factory N°301, Y. Yeskin, who made a point of honour in putting the 93 men of the Lavochkin-Gorbunov-Gudkin team at their ease, drawing up the plans for their «K» project (I-22) «took place in pain». The three men often did not agree among themselves and some components recommended by Lavochkin were contested by Gudkov, or were not unanimously accepted. Thus, according to Gudkov, the wooden fin had to be made entirely of metal. To put an end to these conflicts, the authorities appointed Lavochkin «Chief Designer». The programme

was designated «I-301, a fast fighter made of densified wood». The first prototype was already under development even though the programme was only approved officially in January 1940. Nick-named the «grand piano» because of its carefully polished and varnished cherry-red livery, it was rolled out of the workshop in March.

It was a very simple low cantilever wing monoplane, made mainly of «bakelised» wood for the parts with the greatest loads to bear. The fuselage was of semi-monocoque structure made up of 13 frames, spars and stiffeners. It was covered with sheets of «bakelised» birch

The first I-301 prototype in its very well polished cherry-red livery. The sliding part of the canopy has been removed during the trials. Note the small tail wheel which subsequently turned out to be very fragile. *(J. Marmain)*

veneering placed transversally and shaped on templates. The tail and central section of the wing were incorporated into the building of the fuselage. The wing was built around two spars making a box, and ribs covered with 1/8th-inch bakelised plywood. The horizontal tail surfaces were like the rest. All the moving parts had a metal (Dural) fabric-covered structure. The lower surface hydraulically-controlled split flaps were made of Dural (deflection angles: 15° in flight and 50° for landing). The two single leg undercarriage members with incorporated well doors retracted into wells in the thickness of the wing central section (650 x 200 mm tyres). The tail wheel was made of solid rubber and retracted into the tail (it was subsequently fitted with a tyre).

The engine mounting for the liquid-cooled M-105P was made of densified wood (later steel tubing). Its cowling was made of removable steel panels. It drove a 10-ft diameter three-blade ViSH-61P propeller. The starter was mechanical («Hicks» through the propeller boss) at first then compressed

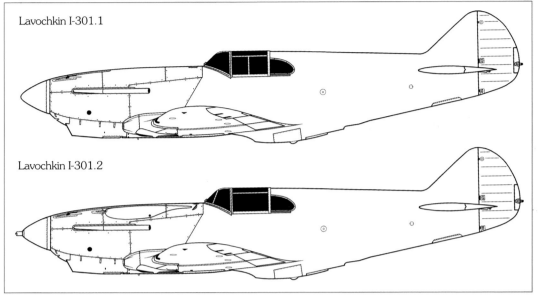

Lavochkin I-301.1

Lavochkin I-301.2

air later. Engine cooling was provided by a radiator placed inside a faired ventral intake made of wood (made of Dural for certain batches). The oil radiator was faired under the nose. The two radiators were fitted with flaps adjusted manually by the pilot. The cockpit was Spartan and had no radio or gyroscopic instruments. The seat was armoured (3/8th inch). The canopy was made of Plexiglas, and comprised a single-piece moulded windshield, a rearwards-sliding canopy with supports and two elliptical glazed side panes. Three fuel tanks were fitted between the wing spars: one in the central section and one in each of the outer wings. They were made of AMTs alloy (aluminium/magnesium) and contained 76 gallons. Four layers of resin-impregnated phenol-formaldehyde sheets protected them. They filled with inert gases from the exhaust as they emptied. Armament comprised a Taubin axial MP-6 23-mm canon with 80 rounds and two heavy BS synchronised machine guns over the engine (220 rounds each). Two synchronised ShKAS were also planned for later.

I-301 N°01 took off for the first time on 30 March 1940 flown by A. Nikashin, the test pilot and Chief-Engineer of the factory. The prototype behaved well in flight and handling was so easy that it was thought that it could be put into the hands of «almost everybody». In spite of all that the prototype did not satisfy the requirements of the original specification. However, Lavochkin, Gorbunov and Gudkov had a good excuse: the I-301 used new experimental materials for its structure; moreover Factory N°301 did not have at its disposal such good infrastructures as its direct competitors (Mikoyan-Gurevich and Yakovlev) and the urgency given to the programme meant that development was too hasty, and there were also several incidents, like the I-301's eventful landing on 11 August 1940 when the pilot, A. Nikashin, blinded by the setting sun, caused a bit of «breakage».

The I-301 underwent «meteoric» trials of only ten days at the NII VVS from 14 June 1940 with the pilots P.M. Stefanovski and S.M. Suprun. It only flew at 365 mph at 15 510 feet (378 mph at 16 335 feet during a «no holds barred» flight) instead of the required 406 mph. It took 5.85 minutes to climb to 16 500 feet (its competitors, I-200 and I-26, were better) and had a range of only 412 miles at cruising speed instead of 500 miles as required; its service ceiling was only 31

Technical specifications

Wingspan: 32 ft. 4 in.	**Max. Take-off Weight:** 6 529 lb.
Length: 29 ft.	**Max. Speed:** 378 mph. at 16 335 ft.
Wing Area: 188.460 sq. ft.	**Service Ceiling:** 31 680 ft.
Weight Empty: 5 451 lb.	**Range:** 347 miles

680 ft instead of the specification's 39 600 ft. Its manoeuvrability in the horizontal plane was adequate but its controls were heavy (lack of trim on the moving surfaces). A whole host of modifications were undertaken in close collaboration with the TsAGI and the NII VVS to rectify the project's main defects.

I-301 N°2 which was fitted with a wing built around a single main spar and a secondary spar, only appeared in November 1940 although it had been ready since October. Meanwhile, the military authorities had requested that new fighters have a range of 625 miles. It was not possible however to redesign the two prototypes' airframes without wasting a lot of time. Whilst waiting for the modifications recommended by the TsAGI and NII VVS studies to be carried out on a new airframe, the I-301 prototype was fitted with an extra 34-gallon fuel tank behind the pilot's seat. Range was improved, and based on the reports by test pilots and a non-stop Moscow to Kursk return flight made by Nikashin previously aboard I-301 N°01 on 28 July 1940, Stalin decided to have the machine produced in four factories (N°21 at Gorki, N°23 at Leningrad, N°31 at Taganrog and N°153 at Novosibirsk). The designation of the prototypes and the future production machines was changed to LaGG-1 and an initial order for 100 pre-series aircraft was placed for operational evaluation (25 to 30 according to the sources). However, no machine was ever actually designated LaGG-1 since the number of modifications which were carried out on the production machines changed it into the LaGG-3. The I-301 was lost on 4 January 1941 following an emergency landing after which it was damaged beyond repair.

NB.: At the time, with the political and military events in Europe, the specifications dictated by the Soviet authorities were deliberately overestimated. In this context, the I-301 prototype was not thought to be a «failure» but a real step forward, compared with the fighters then in service (Polikarpov I-152, I-153 and I-16).

YAKOVLEV

Pre-series I-26 alias Yak-1 (M 105P)
(March 1940)

Serial N°0105, the fifth production series I-26, made by Factory N°301, here during the trials at the NII VVS. Subsequently, the production series machines were re-designated Yak-1. *(J. Marmain)*

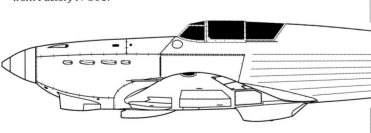

Yakovlev I-26 then Yak-1/05P, first two production batches from Factory N°301.

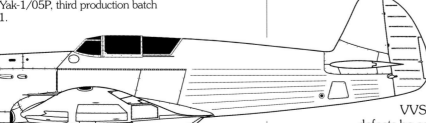

Yakovlev I-26 then Yak-1/05P, third production batch from Factory N°301.

Once the I-26 programme was approved and three prototypes ordered, the government informed Factory N° 301 that it had to make eleven examples (or twelve depending on sources) of a 'military' pre-series in order to define the flying parameters and performances, and reveal any design faults and also so that they could take part in fly-pasts which were very popular in the USSR at the time. Even before the I-26 prototype had made a single satisfactory test flight, the planes were being produced, the first example being completed on 22 March 1940 and delivery of the other ten spread out until June. These planes were still designated I-26, but the reform of the designation system in December gave them the name Yak-1. Naturally they all had the same defects as the prototype I-26. In March-April, four of them were kept at the factory to set up the production series which had to start within three to four months. The first trials confirmed the weakness of the airframe and the wings in particular (the leading edges were reinforced), the inherent defects of the GMP (water overheating and oil leaks) and of the landing gear, and the lack of manœuvrability, etc.

Ten of the eleven I-26s/Yak-1s were then delivered to the 11th IAP at Khodinka in October 1940 and underwent operational trials at the hands of their pilots together with a team detached from the OKB led by K.V. Sinelshchikov. In October and November, before the first snows, these planes carried out 1 222 flights and were tested «under all conditions», including night-flying and simulated combat against I-15s and I-16s. The reports gave a favourable overall

The second I-26 made at Factory N°301 after its undercarriage collapsed on landing on 9 October 1940. *(J. Marmain)*.

impression: the plane had good stability and aerobatic qualities; it could get out of a spin, take off and land easily; it had good in-flight handling qualities, both by day or night and in bad weather, alone or in a group; and its weapons worked without apparent mishaps. These reports however also drew attention to the main defects: weak airframe, engine overheating with oil leaks, unreliable undercarriage, unsuitable tyres (wearing down too quickly); empty cartridge cases ejecting badly. Some of the equipment was missing (radio, generator, landing light, etc.); there were also problems setting the VICh-61P propellers, which meant that several examples were refitted with VICh-21Ps. All these defects prevented the pilots and the ground crews from using these planes to the best of their capabilities. The results of these evaluations, approved by the management of GU VVS-RKKA, recommended that the ten main defects be corrected by the factories in conjunction with the Yakovlev OKB, and a further 53 other defects (out of 93) in the course of production.

MIKOYAN GUREVICH

I-200 prototypes
(«Kh» programme)
(March, May and June 1940)

In the autumn of 1939, when N.N. Polikarpov was part of a large Soviet delegation invited to visit aeronautical creation and production sites (among others) in Germany, two of his colleagues, Kariev and Romodin, revealed his «K» «front line» fighter project, referenced I-200 or «Object 63», to the authorities. He had momentarily put it aside and was going to take it up upon his return. Compared with the Yakovlev I-26 and the Lavochkin-Gorbunov and Gudkov trio's I-301 programmes which fulfilled the same specifications, his estimated performances were better. The engine chosen was the AM-37 with supercharger, tuned up for high altitude flying.

The Soviet government felt that war, which had just started in Poland, would end up drawing the USSR into a more far-reaching conflict, in spite of the pact signed during the night of 23-24 August 1939 with the Third Reich. With this in mind, a modern high altitude fighter was of capital importance, all the more so because the Germans were designing spy planes with a very high service ceiling.

Although the programme developed by Yakovlev was considered as a priority by Stalin (the Lavochkin-Gorbunov-Gudkov programme was only taken into consideration to act as a reserve), the I-200 was just what was wanted to intercept high flying planes. At the time Polikarpov was no longer «flavour of the month» because his I-180 fighter programme was not going well and had already cost the life of the most emblematic of all test pilots, Valery Chalkov in December 1938. Stalin approved the idea of entrusting the development of the I-200 project to the new team led by Artiom Ivanovich Mikoyan who accepted as long as he could work with M.I. Gurevich whom he had befriended when they were both part of Polikarpov's entourage. The «K» project became «Kh», or I-200 and kept the unmistakable Polikarpov stamp in its design.

The OKO-1 was created at Factory N°1 for Mikoyan and Gurevich and 40% of the Polikarpov staff who had followed the project. The team took up the project and lengthened the engine compartment by transferring the oil radiator intake to the left side of the power plant, increased the dihedral angle of the outer wing sections and by increasing the size of the tail surfaces. The «Kh» preliminary study was presented to the authorities at the end of 1939. Stalin, the Communist Party, the NKAP and the VVS all approved it and immediately ordered three prototypes and at the same time appointing Mikoyan and Gurevich Chief Designer and Assistant Chief Designer respectively for Factory N°1 in March 1941. Meanwhile the blueprints had been very quickly finalised. The duo kept the AM-37 engine even though it was in the process of being finished. But this was so fraught with difficulties that the OKO-1 turned to an Am-35A, the only liquid-cooled Vee engine developing enough power to enable the project to meet the specified performances at high altitude.

About a hundred days after the sets of drawings were drawn up, the first I-200 prototype was ready. It was a low cantilever wing of mixed construction.

The structure of the fuselage was made of welded steel tubes for all the front part including the AM-35A engine, covered with removable Dural sheets. The rest was monocoque, made of bakelised wood with plywood skin. The wooden tail was incorporated structurally into the fuselage, but the elevators were made of metal. The moving parts were fabric-covered. The «Clark YH» profile wing was built around a main spar and comprised a central portion entirely made of metal and two outer wing sections made of wood with bakelised

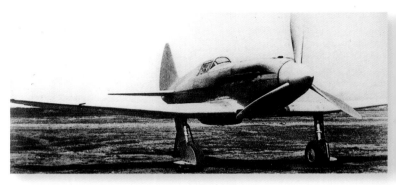

The first I-200 prototype during trials. The right-hand side of the cowling only has the row of exhaust pipes.
(J. Marmain)

The third I-200 prototype, or I-200.3 photographed in front of its hangar. Note that the plane is camouflaged.
(RR)

plywood skin. The ailerons had a fabric-covered Dural structure. The lower surface split flaps were of the «Schrenk» type with 18° and 50° deflection. The controls were pneumatic.

The cockpit was placed to the rear of the wing trailing edge. Its three-piece canopy was made of moulded Plexiglas: windshield, swing-over (to the right) canopy and bevelled fixed rear part. The instruments were very Spartan and there was no radio. The pneumatically activated landing gear comprised two single undercarriage legs which retracted into wells in the wing central section. The shock absorbers were hydraulic and the wheels (with brakes) had 600x180-mm tyres. The tail wheel with its 170x90-mm tyre retracted into the fuselage tail.

The AM-35A engine was not ideal for a fighter as it was heavy (1 826 lb) and was initially designed for bombers. It was mounted on a structure made of welded steel tubes and drove a 10-foot diameter variable-pitch three-blade VISh-22E propeller with the boss made of «Elektron». It was installed in the front part of the fuselage which had the form of a «cone» for better aerodynamic penetration. The oil radiator (9 gallon tank) was cooled by a conduit installed on the left side of the engine with two adjustable flaps on the front. The air intakes for the carburization and the centrifugal supercharger were set into the wing roots. The water radiator was situated in a faired ventral tunnel. Six exhaust pipes came out on either side of the engine compartment. Fuel was contained in three metal tanks: two 16-gallon tanks in the wing central section, another containing 25 gallons between the fireproof bulkhead of the engine and the cockpit.

The planned armament comprised an UBS and two ShKAS machine guns installed above the engine (the AM-35A engine precluded installing an axial gun). The I-200 prototype N°1 (serial N°01) was first tested unarmed in a wind tunnel at the TsAGI and appeared in March 1940. It started its ground trials on the 30th at Khodinka with A.N. Yekatov at the controls and under the supervision of the Chief-Engineer A.G. Brunov. It first took off on 5 April and it took part in the Red Square fly-past on 1 May during the air show (for the workers' holiday). The I-200 N°2 (serial N°02) and N°3 (serial N°03) joined the test programme on 9 May and 6 June 1940 respectively. They were given over to armament trials (N°2) and the series of performance tests (N°3). On 24 May Yekatov reached a maximum speed of 405 mph at 22 770 feet aboard N°1 (406 mph at 23 100 feet at the hands of S. Suprun) and climbed to 16 500 feet in 5.1 minutes. The factory and State trials were carried out simultaneously and ended on 25 August and 12 September respectively.

Although the VVS were satisfied by the trials in general, a host of faults were revealed which were especially due to the dire situation: the engine caught fire and broke; the oil and glycol overheated; the heavy were controls; the plane was unstable while yawing and rolling and tended to go into a spin; there was insufficient visibility both on the ground and in the air

the canopy was not very transparent and could not be opened in flight, etc... Some 112 defects were registered and the final report on the trials recommended that the plane not be «put into the hands of just anybody». But production of the model had already begun under the designation MiG-1. A schedule of modifications classified as «urgent» was started to get rid of all these defects.

At the end of 1940, the Mikoyan-Gurevich team decided to adapt the original AM-37 engine onto the I-200 N°2 airframe. An example of this engine had just been allocated to them and the modifications were made. On 6 January 1941, the test pilot, I. Jukhov took off for the first time. But the factory trials were constantly interrupted by the AM-37 engine which did not work properly and which vibrated too much above 13 200 feet. Dementiev ordered the prototype to be transferred to Factory N°24 «Frunze» where the modifications were carried out. But on 7 May when the trials had been resumed with I.T. Ivashchenko at the controls, the engine broke up and the machine crashed. Although the prototype was destroyed in the crash, the pilot very luckily got out unscathed.

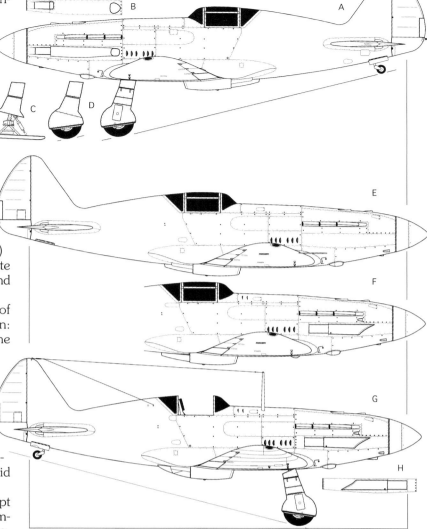

A and E: Right and left profiles of the I-200 N°1 (serial n°1) after modifications.
B drawing of the oil cooling intake for the I-200 prototype before modifications.
C and D: left undercarriage leg of the I-200 prototype before modifications, respectively with ski and wheel.
F: drawing of the front half of the I-200 N°2 (serial N°2) prototype with its second oil cooling intake (the rest of the airframe was identical to that of the first prototype.
G. right profile of I-200 prototype N°3 (serial N°3) tested without any canopy and with a radio transmitter (there was a light of the leading edge of the left wing section).
H: drawing of the right-hand cooling intake on the I-200 N°3.

Technical specifications

Wingspan: 33 ft. 7 in.	Max. Speed: 405 then 407.8 mph.
Length: 29 ft. 11 in.	at 22 770 ft.
Wing Area: 187.706 sq. ft.	Service Ceiling:
Weight Empty: 5 445 lb.	39 600 ft.
Max. Take-off Weight: 6 529 lb.	Range: 456 miles

Two views of the I-200 N°3 prototype with the two lateral fairings for the oil cooling system. The canopy on the first three prototypes of the programme, together with very first examples of the MiG-1, swung open over to starboard. *(J. Marmain)*

SUKHOI

Studies for I-135/M-105P-2TK-2 and I-135/M-106P-2TK-2 and prototype I-135.1, or Su-1
(Studies in March and July 1939)
(Prototype in May 1940)

Technical specifications	
Wingspan: 37 ft. 11 1/2 in.	**Max. Take-off Weight:** 6 325 lb.
Length: 27 ft. 9 in.	**Max. Speed:** 400 mph.
Wing Area: 204.497 sq. ft.	**Service Ceiling:** 35 475 ft.
Weight Empty: 5 489 lb.	**Range:** 331 to 450 miles

(J. Marmain)

The Su-1 with its canopy, but without pressurisation system during its trials.

This poor quality photograph of the Su-1 has been extensively touched up to show the windshield and the rear decking better. The sliding canopy is missing, as is the pressurisation system. The right-hand TK-2 supercharger is clearly visible under the exhaust. *(J. Marmain)*

In March 1939, the specifications issued at the end of 1938 for a «front» fighter were brought up to date. Instead of the M-103A, they proposed using the M-105P engine but only P.O. Sukhoi accepted the version with two TK-2 superchargers and drew up a two-part preliminary study for high altitudes: a model powered by a M-105P-2TK-2 engine (I-135/M-105P-2TK-2) armed with an axial canon, two ShKAS machine guns under the engine cowling and a 220-lb offensive load; and another using the M-106P-2TK-2 (I-135/M-106P-2TK-2) and two extra «Ultra-ShKAS» machine guns. These two parts were presented respectively in March and July 1939.

The semi-monocoque fuselage and the tail were built out of wood with a plywood skin. The wing had a single spar and was made entirely of wood, with a dihedral angle for the outer sections. All the moving parts had a fabric-covered metal structure. The two single undercarriage legs retracted hydraulically towards the rear by turning through 90° and lying flush inside the thickness of the wing central section. The tail wheel retracted into the rear part of the fuselage. The engine was cooled by a ventral tunnel; it drove a VISh-61P propeller and the two superchargers were installed on either side of the engine. A tank containing 550 lb of fuel was installed under the pilot's seat and two drop tanks containing 330 lb of fuel could be carried underwing. The cockpit was equipped with a sliding canopy, but it was not pressurised.

The calculations which went with this project put the estimated maximum speed at 362 to 375 mph at 14 850 ft., 400 mph at 33 000 feet and the service ceiling at 35 475 ft.

The overall project was designated I-135 because it was developed at factory N°135 at Kharkov. It was the plan using the M-105P-2TK-2 which was chosen (the M-106 was not ready) and included in the experimental production programme for 1939-40. In conformity with decree N°330, the I-135.1 (the number of this decree has often been used incorrectly in a lot of documents designating this prototype as I-330), the first prototype appeared on 25 May 1940. The trials started on 11 June and carried on into the spring of 1941. During the trials, the main defects were noted and concerned oil cooling (several types of radiators were tested) and the TK-2s which were not very reliable. The machine, re-designated Su-1 in 1940 was damaged in a crash and repaired in August 1940 but its flight characteristics were generally satisfactory: good longitudinal, directional and yawing stability; easy handling in all situations. On 6 January 1941, the Sukhoi design team was transferred from Factory N°156 (Moscow) to N°289 at Podlipki. During the move, the machine was damaged. Because the TK-2 had been unreliable all the time, the prototype was not repaired and was therefore not present for its State trials, although during the tests it was quite obviously superior, except for vertical manoeuvrability, to the Yakovlev I-26 which had already been put into production. On 16 April, the SNK announced that development of this programme had been halted.

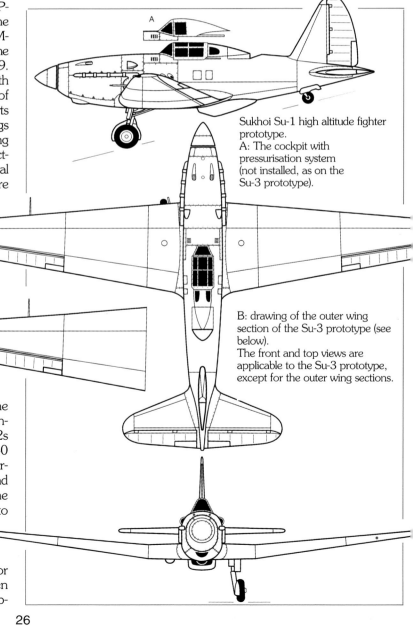

Sukhoi Su-1 high altitude fighter prototype.
A: The cockpit with pressurisation system (not installed, as on the Su-3 prototype).

B: drawing of the outer wing section of the Su-3 prototype (see below).
The front and top views are applicable to the Su-3 prototype, except for the outer wing sections.

PACHININ

I-21 or IP-21 Prototypes (Preliminary study in 1939) (Prototypes in May and October 1940, and January 1941)

Mikhail Mikhailovich Pashinin was one of the builders chosen to develop the new «front» generation of fighters. After being Polikarpov's assistant, he ran his own OKB from 1939 to 1,941in order to design his own model: the I-21 (IP-21 for the OKB). Pashinin presented his programme as «a «diving» fighter whose top speed would reach 593 mph». It was a mixed construction monoplane with a low cantilever wing with asymmetric profile

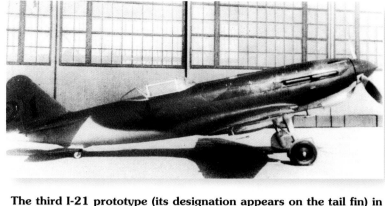

The third I-21 prototype (its designation appears on the tail fin) in front of a hangar at Factory N°21. It was the first fighter to be equipped with an «all-round» vision canopy. *(J. Marmain)*

and plywood-covered metal structure. The wing consisted of three sections: a central section and two outer trapezoidal sections with a dihedral angle. Their leading edge was swept. The trailing edge had trimmed ailerons and split flaps. All the front part of the fuselage was metal: welded steel tubing and removable metal sheets. The monocoque tail and the tail surfaces were made entirely of wood covered with chpon. The engine was to be a Klimov M-107, but Pashinin had to use an M-105P while waiting for the other engine to be finalised. The oil was cooled by means of a radiator under each wing section. The glycol radiator was installed in a ventral intake. The two single undercarriage legs retracted into wells in the wing after turning through 90°. The tail wheel retracted into the end of the fuselage.

The armament chosen was what Stalin wanted: a 20-mm axial canon and two 7.62-mm ShKAS synchronised machine guns above the engine. The single-seat cockpit was placed near the tail with an «all-round visibility» swing-over (to the right) canopy (the first in the USSR) and armoured panes.

The prototype I-21.1 left the workshop on 1 May 1940. Its trials started on the 18th (pilot: P. Stefanovski) and ended in serious damage on 5 July (pilot: P.I. Fokin) which was beyond repair. The plane turned out to be very unstable. The I-21.2, the second prototype, therefore appeared in October after several modifications, such as increased leading edge sweep in order to improve longitudinal and transversal stability, and a shortened fuselage. The dihedral angle on the outer wing sections was increased during the trials on the recommendation of the pilot S. Suprun.

The plane reached 358 mph at 16 500 ft. The third prototype, I-21.3 was built in January 1941 and flew as of 5 April. It differed from the two preceding prototypes for several reasons: the leading edge sweep was increased further; the oil cooler was moved under the nose; the individual exhaust pipes were replaced by manifolds; the tail fin surface was increased and the wingspan was shortened by 5 ft. 1 1/2 in. It was powered by an M-105P and armament comprised an axial BT-23 23-mm canon (or VYa-23) and two ShKAS. During the trials this prototype flew at 362 mph at 15 675 feet. Although stability was greatly improved, the VVS nevertheless turned the I-21 down because they thought that forward visibility was inadequate due to the aft position of the cockpit, take-off and landing distances were too long, landing speed was too high (103 mph) and that it was generally «too complex to pilot». As a result, the order for three pre-series machines was cancelled at the same time as the abandon of the programme was announced.

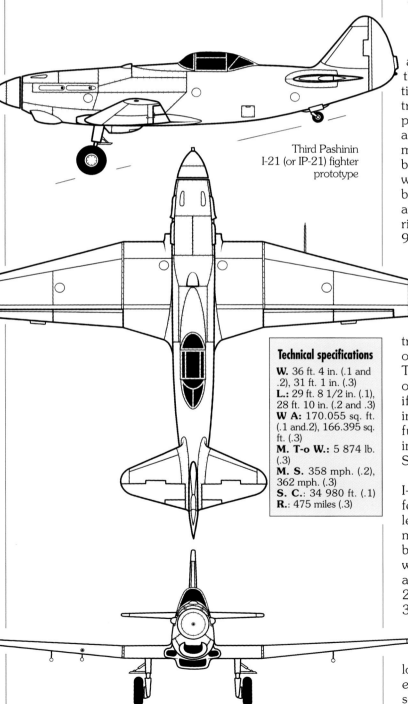

Third Pashinin I-21 (or IP-21) fighter prototype

Technical specifications

W. 36 ft. 4 in. (.1 and .2), 31 ft. 1 in. (.3)
L.: 29 ft. 8 1/2 in. (.1), 28 ft. 10 in. (.2 and .3)
W A: 170.055 sq. ft. (.1 and.2), 166.395 sq. ft. (.3)
M. T-o W.: 5 874 lb. (.3)
M. S. 358 mph. (.2), 362 mph. (.3)
S. C.: 34 980 ft. (.1)
R.: 475 miles (.3)

The third I-21 prototype, before (or after) its first flight (the photo is dated 5 April 1941), at the snowed-over airfield of Factory N°21. *(J. Marmain)*

3-1019c

YAKOVLEV

UTI-26 (I-27) Prototypes
(June and September 1940)

At the same time as the I-26 prototypes, the Yakovlev OKB developed the two-seat UTI-26 version for advanced fighter pilot training. Included in the initial project with the designation I-27, it originated in the I-26.1 prototype, but with the lessons learnt gradually from the I-26.2 trials.

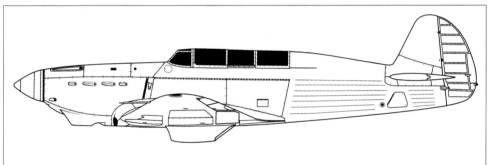

Work on the plane started on 25 January 1940 and was at first considered «illegal», then it was sanctioned by a government decision dated 4 March which wanted to make it into a ground attack plane (Shturmovik). But thanks to his relations with the NKAP, Yakovlev managed to change their minds and the model was kept as a two-seat trainer.

The first UTI-26.1 prototype was finished on 17 June 1940. Based on the same design concepts and technology, and equipped with the same power plant, as the I-26 (M-105P engine, VISh-61 propeller), it was only armed with two 500-round ShKAS machine guns.

Another cockpit with dual controls was installed behind the first. The canopy was lengthened and fitted with a second rearwards sliding section. The wing was placed four inches further back and the side panels were prolonged along the fuselage sides to a point directly underneath the rear of the second cockpit. The rear decking was raised, the fairings for the oil (under the nose) and for the glycol (under the belly) radiators were redesigned. The two men communicated by means of an RPU tube intercom system. For the rest, the various elements were like the I-26 programme.

below, left. **The first two-seat UTI-26 fighter trainer during its factory trials. Each cockpit had a sliding canopy.** *(J. Marmain)*

Below. **The second two-seat UTI-26.2 prototype during evaluation at the NII VVS in mid-winter 1940-41, witness the snowed-over airfield.** *(J. Marmain)*

(J. Marmain).

28

The factory tests were held between 23 July and 25 August 1940 with the pilot P.Y. Fiodrovi (or Fedrovi). During the course of the 20 flights which were made, two types of propellers were tried (with diameters of 9 ft 3 in and 10 ft) but in the end it was the VISh-61P which was chosen. The State trials were held from 28 to 30 August, then from 11 to 19 September at the hands of P.M. Stefanovski and some pilots from 11.IAP so that they could learn to handle their new Yak-1 fighters (see below). All the reports mention numerous defects which were indeed the same as those revealed during the single-seat I-26 prototype trials: faulty undercarriage kinematics and locking system; overheating oil and glycol; bad carburization; defective flap and pneumatic firing controls; no radio or night flying equipment; too much surface deflection; etc. all these defects were considered to be damning for a training plane. As a result, in spite of the interest the VVS expressed for this type of machine, the military refused the prototype as it stood - all the more so as the firing tests had not been carried out - and needed a new example with no defects before approving a potential production series.

The trials were halted on 19 September 1940. The machine was transferred to Kubinka to undergo a new series of evaluations from 21 to 25 September. In spite of its faults, the model was finally thought to be «adequate», so that it could be put into production. This was because it was the only two-seat trainer for training and converting pilots for the conditions imposed by the new «front» fighters. The UTI-26.1 returned to the Yakovlev OKB on 26 September and until the 10 December 1940 it went through a host of different modifications during its 119 test flights (oil and glycol radiators, propellers, undercarriage locking system, etc.).

The second two-seat trainer underwent its factory trials from 16 September to 12 December 1940. It was designated UTI-26.2 and had the benefit of being modified while it was being built: the undercarriage was totally redesigned, eliminating the half-forks, reinforcing the locking system, revising the shock absorbers, fitting bigger tyres (650x200 mm for the main members, 300x125 mm for the retractable tail wheel), locking indicators for the undercarriage and the doors; the anti-nose over angle was increased from 27° to 30°; stability was improved by moving the CG towards the rear (from 26% to 23.2% of the MAC), by increasing the wing section surfaces and the elevators; and modifying the aileron controls and the propeller blades, etc.

The State trials were carried out between 1 January and 14 February 1941 at the NII VVS by the pilot A.G. Kubishin. Some 260

The UTI-26.1 prototype at the LII for its State trials at the end of the summer of 1940. *(H. Leonard)*

acrobatic figures were made (spins, rolls, loops, Immelmanns and tight turns, etc.). The reports noted that the prototype behaved well in flight, that it was stable and manoeuvrable, that it rarely went into a spin and came out of one easily, that take-offs and landings were easy, that on board the controls were well arranged, that the equipment was adequate for the use the plane was put to, and that maintenance was much easier than that of the I-26 single-seater. They also confirmed their decision to order it into production, but based their choice on the I-26.2 after it was finalised. After an extra stay at the NII VVS to study the spin and dive characteristics thoroughly, the prototype was delivered to 12.IAP for pilot and ground crew training.

Technical specifications

Wingspan: 33 ft.	**Max. Take-off Weight:** 6 050 lb.
Length: 27 ft. 11 1/2 in.	**Max. Speed:** 366 mph. at 14 850 ft.
Wing Area: 184.585 sq. ft.	**Service Ceiling:** 31 020 ft.
Weight Empty: 4 798 lb. (.1)	**Range:** 437 miles

YAKOVLEV

I-28 Prototype, or «Yak-5, 1941 model» («Samolyet 28», or I-26V or I-28V)
(July 1940)

In his overall project for a «front» fighter, Yakovlev included a model specially prepared for high altitude flying, intended for the PVO (defence) units for intercepting spy planes and very high-flying bomber formations. The generic designation was I-28 («Samolyet 28»), but period documents also used the reference I-26V and I-28V (V for Vysotny, high altitude). The prototype which was based on the same technological concepts as the I-26 was powered by an M-105PD engine driving a VISh-61Sh propeller, and equipped with a Dollejal E-100 centrifugal two-stage supercharger whose ceiling thresh-

olds were established at 7 755 ft and 21 945 feet thanks to a hydraulic coupling system. This enabled the climb to operational altitude to be reached more steadily. But while the same principle used by the Germans with the DB 601E engine was automatic, that of the M-105PD was controlled manually, complicating the job for the pilot and preventing the engine from being used to its optimum performance limits.

Built from 10 July to 29 October 1940, the I-28 prototype was equipped with a wing copied off the I-26, with the same surface area, but with a span of 32 ft 1 1/2 in (shortened wing tips), and fitted with leading edge slats. The fuselage with its rather deeper, longer canopy and rear decking, the undercarriage and the tail surfaces (entirely made of metal) came from the two-seat UTI-26/Yak-7 (see below) training version.

Armament comprised a ShVAK canon with 120 rounds and two synchronised ShKAS above the engine, each with 750 rounds. The MTOW was higher but the engine was theoretically more powerful at altitude thanks to the E-100 supercharger, allowing the I-28 to be used not only as a high altitude interceptor, but also as a front line fighter.

The first flight took place on 1 December 1940 with Fiodrovi at the controls. It did not last more than twenty minutes because the engine started to «splutter», give off clouds of smoke, vibrate and lose oil; so much so that Fiodrovi was forced to bring the prototype back to ground with a stalled engine. A new M-105PD which had already undergone several modifications was installed in February-March 1941. Then the machine was delivered to the LII NKAP to carry on engine perfection trials during which it was never possible to establish the exact performance parameters.

These trials carried on into 1942 without success, the engine being extremely difficult to finalise.

Subsequently, Yakovlev did what he had done before and once again developed two other high altitude versions based on the Yak-7 (1942) and the Yak-9 (1944).

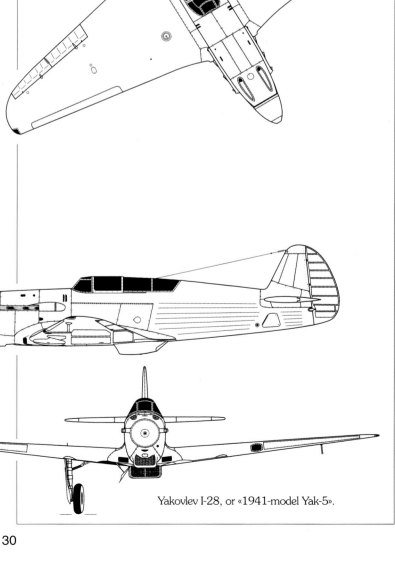
Yakovlev I-28, or «1941-model Yak-5».

Above from top to bottom.
Although the I-28 high-altitude fighter prototype came out of the I-26, it had an M-105PD engine with Dollejal E-100 supercharger. *(J. Marmain)*

Compared with the I-26, the wider oil radiator duct on the I-28 prototype can be clearly seen from this angle.
(J. Marmain)

Technical specifications

Wingspan: 32 ft. 1 1/2 in.
Length: 27 ft. 11 1/2 in.
Wing Area: 109.244 sq. ft.
Weight Empty: 5 390 lb.
Max. Take-off Weight: 6 441 lb.
Max. Speed: 406 mph. at 29 700 ft.
Service Ceiling: 39 600 ft.
Range: ?

Yakovlev I-28, or «1941-model Yak-5».

SUKHOI

Preliminary studies for I-135/M-90-2TK-2 and I-135/M-120-2TK-2
(July 1940)

In a memorandum sent to S.N. Shishkin (VVS) and Leontiev (PGU NKAP), Sukhoi proposed two other variants of the I-135 powered by air-cooled radial engines, the M-90 and the M-120, boosted by two TK-2 superchargers. The preliminary study with the M-90 engine, referenced I-135/M-90-2TK-2 was completed by July 1940. It was built along the lines of the Su-1 and Sukhoi had planned to extend the propeller shaft by almost 16 inches in order to streamline the aircraft's nose better. The superchargers were installed a long way behind the engine, directly below the canopy, on either side of the fuselage. The 660-lb fuel tank was placed under the pilot's seat and two drop tanks could be attached underwing and hold 440 lb of fuel. The pilot was protected by 3/8-inch armour plates on the back of the seat, and by an armoured pane behind his back. Armament comprised four synchronised ShKAS machine guns grouped around the engine (or two ShVAK cannon) and two other ShKAS in the wings (with a total of 6 000 rounds). Considering these features and the estimated performances, the NII VVS decided that the I-135/M-90-2TK-2 was unrealistic and thought the expected performances were unrealisable, all the more so as the M-90 engine was still under development. Moreover, the authorities told Sukhoi he would have just «have to get on with the BB-1 (short-range bombers), the Su-1 (high altitude fighter) and OBSh (heavy ground attack bomber)».

As for the I-135/M-120-2TK-2 preliminary study, whose top speed was estimated at 500 mph at 19 800 feet, the NII VVS's appreciation and decision were the same because the M-120 engine was not yet ready to leave its test bench. This and the superchargers were fitted into the centre of the fuselage, behind the cockpit, the wing and its lift being revised in relation to the position of the power plant. It had retractable tricycle undercarriage, and armament comprised two synchronised cannon under the engine cowling and two ShKAS wing-mounted machine guns. For the rest it was fitted out in the same way as its «brother with the M-90 engine».

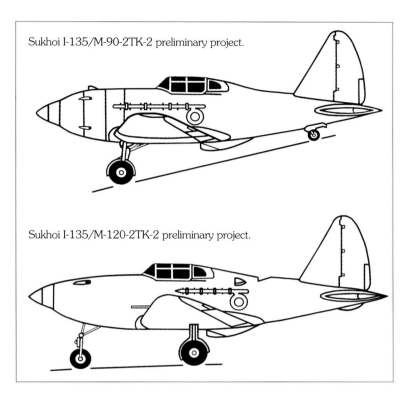

Sukhoi I-135/M-90-2TK-2 preliminary project.

Sukhoi I-135/M-120-2TK-2 preliminary project.

Technical specifications

Wingspan: ?
Length: ?
Wing Area: 193.734 sq. ft.
Max. Take-off Weight: 6 468 lb.

Max. Speed: 418 mph. at 33 000 ft.
Service Ceiling: 41 250 ft.
Range: 343 miles

YAKOVLEV

Yak-1/M-105P and Yak-1/M-105PA
(September 1940 to May 1942)

In May 1940, the government decided to mass-produce the Yak-1/M-105P in four factories: N°47 in Leningrad, N°301 in Moscow, N°292 at Saratov and N°126 at Komsomolsk on the Amur. But the latter factory did not participate in the production because it was already producing twin-engined Ilyushin DB-3F bombers in large numbers. In fact it was Factory N°292 which took up the biggest share of the production: N°301 only produced 117, N°47 only two in 1942 and, before being evacuated because of the German breakthrough, N°30 (Moscow) assembled 65 with parts supplied by N°292. Other factories were envisaged for this production: N°492 at Chkalov and Engels (the factory in fact was never set up), N°448 at Tbilissi, N°131 at Kutaysi, N°153 at Novosibirsk. But these plans were swept aside by the German onslaught on 22 June 1941.

The first batches were just as imperfect as the I-26.2 upon which they were based. The urgency of the situation meant that the lack of «everything or almost everything» prevented production rates from being kept up: engines, propellers, radiators, raw materials, etc. On top of this, the Yakovlev OKB imposed a whole host of modifications with varying degrees of importance (in 1942, 7 023 modifications were carried out during production and assembly of the Yak-1s). The production was organised in such an out-of-date manner and the workers had so little experience that the planes were badly finished: the skin was stuck with low quality products; the engine cowling panels, the undercarriage doors, the inspection panels, the ailerons all fitted badly; the manufacturing tolerances were not respected (for example, the length of the undercarriage legs differed from one plane to another), and the joints between the wings and the fuselage left a lot to be desired, etc.

All these defects, together with the engine problems caused huge differences between one Yak-1 and the next. Speeds varied between 350

and 360 mph depending on the machine which had been produced;
likewise with the quality of the finish (for example the machines produced by Factory N°292 were better made than those from N°301). As
the production settled down, 37 of the 58 major defects were corrected, but some were never got rid of com-
pletely. The oil and the glycol still overheated; the oil leaks were legion, covering
the fuselage right to the tail; the airframe
«moved so much that it lost some of its nuts
and bolts», and its overall strength was below the
specified standard. Moreover each modification
meant the aircraft's mass increased.

Yak-1 serial N°20-29 was thus tested at the NII VVS and weighed 6
490 lb, 552 lb more than the I-26.2. It was from the 29th production batch
that the mass settled down gradually to somewhere around 6 380-6 417 lb.

From the 36th production batch (end 1941), the Yak-1 was powered
by an M-105PA with the same power rating, but performing slightly better at high altitudes, with a new
carburettor and R-7 speed regulator (instead of the R-2) enabling the
plane to fly in negative G situations and on its back. Numerous modifications improved and simplified the model's production,
saving a few more pounds here and there: the cooling intakes were
redesigned; the lower articulated undercarriage doors were eliminated, as was the tail wheel retracting system; an RSI-4 «Malyusha» two-
way radio was installed on every tenth machine (the others only had
a receiver and some had nothing at all); the airframe was insulated. But
the RSI-4's range was inadequate, the quality of the radio link was mediocre
and the defect inherent to the M-105 had not been cleared up (the Klimov
engines suffered constantly from oil leakages). Mass hovered between 6
248 lb and 6 589 lb depending on the batches. The continuous production orders together with others increasing production rates meant
that the factories did not have the time to check the estimates for the mass
or the weight of components supplied by their subcontractors.

On the eve of the German invasion, 425 Yak-1/M-105P had been tak-
en on by the VVS. These machines and those that followed during the
first months of the war were inferior in quality to the I-26.2 prototype and
as a result performed less well. Although they were slightly faster than the
Bf 109Es and Fs at low altitudes, they were outclassed in climbs and in
dogfights above 6 600 feet; they were also less reliable. Up to April-May
1942, some 2 947 M-105P and PA-powered examples rolled off the production lines. Although the Yak-1/M-105P and PAs produced in 1940
and 1941 were armed with an axial canon and two synchronised ShKAS
under the engine cowling, most of the Yak-1/M-105PAs made in 1942
had their two ShKAS replaced by a heavy 12.7-mm UBS machine gun.

On 23 September 1941, the GKO ordered Factory N°292 to adapt its
production for fitting RS-82 rocket launchers under the wings of the Yak-

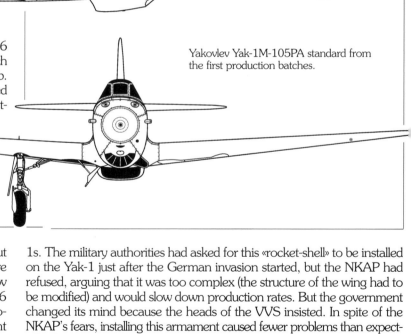

Yakovlev Yak-1M-105PA standard from
the first production batches.

1s. The military authorities had asked for this «rocket-shell» to be installed
on the Yak-1 just after the German invasion started, but the NKAP had
refused, arguing that it was too complex (the structure of the wing had to
be modified) and would slow down production rates. But the government
changed its mind because the heads of the VVS insisted. In spite of the
NKAP's fears, installing this armament caused fewer problems than expected. The wing structure was not altered, but an extra plywood reinforce-
ment panel was mounted on the underside of each section for the fitting
of the rocket (or bomb) launchers. The trials showed that firing the rockets did not cause any damage to the underwing skin surfaces. But they did
weigh the Yak-1 down (with six rocket launchers, the MTOW increased
to 6 589 lb), and reduce its overall performances and its in-flight behaviour. Although a direct hit invariably destroyed the enemy, the RS-82s scat-
tered too much because they were not guided and therefore turned out to
be relatively ineffective in a dogfight. On the other hand, against ground
targets, especially if all fired at the same time, they were very effective. Production of RS-82 rocket-equipped Yak-1s only concerned examples from
N°43 batch (October 1941) to N°65 (May 1942). The pilots very quickly
caught on to the fact that they were at a disadvantage in a dogfight with
the enemy and would get rid of their rockets as quickly as possible to get
the Yak-1's performances back up to par and fight or get away.

MiG-3

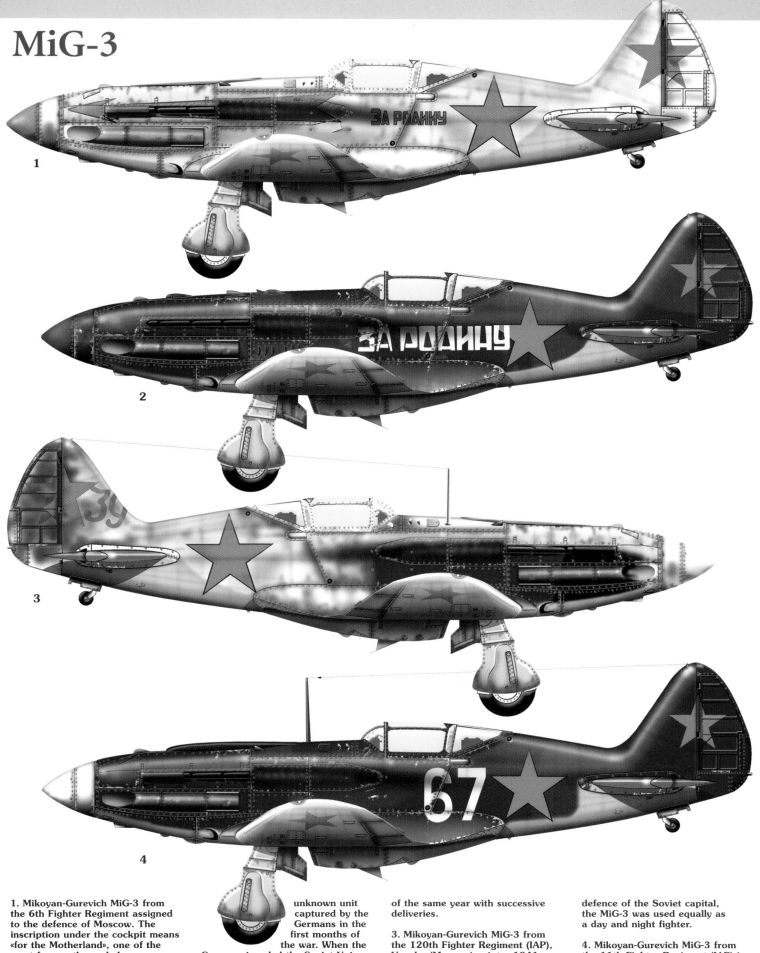

1. Mikoyan-Gurevich MiG-3 from the 6th Fighter Regiment assigned to the defence of Moscow. The inscription under the cockpit means «for the Motherland», one of the most frequently-used slogans on Soviet equipment (aircraft but also armoured vehicles, lorries, etc.) during the Great patriotic War.

2. Mikoyan-Gurevich MiG-3 from an unknown unit captured by the Germans in the first months of the war. When the Germans invaded the Soviet Union in June 1941, more than 1 400 examples of this plane had been delivered; these represented only 10% of VVS strength, this figure rising to more than 40% at the end of the same year with successive deliveries.

3. Mikoyan-Gurevich MiG-3 from the 120th Fighter Regiment (IAP), Venuku (Moscow), winter 1941-1942. The temporary water-based whitewash, officially called MK-7, has been partly rubbed off revealing the original green and black camouflage underneath. During the defence of the Soviet capital, the MiG-3 was used equally as a day and night fighter.

4. Mikoyan-Gurevich MiG-3 from the 11th Fighter Regiment (IAP) in 1943. Withdrawn from operational frontline regiments at the beginning of 1944, the MiG-3 was used until the end of the conflict by Soviet defence units (PVO).

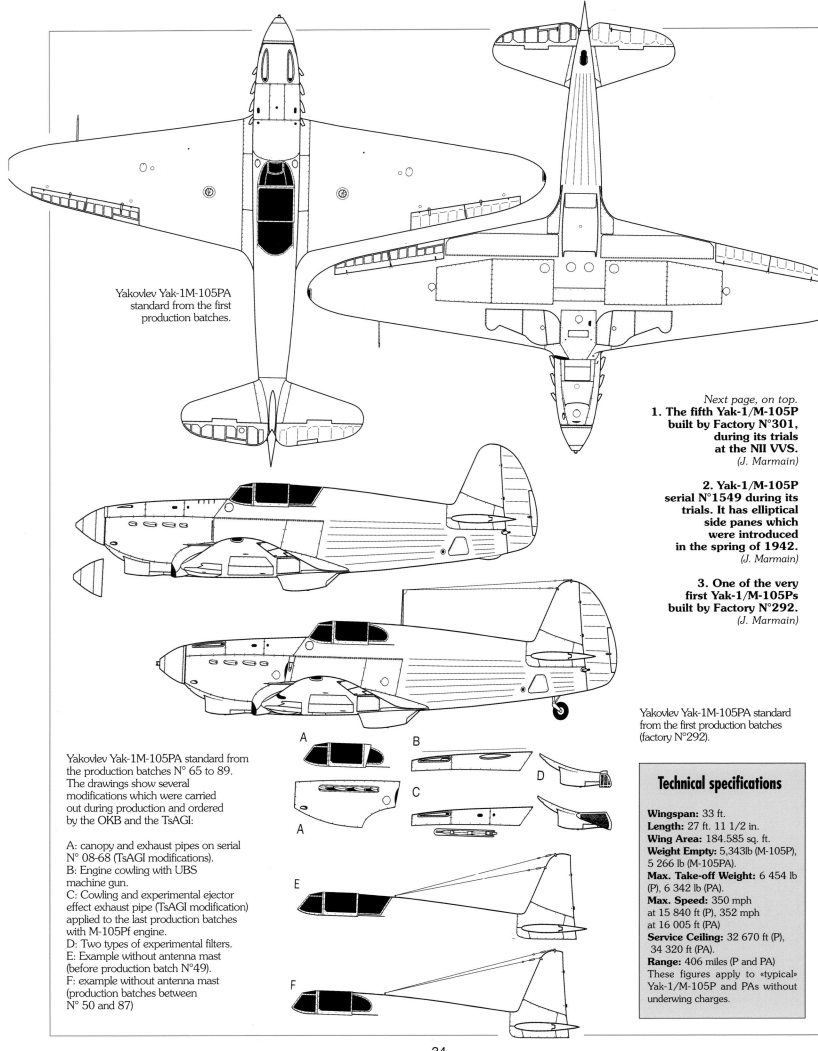

Yakovlev Yak-1M-105PA
standard from the first
production batches.

Next page, on top.
**1. The fifth Yak-1/M-105P
built by Factory N°301,
during its trials
at the NII VVS.**
(J. Marmain)

**2. Yak-1/M-105P
serial N°1549 during its
trials. It has elliptical
side panes which
were introduced
in the spring of 1942.**
(J. Marmain)

**3. One of the very
first Yak-1/M-105Ps
built by Factory N°292.**
(J. Marmain)

Yakovlev Yak-1M-105PA standard
from the first production batches
(factory N°292).

Yakovlev Yak-1M-105PA standard from
the production batches N° 65 to 89.
The drawings show several
modifications which were carried
out during production and ordered
by the OKB and the TsAGI:

A: canopy and exhaust pipes on serial
N° 08-68 (TsAGI modifications).
B: Engine cowling with UBS
machine gun.
C: Cowling and experimental ejector
effect exhaust pipe (TsAGI modification)
applied to the last production batches
with M-105Pf engine.
D: Two types of experimental filters.
E: Example without antenna mast
(before production batch N°49).
F: example without antenna mast
(production batches between
N° 50 and 87)

Technical specifications

Wingspan: 33 ft.
Length: 27 ft. 11 1/2 in.
Wing Area: 184.585 sq. ft.
Weight Empty: 5,343lb (M-105P),
5 266 lb (M-105PA).
Max. Take-off Weight: 6 454 lb
(P), 6 342 lb (PA).
Max. Speed: 350 mph
at 15 840 ft (P), 352 mph
at 16 005 ft (PA)
Service Ceiling: 32 670 ft (P),
34 320 ft (PA).
Range: 406 miles (P and PA)
These figures apply to «typical»
Yak-1/M-105P and PAs without
underwing charges.

At first, the number of rocket launchers was reduced to four (plus two bombs), but from 12 May 1942, the GKO decided to abandon this armament scheme on the Yak-1 after 1 148 examples had been equipped in this manner.

On 26 April 1942, the GKO ordered Factory N°292 to equip ten Yak-1s with four underwing rocket launchers. But by 25 May only one example had been fitted out, the engineers from the Yakovlev OKB having succeeded in the meantime in convincing the decision makers in high places that they were making a bad choice by lowering the aircraft's performances with the launchers. However, on 2 May 1942, another decision from the GKO repeated the order to install the rocket launchers under the wings of the «front» fighter for secondary bombing missions. The Yak-1s were fitted out with two BI-42 bomb launchers for 55 lb to 220 lb FAB projectiles (demolition) from batch N°80 onwards. But as the order was retroactive, all the Yak-1s from batches N° 5 to 126, then 148 to 192 - the last - were thus equipped (batches N° 127 to 147 escaped because

they were part of the airframe lightening programme). But whether powered by M-105P and PA or by the M-105PF (see below), the Yak-1s were clearly still underpowered with these loads and this totally ruined their performance and flight handling. With two 220-lb bombs, the typical MTOW was 6 899 lb, the take-off run was lengthened by 330 feet and the top speed and the rate of climb were greatly reduced (some reports noted that 550-lb bombs were carried). Moreover no specific bombing sights were available for the pilots who had to «trust in their flair» when aiming at ground targets. In fact, although most of the Yak-1s were equipped for tactical bombing, they were hardly ever used in this role. In all, 7 509 machines were fitted with bomb launchers.

NB.: During the winter of 1941-42, various Yak-1s were tested with the bombs and rockets simultaneously to determine exactly how they affected flight characteristics and how effective they were tactically. Among these Yak-1s was serial N° 38-55 which carried out 27 flights with test pilot A. G Proshakov at the controls at the NII VVS from 7 March to 24 April 1942. The true number of Yak-1s produced up to July 1944 will never be known exactly. The most often published figure is that of 8 670 examples of all types, in 192 batches, prototypes included (8 734 or 8667, depending on the sources), of which 2 998 Yak-1/M-105Ps and PAs.

B ISNOVAT

SK-2 Prototype
(Autumn 1940)

The SK-1 experimental prototype with cockpit closed. It was the forerunner of the SK-2. In flight, forward visibility was almost inexistent. *(J. Marmain)*

In 1938, Matus Ruvimovich Bisnovat (or Byesnovat), one of V.K. Tairov's assistants (Polikarpov OKB) was allowed to create his own OKB in order to work out new wing solutions for heavy loads, structural forms and types of controls and to test them under real flight conditions at high speeds. He conceived the SK-1 (SK for Skorostnii Krylov - high speed wing) according to his own aeronautical and aerodynamic ideas: powerful engine, very streamlined airframe, wings with span and surface area reduced to the minimum, retractable undercarriage and all-metal construction. The engine was an M-105 driving a VICh-52 propeller with a cone-

shaped boss, cooled by a ventral radiator with a frontal area of only 1.829 sq. ft. attached to an airflow compression system. The air intake for the carburization was very tightly faired on the top of the engine cowling which itself fitted very closely. There were four ejector exhaust pipes.

The semi-monocoque fuselage had an ovoid cross-section. Its frame was just big enough to allow the pilot to get into the cockpit which had no canopy so as not to create any «parasitical protuberance». Its structure was made of metal with stressed skin. The low NACA-230 profiled single spar wing was made of wood in the end and very carefully varnished and polished. The two single undercarriage legs and the tail wheel were retractable. Ready at the end of 1939, the SK-1 was tested by G.M. Shiyanov in January 1940 with the undercarriage lowered since it was fitted with skis in place of the wheels. When taking off and landing, Shiyanov could raise his seat so that his head stuck out above the upper contour of the fuselage behind a very small windshield which was extended automatically, giving some forward visibility. Otherwise he flew almost «blind and on instruments» as only the sides of the fuselage were glazed. In spite of the fixed undercarriage the machine reached 360 mph at very low altitude, handling was easy and in-flight behaviour was close to «perfect».

The excellent quality of his work enabled Bisnovat to build his SK-2, a fighter following the «K» programme specifications. Copied from the SK-1, it differed in having a conventional cockpit, with a canopy which swung open to the right and could be released in an emergency; the cockpit was placed very close to the tail which had been enlarged slightly; the undercarriage was fitted with wheels and the size of its ventral radiator was increased; its oil radiator was repositioned under the nose; the air intake was replaced by two gills in the wing roots. Two heavy machine guns or two ShVAK cannon or one ChKAS were planned but not installed. Shiyanov tested the SK-2 from November 1940 onwards and flew at 412.5 mph at 16 170 ft. Its behaviour was just as pleasing as the SK-1 but it had an accident in December (a forced belly-landing).

The SK-2 fighter prototype, derived from the previous SK-1. The photograph is dated 23 December 1940 when the plane was going through very satisfactory trials. *(J. Marmain)*

After it was repaired, the VVS thought its landing speed and its wing area were too high as were the landing and taking off distances. Moreover its range was clearly inadequate. So the plane was turned down by the military in December 1940 and all Bisnovat's work was cancelled.

Technical specifications

Wingspan: 24 ft. 1 in.
Length: 27 ft. 4 in.
Wing Area: 103.001 sq. ft.
Weight Empty: 4 070 lb.

Max. Take-off Weight: 5 060 lb.
Max. Speed: 412.5 mph at 16 170 ft.
Service Ceiling: 33 990 ft.
Range: ?

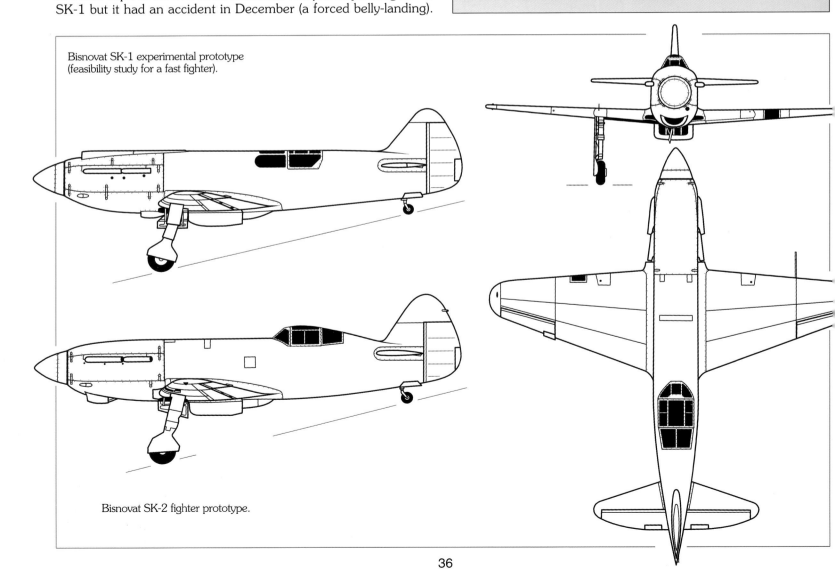

Bisnovat SK-1 experimental prototype (feasibility study for a fast fighter).

Bisnovat SK-2 fighter prototype.

BOROVKOV - FLOROV

«Object 10» and «Object 11» Projects
(Autumn 1940)

In Autumn 1940, the A.A. Borovkov and I.F. Florov constructor partnership envisaged developing two projects for biplanes equipped with ramjets based on their previous I-207 fighter project. This was started in 1937 and gave rise to several interesting prototypes from an experimental point of view; they had similar dimensions to those of the Polikarpov I-153 but without the stepped upper wing or struts. Although the programme did not give rise to any series production despite the VVS's interest in a dive-bomber version (an order for 200 machines was not fulfilled), the new decisions taken at the Kremlin meeting in January 1939 authorised the two men's design team to continue its efforts to find new aeronautical solutions. As a result and because the I-207 N°3 prototype had been tested with Merkulov ramjets, Borovkov and Florov thought they could make a version with an internally-installed ramjet, inside the airframe called «Object N°10». The aim was to show the authorities that a biplane could reach the same speeds as a monoplane and be more manoeuvrable, by having a perfectly streamlined airframe and by getting rid of the struts and all the other usual wiring, so that the design would produce as little drag as possible.

So that «Object» 10 could fly as fast as the new monoplane fighters, Borovkov and Florov installed one of Merkulov's «DM» ramjets in the rear part of the fuselage behind the pilot's seat. Thus this back-up engine would not produce any drag in flight when it was not being used; when the pilot spotted an intruder, or wanted to escape from one, and once the pilot started it, the auxiliary engine enabled the plane to reach an estimated speed of 525 mph.

The design was in the form of a biplane without wires or struts; the wings were in the shape of very flat Ws (upside-down for the upper wing, right way up for the lower wing). The engine selected was an M-71 with a propeller boss which contributed to the aircraft's streamlining. The aircraft's cross-section was round and tapered gradually to the tail where it ended in the exhaust pipe for the ramjet. The cockpit had a canopy and was located almost at the base of the very slender tail. Under the cockpit, the faired air intake which could be closed, supplied the ramjet which used the same fuel as the M-71. The tailplane was positioned just above the exhaust pipe and its position in the fuselage precluded any tail wheel. So the machine was fitted with retractable tricycle undercarriage and a little tail skid at the rear. Three versions were planned: a very manoeuvrable high-speed fighter, an escort fighter and a dive-bomber. The armament consisted of two ShKAS machine guns and one BS machine gun, which could be easily replaced in the units by two 23-mm cannon.

At the same time as «Object N°10», Borovkov and Florov conceived «Object N°11» which was similar to the previous one but with two DM ramjets installed side by side in the rear part of the fuselage. This time the undercarriage was classic and retractable, the tail wheel being installed between the two ramjets.

The intake for their air supply was at the beginning of the fuselage under a large propeller boss which contributed to the streamlining of the design.

Unfortunately Borovkov and Florov came up against the incomprehension of the authorities, for in the autumn of 1940 when they submitted their two projects nobody among the military seemed to be backing the biplane concept any more and A.S. Yakovlev, the assistant head of NKAP for the experimental section, warned Borovkov and Florov that neither of the two designs would be put on the list of future developments.

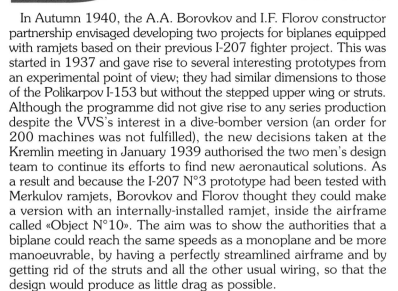

Borovkov-Florov «Object N°10» project.

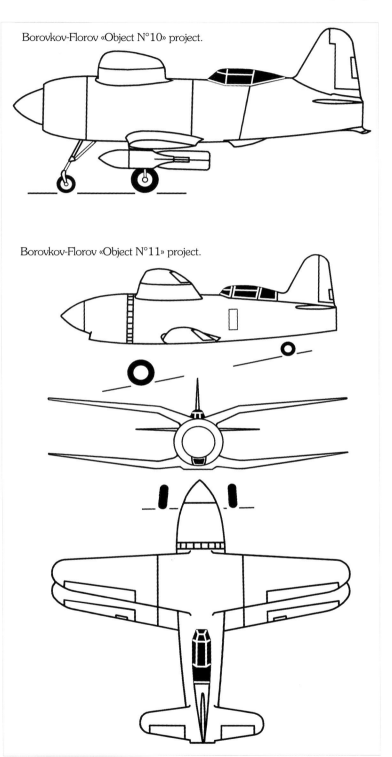

Borovkov-Florov «Object N°11» project.

Technical specifications

Wingspan: 31 ft. 4 in. (10), 28 ft. (11).
Length: 27 ft. 6 in. (10), 25 ft. 11 in. (11).
Wing Area: 258.312 sq. ft. (10), 236.786 sq. ft. (11)
Weight Empty: ?.

Max. Take-off Weight: 7 700 lb. (10), 7 150 lb. (11)
Max. Speed: 468.75 to 525 mph.
Range: 500 miles (10 and 11)

MIKOYAN-GUREVICH

MiG-1
(Autumn 1940)

The host of defects recorded at the trials of the three I-200 prototypes gave rise to a programme of modifications classified as «urgent». Among the essential changes to be carried out were: installing leading edges slats to improve stability; increasing the size of the tyres; protecting the fuel tanks and increasing their capacity, to give a range of 625 miles; redesigning the cockpit canopy; redesigning the power plant's cooling system. A second conduit for cooling the oil was inserted on the right-hand side of the engine with two flaps for regulating the evacuation of the air at the end of both conduits and not at the beginning). The ventral tunnel for the glycol radiator was lengthened and the canopy was redesigned to slide backwards. While these modifications were being carried out on I-200 N°3, 100 examples of the same machine were ordered of which 25 were already being built in December 1940 under the designation MiG-1. A sliding canopy was only installed on the ninth example, but the leading edge slats were absent. Armament was grouped together over the engine and comprised a UBS heavy machine gun slightly off-centre to the left (300 rounds) and two ShKAS (375 rounds each). The MiG-1 could carry two 110- or 220-lb FAB bombs in the secondary infantry support role.

The first 25 MiG-1s were transferred to Yevpatoria in the Crimea, under better weather conditions than at Moscow. They were evaluated operationally by the pilots of 146.IAP commanded by Major Orlov who was joined by S. Suprun and the engineers Nikichenko and Kariev. In February 1941, they were moved to the Kachinks Military School. The modifications had made them heavier, reducing their range and top speed (362 mph at 23 760 feet). The reports from the pilots did not contain just praise however, although the planes were already being mass-produced. They gave rise to another programme of «urgent» modifications which ended up changing the MiG-1 into the MiG-3.

Technical specifications

Wingspan: 33 ft. 7 in.	**Max. Take-off Weight:** 6 817 lb.
Length: 26 ft. 11 in.	**Max. Speed:** 392 mph at 23 760 ft.
Wing Area: 187.706 sq. ft.	**Service Ceiling:** 39 600 ft.
Weight Empty: 5 724 lb.	**Range:** 362 miles

MIKOYAN-GUREVICH

IP-201 (ex I-200 N°3) Prototype
(Autumn 1940)

In the summer of 1940, the armourers Ya. G. Taubin and M.N. Baburin brought out a new canon: the 23-mm MP-3, or PTB-23 designed by OKB-16 at the NKVD. They installed it in a container fixed under a section of MiG-1 wing which then served as a test bench so as to increase the armament of the Mikoyan-Gurevich OKB's new «front» fighter

whose fire power was under question. The plan was to have two underwing cannon on the new machine. The model was subjected to close study by a commission led by B.N. Yurev; although the initial calculations revealed a 9 mph loss of speed, which after all was thought to be negligible for a machine showing a top speed of 406 mph, those made by the Yurev team indicated that the loss was higher, perhaps some 21 mph slower. Despite this, the authorities decided to start «Project IP-201» (IP for Istrebityel Pushchni - fighter equipped with cannon) and

allowed experiments with the I-200 N°3 prototype to start.

Support for the MP-3 was not unanimous among the military authorities since its 300-rpm was considered too slow. However, at the end of September 1940, the prototype, rechristened IP-201 for the occasion, was submitted to a series of modifications so that it could be fitted with two containers holding MP-3s under the wings and eliminate the two ShKAS machine guns on the engine (the UBS was kept). This work was approved on 12 October because meanwhile, Taubin and Baburin had improved their canon and presented the MP-6 whose rate of fire was double that of the previous MP-3. This time the authorities seemed to be happy; after having approved the MP-6, the Sovnarkom told all the aircraft builders on 16 November to use the new canon when doing their tests on their combat planes.

Installing the new canon was not easy and deformed the wing so much that a new series of modifications had to be undertaken to restore the profile before the definitive «graft» could be made, and succeed. On 1st December, piloted by V.N. Gurski, the IP-201 took off for the first and last time under that designation and with its new armament. The flight ended with a forced landing as a result of problems with the flow of fuel from the main tank. The IP-201 project was abandoned as quickly as it had been initiated, because the trials on other machines were so disappointing that the NKAP and

the VVS did not want to insist. The IP-201 was repaired and brought back to I-200 N°3 standards.

Taubin and Baburin were arrested on 15 May 1941 and executed. The charges against them, apart from the failure of the MP-6, included influence peddling. The authorities, charmed by the MP-6's characteristics, had put all their expectations into this new canon and had allowed themselves to be convinced by the two armourers of the absolute necessity of changing all combat aircraft armament in favour of the MP-6.

MIKOYAN -GUREVICH

MiG-3
(December 1940)

While the hundred or so MiG-1s were being built, the OKO-1 revised the model's specifications, using the reports from prototype trials and wind tunnel tests at the TsAGI to work on. The schedule of modifications was extensive. Apart from those concerning the canopy and the power plant's cooling system,

OKO-1 applied the following changes: replacing the propeller by a VISh-61Sh; adding a 55-gallon tank under the pilot's feet; transferring inert gases from the exhaust to the tanks and installing self-sealing material; increasing the dihedral angle on the outer wing sections (to 6%) and fitting leading edge slats; fitting 650 x 200 mm tyres on the wheels and getting rid of the articulated part of the wheel well doors; enlarging the bevelled glazed panel behind the canopy; installing an 8-mm thick armoured plate on the back of the pilot's seat; replacing the PBP-1 sights with a PBP-1A set which were more accurate; installing an RSI-3 radio transmission system (later an RSI-4 system).

With all these changes, the model was re-designated MiG-3 as of the 101st airframe coming off the production lines. In theory the armament was not changed, but the VVS thought it insufficient and insisted that OKO-12 add two UBK machine guns in detachable underwing pods. These weighed the machine down so much that in the units the pilots more often than not had them removed to restore the MiG's performance and manoeuvrability. The bomb loads varied: 3 1/2-lb to 220-lb bombs up to a maximum of 484 lb, or two VAP-6M or ZAP-6 dispensers (chemical products or napalm) or eight unguided RS-82 rockets. On the other hand, leading edge slats were not fitted.

Ten of the eleven MiG-3s which came off the production lines at the end of December 1940 took part in an operational evaluation programme which ended badly for one of Factory N°1's pilots. On 13 March 1941, the rotor of the centrifugal supercharger of one of the MiG-3s came undone, pierced the armoured plate, then the front tank and reached the cockpit fatally wounding the pilot on the way. In spite of the modifications that were made, the MiG-3 was still a difficult machine to handle. Over-sharp correction on the joystick risked sending it into a spin. On 12 January 1941 the pilot, V. Kuleshov, was killed when the

aircraft went into a spin. He tried to bale out but it was too late. The mass of the MiG-3 increased but its top speed did too, to 400 mph at 25 740 feet during the trials. On the other hand, its range was still lower than the 625 miles that were required: only 535 miles.

The first fighter units received their MiG-3 fighters from the spring of 1941 (normally the MiG-1s were only used for the pilots to familiarise themselves with the machine). The government asked for production rates to increase because of the way the war was unfolding in Europe; so at the end of March, 473 machines had left the factories, of which 200 had already reached the front line units. The premise that war was imminent meant that they were destined to serve in the border units. A lot of accidents and incidents were caused by the pilots' lack of experience and training with the new flying techniques, but little by little they managed to master their new mounts.

On the day of the German invasion, 22 June 1941, the VVS took delivery of the new fighters (LaGG-3, Yak-1 and MiG-3) but they only represented 37% of the total strength, of which 90% were MiG-3s (the VVS had accepted 917 on 22 June). The remaining 63% were old I-152s, I-153s and I-16s together with a few antique I-5s. During the German onslaught, the MiG-3s became priority targets, as much on the ground as in the air. But the improvements for better high altitude performance, the numerous design defects still not corrected, the bad finish on the skin and the extra weight all reduced their speed and range;

A brand-new MiG-3 without any operational markings and waiting to be assigned to a unit. The shape of the frontal opening of the left-hand fairing for the oil cooler is not the same as the one on the right. *(J. Marmain)*

Technical specifications

Wingspan: 33 ft. 7 in.	**Max. Take-off Weight:** 7 370 lb.
Length: 27 ft. 3 in.	**Max. Speed:** 400 mph at 25 740 ft.
Wing Area: 187.706 sq. ft.	**Service Ceiling:** 39 600 ft.
Weight Empty: 5 871 lb.	**Range:** 512 miles

From left to right.
A MIG-3 at its joint factory and NII VVS trials at Katcha in February and March 1941. These trials were to find out far it could fly. *(J. Marmain)*

With the inscription *"Death to the German Occupiers"* painted on its back, this MiG-3 is waiting to take off. Note the position of the antenna mast. *(J. Marmain)*

they were therefore unable to fight at low and medium altitudes; all the more so as the pilots did not want to use the underwing pods containing the UBK machine guns (they were replaceable by 20 or 23-mm cannon) which made the plane even less manoeuvrable at those altitudes. OKO-1 ended up recommending the pilots not to use them and to avoid filling the fuselage tanks completely in order to save about 255 lb.

At the end of May 1941, five MiG-3s were taken from the production lines in order to undergo a new series of modifications: better trimming on the ailerons; tail surface dimensions reviewed; leading edge slats (which were not fitted to the series machines) fitted, etc. The tests carried out by NII VVS and LII VVS pilots gave very favourable results. These unfortunately did not have an immediate effect on the production series because in the meantime the war against Germany had started.

The scope of the destruction caused to the VVS by the Luftwaffe meant that the MiG-3s were reassigned to defence units (PVO). Their mission was to intercept the waves of bombers and reconnaissance planes flying high (some carried out very successful night missions). At the end of the summer of 1941, new modifications were introduced: fitting (at last) leading edge slats on all production machines; installing automatic variable pitch propellers; increasing the engine gearing ratio; redesigning the fairings for the fixed weapons, etc. The MiG-3's stability, its manoeuvrability and engine reliability were all improved, as was its speed at altitude, at the cost of a reduced rate of climb.

On 3 July 1941, the NKAP ordered four MiG-3s to be modified and equipped with specially adapted AFA-1 cameras by the design team. These machines were for reconnaissance missions and were tested by the GK NII VVS. After a fifth machine had undergone the same changes and tests, the design was adopted officially, to be applied operationally.

Although production rates were reaching their limit at Factory N°1 in August, the fate of the MiG-3 was already sealed: the military decided it had to go, with Stalin's approval. The VVS needed assault planes like the Ilyushin Il-2 with AM-38

engine (a variant of the AM-35 for low altitudes). So as to be able to do this, production capacity had to be found somewhere. With the evacuation eastwards of the vital factories threatened by the German breakthrough, the «death» of the MiG-3 was just a quick as its birth. In December 1941, Stalin ordered its production to be halted. The USSR did not need high-altitude fighters, but Il-2s and AM-38 engines «as essential to the Red Army as oxygen and bread».

Before the production of the MiG-3 was stopped, OKO-1 brought out a new variant of the MiG-3 on which the improvements already mentioned had been carried out, together with a propeller with bigger blades, exhaust pipes with redesigned fairings and six RS-82 rockets. 49 of these machines rolled out of the factory up to the end of October and a further 182 later. The decision to bury the MiG-3 and its engine was made official on 23 December 1941. The last examples were delivered at the beginning of 1942 just before Factory N°1 returned to Khodinka, the German threat to Moscow having in the meantime receded and moved to the south, towards Stalingrad. The total production amounted to 3 222 machines, prototypes, MiG-1 and MiG-3 included.

NB: OKO-1 studied 16 different weapon arrangements of which some were tested. One machine was armed with five heavy machine guns, another tried out only two, then two 20-mm cannon. But the tests were not conclusive.

NB. According to some sources, the MiG-3s were never equipped with leading edge slats, except on some prototypes of which one was tested in 1940 with slats covering the whole span of each outer section (which was subsequently shortened) within the framework of the I-210 programme.

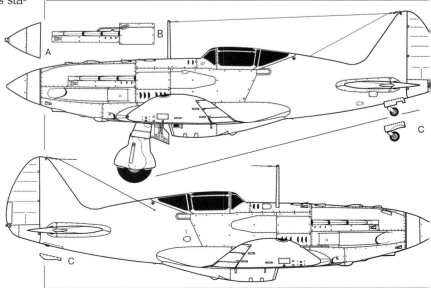

A MiG-3 with its heavy machine guns installed in underwing containers. They were not used very much because they reduced the aircraft's performance too much.
(J. Marmain)

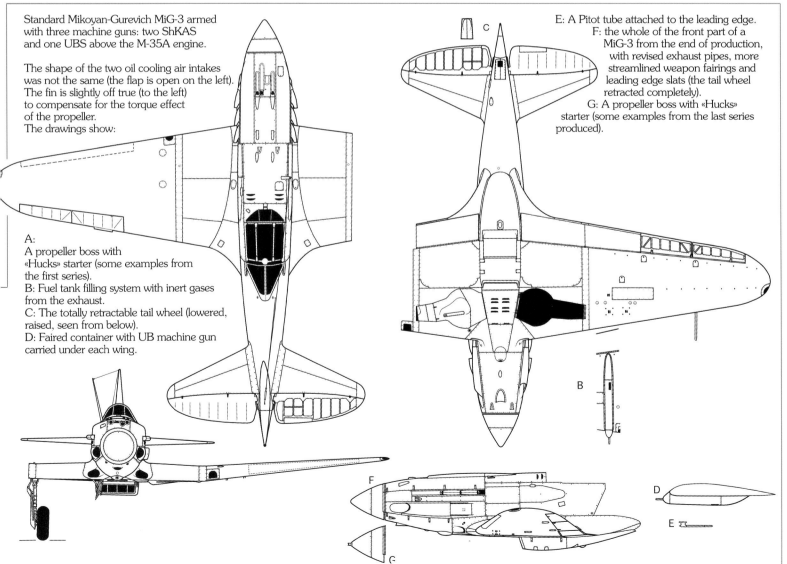

Standard Mikoyan-Gurevich MiG-3 armed with three machine guns: two ShKAS and one UBS above the M-35A engine.

The shape of the two oil cooling air intakes was not the same (the flap is open on the left). The fin is slightly off true (to the left) to compensate for the torque effect of the propeller.
The drawings show:

A:
A propeller boss with «Hucks» starter (some examples from the first series).
B: Fuel tank filling system with inert gases from the exhaust.
C: The totally retractable tail wheel (lowered, raised, seen from below).
D: Faired container with UB machine gun carried under each wing.

E: A Pitot tube attached to the leading edge.
F: the whole of the front part of a MiG-3 from the end of production, with revised exhaust pipes, more streamlined weapon fairings and leading edge slats (the tail wheel retracted completely).
G: A propeller boss with «Hucks» starter (some examples from the last series produced).

L AVOCHKIN
GORBUNOV - GUDKOV

LaGG-3 «Type 31»
(December 1940 to 1944)

The modification schedule planned for putting the finishing touches to the I-301 (LaGG-3) enabled 440 lb to be saved on the overall structure, which was a «too robust» design. The wing design (NACA profile 23016 at the wing roots and NACA-23010 at the tips) was revised to include two further 12 1/2 gallon tanks in the outer sections (total capacity rose to 100 gallons) and automatic slats on the leading edges (from the 34th batch onwards). A whole series of different arrangements of weight trims on the movable surfaces were tested with the I-301 prototypes, of which several were retained for the production series: counterweight on the top and the base of the tail fin (on the top only as of the 7th batch, rudder with flush wing slats as of the 23rd batch), internal pendulous (then axial) counterweight system for the elevators. The standard armament was decided upon: one axial ShVAK canon with 120 rounds (one axial UBS for the first examples of the series) and two synchronised ShKAS machine guns over the M-105P or PA engine (325 rounds per weapon). Three to four unguided RS-82 rockets or various bombs or two 17 1/2- or 22-gallon drop tanks could be carried under each wing.

While waiting for the new model designated LaGG-3 «Type-31» to be finalised, the two prototypes continued their tests, exploring the different flying and instrument characteristics (spins, dives, armament, on-board instrumentation, etc). I-301 N°01 was lost on 4 January 1941 following a forced landing (engine problems) which damaged it beyond repair. As I-301 N°02's wing could not take the extra two tanks, the authorities decided to continue the tests with a LaGG-3 from the very beginning of the production series.

In the autumn of 1940, the Lavochkin-Gorbunov-Gudkov threesome split up. Getting the production lines in the designated factories started was difficult considering the materials used for producing LaGG-3s. Gudkov remained in Moscow whereas Lavochkin was transferred to Gorki (Factory N°21), the principal production site. Gorbunov had to supervise the one at Taganrog (Factory N°31). From then on each of them undertook separately, and sometimes in competition with the other two, the development of the LaGG-3, depending on the military authorities' requirements. Lavochkin nevertheless remained the «the system's boss».

The first LaGG-3 rolled out of the Leningrad factory (N°23). Nikashin tested it in December 1940. As soon as they were built, the following

Top.
A LaGG-3 from the very first series, without the sliding part of its canopy, testing the flow of air on the wing and skin resistance. Note the two counter-weights on and under the rudder.
(J. Marmain)

models were sent to their units in Soviet Asia (Stalin was worried lest the presence of Japanese troops in Manchuria start another war) where the pilots reported a number of imperfections: oil leaks, broken connecting rods, badly made hydraulic systems, overheating engine. Only 65 machines were built at Leningrad before the factory was evacuated to Novosibirsk where it merged with N°153. Factory N°21 finished its first Lagg-3 in January 1941. It was tested on the 23rd then, after a short factory test programme, it was transferred to the NII VVS for approval between February and April. The same defects were noted and in spite of the initial «diet», it had put on weight, some 880 lb caused by the installation of various items of equipment and the increase in fuel capacity. Thus several other LaGG-3s were «prototypes used to rectify the major defects urgently» (apart from those already mentioned): the landing gear was defective, the tail wheel was broken (fragile retracting and locking mechanisms); the canopy was badly fitted and was not very transparent; the metal sheet on the engine cowling and the stressed skin were badly finished; etc.

In February 1941, no less than 2 228 different modifications were recorded by Lavochkin's OKB and had to be introduced into the series. Despite the military's «doubts» about the LaGG-3's effectiveness, its strength and the modernity of its design (which had already enabled a

Technical specifications	
Wingspan: 32 ft. 4 in.	**Max. Speed:**
Length: 29 ft. 1 1/2 in.	359 mph at 16 500 ft
Wing Area: 188.460 sq. ft.	(first batches, 1941),
W. E.: 5 660 lb (first batches, 1941),	334 mph at 16 500 ft (1941),
5 742 lb (1941),	323 mph at 16 830 ft (1942).
5 568 lb (1942).	**S. C.:** 30 000ft (first batches, 1941),
Max. Take-off Weight:	30 690 ft (1941 and 1942).
7 361 lb (first batches, 1941),	**Range:** 543 miles (first batches, 1941),
7 216 lb (1941),	440 miles (1941)
6820 (1942).	and 291 miles (1942)

Top.
**A LaGG-3 from the 23rd production series
with two bomb-launchers and six RS-82 rocket-launcher rails.
It is fitted with skis for taking off and landing in the snow.**
(J. Marmain)

Above.
**An example from the 66th and last production batch
of the LaGG-3 fighter, recognisable by its canopy with a double
rear frame support.** *(J. Marmain)*

Right.
**A LaGG-3 from the 23rd series fitted with skis.
It still has a counterweight on the top of the rudder,
a feature which disappeared during this production batch,
being replaced by a rudder with a flush slat.** *(RART)*

lot of changes and developments to be undertaken) made it indispensable for re-equipping VVS fighter and interception units. But these doubts were however justified. The models tested only flew at 360 mph at 16 500 feet and getting to that height took 6.8 minutes. Moreover, the engine overheating problems, the continual oil leaks and hydraulic system failures prevented the pilots from exploiting the full operational potential of the LaGG-3.

At Taganrog, Gorbunov was confronted with the same teething problems when setting up mass-production of the LaGG-3, which were compounded by the fact that the factory mainly produced planes made of metal. The stream of modifications which came from the Lavochkin OKB did not simplify matters and some of them, recommended by Gorbunov himself, were very seriously challenged. As for Factory N°153, it only started to produce LaGG-3s after the evacuation caused by the German invasion. Having merged with several other factories, it became a huge complex. The first LaGG-3s delivered were so bad that none of them could be declared «fit for service».

No other plane among those approved in 1939 was beset by so many problems as was the LaGG-3. The increase in the factories' production rates was followed by a host of defects. They were caused by teams of workers who knew hardly anything about aircraft manufacturing techniques and particularly those of the Lavochkin fighter. Because of the number of problems posed by the machine (certain accidents were fatal during training), the pilots called it the «guaranteed varnished coffin» (in Russian Lakirovanny Garantirovannyi Grab, or LaGG) because its in-flight behaviour turned out to be quite unpredictable, strange and so bronco-like, with a tendency to rear up and want to stall, with consequent loss of stability (whence the fitting of counterweights on the moving surfaces).

However, little by little, despite a top speed only obtained in a free dive (the LaGG-3 tested in the summer of 1941 only reached 335 to 343 mph compared with the prototype's 365 mph) caused by its mass and the lack of power from the M-105P, despite power plant vibration during dives and various other defects, the quality of the LaGG-3's manufacture evened up and the pilots started to feel better flying it. The plane now had the benefit of a radio transmission system, the canopy was larger and the windshield was armoured, the hydraulic system was made more reliable, the counterweights were replaced by axial trim (elevators) and flush slats (steering, on the 23rd production batch) and filling the tanks by inert gases was standardised.

The government ordered 66 batches which underwent a host of successive changes among which the most important were (from batches): N°1 to N°3 powered by an M-105P engine, N°4 to N°28 powered by an M-105PA engine, and N°29 to N°66 with an M-105PF (mounting made of welded steel, 10-foot VISh-61P variable pitch propeller with hydraulic controls); N°1 to N°4 with armament

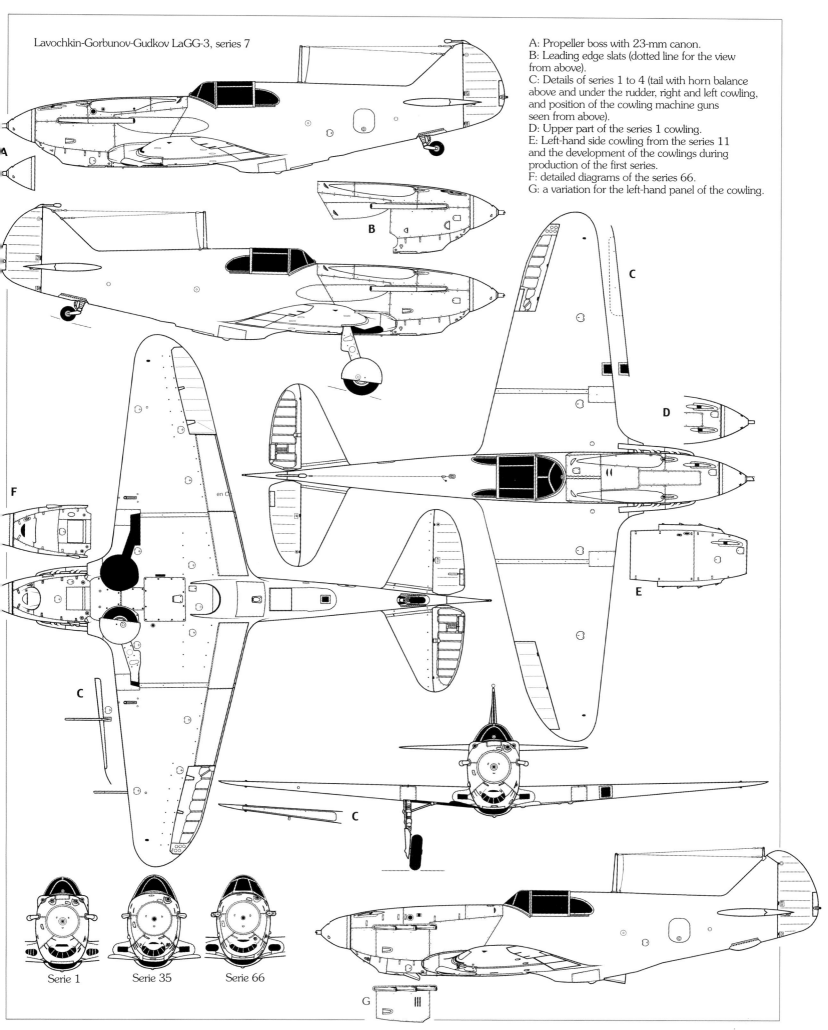

Lavochkin-Gorbunov-Gudkov LaGG-3, series 7

A: Propeller boss with 23-mm canon.
B: Leading edge slats (dotted line for the view from above).
C: Details of series 1 to 4 (tail with horn balance above and under the rudder, right and left cowling, and position of the cowling machine guns seen from above).
D: Upper part of the series 1 cowling.
E: Left-hand side cowling from the series 11 and the development of the cowlings during production of the first series.
F: detailed diagrams of the series 66.
G: a variation for the left-hand panel of the cowling.

Serie 1   Serie 35   Serie 66

45

comprising one axial UBS, two UBS and two ShKAS machine guns under the cowling (the UBS was sometimes not fitted and the lower balance horn disappeared from batch N°7 onwards); from batch N°8, an axial ShVAK canon, a UBS under the cowling and from batch N°11, six to eight RS-82 rockets or two FAB-50 (demolition), FAB-50M or AO-25M (fragmentation), ZAB-50TG (incendiary), TShAB-25R-5 and AOTSh-25 (phosgene, mustard gas, napalm), VAP-6M and ZAP-6 (chemical) bombs under wing; batch N°23: the elimination of the balance horn, replaced by flush slats (rudder) and modified rear structure on the cockpit canopy; batch N°29 powered by an M-105PF engine with three exhaust pipes per bank; batch N°33 with VISh-105V propeller; batch N° 34 with NS-37 axial canon and one UBS under the cowling; batch N°35 with widened and lengthened (rearwards) ventral radiator, retractable tail wheel; batch N°66 with lightened airframe, armoured windshield (flat plates), revised canopy (this was the fastest batch - 431 mph with eight exhaust pipes, redesigned ventral tunnel and nose radiator). Depend-

ing on supply and availability, VYa cannon could replace the ShVAKs and some examples were armed with three UBS and two ShKAS. Finally the rockets and bombs could be replaced by two underwing gondolas containing a UBS (rarely used) each or two drop tanks.

Certain machines made by Factory N°21 were equipped with fuel tanks made of densified wood because the deliveries of AMTs aluminium were rare for a while after the factory was evacuated. Others were fitted with wooden VISh-105PD or VS propellers for the same reasons (with a loss of about 15 mph).

The mass production of the LaGG-3 was stopped in 1944 after the 6 528th was finished. Factory N°23 built 65 in 1941; N°21 made 1 659 in 1941 and 1 924 in 1942; N°31 produced 474 in 1941, 782 in 1942, 1 065 in 1943 and 229 in 1944 (it was the last to stop production); and N°153 built 265 in 1941 and 65 in 1942. Out of this total only 5 924 were actually accepted by the VVS. Among the others, some took part in experimental programmes; others were brought up to La-5 standards.

BOROVKOV - FLOROV

Project «D», aka IS-207
(End of 1940)

At the end of 1940, A.I. Borovkov and I.F. Florov's OKB-207 planned to develop a fighter-interceptor based on the use of two Merkulov DM-12 ramjets to increase the aircraft's top speed and rate of climb. The preliminary design, referenced as «D» was a twin-boom, twin tail monoplane with central fuselage in the form of a bullet ending with a compartment housing a Shvetsov M-71 pusher engine. The wing was a very flat «w» with a laminar profile. Its 18°-swept leading edge had automatic slats. The two Ramjets were housed in the booms supporting the tail. The rectangular tail plane was positioned high on the fin. The cockpit and the very long streamlined canopy were incorporated into the nose of the nacelle. So that the pilot could survive in an emergency, the whole of the front section including his seat was ejected downwards to avoid getting caught up in the four-blade pusher propeller. The plane had retractable tricycle undercarriage. Two 37-mm cannon and two ShKAS machine guns were installed under the cockpit and fired through the nose. The whole of the front part of the nacelle could be disconnected and pushed forwards along built-in rails to give good access to all the on-board equipment and the armament.

On the evidence obtained from the configuration, the new conception and the announced estimated speed of some 531 mph, the «D» was officially approved by the NKAP at the beginning of 1941 and given the designation IS-207. The plans were finished in the spring but it was obviously going to take a lot of time to realise this rather «futuristic» interceptor and its Ramjets which were still being developed. The beginning of the German invasion of the USSR put all Soviet experimental aviation policies into question. All of a sudden, in July, like many others, Borovkov and Florov's work was cancelled and their OKB disbanded.

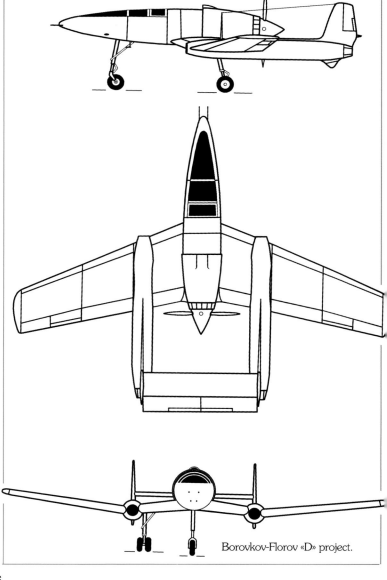

Borovkov-Florov «D» project.

Technical specifications

Wingspan: 47 ft. 10 in.
Length: 35 ft. 6 in.
Wing Area: 376.705 sq. ft. or 322.890 sq. ft. depending on the source.
Max. Take-off Weight: 11 550 lb.

or 13 200 lb depending on to the source.
Max. Speed: 412.5 mph at 20 295 ft (without the DM-12s), 523 mph (with the DM-12s - estimates).

LaGG-3

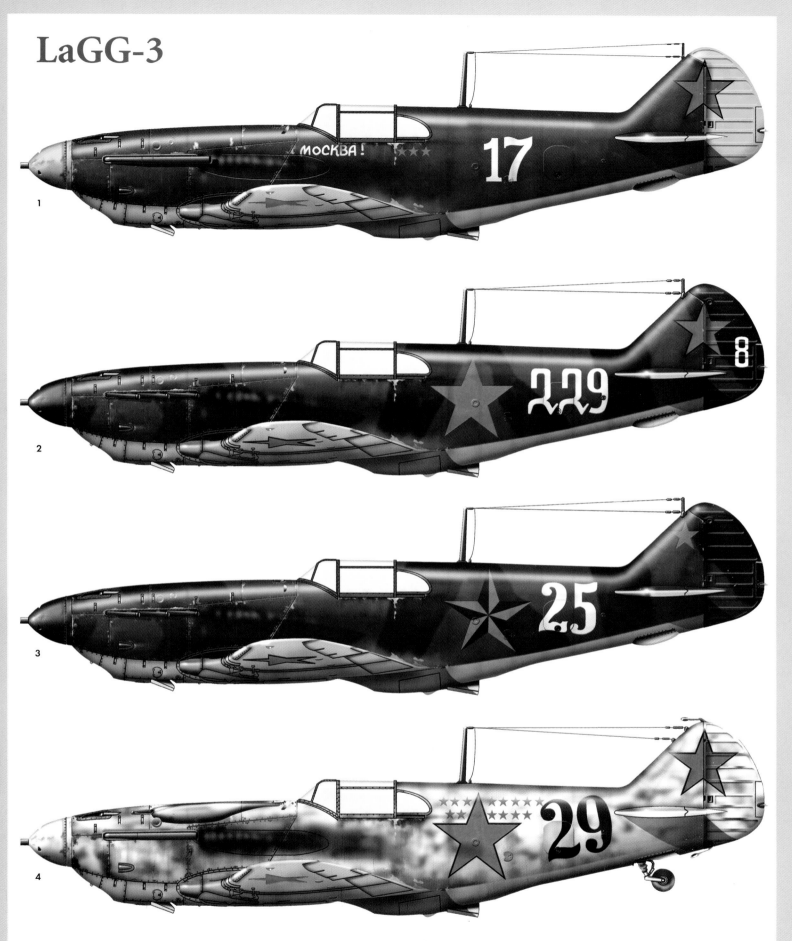

1. LaGG-3 from an unknown unit assigned to the defence of Moscow, as shown by the inscription below the canopy. The very sober dark green-based camouflage on the upper surfaces was only enhanced by the propeller boss and the rudder, both painted yellow.

2. LaGG-3 Type 29, from an unidentified unit.

The three-figure individual number is unusual for a machine belonging to a fighter regiment.

3. LaGG-3 Type 29, from an unidentified unit, captured on the Eastern Front by the Germans. The fuselage star, with black shading to give the effect of relief, was nicknamed the «Kremlin Star».

4. LaGG-3 flown by Captain Gerasim A. Grigoriev, from the 178th Fighter Regiment (IAP), Moscow Defence Zone, January 1943. Although the upper surfaces of the aircraft have been temporarily camouflaged in white, the pilot's kills have been preserved on the rear of the fuselage, represented by red stars.

47

MOJAROVSKI
VENYEVIDOV
Bsh-MV «Kombaïn» Project
(End of 1940)

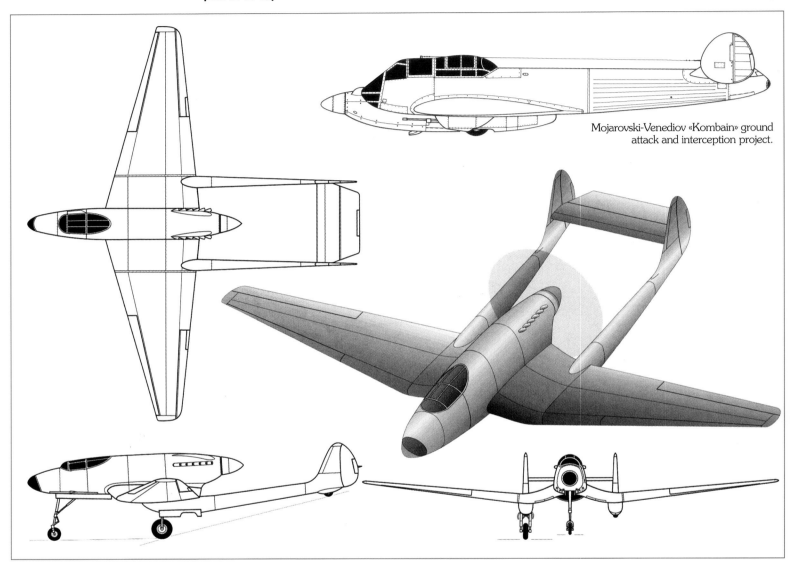

Mojarovski-Venediov «Kombain» ground
attack and interception project.

The Bsh-MV «Kombaïn» project designed by the armourer partnership of G.M. Mojarovski and I.V. Venyevidov who were combat aircraft armament specialists (turrets, mountings, frames, etc.) was based on the then revolutionary concept of a special mobile mounting for following a target on the ground designated «KABB». It comprised two ShVAK cannon and two ShKAS machine guns with a downwards deflection of 30°. This weapons system was intended for ground attack planes (the Sturmoviks) which the VVS greatly needed.

In order to demonstrate the feasibility of their idea, at the end of 1940 Mojarovski and Venyevidov worked with A.A. Archangelski on building a plane specially designed to be equipped with this new system. They conceived a monoplane made entirely of metal, with a twin boom and twin tail configuration, with a low «w» wing and central fuselage powered by a Mikulin AM-38 pusher engine. The project's configuration suggests a retractable tricycle undercarriage. The bomb load was carried in bays in the central section of the wing and under it: up to 1 320 lb. of bombs, or 330 lb and six unguided RS-82 or RS-132 rockets. The single-seat cockpit was positioned in the front of the nacelle with a «car-type» door and a canopy (swinging over to the left).

The «KABB» was installed under the cockpit and could be blocked at 0° so that the BSh-MV could also be used as a fighter or interceptor against aerial intruders. During the development of the programme, the «KABB» system was tested on a modified light twin-engined Yak-2 bomber in April 1941. Although the tests were convincing, in the end the BSh-MV was not built because the threats of invasion meant that priority had to be given to other aeronautical concepts which were needed more urgently, but also because the technology for the BSH-MV/KABB association which had yet to be developed from the industrial point of view, was still too complex and required too much time to perfect (the «KABB» system was tested again on a Douglas A-20G «Boston» in 1944).

Technical specifications

Wingspan: 45 ft. 8 in.	**Max. Speed:** 375 mph (estimate).
Length: 37 ft. 2 in.	*No other figures are available*

1941

Mikoyan-Gurevich MiG-3 from the 7th Fighter Regiment (IAP), Leningrad Front, July 1942. The camouflage on this aircraft was particularly original because it was made of black zebra-like stripes painted over the brown and dark green background. In order to be able to bale out more easily, the pilots sometimes took the cockpit canopy off their fighters, a practice carried out even in winter.

GLOSSARY

POLIKARPOV

I-185/M-81 («RM» or 02, sometimes I-187) Prototype, ex-I-185/M-90 (January 1941)

The I-185/M-81 prototype in March 1941, a short while before the flight ban imposed by Yakovlev. The prototype had only flown once and the engine was not mass-produced. The photographs are dated 5 March 1941 and were classified «Top Secret». *(RART)*

As the M-90 engine was not available, Polikarpov planned to install either the M-71 initially recommended by A. I Shakurin, or an M-82 on the first unfinished airframe of his I-185 programme. But these were not ready and the design team had to fall back on the less powerful M-81 at the end of 1940 in order to start the trials. So the I-185/M-90 was rechristened «RM» (or «02») but its designation was in fact I-185/M-81 (certain documents mention the designation I-187). The fan incorporated with the propeller disappeared but the rest of the airframe only underwent the modifications needed to streamline the new engine which included a different fairing for the carburization intake, a single exhaust outlet on either side of the fuselage and a conventional propeller boss. The prototype was only test-flown once, on 11 January 1941,

The Polikarpov I-185/M-81 (sometimes I-187) prototype, ex-I-185/M-90. The tail wheel was tiny.

during which the aircraft did not exceed 303 mph at low altitude. In fact the engine was not thought to be powerful enough (1 300 bhp/969 kW rated power) and A.S. Yakovlev forbade its use on 21 March, particularly as the authorities had decided not to mass produce it. The test report however did note the prototype's good behaviour in flight. The M-81 was removed in April and subsequently replaced by an M-71.

Technical specifications

Wingspan: 32 ft. 4 in.	**Max. Take-off Weight:** 7 053 lb.
Length: 26 ft. 6 in.	**Max. Speed:** 309 mph at 0 ft.
Wing Area: 167.149 sq. ft.	
Weight Empty: 5 176 lb.	*No other figures available.*

POLIKARPOV

«1941» I-185/M-71 Prototype (ex-I-185/M-81) (April 1941)

Just after the only test flight of the I-185/M-81, an M-71 engine was delivered to the Polikarpov OKB on 16 February 1941. It was only a pre-series example which had been declared «fit for flying», and it was mounted in place of the M-81 and the plane tested on 8 April. The trial flight ended with an emergency landing because the propeller raced out of control; this was caused by a fault in the functioning of the pitch mechanism. Next it was the carburization which turned out to be defective and the M-71 gave up the ghost. No other example of the engine was available before the Germans invaded the USSR at the end of June 1941, so the prototype did not undergo any more factory trials until October and the delivery of another M-71. Subsequently, the machine was evaluated operationally by the 728.IAP on the Kalinin front together with the 2nd and 3rd prototypes, respectively powered by an M-82A and an M-71 (see below).

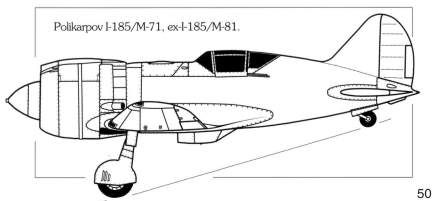

Polikarpov I-185/M-71, ex-I-185/M-81.

The I-185/M-71 prototype, ex-I-185/M-90 then I-185/M-81, photographed during its evaluations on 11 October 1941. The machine is equipped with the second engine, the M-71.
(RART)

Technical specifications

Wingspan: 32 ft. 4 in.   **Wing Area:** 167.149 sq. ft.
Length: 26 ft. 6 in.   *No other details available*

YAKOVLEV

Yak-7UT/M-105PA, and Yak-7UTI (or Yak-7R) photographic reconnaissance prototypes
(April and August 1941)

Before war was declared between Germany and Russia, the two-seat UTI-26 was the only plane designed for training pilots for the new «front» fighters (there had been an attempt to convert the LaGG-3 into a two-seater but without success). Making it was entrusted to Yakovlev because he had experience in this domain, having developed a fighter training monoplane in 1936 which was mass-produced for the VVS. Although it was still not perfect, the UTI-26 gave rise to the Yak-7UTI series which was different in that it had a fixed tail wheel and its armament was reduced to one ShKAS with 500 rounds installed over the engine. Its M-105PA engine, driving a VISh-61P propeller, was restricted to 2 350 rpm in order to avoid the continual power plant overheating problems. But the oil leaks persisted, just like the other main defects of the UTI-26.2 prototype on which the Yak-7UTI was based.

On 7 March 1941, the NKAP gave the green light for the production of 600 aircraft to start at the end of the year at Factory N°301, which then stopped producing the Yak-1 in April. The first example (serial number 01-02) was tested by P.Y. Fiodrovi on 18 May at Moscow Central Airfield. But the invasion of the USSR by German troops interrupted production of the model in September and disrupted planning because the factory was evacuated to Novosibirsk where production took up again at Factory N°153 in November. So in all only 186 examples were built, of which 145 in 1941, since priority was given to fighter production. Seven months went by before a new version of the two-seater was built (Yak-7V, see below). The story goes that all Lavochkin, Mikoyan-Gurevich and Yakovlev fighter pilots started on Yak-7UTIs (and Yak-7Vs) before going solo.

Some were used for rapid liaison, transporting high ranking

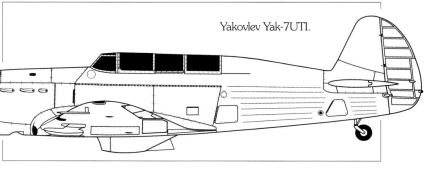

A rare photograph of a Yak-TUTI during its evaluation in mid-winter. The undercarriage is retractable and the Pitot tube has been installed under the left outer wing section. *(RR)*

Technical specifications

Wingspan: 33 ft.	**Max. Take-off Weight:** 6 160 lb.
Length: 28 ft.	**Max. Speed:** 366 mph at 14 850 ft.
Wing Area: 184.585 sq. ft.	**Service Ceiling:** ?.
Weight Empty: 5 027 lb.	**Range:** ?

Yakovlev Yak-7UTI.

front-line officers. Others carried out artillery fire correction missions in the Gachina region and during the siege of Leningrad. In August 1941, Factory N°301 adapted two Yak-7UTIs for photographic reconnaissance. They were equipped with an AFA-IM camera and a «Mayutka» RSI-4 transmitter. The airframe was very well insulated, the wings had leading edge slats, the pilots' seats

and the canopy were armoured and armament consisted of only the axial ShVAK canon with 120 rounds. They were submitted to the NII VVS for evaluation with a special brigade in September but the need to give priority to fighter production prevented them from being produced. The two prototypes were sometimes referenced as Yak-7R.

YAKOVLEV ★

I-30.1 and I-30.2 «Double» prototypes, or «Yak-3 1941- model» («Samolet 30», I-26U) (April and May 1941)

In answer to the criticisms aired by the pilots concerning the problems with the I-26/Yak-1 fighter, Yakovlev replied that all the defects would be corrected with the appearance of the I-30. This was the fourth part of the original «front» fighter programme presented by Yakovlev («Samolet 30», or I-26U depending on the documents) and in his design, he incorporated all the improvements dictated by the I-26, UTI-26 and I-28 trials. Two prototypes were ordered. Based on the Yak-1, the model was however a completely new machine. Its silhouette was more aerodynamic, with a single-seat cockpit with better designed and better positioned controls, and a slightly lower three-piece canopy. Particular care had been taken with the airframe insulation and sealing, so that the on-board RSI-4 radio («Mayutka» receiver and «Orel» transmitter) would be as effective as possible (125 miles' range at 13 200 feet).

The wing was still of monobloc construction and was copied from that of the I-28, but it was made entirely of metal and was in three parts: a central section without dihedral and two removable outer sections with a dihedral angle and automatic leading edge slats. The tail and the landing gear were those of the UTI-26/Yak-7 (see below).

Originally the engine was an M-105PD but it was not really ready and was unreliable, obliging the OKB to plan for it to be replaced by an M-105P driving a metal three-blade VISh-61Sh (ShA depending on the sources) propeller. The engine mounting and cowling were simplified for better production and to give easier access to the power plant. The exhaust pipes were faired and propulsive. The oil and glycol radiator intakes were fitted with filters and grills. The gills at the wing roots were redesigned. The four self-sealing wing tanks contained 842 lb of fuel and a little 6 1/2 gallon distribution tank enabled consumption to be controlled. A warning light told the pilot when there were only 11 gallons of fuel left in the left and right

Technical specifications

Wingspan: 32 ft. 2 in.
Length: 27 ft. 11 1/2 in.
Wing Area: 184.585 sq. ft.*
Weight Empty: 5 610 lb.
Max. Take-off Weight: 6 886 lb.

Max. Speed: 357 mph at 16 170 ft.
Service Ceiling: 29 700 ft.
Range: 609 miles
186.845 sq. ft. according to some sources.

tank groups. The oil tank contained 77 lb.

Armament was particularly powerful: an axial ShVAK canon with 120 shells, two synchronised ShVAK cannon at the beginning of the wing outer sections with 120 shells each. The fitting of the fuselage weapons was designed in such a way that they remained in place even when the engine was removed. The set of on-board instruments was very complete with a joystick copied from the Messerschmitt Bf 109, but there was no radio-compass which prevented the plane from flying in overcast conditions or at night.

The factory trial programme started on 5 April 1941. The plane was fitted with wooden outer wing sections without leading edge slats. The I-30.1's first flight took place on 12 April 1941 at the hands of Fiodrovi. Its M-105PD engine with Dollejal E-100 supercharger was not very reliable and was replaced with an M-105P with which it carried out its trials at the NII VVS from 17 June onwards. This time, the outer wing sections were made of metal and the leading edge slats had been installed. From the outset, and despite the increase in the estimates for the mass caused by the armament and the various modifications which had been carried out, in comparison to the Yak-1, the prototype turned out to be an excellent gun platform: very stable and very manoeuvrable. The leading edge slats made up for a lot of mistakes and enabled the plane to be flown at its

The I-30.1 prototype with its partitioned nose duct, its landing light, its Pitot tube and its two wing-mounted cannon, during its trials in the spring of 1941. (J. Marmain)

The I-30.1 prototype, «all flaps out at 15°». Note the camouflage scheme and that, as was often the case with Yakovlev, the prototypes had no markings. (J. Marmain)

The I-30.2 «Double», the second prototype in the «1941 Yak-3» programme. The elimination of the cooling duct for the oil in favour of openings in the central wing section leading edges enabled the front of the prototype to be considerably streamlined, giving it a sort of «Spitfire-look». The machine was equipped with RSI-4 radio transmission with antenna installed on the back. *(J. Marmain)*

minimum speed (78 mph) without stalling. Range went from 437 miles to 609 miles. On the other hand, general perform-ance turned out to be slightly lower than that of the I-26. Acro-batic figures were impracticable above 26 400 ft and landing speeds were higher, though the landing run did not increase because of the effectiveness of the brakes.

On 21 April 1941 the government gave the plane the designation «Yak-3, 1941 model», which was to be mass-produced in Moscow (factory N°81, at Saratov (N°292) and Khabarovsk (N°83) from 1 May, and 250 examples were to be made in 1941. The I-30.1 proto-type was allocated to Factory N°292, to be used for production. When hostilities started with Germany on 22 June, some airframes were already being made. But no pro-duction was carried out and no complete example saw the light of day. The destruction caused by the Ger-man onslaught, the evacuation of the vital factories eastwards and the lack of light alloys were responsible for this. However, on 19 December 1941, the government ordered the produc-tion of a further 1 100 machines for 1942, but the order was cancelled in March for the reasons which have already been mentioned. In 1942, the I-30.1 was modified to serve as a per-sonal plane for V.I. Stalin, Colonel and commanding officer of 434.IAP. Stalin's son had an M-105PF installed and had all the weapons removed except for the axial canon. The two outer wing tanks were also removed, bringing the capacity down to 594 lb. 891 lb were thus saved on the aircraft's mass, bringing the CG down to 21.1% of the MAC (against 23.2% before) and raising the speed to 365 mph, the same as the I-26.1 prototype.

In the meantime, the Yakovlev OKB finished the second prototype in May 1941. Designated I-30.2 «Double», it was similar to the previous aircraft but had a very slight-ly revised canopy (this was recommended for all fighters produced for the VVS, as were the wing-mounted weapons),

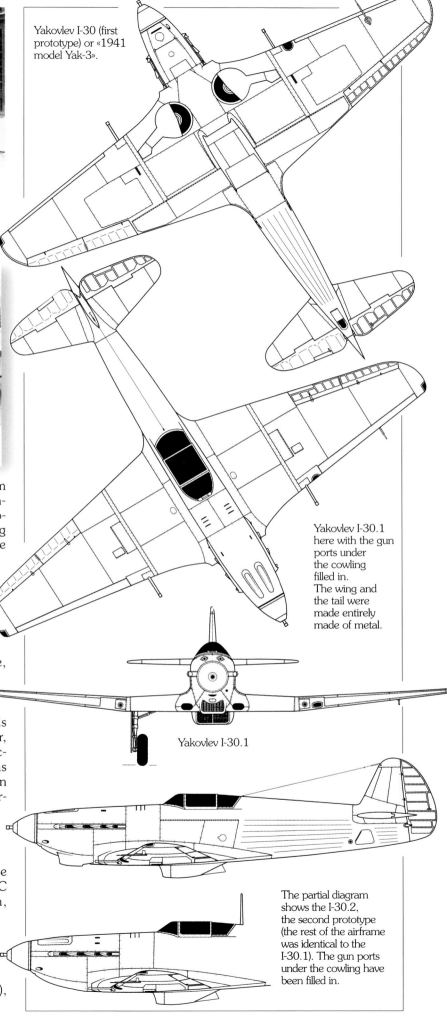

Yakovlev I-30 (first prototype) or «1941 model Yak-3».

Yakovlev I-30.1 here with the gun ports under the cowling filled in. The wing and the tail were made entirely made of metal.

Yakovlev I-30.1

The partial diagram shows the I-30.2, the second prototype (the rest of the airframe was identical to the I-30.1). The gun ports under the cowling have been filled in.

a shallower ventral intake installed further back under the belly. The oil radiator disappeared in favour of openings on the leading edges of the central wing section, making the whole of the underside of the engine section very streamlined aerodynamically. As for the I-30.1, the M-105PD was replaced by an M-105P which was still being tested. Armament was copied from that of the first prototype, but included four machine guns under the cowling which, according to the sources, were not installed (the rest of the armament was). In December 1942, during the trials at LII NKAP, P.I. Fiodrovi took off badly, stalled, fell to the ground, rolled over and seriously damaged the aircraft. The authorities ordered it to be scrapped and no further tests or development were carried out on the I-30 programme.

POLIKARPOV

ITP (1) and ITP (2) Preliminary studies (During 1940) and ITP (M-1) ITP (M-2) (May 1941 and November 1942)

Technical specifications	
Wingspan: 33 ft.	**Max. Speed:** 356 mph. at 16 500 ft. (1),
Length: 29 ft. 6 in.	418 mph. at 24 420 ft. (2)
Wing Area: 177.051 sq. ft.	**Service Ceiling:** 33 000ft. (1), 38 775 ft (2)
Weight Empty: ?	**Range:** 850 miles (1), 993 miles (2).
Max. Take-off Weight: 6 930 lb. (1), 7 803 lb. (2).	*The figures are estimates.*

Frustrated by being forced to give up and hand over his high altitude fighter «K» programme, Polikarpov used it to study another referenced «ITP» (Istrebituel Tyajelyi Pushechnyi, or heavily armed fighter) according to new specifications issued during 1940 for a heavy single-seat fighter armed with two 37-mm cannon. The preliminary study represented a low cantilever wing monoplane of mixed construction looking rather like a Curtiss P-40, and was made up of two parts: ITP (1) powered by an M-105P engine and ITP (2) by an AM-37P engine. Submitted to the authorities with a list of the characteristics and estimates for the performances for each part, in the end the programme was not pursued with those engines.

In 1941, the ITP changed power plants. Although the drawing up of the plans started as early as November 1940, building work on the prototype only began in May 1941. It was designed around an M-107P which was still experimental, and equipped with an axial ShK 37-mm canon with 40 rounds. The semi-monocoque fuselage was made of wood and covered in plywood. The cowling made of Dural sheets was very well streamlined around the engine. The exhaust gases were evacuated by two rows of individual pipes. The faired intake for the oil radiator under the nose ensured the supply of air for the carburization. Two radiators incorporated in the central wing section (without dihedral) cooled the glycol by means of two large rectangular gills set into the wing roots. The flow of hot air escaped underneath.

Three shots of the ITP (M-1) prototype during its trials in 1942 in Novosibirsk. The M-107P engine (replaced by an M-107A at the end of the year) and the individual exhaust pipes were extremely well enclosed as far as bodywork was concerned. Unfortunately this power plant and the 37-mm (then 20-mm) axial canon worked badly and the machine did not go through its State trials. *(J. Marmain)*

Technical specifications

Wingspan: 33 ft.
Length: 29 ft. 6 in. (M-1),
     30 ft. 4 in. (M-2)
Wing Area: 177.051 sq. ft. (M-1),
     177.589 sq. ft. (M-2)
Weight Empty: 6 512 lb. (M-1),
     6 402 lb. (M-2)
Max. Take-off Weight: 7 405 lb. (M-1),
     7 854 lb. (M-2)
Max. Speed: 409 mph. at 20 790 ft. (M-1),
     406 mph (M-2)
Service Ceiling: 34 320 ft. (M-1),
     37 950 ft. (M-2)
Range: 800 miles (M-1), 612 miles (M-2)

The two-spar wing was made entirely of metal (NACA-230 profile). The outer sections had a dihedral angle of 5°30'. There were automatic leading edge slats and the two fabric covered ailerons and split flaps were fitted to the trailing edge. The wooden tail was the same as those in the I-185 programme. The moving parts were fabric-covered. Two fuel tanks with a total capacity of 138 gallons were set into the wing central section.

The retractable undercarriage comprised two single members with oleo-pneumatic shock absorbers and a tail wheel. The cockpit and the canopy were the same as those of the I-185/M-82A (see below). Armament comprised two synchronised ShVAK cannon (200 rounds each) installed in the sides of the fuselage, and 880 lb of bombs or eight RS-82 rockets could be carried overweight underwing.

In October 1941, although the government had ordered the factories which were essential to the survival of the USSR to be evacuated in the face of the German threat, the ITP (M) was only half complete. Polikarpov's installations were transferred to Novosibirsk where the prototype was finished at the beginning of 1942. Its first flight took place on 23 February at the hands of A.N. Nikashin. The plane lacked stability and turned out to be less manoeuvrable than a standard Yak-1 fighter. The M-107P's unreliability was desperately obvious, but the trials revealed that the performances were very encouraging when it worked well. At the end of 1942, it was replaced by an M-107PA with which the aircraft underwent a new series of tests.

The ammunition supply for the ShK-37 functioned badly and its recoil was too heavy. It was replaced by a ShVAK (200 rounds) when the aircraft went through a series of modifications to reduce weight and save some 440 lb in flying order. But no performances were recorded officially because the authorities ordered the machine to do its static tests first. The ITP (M-1) was not accepted by the VVS for two important reasons: the power plant caused too many problems and Yakovlev had already developed the YaK-9T fighter with a perfectly reliable N-37 axial canon. As a result the «ITP» programme was officially abandoned.

Before that, a second prototype initially intended for the static tests was built at Novosibirsk. It was identical to the preceding prototype and in 1942, when new specifications for a high altitude fighter (in fact, they were only a newer version of the ones which had given rise to the «K» and «Kh» programmes in 1939-40) were issued, the prototype was improved so it could be used in this role and compete with the I-231 (2D) prototype designed by Mikoyan and Gurevich.

The planned engine was the AM-37. Designated M-2, or ITP (M-2), the machine was transferred to Moscow in December 1942 (the German threat to the town and the region had in the meantime receded) where the power plant was replaced by an AM-39A which was still at an experimental stage. Installing the engine needed the fuselage to be lengthened slightly and a few bosses on the cowling, which was now closer-fitting than that of the M-1. The increase in the mass caused by the AM-39A was compensated by replacing the axial ShK-37 canon with a ShVAK. The loads carried were the same as for the M-1.

The various modifications and adaptations needed to respect the specifications and the delay with the AM-39A put the trials off until 23 November 1943. These were carried out by N.V. Gavrilov until June 1944 during which the engine turned out to be very unpredictable and prevented the plane from obtaining the performances that Polikarpov was expecting, in spite a top speed of 406 mph at 8 250 ft. The cloud the designer was under at the time did nothing to improve his relationship with the engine designers, Mikulin and Klimov, whose efforts were clearly directed towards other officially «more acceptable» aircraft manufacturers. As a result, the ITP (M-2) was turned down in June 1944 at the end of its factory tests.

The ITP (M-2) prototype in 1944. It was equipped with an AM-39A engine and an even closer-fitting cowling than that of the ITP (M-1). The axial canon was a 20-mm ShVAK (here it has not been installed since the tip of the barrel cannot be seen sticking out through the propeller boss). *(J. Marmain)*

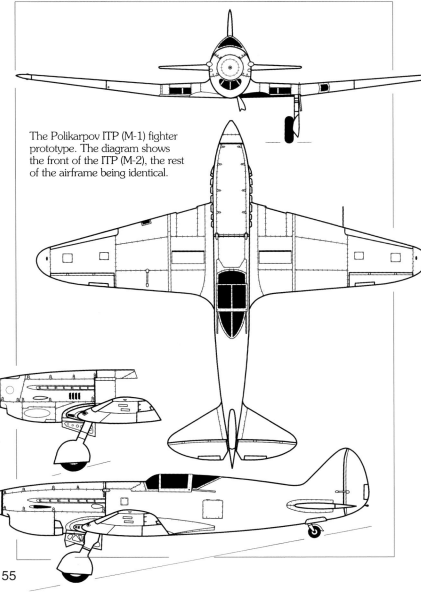

The Polikarpov ITP (M-1) fighter prototype. The diagram shows the front of the ITP (M-2), the rest of the airframe being identical.

MIKOYAN -GUREVICH

MiG-3/AM-37 Prototype («Object 72», or MiG-7) (May 1941)

In April 1941, the AM-37 engine which from the start was intended for the I-200 took its State homologation trials and was to be produced in great numbers. One example was delivered to the Mikoyan-Gurevich team and was tested without great success aboard the I-200 N°2 prototype (see below). On 26 April, the NKAP ordered a standard MiG-3 to be fitted with a new AM-37 at Factory N°1 and undergo tests at the hands of the pilot, N.P. Baulin (or A.I. Jukov according to some sources). Fitting this engine did not cause any particular problems because it was the same size as the AM-35A and the engine mountings did not have to be changed. OKO-1 referenced the machine as «Object 72», and the military authorities gave it the designation MiG-7 (the first use of this designation);

the designation MiG-3/AM-37 was also found in some documents.

The trials starting in May 1941 were not satisfactory. Longitudinal stability on the MiG-3 left a lot to be desired and in particular, the engine was very difficult to get right; it was not particularly reliable and only a radical redesign of the airframe could improve matters. But at the time, Mikoyan and Gurevich preferred to use the engine for the DIS-200 twin-engined escort fighter and give up on a MiG-3 with this engine, at least until the engine was improved. The airframe was taken to a repair workshop in the Moscow area and was brought up to normal standards. As for the AM-37 engine, production was cancelled because the USSR was invaded by German troops, and the authorities ordered Mikulin to put all his efforts into producing the AM-38, which was a priority for the Ilyushin Il-2 (Sturmovik) ground attack aircraft. No other details or figures are available.

GUDKOV

K-37 Prototypes (Gu-37, or LaGG-3K-37) (June 1941)

The K-37 prototype, or LaGG-3K-37, alias Gu-37 with its 37-mm ShK-37 whose barrel can be seen sticking out through the propeller boss. Its size made Gudkov place the cockpit 13 1/2 inches further back. *(RART)*

Technical specifications

Wingspan: 32 ft. 4 in.
Length: 27 ft. 3 in.
(not including the ShK-37 barrel)
Wing Area: 189.644 sq. ft.
Max. Take-off Weight: 7 398 lb.
No other figures.

At the end of May 1941, a secret decision by the Government recommended that a plan to improve the LaGG-3 be urgently drawn up, even at the cost of slowing down the aircraft's production rates. But this was not followed up because German troops started to sweep over the Russian plains on June 22. The VVS's strength was destroyed in the first few days and it was no longer a question of speeding up the supply of new machines for the air force regiments. The LaGG-3s were imperfect fighters, designed and produced quickly and were outclassed by their German equivalents. They were assigned particularly to the bomber interceptor and ground attack roles, tasks which suited the robustness of their airframe.

Remaining in Moscow after separating from Lavochkin and Gorbunov, Gudkov was the first to develop a special version for ground support. He took three LaGG-3 airframes from the beginning of the production series (with M-105P engines) and equipped them with an axial 37-mm Shpitalny ShK-37 canon with 21 rounds and a UBS under the cowling. The barrel of the ShK-37 was so long that Gudkov had to modify the front of

the fuselage in order to install the oil radiator, the fireproof partition and the cockpit 12 inches further aft. The first of the three prototypes, designated K-37 (or Gu-37, or LaGG-3K-37 depending on the documents of the period, the «37» for the calibre of the axial canon) was built at Factory N°23. It was ready in June 1941 and carried out 58 test flights of which 54 alone were for firing the axial canon. The two other prototypes followed closely on its heels and were tested operationally on the Viasm front where they got encouraging results, as much against the bombers as against armoured ground targets. A batch of twenty K-37s was produced by Factory N°21 before it was evacuated eastwards on 16 October. These machines were put at the disposal of the 43rd Air Force Division (43.AD) operating temporarily over the Moscow front and had a «certain success». But the ShK-37 canon was full of design and construction defects. Shpitalny was nevertheless convinced that his canon was effective and reported to Stalin that «his cannon had destroyed five medium tanks» ignoring the fact that at the time he made that remark the flight operating the K-37s had virtually ceased to exist.

MIKOYAN-GUREVICH

MiG-3/AM-38 prototype and conversions (July 1941)

Technical specifications

Wingspan: 33 ft. 6 in.	**Max. Take-off Weight:** 7 095 lb.
Length: 27 ft. 3 in.	**Max. Speed:** 370 mph at 11 220 ft.
Wing Area: 187.706 sq. ft.	**Service Ceiling:** 31 350 ft.
Weight Empty: 5 680 lb.	**Range:** ?

As German troops were sweeping everything in front of them, Mikoyan and Gurevich felt that despite its modernity, the MiG-3 was not the ideal fighter-interceptor for opposing the Luftwaffe. Basing themselves on rumours going around in high places, they thought the project would be cancelled because of the defects inherent in its hastily put together design. (Semyon was the brother of Anastasias who was very close to Stalin). In July, they proceeded to install an AM-38 engine in a MiG-3 airframe. This power plant was a priority for the Ilyushin Il-2 ground-attack aircraft but its power (1 600 bhp at take-off) and its very good performances at medium and low altitudes - the heights at which most of the dog-fighting took place - corresponded better to countering the Messerschmitt Bf-109 E and F fighters, the second of which had just arrived on the Eastern front.

The Am-38 was developed from the AM-35A and caused no problems when installed onto the MiG-3 airframe. But the exhaust piping was redesigned and the injection of inert gas into the fuel tanks was removed, as was the possibility of carrying external loads. The prototype, refe-

One of the 18 MiG-3s equipped with an AM-38 engine (or it maybe the prototype), recovered at the font, repaired and reconditioned. Some of them were armed with two 20-mm cannon.
(J. Marmain)

renced MiG-3/AM-38, was ready at the end of July and took off for the first time at the beginning of August at the hands of test pilot I.K. Stankevich of the LII VVS. Up to the 17th, several pilots from the LII NKAP and the NII VVS tested it and noted that it turned better and faster than the standard MiG-3 up to 13 200 feet. Moreover the trial reports mentioned the fact that it outclassed the most recent versions of the Messerschmitt Bf-109 (F-2 and F-4). But nothing had been done to improve the cooling capability of the engine; this caused seriously high temperatures for the power plant, both on the ground and in the air.

The attempt to adapt the MiG-3 to the AM-38 engine was recommended for mass-production, but Stalin would not hear of it. He opposed production of any new combat machine whatever the category and so the AM-38 engines remained a priority for the Il-2s. Because there was no other engine, the programme was buried. However, a repair workshop at the front installed damaged AM-38s which had been repaired and verified onto eighteen MiG-3s (it is not known when). Several of these machines without any specific designation were rearmed with two 20-mm cannon and affected to defence (PVO).

POLIKARPOV

I-185/M-82A, or «I» prototype (Third airframe) (July 1941)

The M-82A radial engine with two-stage supercharger was approved in 1940. Its performances were so promising that the authorities recommended it to all aircraft builders at the time when the west of the USSR was being invaded by German troops, threatening all the armament production sites and especially the liquid-cooled Vee engines. It was planned to test it in the context of the I-185 programme; so the third airframe was brought up to standard at the end of 1940. But the M-82A did not reach Polikarpov until the spring of 1941. Although the machine was referenced «I» by the OKB, its designation was in fact I-185/M-82A. Less bulky than the M-71, the M-82A enabled the engine com-

partment of the airframe to be refined and to extend the fuselage. The canopy was redesigned to reduce drag and its three sections were moulded from a single piece. The air intakes for the carburization were set into the wing roots and the size of the ventral tunnel was reduced. The propeller boss was more pointed. The armament was entirely redesigned: three synchronised ShVAK cannon grouped around the engine, with a total of 560 rounds. Four FAB-100 bombs or eight RS-82 rockets were carried underwing.

The machine was only ready on 19 July 1941 and after a few factory tests carried out by Yuliakin, it was transferred to the LII in September 1941. A certain number of difficulties constantly put off the flights until at the beginning of October the factories were ordered to evacuate, threatened as they were by German troops. The factory trials continued in February 1942 and finished on 28 March. There followed a new series of tests at the NII VVS

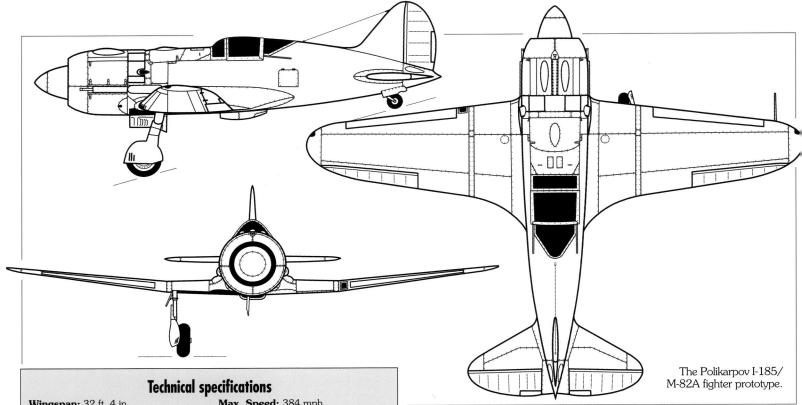

The Polikarpov I-185/
M-82A fighter prototype.

Technical specifications

Wingspan: 32 ft. 4 in.
Length: 26 ft. 9 in.
Wing Area: 186.738 sq. ft.
Weight Empty: 5 361 lb.
Max. Take-off Weight: 7 321 lb.

Max. Speed: 384 mph.
at 21 681 ft.
Service Ceiling: 36 300 ft.
Range: 656 to 862 miles
(depending on the sources)

from 23 April to 5 July which resulted in satisfactory reports. The prototype was sent to the front at Kalinin in November to be evaluated operationally by the pilots of the 728.IAP together with two I-185 prototypes powered by M-71s (see below). The reports estimated that the M-71-powered I-185 should be mass produced

The I-185/M-82A prototype during its trials at the beginning of 1942 where it gave excellent performances. The machine was then evaluated by the 728.IAP, but was not mass-produced in spite of favourable reports from the pilots who tried it out. *(J. Marmain)*

and also that although it performed less well, the M-82A powered version outclassed all the operational Soviet and foreign fighters, and that the two versions could be put at the disposal of trained, but not necessarily very experienced pilots. They concluded that the I-185 fighter was very modern, very manoeuvrable and easy to pilot, fast, very well armed and very robust. But at the time, Stalin refused obstinately to put a new fighter model into production, all the more so as Lavochkin had succeeded in adapting the M-82A to his LaGG-3 airframe, thus producing the La-5 which had the advantage of using fewer strategic materials than the I-185. Finally no aircraft production factory was yet «officially available» to produce the I-185 in any numbers, be it with an M-82A or an M-71.

GUDKOV

Gu-82 Prototype
(September 1941)

Before Gorbunov attacked the difficult problem of replacing the M-105 engine by an M-107 on the LaGG-3 airframe (see below), his colleague Gudkov started a study for an M-82-powered version at Factory N°301 in March 1941. Recently approved, this engine

had only been used to power single-engined Su-2 close range bombers. With the German invasion in June 1941, the Soviet government issued specifications to encourage builders to use the M-82 which, with its 1 400 bhp rating on take-off, was an alternative in the case the M-105 became unavailable. The M-82s were available in large quantities and were being made out of range of the Luftwaffe bombers.

Two prototypes were built. Designated Gu-82, they were armed differently. The first was fitted with four heavy machine guns and the second with two synchronised ShVak cannon and two BSs. The first took off in September 1941. Grafting an engine with such a large diameter (4 ft 3 1/2 in) on such a fine airframe as that of the LaGG-3 was not done without any headaches. Gudkov's team merely took the whole of a Su-2 power plant, mounting and accessories included, and fitted it onto a LaGG-3 by lengthening the engine cowling and by fixing it as best as possible to the ovoid cross-section of the rest of the fuselage. The oil radiator was transferred under the belly and a long air intake under the cowling supplied the centrifugal supercharger. The wings were also reworked and the wingspan reduced slightly. To improve visibility to the rear, part of rear decking was glazed. The factory tests were brief but showed that the first Gu-82 prototype behaved well in flight. The breakthrough by German troops up to the gates of Moscow obliged the Gudkov OKB to pack up and leave. The Gu-82s were crated and shipped to Novosibirsk, then to Gorki where they were never put back into working condition. Thus no official test programme was undertaken. However, on 12 October 1941, just before the move, basing themselves on the rare flights that did take place, the authorities had already toyed with the idea of possibly replacing the LaGG-3 (already under threat because of its defects) with the Gu-82 on the Gorki assembly lines; the VVS were perfectly aware of the new fighter's potential once its flaws could be ironed out.

Designated as the Gu-82, Gudkov's prototype was very similar to the La-5/M-71 which was fitted with an air intake under a similar engine cowling. The two machines are often confused, but the rear of the Gu-82 was not cut down.

(G. Gorokhoff)

Technical specifications

Wingspan: 32 ft. 4 in. **Max. Speed: 358** mph.
Length: 28 ft. 10 in.
Wing Area: 188.460 sq. ft. *There are no other figures.*

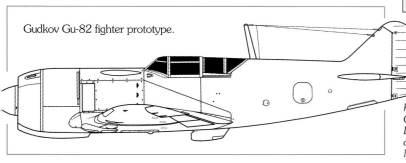

Gudkov Gu-82 fighter prototype.

NB.: The sources do not all agree with each other. According to some, only one prototype was built in the autumn of 1941, armed with two ShVAK cannon and two BS. Moreover, the information that said that Gudkov simply took the power plant from an Su-2 can not be checked anywhere in Soviet documents. Gudkov apparently only consulted the Su-2's technical documents concerning installation of the power plant and its cowling, and only adapted the latter to his Gu-82. Finally nothing is known of the second prototype's history. At the time the Gu-82 was being developed, Gudkov was under a lot of pressure from Yakovlev and Lavochkin. They had a lot of influence with the authorities, which was not Gudkov's case. So the successful adaptation of an M-82 engine onto a LaGG-3 airframe was purely and simply taken over by the Lavochkin OKB and used for the La-5 design.

POLIKARPOV

I-185/M-71 Prototype (third airframe)
(September 1941)

Built in 1940, the third airframe of the I-185 programme had to be used as a test bench for the M-71 engine. Designated I-185/M-71, it was similar to the previous prototype except for the engine cowling which had a wider diameter, and the longer, but shallower ventral tunnel for the oil radiator. The wing structure had been modified. It was built around a single main spar made of steel, and another auxiliary one together with a subsidiary structure. The incidence of the length of chord was 1° 30'. Armament comprised two UBS (400 rounds) and two ShKAS (1 400 rounds) all synchronised. The bomb load was two FAB-250s, four FAB-100s or eight RS-82 rockets.

As the engine was not available for this prototype before the German invasion, the factory trials were only started in September 1941. They turned out to be hectic because of the power plant's teething problems. Then the machine was sent to the Kalinin front were it was evaluated by the pilots of 728.IAP along with the I-185 prototype powered by an M-82A engine, and the first airframe also powered by an M-71. Armament was replaced by three synchronised ShVAK cannon. The trials at the «front» confirmed its excellent operational characteristics, and its performance and powerful armament were very much appreciated by the pilots who flew it.

The I-185/M-71, ex-I-185/M-81, at the trials in April 1941 when the snow still covered the field.
(J. Marmain)

Technical specifications

Wingspan: 32 ft. 4 in. **Max. Speed:** 387 mph at 20 295 ft.
Length: 26 ft. 6 in.
Wing Area: 167.149 sq. ft. *No other figures available*

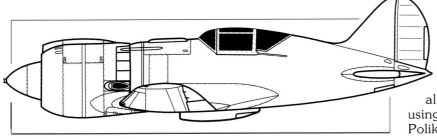

In spite of the numerous problems getting the M-71 operational, the model was recommended for mass production. But this did not happen because of the engine's unreliability and the bad relations between Polikarpov and his regulatory authorities (Shakurin and Yakovlev), all the more so as Lavochkin had already made his La-5, using an M-82A engine although it did not perform as well as Polikarpov's fighter.

YAKOVLEV

Yak-7/M-105P (September 1941)

Detached to head a team from the Yakovlev OKB at Factory N°301 and supervise the organisation of Yak-7UTI production, K.A. Sinelshchikov had the bright idea of converting the two-seater into a single-seater because the fighter regiments needed to be re-equipped with new materiel at the start of the invasion by Germany, whose troops and aeroplanes swept aside everything in front of them. The Yak-7UTI, serial number 04-11 was fitted an armoured plate over the rear position, self-sealing tanks which filled with inert gas as they emptied, three «RO» rocket-launchers under each wing section for as many RS-82 rockets (they could be replaced with bombs), an axial ShVAK canon with 120 shells and two ShKAS under the cowling, each with 750 rounds. The engine was an M-105P but no other major modifications were carried out and the new model was designated Yak-7/M-105P. Yakovlev was not informed of the conversion made by Sinelshchikov and when he learned of it he remained sceptical and at first pretended to ignore it. But the huge losses suffered by the VVS brought him very quickly back to reality.

After very brief factory trials under the supervision of the technical management of the Yakovlev OKB (the rocket-launchers were not fitted for the trials) during which the machine turned out to be better than the single-seat Yak-1, thanks to the modifications already applied to the UTI-26 (revised undercarriage, bigger wheels and tyres, more efficient brakes, engine mounting easier to remove, improved anti-nose over angle, CG placed at 20/21% of the MAC, revised elevators, etc.). Yakovlev submitted the model to the authorities who approved it immediately. The GKO and the NKAP issued decrees respectively on 14 and 23 August and 14 and 26 August 1941 for the Yak-7 to be produced by Factories N°301 and N°153, suggesting in the same breath that a variant with M-107 engine be also studied.

It was only in September 1941 that the rocket-launchers were installed under the wings of a Yak-7, serial N° 06-05, produced by Factory N°301. The firing tests were a success at the scientific trials Polygon for aircraft armament (NIPAV) and did not affect the flight characteristics and the general performances of the Yak-7 in any way, all the more so

A series of Yak-7s coming out of the factory at Novosibirsk. They were based on the Yak-7UTI, but underwent a lot of modifications which had made them in fact into single-seaters (the rear space being used for installing all sorts of extra equipment. Note the partitions for the oil and glycol radiators. *(J. Marmain)*

as the plane's stability, which was far better than that of the Yak-1, the LaGG-3 and MiG3, caused less of a scattering effect.

The tide of German troops which surged towards Leningrad, Moscow and the Crimea disrupted the production plans for the Yak-7 because Factory N°301 had to be evacuated to Novosibirsk where it merged with N°153. Thus only 62 aircraft were produced in 1941; 51 in September-October by Factory N°301 and 11 by Factory N°153 in December. The test pilot A.N. Lazarev tested serial n° 04-11 at the NII VVS in Novosibirsk and noted its good flight characteristics, how easy it was to get out of a spin, how well it behaved when diving, characteristics

One of the very first Yak-7s (serial N°01-70), right profile. Note the absence of nationality and unit markings, as well as wheel well doors. The rear canopy does not look as though it fits properly. *(J. Marmain)*

Technical specifications	
Wingspan: 33 ft.	**Max. Take-off Weight:** 6 512 lb.
Length: 28 ft.	350 mph at 16 500 ft. Service Ceiling:
Wing Area: 184.585 sq. ft.	30 525 ft.
Weight Empty: 5 449 lb.	**Range:** 402 miles.

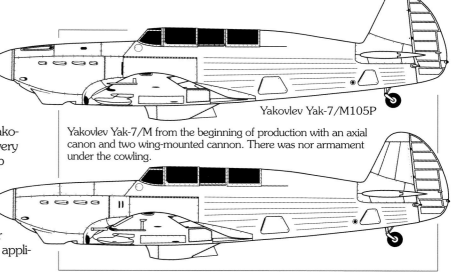

Yakovlev Yak-7/M105P

Yakovlev Yak-7/M from the beginning of production with an axial canon and two wing-mounted cannon. There was nor armament under the cowling.

which he considered safer than those of the Yak-1. But the inherent defects of the power plant persisted; others affected the tyres, the M-105P engine piping, the landing gear locking system and the tail wheel. Moreover, the MTOW of the production series Yak-7s had increased which made their general performance drop.

Despite these defects and the very limited production run, Yakovlev and the authorities agreed that Sinelshchikov had had a very good idea in converting the two-seaters into single-seaters; on top of that, maintaining the rear cockpit position enabled the Yak-7 to be more adaptable than the other «front» fighters as it could carry freight or a man (a good point when it was a question of frequently moving from one airfield to another in a hurry), extra instruments, or an extra fuel tank or one camera (or more), thus opening the way to other operational applications for the aircraft.

YAKOVLEV

Yak-7M/M-105PA Prototype
(September 1941)

A second single-seat version of the Yak-7UTI two-seater was designed in September 1941 by a team of engineers from the Yakovlev OKB attached to Factory N°292 where it was supervising the setting-up of the Yak-1 production series. A damaged Yak-7UTI (serial N°05-12) underwent a series of repairs and modifications which were more extensive than those carried out by Sinelshchikov at Factory N°301. The engineers took into account the lessons learnt from experiments with the I-28 and I-30 and made the following alterations: an M-105PA was installed; the seat and the controls in the rear cockpit were removed and replaced by an 18-gallon tank; the front seat was fitted with armour plating; the wingspan was reduced to 32 ft 1 1/2 in.; the outer wing sections had leading edge slats and an FS-155 landing light was fitted; armament consisted of three ShVAK cannon: an axial one with 120 shells and two at the beginning of the wing outer sections with 110 rounds each. On the other hand, the two ShKAS under the cowling were removed. The capacity of each tank was reduced by 5 gallons, the aileron articulations were revised and the surface of the split flaps was increased.

The firepower of the new prototype designated Yak-7M (M for «modified»), intended for bomber interception and possibly ground attack was heavier than any other Soviet fighter then in service. The cannon were reliable down to a temperature of -30° and were sighted at 1 320 ft. The wing-mounted cannon could be used singly or together. But all these modifications had caused a 792-lb increase in MTOW, compared with the Yak-7UTI, mainly because the structure and the mountings for the cannon and ammunition were redesigned.

Homologation tests started on 5 October at Chkalovskoya (Moscow). On the 16th, A.G. Prochakov took the prototype up towards Sverdlovsk. On landing at Kazan, the right undercarriage member collapsed because of a defect in the undercarriage pneumatic system. The machine was repaired and the trials only resumed on 31 October, lasting until 27 December. In spite

Yak-7UIT serial N° 05-12 repaired after an accident and changed into a Yak-7M prototype. The wing-mounted cannon are clearly visible. Note the rectangular shape of the two grills at both wing roots. (J. Marmain)

Technical specifications

Wingspan: 32 ft. 2 in.	**Max. Take-off Weight:** 6 952 lb.
Length: 28 ft.	**Max. Speed:** 347 mph at 16 830 ft.
Wing Area: 184.585 sq. ft.	**Service Ceiling:** 28 875 ft.
Weight Empty: 5 803 lb.	**Range:** 468 miles.

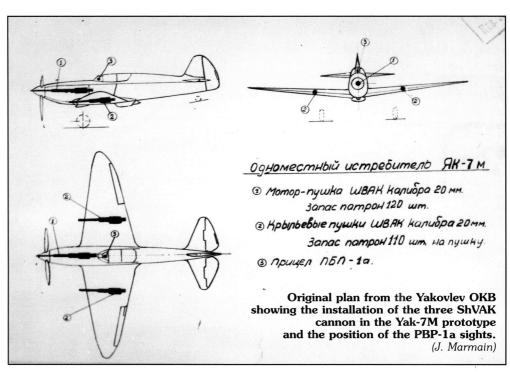

Одноместный истребитель ЯК-7 М

① Мотор-пушка ШВАК калибра 20 мм. Запас патрон 120 шт.
② Крыльевые пушки ШВАК калибра 20 мм. Запас патрон 110 шт. на пушку.
③ Прицел ПБП-1а.

Original plan from the Yakovlev OKB showing the installation of the three ShVAK cannon in the Yak-7M prototype and the position of the PBP-1a sights.
(J. Marmain)

of the Yak-7M's portliness, they revealed excellent handling and manœuvrability characteristics thanks to the installation of the automatic slats. Going into a spin was only possible if deliberately tried and stability, especially in a roll, was perfect. But the positive points stopped there. The Yak-7M was definitely less controllable when the slats got blocked (soft, heavy controls with a pronounced tendency to tip over), the wing cannon were badly synchronised, the landing and take-off distances were increased and landing speed was considered as «frightening» (119 mph).

Despite a drop in performance compared with the Yak-7UTI, the reports recommended that the model be nonetheless produced. But the only positive point to be retained by the authorities was the 18 gallon tank installed in the rear cockpit, since the wing cannon were considered to be too inaccurate to be kept, all the more so as mass-production of the ShVAK was not sufficient enough at the time; and the leading edge slats were not required in the specifications issued by the VVS. Moreover, Factory N°153 was getting ready to mass-produce the M-105PA-powered Yak-7 and Stalin had formally forbidden any new technological ideas to be introduced until the military situation turned in favour of the Russian troops.

YAKOVLEV

Yak-1/M-105PA «Winter version» (November 1943)

The «Winter version» variant of the Yak-1/M-105PA was produced during the winter of 1941-42 with skis instead of wheels, a system to dilute the oil with petrol, anti-freeze for the glycol, protection for the piping, the radiators and the whole power plant when not running, and washable Type MK-7 white paint, which unfortunately was very rough, as camouflage. The lack of rubber for making the tyres and operating from snowed-over, badly prepared airstrips caused this variant to be made with its own designation. The government grasped the need in mid-August 1940 and asked all the builders of «front» fighters to set about studying sets of skis to equip their models for winter operations.

The Yakovlev OKB designed retractable skis, 5 ft 5 1/2 in long by 24 in wide for a total weight of 283 lb (including fixed tail ski) which retracted up under the wing roots. Beforehand trials had been carried out with the I-26 prototype and the Yak-1/M-105PA serial N° 38-55 was tested at Saratov in November 1941 (18 factory and State test flights, 50 take-offs and landings). Although the general flight characteristics remained almost unchanged, the drag caused by the retracted skis slowed the model down by 18 3/4 mph to 25 mph and its manœuvrability suffered as a result. On the other hand, because of the friction caused by the skis on the snow, landings were shorter. On 25 February 1942, 830 examples of the «winter version» came off the production lines, although the GKO ordered production to be abandoned shortly beforehand, preferring to order the units to form maintenance battalions to clear the landing strips. Subsequently, skis which were jettisonable after take-off were tested. These were not produced in numbers because it was clear that it was better to have them when landing rather than taking off, to avoid the dangers of nose-overs.

(J. Marmain)

«Winter version» Yak-1 serial N° 30-55 being tested with skis. Some 830 examples were built and equipped in this way during the winter of 1941-1942.

(J. Marmain)

A. Yak-1 undercarriage with the rarely-used skis which were jettisoned on take-off.

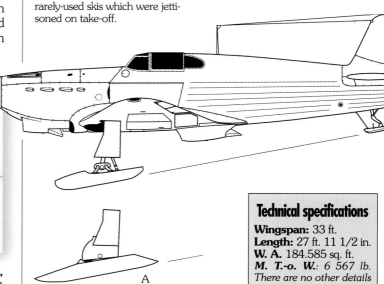

A

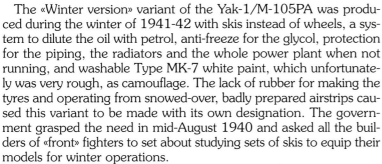

(J. Marmain)

Yak-1 serial N° 30-55 with skis and rocket launchers under the wings, being tested right in the middle of winter (1941/1942). From 12 May 1942, the Yak-1s no longer carried these offensive weapons but still carried bombs instead of the RS-82 rockets. (J. Marmain)

Technical specifications
Wingspan: 33 ft.
Length: 27 ft. 11 1/2 in.
W. A. 184.585 sq. ft.
M. T.-o. W.: 6 567 lb.
There are no other details

Yak-1

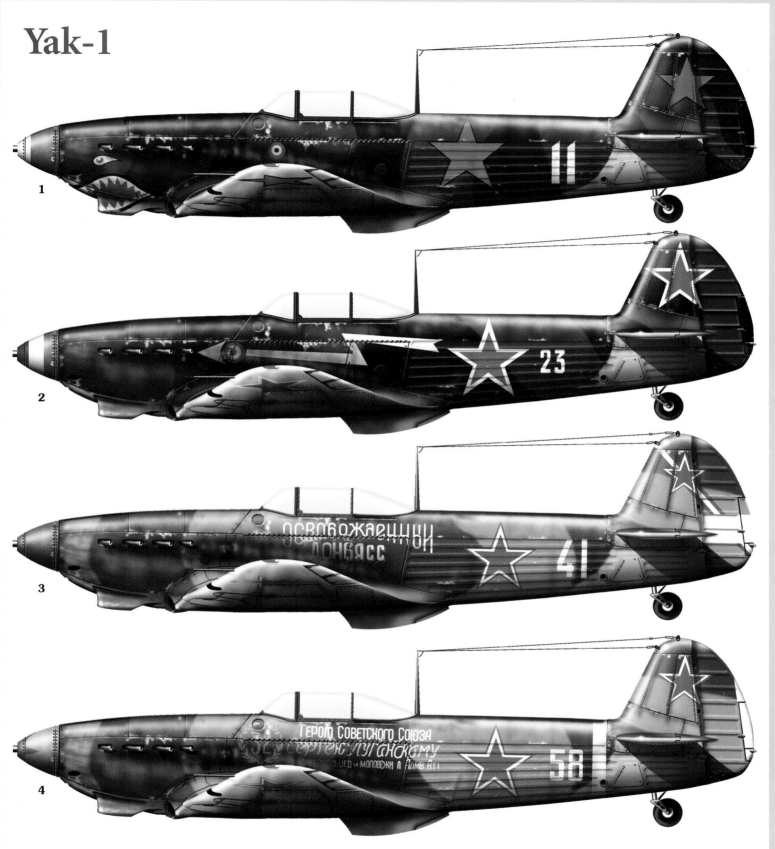

1. Yakovlev Yak-1b piloted by Albert Durand from the *Normandie* group in May 1943. This unit was created in 1942 and was made up of French volunteers fighting alongside the Soviet troops, as the little roundel under the windshield indicates. The red stars were edged with black; this emblem was not painted on the top surface of the wings which was common practice in the Red Army Air Force during the whole on the «*Great Patriotic War*».

2. Yakovlev Yak-1b from the «*Normandie-Niemen*» Regiment. Officially named the «Groupe de Chasse N°3» and attached to the 303rd Fighter Division whose emblem was an arrow in the shape of a bolt of lightning, the «*Normandie*» became the «*Normandie-Niemen*» at the end of July 1944 with Stalin's special authorisation after Soviet troops had successfully crossed the river. The machines of the 2nd Escadrille («*Le Havre*») normally bore a fuselage code going from 16 to 27 as here.

3. Yakovlev Yak-1b from the 3rd Squadron of the 367th Fighter Regiment (IAP). The grey-based camouflage was worn by Soviet aircraft from the second part of WWII. The inscription in Cyrillic means «*Donbass freed*», this fighter having been financed with donations from the inhabitants of the Donetz basin mining region, now in the Ukraine.

4. Yakovlev Yak-1b flown by Sergei D. Lugansky, commanding the 152nd Guards Fighter Regiment. A laurel wreath surrounding the number of kills, obtained at the time by this ace who ended the war with 37 victories, has been painted on the fuselage; the inscription reveals that the machine was supplied thanks to donations from the inhabitants of the town of Alma Ata.

MIKOYAN -GUREVICH

I-210 Prototype, or MiG-3/M-82A
And pre-series MiG-9 («IKh» Programme)
(November 1941)

Soviet combat aircraft were given a new designation system in 1940. But as was still their habit, Mikoyan and Gurevich continued to apply the old method of referencing its prototypes. Thus, when their own OKB also got down to adapting the M-82A engine to the MiG-3, the resulting programme was designated «IKh» or I-210. Mikoyan and Gurevich hoped to prolong the life of their fighter in this way and entrusted I.G. Lazarev with the adaptation. He grafted the M-82A onto the front of the fuselage structure with a minimum of modifications (VICh-105V propeller). He designed a cowling which fitted very tightly and was as well-sealed as possible, redesigned the central section of the wing. The rest of the elements were those of the standard MiG-3 so as to make continued series production easier.

The NII VVS approved the preliminary study on 23 August 1941 and ordered five prototypes with increased firepower compared with the MiG-3. These machines were built in November and December at Kuibishev where the Mikoyan-Gurevich OKB had been evacuated. The increase in size of the cross-sectional frame at the front of the fuselage enabled a more spacious cockpit to be fitted with a bigger canopy. The tailfin surface was increased for better stability in yawing but fuel capacity was reduced. The oil radiator was moved to a position under the engine and the outer wing section leading edges were fitted with automatic slats. Carburisation was fed air by two intakes on the cowling. Exhaust was by means of a big pipe on either side of the engine, behind the ring of flaps which regulated the flow of the cooling air exhaust. Armament consisted of three heavy UBS machine guns (one in the fuselage axis and two on either side.

The first flight of the I-210, or MiG-3/M-82A took place at the hands of test pilot Golofastov (NII VVS) on 2 January 1942 and was very disappointing. In spite of the increase in available power, the plane did not fly faster than a standard MiG-3 and climbed less high. The tail vibrated and its handling was very uncertain. Moreover it was less manoeuvrable than the MiG-3. The prototype underwent

(J. Marmain)

Adapting an M-82 engine onto a MiG-3 airframe was carried out in the autumn of 1941. The prototype and the four other examples which had been ordered were designated I-210, or MiG-3/M-82A, sometimes MiG-9. *(J. Marmain)*

wind tunnel tests at the T-101 at TsAGI which revealed that the engine compartment was not air-proof enough and caused a lot of drag. Lazarev designed a «Mercier» type cowling and modified the propeller shaft to lengthen the model's nose. But despite this, the five prototypes were failures since only their range was very much better than that of the MiG-3. They were nevertheless tested operationally on the Kalinin front and had the advantage of two extra ShKAS machine guns installed above the lateral UBS, and a mechanical «Hicks» starter at the tip of the propeller boss. Certain period documents mention the building of ten pre-series examples referenced as MiG-9s.

Mikoyan-Gurevich I-210. The dotted lines show the two other guns installed during the operational trials (on either side of the engine).

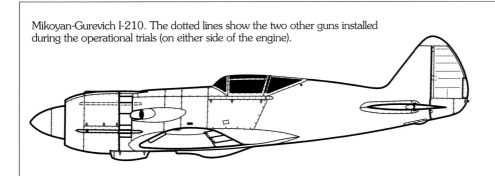

Technical specifications

Wingspan: 33 ft. 7 in.	**Max. Take-off Weight:** 7 440 lb.
Length: 26 ft. 7 1/2 in.	
Wing Area: 187.706 sq. ft.	**Max. Speed:**
Weight Empty: 5 984 lb.	353 mph. at 20 295 ft.
Service Ceiling: 28 710 ft.	**Range:** 668 miles

LAVOCHKIN

LaGG-3/M-82 or LaG-3/M-82
Prototypes (L-82 Programme)
(December 1941)

At the end of 1941, Lavochkin arrived at factory N°21 at Gorki. He was in the military authorities' and the politicians' bad books despite open good relations with people within the NKAP among whom Shakurin. The difficulties in perfecting the LaGG-3 had pla-

(continued on page 66)

TOMASHEVICH

Prototype «110» («Object 110» or I-110) (December 1941)

Tomashevich's «110» with its impressive partitioned radiator fairing under the nose. *(J. Marmain)*

The «110» (or I-110) prototype designed by Tomashevich at Omsk in 1941. *(J. Marmain)*

Curtiss P-40, of which several dozen examples were sent to the USSR by its Allies. The fuselage, the wings and the tail were of mixed construction and fabric covered with bakelised plywood skin. The cockpit was equipped with a sliding canopy. The armament comprised an axial ShVAK canon installed in the Vee of the engine and two synchronised UBSs under the engine cowling. The two single leg undercarriage members retracted towards the fuselage into the thickness of the central part of the wing. The tail wheel disappeared into the fuselage.

The engine was an M-107P cooled by a very impressive circular radiator, faired and installed under the nose. The trials took place from December 1941 onwards. Although the «110» was very easy to handle, it turned out to be heavy and performed less well than the mass-produced Yakovlev and Lavochkin fighters. Moreover the M-107P was still not very reliable and there were a number of problems getting it ready. Finally, at the time, Stalin was against creating another new plane. So the «110» programme was abandoned in 1943.

In 1938, D.L. Tomashevich was Polikarpov's right-hand man, responsible for the I-180 programme whose first prototype crashed on 15 December when it was being tested by the most emblematic of Soviet test pilots, Valery Chkalov. Accused of «sabotage», Tomashevich was immediately imprisoned in «Department 29» (or TsKB-29-NKVD) which regrouped all the builders and their personnel who were victims of the Stalin purges. There, the Study Brigade N°101 was to have been his, to develop a new «front» fighter. But the size of the programmes in progress meant he was affected to Tupolev (Brigade «103») and the «101» Brigade was never created.

In 1941, Tomashevich was deported to Omsk (Zavod 266) where he developed the single-seat fighter, «110» (Object «101» or I-110). It was a concept that was clearly influenced by the American

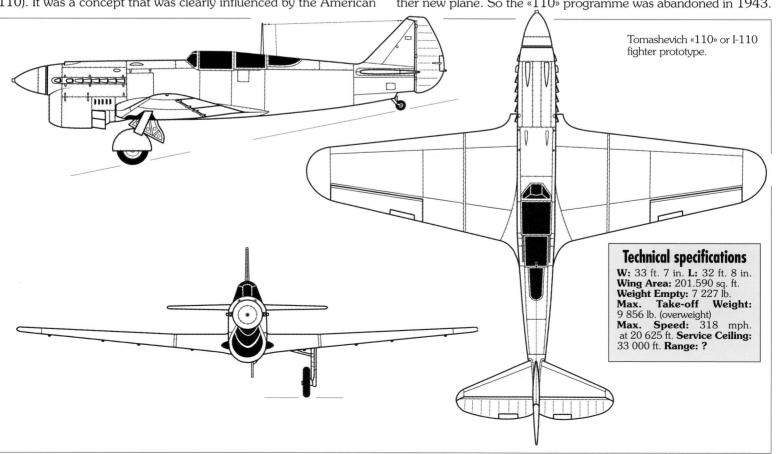

Tomashevich «110» or I-110 fighter prototype.

Technical specifications
W: 33 ft. 7 in. **L:** 32 ft. 8 in.
Wing Area: 201.590 sq. ft.
Weight Empty: 7 227 lb.
Max. Take-off Weight: 9 856 lb. (overweight)
Max. Speed: 318 mph. at 20 625 ft. **Service Ceiling:** 33 000 ft. **Range:** ?

Lavochkin LaGG-3/M-82 (or LaG-3/M-82).

Technical specifications

W.: 32 ft. 4 in.	**Max. Take-off Weight:**
L.: 28 ft. 9 in.	7 436 lb.
Wing Area:	**Max. Speed:** 375 mph.
188.460 sq. ft.	at 21 285 ft.
Weight Empty: 6 138 lb.	**Service Ceiling:** ? **Range:** ?

ced him in a difficult position and the transfer of a part (only) of his OKB the previous year did nothing to improve matters. The team was not really welcome at Gorki.

It was here that Polikarpov's I-16 and Pashinin's I-21 were also being developed. Moreover the authorities seemed to want to stop series production of the LaGG-3 in 1942 and it was Yakovlev's ambition to set up his own OKB for his own fighter. It was in this context that Lavochkin got down to studying the conversion of his airframe to take the enormous M-82 much later than Gorbunov, Gudkov, Mikoyan-Gurevich and Yakovlev. At first, it seemed impossible. The M-82's diameter was 18 inches bigger than the ovoid frame of the LaGG-3's frontal cross-section. And it was 550 lb heavier than the M-105 which necessarily meant moving the CG. The axial canon could not be installed. The modifications that had to be made to the airframe of the LaGG-3 seemed to him to be insurmountable and he recommended concentrating the OKB's efforts on developing a new version with the M-107 engine.

But S.M. Alexeyev, the head of the design team at Factory N°21 and Lavochkin's assistant, thought that transforming the airframe to take the M-82 would not cause so many problems. He obtained permission to second two or three members of the team to this programme, all the more so as the «boss» had met Shvetsov, the engine designer, during a conference at the NKAP where Shvetsov agreed to supply «an M-82 model» so as to be able to carry on study work. V.I. Valedinski (detached from the Shvetsov OKB) and K. Slepnev (head of the engine department at Factory N°21) joined Alexeyev's little group which had the job of doing most of the conversion work on the front of the fusela-

ge for this new programme which was given the reference «L-82».

Unlike Gorbunov and Gudkov who only tried to replace the M-105 with an M-82, the Alexeyev team looked at the problem from another point of view. So as not to have to redesign the whole front part of the LaGG-3 airframe, it designed a connecting section which gradually got rounder and extended the fuselage from the front of the cockpit, over the former structure (which subsequently disappeared). Moving the CG was summarily made up for by transferring the oil radiator into an intake under the engine cowling, by suppressing the ventral intake which was no longer needed and by installing two synchronised ShVAK cannon under the upper part of the cowling. This fitted the shape of the M-82 very closely and included two side flaps regulating the flow of cooling air into the engine and the exhaust.

At first the work was carried out «illegally» because of the hostility shown by the Gorki management to the Lavochkin team which had been relegated to a «corner» of the factory, and because of Yakovlev's stranglehold on the factory, but then the authorities gave the Lavochkin team the go-ahead to present their results for February 1942. The prototype LaGG-3/M-82 (or LaG-3/M-82 depending on the sources) was finished in December 1941. Apart from the connecting section, the machine was fitted with automatic leading edge slats. The M-82 engine drove a three-blade 10 ft 3 in VISh-105P propeller with hydraulic pitch control, a double starter (compressed air and «Hicks» mechanical on the propeller boss); the pilot's seat was armoured (3/8 inch thick) and the two cannon could fire 170 rounds each. The fuel was held in five tanks with a total capacity of

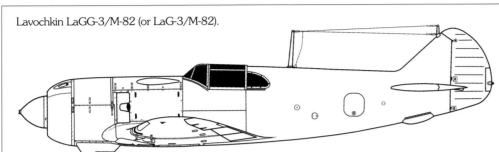

The hinged and removable panels covering the power plant on the LaGG-3/M-82A prototype gave easy access to the M-82A and the guns, except for the lower half.
(J. Marmain)

**The LaGG-3/M-82A being tested with skis, and mounted
on trestles to test the landing gear kinematics.
The photograph has been stamped «secret».** *(J. Marmain)*

**The LaGG-3/M-82A which arose from a LaGG-3 airframe
and a Shvetsov M-82 air-cooled radial engine. The trials were only
reasonably successful but sufficiently promising to give rise
to the future La-5.** *(J. Marmain)*

Right.
**The LaGG-3/M-82A here during its initial trials (the photograph
has been classified «secret») was slightly shorter than a standard
LaGG-3. Alexeyev and his team succeeded in «marrying»
the engine to the ovoid frames of the LaGG-3 airframe.**
(J. Marmain)

103 gallons. For the rest, the prototype's airframe was identical to the LaGG-3's.

The management of Factory N°21 was so worried about having to answer for Lavochkin's work that it refused to move the prototype into a hangar.

This uncooperative and negative altitude together with a very harsh winter and various technical problems caused the trials to put back to March 1942. It was G. Mischenko who took over the test after the death of Y. Stankevitch aboard LaGG-3 «Sparka» on 14 February 1942 (see below). His opinion was lukewarm for although the LaGG-3/M-82 behaved well, flew faster at low-altitudes and climbed faster than a standard LaGG-3, take-off and landing distances were too long. The different aerodynamic trimming for the moving surfaces did not please him and the engine cylinders were not all cooled equally. As a result there was a whole series of modifications to be made on the engine, the ailerons and the moving surfaces trim.

In April, the government decided to transfer the Lavochkin OKB to factory N°31 (where Gorbunov was already installed), to stop LaGG-3 production and impose Yak-7B production at Factory N°21 from May onwards. Valedinski advised Shvetsov that the M-82 adaptation on the LaGG-3 was worthwhile and he repeated the information in high places. Stalin listened all the more carefully as the test

pilot, Nikashin, who had tested the prototype with Fedorov at the end of March, also spoke well of it. As a result, an emergency programme was decreed to enable the Lavochkin team to have all the necessary priorities and prerogatives, to end all the harassment from Factory N°21's management, and to undertake a series of tests from the end of April with test pilots from LII VVS (A. Yakimov) and NII VVS (A. Kubishkin).

Eleven flights were made between 9 and 14 May. In spite of some defects (joystick hardness, excessive temperature in the cockpit, oil overheating and leaking, the need to fit a frontal ring of cooling flaps to regulate engine cooling, reduced handling qualities compared with the LaGG-3, etc.), the LaGG-3/M-82 was «judged promising» (higher top speed, good range for a fighter, excellent manœuvrability in the vertical plane, etc.) This opinion radically changed the fate of the Lavochkin OKB and that of the fighter. The authorities reattributed control of the factory to Lavochkin and designated it to produce the new model in numbers from July 1942 (with factory N°31). They

NB: Certain sources indicate that two LaGG-3/M-82 prototypes were made, the second with the oil radiator positioned very far forward under the engine cowling. But it was more likely that this «second prototype» was one of the very first of the pre-series machines (or from the batch of LaGG-3s given over to development work on the La-5) affected to the various test programmes to perfect the La-5.

YAKOVLEV

**The Yak-7/M-82A prototype being built.
Note the «all-round» visibility canopy.** *(J. Marmain)*

Yak-7/M-82A Prototype
(December 1941)

Even though Yakovlev did not want to replace the M-105PA with the powerful Shvetsov M-82A engine (unlike Lavochkin and Mikoyan-Gurevich who did not any other choice to «save» their models) the modification was tried out in August 1941. A Yak-7 airframe was taken from the production line and subjected to extensive modifications: to the frame of the whole of the front part of the fuselage so as to be able to take the diameter of the M-82A (9 ft 3 in-diameter AV-5L-127 propeller with boss); to the NACA engine cowling with its ring of adjustable flaps and hot air extraction flaps, to the two exhaust manifolds (one for seven pipes) and to the cockpit which was raised. Wings with a 32 ft 2 in span were installed with a reduced wing area (redesigned wingtips), similar to the I-28 with leading edge slats, bigger ailerons, reinforced skin and two extra 9-gallon fuel tanks in the central section; the frames of the rear fuselage were reduced and an 18-gallon tank was installed behind the cockpit. This now had an armoured all-round visibility canopy and an armoured seat which was raised 4 inches for better forward visibility. It was equipped with an RSI-4 radio and RPK-10 radio-compass (ADF antenna loop was hidden in the fuselage); an OP-295 radiator

Technical specifications	
Wingspan: 32 ft. 2 in.	**Max. Take-off Weight:** 7 414 lb.
Length: 28 ft. 10 in.	**Max. Speed:** 357 mph at 9 438 ft.
Wing Area: 184.585 sq. ft.	**Service Ceiling:** 33 000 ft.*
Weight Empty: 6 039 lb.	***Range:*** *437 miles* *Estimates*

The Yak-7/M-82A during its trials at the LII in the spring of 1942. The propeller was not good enough and the modifications were too extensive for the authorities to consider mass-producing it. (J. Marmain)

with ventral tunnel was installed just behind the engine cowling. Armament comprised two wing-mounted ShVAK cannon with 100 rounds each and a UBS (on the fuselage side with 260 rounds), installed on reinforced mountings. Six RS-82 rockets could be carried underwing.

The prototype, designated Yak-7/M-82A, was in fact a totally new machine. It was built from August onwards but was only finished at Novosibirsk in December 1941 after the factory was evacuated. It underwent its factory trials from 23 January to 13 May 1942, but P.I. Fiodrovi only carried out 17 flights because three M-82As (four, depending on the sources) were «worn out» during these trials. They came from the very first production batches and were not yet very reliable. The oil and fuel piping burned and the propeller was not suitable. Performances were only measured during two flights and turned out to be disappointing: 357 mph at 9 348 feet using the first stage of the centrifugal supercharger (the second was just not reliable) instead of the 384 mph at 21 120 feet the engineers had predicted. They were measured without the UBS canon (or without any armament at all, depending on the sources) and with reduced fuel capacity in order to bring the MTOW down from 7 414 to 7 172 lb and in order to reposition the CG at 24.7% of the MAC (it was too far forward when the aircraft was fully laden).

The reason that the programme failed, apart from the defective supercharger, was because of the choice of propeller whose performance was totally inadequate. Another one with a 10 ft 6 in diameter was considered but the height of the undercarriage

ruled it out. A 10-ft propeller could have been used but the ground clearance would have been very small in this case the plane would not have been able to lift its tail for take-off. As a result on 24 May 1942 all work was abandoned and the prototype was taken to an experimental workshop where it underwent extensive modifications (see below).

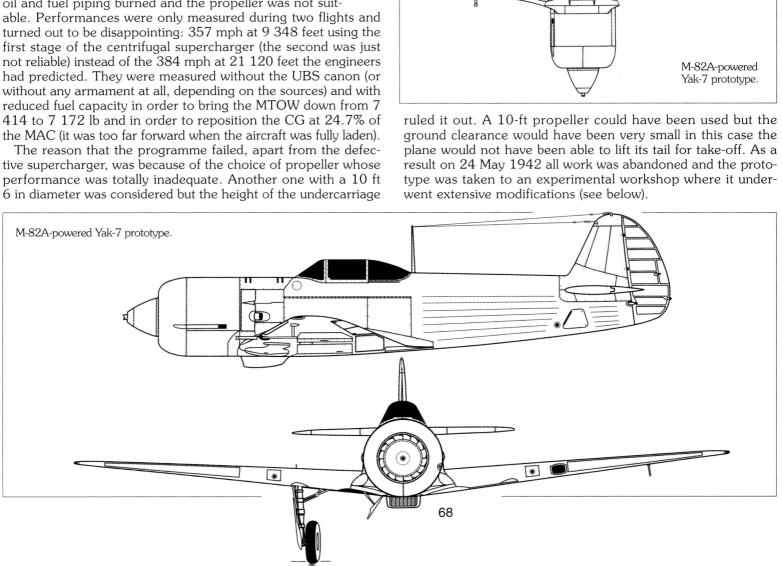

M-82A-powered Yak-7 prototype.

M-82A-powered Yak-7 prototype.

KOCHERIGIN

Several studies without designations (During 1941)

In 1941 the NKAP ordered Kocherigin to develop an experimental fighter powered by a 36-cylinder (in 6 banks) M-300 engine, designed by A. Bessonov and tested at the TsGAI bench where a power rating of 3 000 bhp was expected (no other details). During the same year, Kocherigin «privately» drew up several other preliminary studies for fighters and interceptors equipped with M-105P and M-107P engines with axial cannon (no other details).

MIKOYAN-GUREVICH

«KhS Object» or MiG-3 with pressurised cockpit (During 1941)

Although designed to operate at high altitudes, the MiG-3 was not however equipped with a pressurisation system so as to be able to intercept German spy planes flying at the limit of the stratosphere. The VVS did not hide their desire for a pressurised version of the MiG-3 fitted out with a cockpit designed by A. I Shcherbakov at Factory N°482 at Vladikino (a Moscow suburb). But in 1941, Factory N°1's only priority was to produce standard MiG-3s in great numbers and the «KhS Object» project with pressurisation was just not on the agenda, particularly with all the terrible fighting going on since 22 June. The pressurised fighter project was not ordered by the NKAP until 1943 and then gave rise to the I-222 (3A) programme (see below).

MiG-3SPB Project (During 1941)

During the thirties, V.A. Vachmistrov made a name for himself by designing his famous «Zveno» composites, comprising a heavy bomber (at first a twin-engined TB-1 then a four-engined TB-3) and several fighters (two to five). These were true «flying aircraft carriers» and were more or less successful from an experimental point of view, before they were turned down by the authorities because of their vulnerability. However, at the beginning of the Great Patriotic War, the Navy Air Force used the last of Vachmistrov's models, the «Zveno SPB» which was designed to be used against targets which were extremely difficult to reach by normal airborne means. For the occasion, the TB-3 carried two I-16 SPB (SPB for Skorosnoy Pikiruyushchi Bombardirovshchik - rapid dive bomber) fighters each equipped with two 550-lb bombs underwing. The idea was to carry the planes in as close as possible to the target, release them and thus make a surprise attack. This tactic was used several times against the port of Constanza and the Chernavoda Bridge which concealed a pipeline under its double surface carrying Rumanian oil from the oilfields at Ploesti to the port. Thanks to the «Sveno», the bridge was hit and the pipeline seriously damaged. The port itself was attacked several times with significant damage both in the port and out in the roads.

Vachmistrov planned to modernise his «Zveno SPB» by using the modern four-engined TB-7 (or Pe-8) bomber and two MiG-3s transformed into MiG-3SPB dive-bombers. Like the preceding I-16SPBs, they carried two 550-lb FAB-250 bombs underwing. Preliminary work was done on a Pe-8 at Factory N°124 «imeni G.K. Ordjonikidze» at Kazan but was finally abandoned, relegating the MiG-3SPB model to the list of aborted projects.

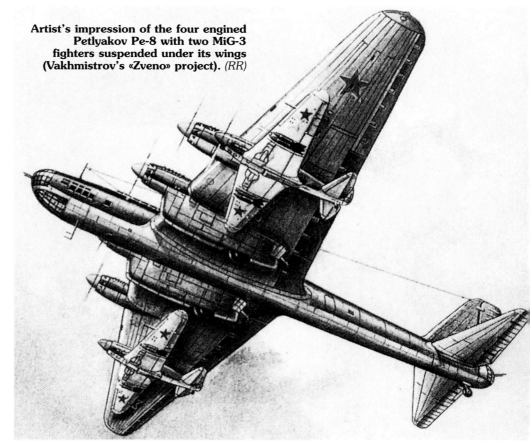

Artist's impression of the four engined Petlyakov Pe-8 with two MiG-3 fighters suspended under its wings (Vakhmistrov's «Zveno» project). (RR)

1942

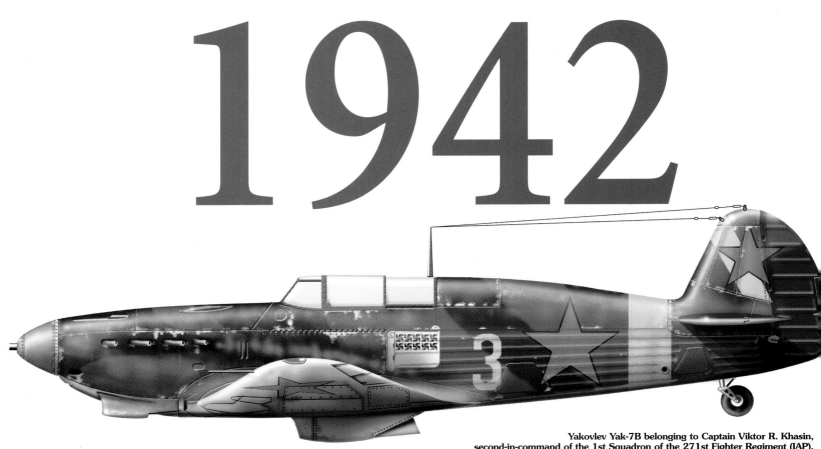

Yakovlev Yak-7B belonging to Captain Viktor R. Khasin, second-in-command of the 1st Squadron of the 271st Fighter Regiment (IAP), 274th Fighter Division (IAP), Kalinin Front, end of 1942. This plane still bears the characteristic camouflage from the beginning of the war (dark green and black with pale blue undersides), the pilot's tally being shown in quite an unusual manner. Khasin, who finished the war with 28 confirmed kills, was made a Hero of the Soviet Union.

GLOSSARY

YAKOVLEV

UTI-26.2/2DM-4S or UTI-26PVRD Prototype (Beginning of 1942)

The first DM-4S ramjets from the engine builder I. A Merkulov which were declared «fit for service» were built at the beginning of 1942. As with other projects and experimental programmes, the Yakovlev OKB took part in the development of «jet aviation in the USSR», at first in «accelerator trials». For the Yak fighter had to fly not only higher but faster. The UTI-26.2 prototype which was then being evaluated with 12.GvIAP (PVO) in Moscow, was fitted with two of these ramjets under the outer wing sections for testing (in certain sources and documents, the reference given is sometimes UTI-26.2/2DM-4S or UTI-26PVRD). The DM-4S measured 5 feet long, 20 inches in diameter and weighed 99 lb. Its «average» fuel consumption was from 24 to 26 1/2 lb per minute. But the programme was very quickly stopped because the two DM-4Ss moved the CG too far forward (the plane nosed over at the slightest turbulence) and because the fuel tanks were not protected from the danger of fire; the installation vibrated a lot, causing the piping to break (the two DM-4Ss used the same fuel as the M-105P engine). The dimensions were those of the UTI-26.2. No other figures are available.

GORBUNOV

«Lightweight» LaGG-3 Prototypes (Beginning of 1942)

At the beginning of 1942, at Tbilissi where Factory N°31 had been evacuated, Gorbunov was ordered to try and improve the performances of the LaGG-3 in order to satisfy the original specifications. He had an M-105PF engine at hand, but in order to lighten the structure of the LaGG-3, he had to whittle everything down: the armament which only comprised an axial MP-20 canon, lighter than the ShVAK, and a synchronised UBS under the cowling; the on-board equipment which was reduced to the strictest minimum; the general structure whose mass he managed to reduce by saving some 66 lb in the composition of the tail surfaces (the wood was less dense).

Gorbunov applied these changes to LaGG-3 serial N° 2444. The machine now only weighed 6 303 lb, i.e. 880 lb less than a standard LaGG-3 produced by Factory N°21. At the time, and almost daily, Gorbunov visited Colonel E. Kondrat, the commanding officer of a fighter regiment at Taganrog whose job was to train pilots on LaGG-3s. He persuaded Kondrat to get his regiment to test the LaGG-3 «oblegchennyi» or «lightened» prototype (no suffix or specific designation was granted to him). The trials revealed that the aircraft handled better, but its top speed settled at 352 mph at 9 900 feet, or the same speed as a LaGG-3 built at the beginning of 1942. Unfortunately the programme ended in tragedy: V. Guzin who headed the trials was killed because he was not able to get out of the plane after the fuselage broke in two just as it started pull out of a dive. Clearly the less dense wood turned out to be weaker than Gorbunov thought.

Technical specifications

Wingspan: 32 ft. 4 in.	**Max. Take-off Weight:** 6 303 lb.
Length: 29 ft. 1 in.	**Max. Speed:** 352 mph at 12 870 ft.
Wing Area: 188.567 sq. ft.	**Service Ceiling:** 10 200 ft.
Weight Empty:	**Range:**

LaG-5 Prototype (Beginning of 1942)

At Tbilissi, Gorbunov tried to adapt an air-cooled double-row radial engine onto to a LaGG-3 airframe just like Gudkov. He had a 1 700 bhp-rated (at take-off) M-82A at his disposal, but did not succeed in joining the engine to the fuselage as well as his colleague

Technical specifications

Wingspan: 32 ft. 4 in.	**Max. Take-off Weight:** 7 277 lb.
Length: 28 ft. 8 1/2 in.	**Max. Speed:** 346 mph. at 21 450 ft.
Wing Area: 188.460 sq. ft.	**Service Ceiling:** 31 350 ft.
Weight Empty: 5 731 lb.	**Range:** 409 miles

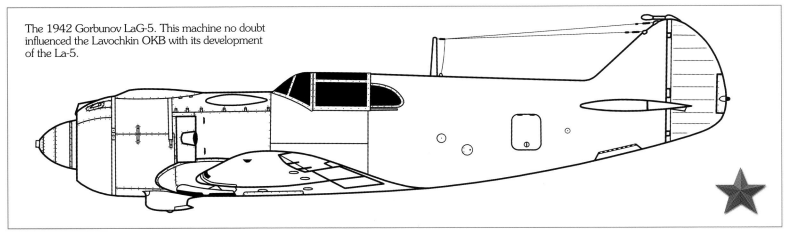

The 1942 Gorbunov LaG-5. This machine no doubt influenced the Lavochkin OKB with its development of the La-5.

had done. Two cannon were installed above the engine and the wingspan was only 28 ft 8 1/2 in for the same wing area (188.460 sq. ft.). The air intake for the carburization was half sunk into the top of the engine cowling and the oil radiator was moved under the nose. For the rest, the airframe was similar to that of a standard LaGG-3.

Designated LaG-5, the prototype was tested at the beginning of 1942. The badly fitting seals and panels of the power plant generated a lot of drag and reduced the top speed to 346 mph at 21 450 feet. The machine was nevertheless approved during the year, but no production series was decided upon because in the meantime, the Lavochkin OKB had also made a conversion attempt using the M-82 engine, but successfully thanks to Alexeyev's determination. It seems that Gorbunov's attempt (his prototype disappeared out of

sight) was taken up by Lavochkin, or that some form of collaboration took place between the two men through the good offices of Alexeyev, because the engine compartment and its fairing, and the lay-out of the air duct and the supercharger of the production series La-5 were very similar to the LaG-5's, and this particular designation is very often found among production reports of the first production batches.

NB. Most of the documents about the transformation of the LaGG-3 into a La-5 no longer mention the Gorbunov LaG-5. However, quite a few sources mentioned Gorbunov's conversion and the designation LaG-5 does appear clearly in numerous period documents, including diagrams and plans. It is not impossible that Lavochkin, through his influence in high places, managed to get Gorbunov's prototype purely and simply «forgotten» in the historical reports recording the transformation of the LaGG-3 into a La-5, or that his own design team took the credit for the machine.

LAVOCHKIN

LaGG-3-37 and LaGG-3 batch N°34
(Beginning and December of 1942)

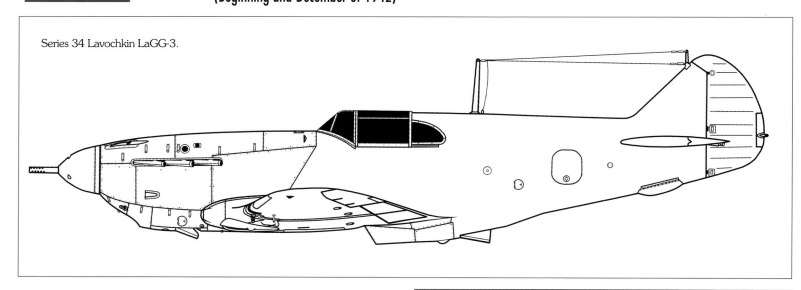

Series 34 Lavochkin LaGG-3.

The experiment, which was attempted by Gudkov and which succeeded, to adapt the ShK-37 axial canon in August 1941 was taken up by Lavochkin after the factories were evacuated to the East. At first, twenty LaGG-3 airframes with M-105PF engines were adapted to take the same canon at the beginning of 1942. These planes were tested operationally by 42.IAP under Colonel F. Shinkarenko on the Briansk front with convincing results. But the pilots thought that the twenty or so rounds they had were not enough. Designated LaGG-3-37, these machines were afterwards transferred to the 219.IAP (Stalingrad front) in September where their pilots obtained even more spectacular results although the LaGG-3-37 did have to be given fighter cover.

In December 1942, a first batch of NS-37 cannon which were more modern and lighter, designed by Nudelman and Suranov and recently officially approved, was produced in order to replace the ShK-37 of which production had been stopped because it was not reliable and tended to jam too often. They were installed on the forty or so LaGG-3s which made up Batch N°34. The barrel of the NS-37 was much shorter which made it unnecessary to move the radiator, the fire-proof bulkhead and the cockpit further back. As soon as they were built, these machines joined their predecessors on the Stalingrad front. But only Batch N°34 was equipped with this weapon (with a UBS under the engine cowling).

NB. Most of the sources attribute the production of these twenty machines with ShK-37 canon to Gudkov following experiments with three prototypes equipped in the same manner (see K-37).

Technical specifications

Wingspan: 32 ft. 4 in.
Length: 29 ft. 1 1/2 in.
Wing Area: 188.460 sq. ft.
Weight Empty: 6 230 lb.
Max. Take-off Weight: 7 398 lb.

Max. Speed: 350 mph. at 13 530 ft.
Service Ceiling: 29 700 ft.
Range:
These figures correspond to the LaGG-3-37s from Batch N°34.

The LaGG-3-37 prototype or the first of the 20 examples armed with a ShK-37 axial canon, recognisable by its long barrel sticking out of the propeller boss. Series 34 was equipped with 37-mm NS-37 cannon which were lighter and more reliable and which had a shorter barrel. *(J. Marmain.)*

YAKOVLEV

Yak-7A/M-105PA
(January 1942)

The designation Yak-7A/M-105PA was allocated to the Yak-7s built by Factory N°153 from January 1942 onwards. Several modifications recommended by the TsGAI and the NII VVS were introduced progressively to correct the defects and improve the model: filling the fuel tanks with inert gases taken from the exhaust, and no longer with Anazot which was frequently unavailable (from batch N°14 onwards); insulating the airframe (from batch N°15); changing the pneumatic ammunition supply for a mechanical one (from batch N°15, from the 31st machine onwards); replacing the electric fuel gauges by mechanical ones on the upper wing surface, visible from the cockpit (from batch 16); installing an RSI-4 «Malyutka» receiver and an RSI-3 «Oriol» (batch N°16 from the 31st machine) and modifying the cockpit instruments; replacing the glazing of the rear cockpit by a fairing made of plywood which swung open to the right, and modifying the exhaust pipes (batch N°17); re-instating the retractable tail wheel and closing off the undercarriage well completely (batch N°19).

The locking system for the canopy was improved, the diameter of the gun ports was reduced, the empty shell cases were collected, the air supply to the supercharger could be modified to reduce the take-off distance and the flaps could be positioned at 5° or 55° only, the 15° position being suppressed. Finally the tail was made entirely of metal.

As usual, these changes meant an increase in the take-off weight, so that the Yak-7's performances were not as good as the I-26.2 prototype, but nevertheless better than those of the Yak-7 with skis. All the Yak-1s and Yak-7s could be fitted with skis during the winter and were painted white.

The skis were made of strips of Siberian wood stuck together with casein or TsIAM glue, nailed, screwed and fitted with light alloys to slide better.

A Yak-7A with the rear part of the canopy replaced by a plywood fairing. The plane is equipped with a radio transmission system. *(G. Gorokhoff)*

The mass of the whole ski (and tail skid) arrangement was 284 lb, ChroManSil tube fittings included.

The first Yak-7A built by Factory N°153 was serial N°14-11. It was tested from 16 January to 22 February 1942 with wheels and with skis.

Thirty flights were carried out to determine the aircraft's performances and test the weapons (an axial ShVAK canon with 120 shells and two ShKAS under the cowling with 1000 rounds), and a further 288 very short flights to establish the effectiveness of the skis. In all 277 aircraft were built of which 13 in January-February and 267 until May 1942.

Technical specifications

Wingspan: 33 ft.
Length: 28 ft.
Wing Area: 184.585 sq. ft.
Weight Empty: 5 550 lb.
Max. Take-off Weight: 6 617 lb.
Max. Speed: 325 mph. at 16 500 ft*, 346 mph at 16 335 ft**

and 357 mph at 16 500 ft***
Service Ceiling: 30 525 ft.
Range: 368 miles
* with skis, beginning of the production run
** with skis, end of production
*** with wheels.

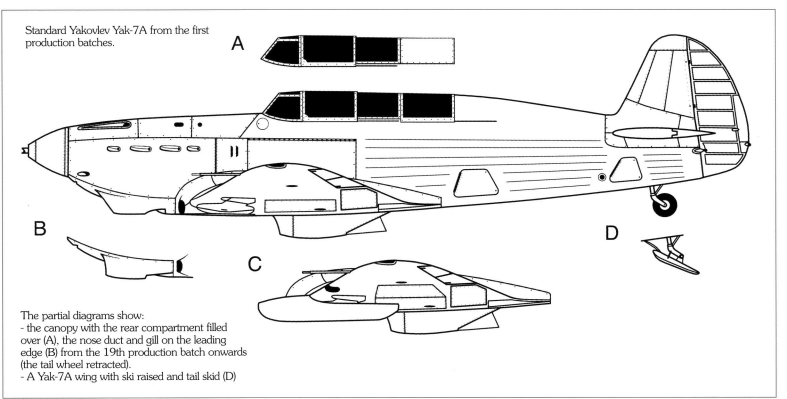

Standard Yakovlev Yak-7A from the first production batches.

A

B   C   D

The partial diagrams show:
- the canopy with the rear compartment filled over (A), the nose duct and gill on the leading edge (B) from the 19th production batch onwards (the tail wheel retracted).
- A Yak-7A wing with ski raised and tail skid (D)

YAKOVLEV

Yak-7V/M-105PA and Yak-7V/M-105PF
(February 1942 and during 1943)

Technical specifications

W.: 33 ft. **L.:** 27 ft. 11 1/2 in.
Wing Area: 184.585 sq. ft.
Weight Empty: 4 862 lb.
Max. Take-off Weight: 5 995 lb.

Max. Speed: 295 mph. at 16 500 ft
Service Ceiling: 32 670 ft.
Range: 384 miles
estimations

Above, from left to right.
A Yak-7V from the last production batches, here at Tula in the winter of 1943/1944. Note the installation of the exhaust pipes.
(H. Leonard)

A Yak-7V with fixed ski undercarriage photographed in the winter of 1942/1943.
(H. Léonard)

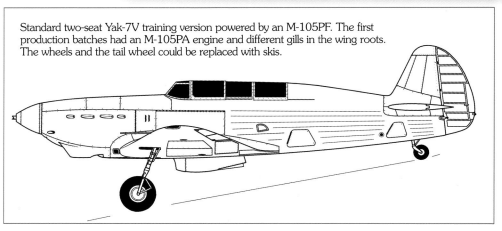

Standard two-seat Yak-7V training version powered by an M-105PF. The first production batches had an M-105PA engine and different gills in the wing roots. The wheels and the tail wheel could be replaced with skis.

The destruction caused by the German invasion and the evacuation of the factories eastwards temporarily stopped production of the Yak-7UTI in favour of single-seat fighters. Since the VVS still needed such a machine, the studies for a new version started at the beginning of 1942. To simplify production, lighten the airframe and reduce production costs but increase the production rates, the new model was designed with fixed undercarriage. This idea had been suggested by Cherenko, the head of a brigade from Factory N°301's SKB (design team) in a report sent to the authorities on 5 August 1941. The Yakovlev OKB took it up, considering that the machine did indeed not need retracting undercarriage to train and familiarise the young pilots who had been certified on UT-1 for fighters, and for training pilots for the front. The undercarriage retraction and lowering mechanism was removed as was the armament; the general structure was simplified and lightened. The wheel wells were closed over, the shock absorbers were reinforced, the tail wheel was fitted with a 300 x 125 mm tyre and a steel fork (it was made of Dural previously); a manual brake was installed in the rear cockpit for the instructor. Oxygen equipment was removed and on-board instrumentation was reduced to the bare essentials. The system for filling the tanks (which had a total capacity of 60 gallons) with inert gases was removed.

The Yak-7V/M-105PA prototype (serial N° 18-40) underwent 23 factory and State trial flights from 18 February to 24 March 1942 at Novosibirsk with and without skis at the hands of P.I. Fiodovri and some of the factory pilots, some from NII VVS and also from 19 and 20.ZAP (air reserve regiments). It was slower than the Yak-7UTI because the fixed undercarriage caused a lot of drag, but without altering the handling. However, the absence of RPU intercom made communication between the pupil and the instructor almost impossible, all the more so as a partition separated the two cockpits (this was eliminated during production). The canopies were nearly always bolted open as seeing through the Perpsex glazing was very problematic. Braking was delicate flying solo but in flight the plane was even more stable. The simplicity of the airframe enabled the plane to do all sorts of acrobatics, spins and dives. The model, judged ideal for training pilots was mass-produced from May 1942 to December 1943 numbers depending on the VVS's needs, with M-105PA and M-105PF engines (Yak-7V/M-105PF). In all 510 examples were built and 87 Yak-7Bs were converted to Yak-7V standards. The wheels could be replaced with skis (likewise for the tail wheel).

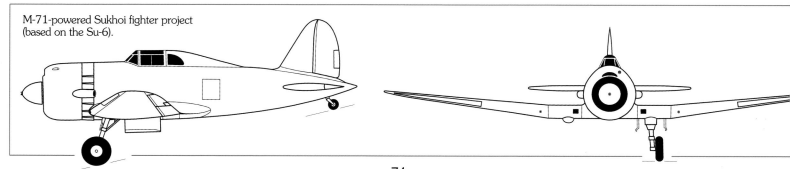

M-71-powered Sukhoi fighter project (based on the Su-6).

LAVOCHKIN

LaGG-3 «Sparka» Prototype

On 14 February 1942, the test pilot, Y. Stankevitch was killed in an accident trying out a two-seat prototype based upon the LaGG-3. This model was designed within the framework of the development plans for a rapid liaison aircraft between Gorki and Moscow and not as a training aircraft for fighters. The prototype was christened «Sparka», a term which is generally translated by «tandem». A second cockpit for the passenger was installed behind the pilot's and could also carry freight. The airframe was no doubt taken from a batch in the middle of the production series with three exhaust pipes on either side of the engine (they were manifolds on the preceding batches), a rudder with an overlapping slat and leading edge slats. The tail wheel was retractable and the canopy had been extended to cover the second cockpit (there is no indication how one got into this cockpit). The death of Stankevitch put paid to the «Sparka» programme: it is not known whether it was designed as a single example for the factory or for mass-production for rapid front line communication. Certain documents maintain that the «Sparka» was developed by Gorbunov and not by the Lavochkin OKB. There are no other details or figures.

Certain recent sources state that two two-seat prototype trainers were produced based on the LaGG-3 (from the first production batches with tubular manifolds for the exhaust, but without any rudder trim) intended for conversion and training fighter pilots and designated LaGG-3UTI. Apparently the first crashed killing its pilot, Popovitch. As for the second, no details are known. The model did not give rise to a production series and the first true two-seat training version appeared later with the appearance of the La-5. It is not impossible that the term «Sparka» was assimilated to the LaGG-

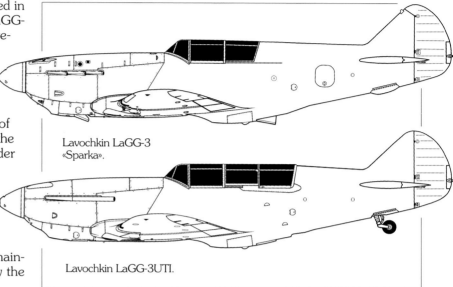

Lavochkin LaGG-3 «Sparka».

Lavochkin LaGG-3UTI.

3UTI but in that case the machine that crashed would not have killed the same pilot!

NB: The two-seat model, of which two types of plans have been published by the specialist press, both Russian and Western, is rather a grey area. The first type corresponds to the «Sparka» aboard which the pilot Stankevitch was killed. The second really does show a two-seat version, no doubt the LaGG-3UTI; but other sources say that only one prototype was built and that «Stankevitch was killed flying it».

SUKHOI

Preliminary study and unfinished prototype without designation with M-71 engine, based on the Su-6 (February 1942)

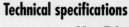

Technical specifications

Wingspan: 39 ft. 11 in.	**Max. Take-off Weight:** 8,305lb.
Length: 29 ft. 1 1/2 in.	**Max. Speed:** 376 mph. at 19 800 ft.
Wing Area: 242.167 sq. ft.	**Service Ceiling:** 27 720 ft.
Weight Empty: 6 257 lb.	**Range:** 475 miles

On 25 February 1942 (on the 27th according to other sources), Sukhoi presented P.I. Fiodorov, the then Head of the NII VVS, with the preliminary study for a fighter-interceptor based on the Su-6 ground-attack bomber powered by an M-71F engine, with a low cantilever wing, armoured cockpit and swing-over canopy. The initiative for developing such a heavily armoured aircraft (the armour weighed 297 lb, the plates were 3/8th to 1/2 in thick in places), was due to the test pilot P.M. Stefanovski who, in his evaluation report on the ground attack model, recommended that the version be fitted with two 37-mm cannon to intercept enemy Ju-87, He-111 and Fw 200 bombers. But the preliminary study's armament only comprised two 23-mm wing-mounted ShVAKs or VYas (160 shells) and a 12.7-mm synchronised UBS machine gun on the engine (30 rounds), whereas NS-37 or Sh-37 cannon would have been more appropriate. For the secondary support role, the model could carry 440 lb of bombs or six RS-82 (or RS-132) rockets. The fuel tank was incorporated in the fuselage and the oil radiator in the central wing section.

When the military authorities studied this preliminary project with no specific designation they concluded that the theoretical perfor-

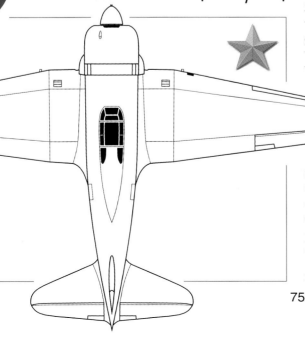

mances were probably inferior to those of Polikarpov's I-185 with the same engine (even though the M-71 engine did seem to be perfect for the role), that the VYa cannon's rate of fire was too slow for the use they were to be put to and above all that the plane was too massive to intercept intruders even those slower than itself. The preliminary study was rejected by A.I. Repin, on 11 July 1942 even though Sukhoi had started building a prototype. This was stopped immediately and the project «buried».

YAKOVLEV

Yak-1/M-105PA and Yak-1/M-105PF «light» prototypes (March and September 1942)

Technical specifications

Wingspan: 33 ft.
Length: 27 ft. 11 1/2 in.
Wing Area: 184.585 sq. ft.
Weight Empty: 5 170 lb.
Max. Take-off Weight: 6 116 lb.

Max. Speed: 370 mph. at 12 540 ft.
Service Ceiling: 36 300 ft.
Range:
These figures are for the «light» Yak-1/M-105PF.

In 1942, the VVS lived in dread of the German Messerschmitt Bf 109F (F-2 and F-4 versions). At the same time as the Yak-1/M-105PF was designed, on 14 March 1942, the GKO decided to entrust the Yakovlev OKB with the design of a «light» version for pure interception, to be delivered by 1 April. The programme was classified as «experimental» and the lightening of the plane comprised 25 modifications including getting rid of the ShKAS machine guns and replacing the sights; getting rid of one of the oxygen bottles, the glycol radiator filter and grill, the Anazot tank filling system and the rocket launchers (which could be refitted if needed); and replacing the wooden tail surfaces with all-metal ones. Ten machines were thus modified in the factory between 21 and 24 March 1942 («light» Yak-1/M-105PAs). In May, aircraft serial N° 33-60 (60th batch) underwent factory trials, but no State trials were made because the metal tail surfaces were not available before April. The ten machines were delivered directly to 12.GvIAP (Moscow Defence) for operational evaluation.

In September 1942, twenty other fighters were subjected to the same «diet». This time it was the Yak-1/M-105PF from Batch N°96 intended for the Stalingrad front at the request of headquarters. Two months earlier, two Yak-1s had tried to intercept a new Messerschmitt Bf 109G in

the Stalingrad sector. Just as they were about to shoot it down, the German fighter brutally accelerated and escaped. Informed of this, the Party Secretary, G. Malenkov told the two pilots off but their commanding officer, General S. Rudenko, rushed to their defence explaining how the Yak-1's performance had deteriorated because of the bad visibility through the canopies which meant that the pilots had to fly with the cockpit open, the bad finish of the fabric and skin, the undercarriage well doors and the flaps (among others). Malenkov was not convinced and ordered pilots from 434.IAP to carry out tests; they proved Rudenko right.

The argument gave rise to twenty other «light» Yak-1/M-105PFs equipped this time with metal tail surfaces. The antenna mast was removed, as was the generator and the night-flying equipment, and together with all the modifications that been done to lighten the machine, the result was that the MTOW dropped to 6 116 lb compared with the 6 417 lb of Yak-1 Serial N°15-69. Serial N° 45-96 took its State trials between 12 and 17 October 1942 at the LII NKAP. The twenty machines were delivered to the 512 and 520.IAPs of the 16th Air Army where they were very much appreciated by the pilots who thought however that the armament was inadequate. The climb rate was exceptional and between 6 600 and 9 900 feet, these machines were comparable to the Bf 109F-4 and G-2 in horizontal and vertical manœuvrability and often managed to get onto their tails (while two of them were being ferried, their pilots managed to shoot two Bf 109G-2s down). Although these machines were not followed up by mass-production, the lessons learnt during their operational use (the two regiments obtained better results than with their standard Yak-1s) were used in the design of the future Yak-3.

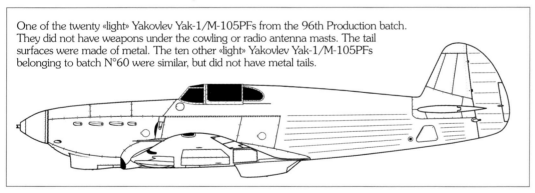

One of the twenty «light» Yakovlev Yak-1/M-105PFs from the 96th Production batch. They did not have weapons under the cowling or radio antenna masts. The tail surfaces were made of metal. The ten other «light» Yakovlev Yak-1/M-105PFs belonging to batch N°60 were similar, but did not have metal tails.

YAKOVLEV

Yak-7B/M-105PA (April 1942)
Yak-7B/M-105PF Prototype
Yak-7B/M-105PA and PF series, and
Yak-7B/MPVO (May and August 1942)

In close collaboration with all the design teams, the TsAGI carried out research in order to improve the Yak-7 and recommended that firepower be increased by replacing the two ShKAS on the cowling by two UBS with 400 rounds (260 for the left hand one and 160 for the right). It was powered by an M-105PA with

a ShVAK axial canon and 120 rounds. Six RS-82 rockets or two 55 to 220-lb bombs could be carried underwing but the rockets were no longer mounted on the Yakovlev fighters, respecting the decision taken by the GKO on 10 April 1942. The new version was designated Yak-7B/M-105PA and had been modified slightly, viz. widening and refining of the oil and glycol radiators, which were slightly tilted downwards, with larger adjustable flaps.

The proofing and the insulation of the airframe was improved, the tail wheel was now totally retractable; joints and skin were more carefully made; the panels on the engine cowling fitted better; the propeller reduction gear worked better; the settings for the lowering and raising of the undercarriage were more precise and bet-

Yak-7

1. Yakovlev Yak-7B belonging to Lieutenant Viktor A. Orekhov, 434th Fighter Regiment, Stalingrad Front, 1942. The front of this fighter, decorated with five kills has been painted red, perhaps for easy identification.

2. Yakovlev Yak-7B flown by Major Alexander N. Kilaberidze, commanding the 1st Squadron of the 65th Guards Fighter Regiment, Baltic Front, October 1944. This particularly colourful fighter, still bearing its green and black camouflage from the beginning of the war, bears «for Brother Chota» below the cockpit and «Westwards» inside the white arrow.

3. Yakovlev Yak-7B financed by the Komsomol (Federation of Young Communists) from the Kubass region. The insignia of the KIM (International Communist Youth Movement) has been painted inside the star.

4. Yakovlev Yak-7B from the 42nd Fighter Regiment (IAP). The pilot's kills are represented by swastikas and not by the usual red stars.

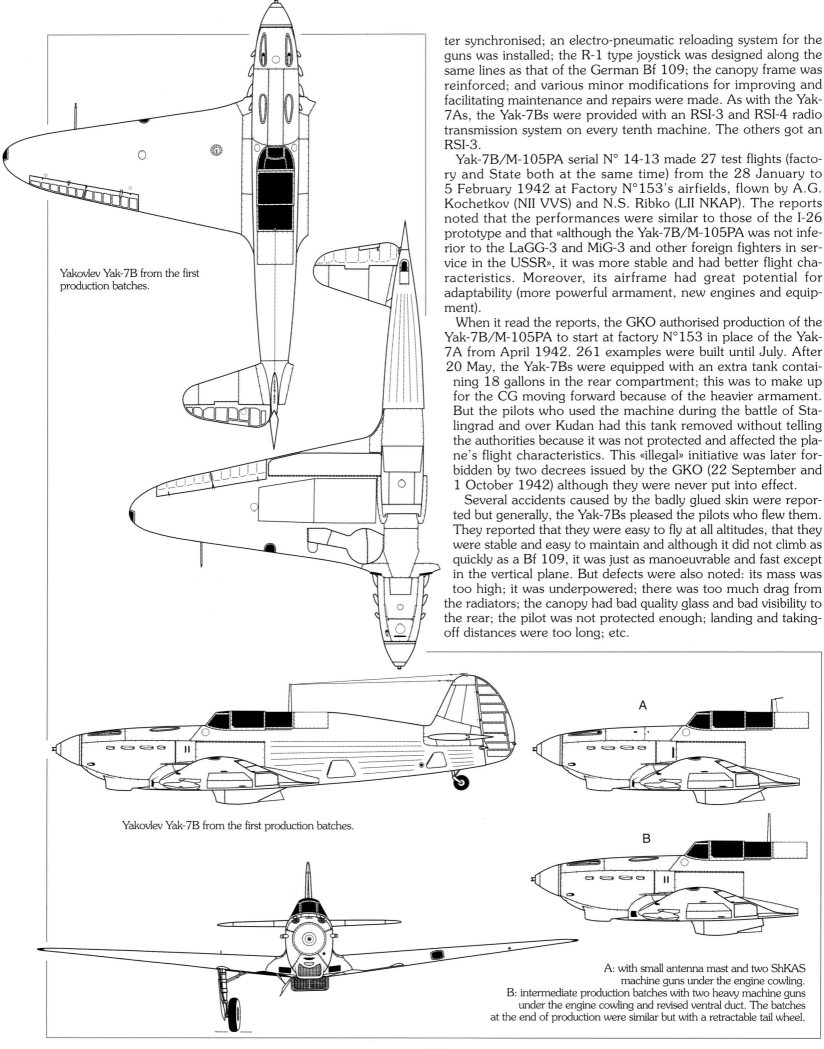

Yakovlev Yak-7B from the first production batches.

ter synchronised; an electro-pneumatic reloading system for the guns was installed; the R-1 type joystick was designed along the same lines as that of the German Bf 109; the canopy frame was reinforced; and various minor modifications for improving and facilitating maintenance and repairs were made. As with the Yak-7As, the Yak-7Bs were provided with an RSI-3 and RSI-4 radio transmission system on every tenth machine. The others got an RSI-3.

Yak-7B/M-105PA serial N° 14-13 made 27 test flights (factory and State both at the same time) from the 28 January to 5 February 1942 at Factory N°153's airfields, flown by A.G. Kochetkov (NII VVS) and N.S. Ribko (LII NKAP). The reports noted that the performances were similar to those of the I-26 prototype and that «although the Yak-7B/M-105PA was not inferior to the LaGG-3 and MiG-3 and other foreign fighters in service in the USSR», it was more stable and had better flight characteristics. Moreover, its airframe had great potential for adaptability (more powerful armament, new engines and equipment).

When it read the reports, the GKO authorised production of the Yak-7B/M-105PA to start at factory N°153 in place of the Yak-7A from April 1942. 261 examples were built until July. After 20 May, the Yak-7Bs were equipped with an extra tank containing 18 gallons in the rear compartment; this was to make up for the CG moving forward because of the heavier armament. But the pilots who used the machine during the battle of Stalingrad and over Kudan had this tank removed without telling the authorities because it was not protected and affected the plane's flight characteristics. This «illegal» initiative was later forbidden by two decrees issued by the GKO (22 September and 1 October 1942) although they were never put into effect.

Several accidents caused by the badly glued skin were reported but generally, the Yak-7Bs pleased the pilots who flew them. They reported that they were easy to fly at all altitudes, that they were stable and easy to maintain and although it did not climb as quickly as a Bf 109, it was just as manoeuvrable and fast except in the vertical plane. But defects were also noted: its mass was too high; it was underpowered; there was too much drag from the radiators; the canopy had bad quality glass and bad visibility to the rear; the pilot was not protected enough; landing and taking-off distances were too long; etc.

Yakovlev Yak-7B from the first production batches.

A

B

A: with small antenna mast and two ShKAS machine guns under the engine cowling.
B: intermediate production batches with two heavy machine guns under the engine cowling and revised ventral duct. The batches at the end of production were similar but with a retractable tail wheel.

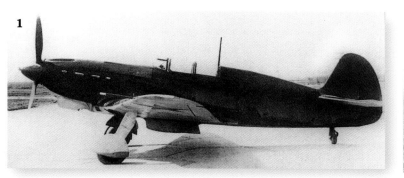

1. One of the very first Yak-7Bs powered by an M-105PA engine built at Factory N°153 at Novosibirsk, during its trials at the NII VVS. *(J. Marmain)*

2. Yak-7B/M-105PA serial N°02-66 without its undercarriage doors. Note the partitioned nose radiator. *(J. Marmain)*

3. Yak-7B/M-105PA serial N°23-03 (3rd production batch, 22nd aircraft) during its trials at the NII VVS. The undercarriage doors are now one piece instead of two (two for the preceding versions) and the space behind the cockpit has been faired over, usually with wood but sometimes with metal; it could be used to take various items or a mechanic from one field to another. *(J. Marmain)*

4. A Yak-7B/M-105PF from the last production batches fitted with skis for the winter, but without radio. The exhaust pipes are faired and the rear part of the canopy has been replaced by a plywood fairing. *(J. Marmain)*

5. This Yak-7B (M-105PA or PF) carries six RS-82 underwing. This type of weapon was not used very often by the Yakovlev fighters and was finally removed during 1942. *(J. Marmain)*

The Yak-7B/M-105PA as clearly underpowered and it was on Yakovlev's insistence that the engine builder, Klimov, accepted to increase the admission pressure of the supercharger outlet on the M-105PA first from 950 mm Hg to 1 000mm Hg, then to 1 050 mm Hg, and modify certain elements and the carburization which in fact all contributed to the creation of the M-105PF, which was 130 bhp more powerful at altitude (see below). This new engine was first tested on Yak-7A serial N° 22-41. The results were apparently so spectacular that the NKAP made Klimov start production of the new engine immediately.

The M-105PF was installed aboard the Yak-7s from Batch N°22 onwards. This change was made together with a certain number of other measures intended to improve the model which was referenced Yak-7B/M-105PF (with the same armament as the previous machine).

The airframe structure was lightened without changing the coefficient of rigidity or the operational or maintenance characteristics; the back of the seat was changed for another which was lighter; it could also be adjusted in flight. The rear glazing was replaced by a moulded plywood fairing; the rear decking was redesigned. The undercarriage well doors were lightened. Underwing fixation points and the pneumatic firing system were suppressed. The ViSH-61P propeller was improved; the R-1 joystick was generalised. In fact although this weight-saving programme only saved 66 lb or so on the MTOW, everybody maintained that the performance of the «Yak-7» would be improved with the M-105PF

engine. Serial N° 22-41's trials from 30 May to 9 June 1942 with the pilots P.I. Fiodrovi (NII VVS) and A.N. Lazarev (Factory N°153) showed an increase in speed of 18 mph at 9 240 ft and 22 mph at the first levelling-off height (12 738 ft) for a top speed of 372 mph. Above this height, the M-105PA's and PF's speeds were similar. On the other hand, the model climbed much faster up to 16 500 ft and it was more manoeuvrable both in the horizontal and vertical planes. But its range was reduced because the tank in the rear compartment had been removed. This improved stability, but moved the CG too far forward (during the ground tests several ground crew were obliged to literally sit on the tail). The M-105's usual defects persisted (oil and glycol overheating, oil leaks, etc); fuel supply was irregular from the right and left tanks (at least until 1943 when the supply system was redesigned so that the pilot could go from one tank to the other without any problems).

The elevators were less effective; the brakes were to be used cautiously; the radio's range was inadequate (31 to 50 miles for contact with the ground depending on altitude, 9 to 12

Technical specifications

Wingspan: 33 ft.	356 mph. at 12 045 ft.**
Length: 28 ft.	**Service Ceiling:** 33 000ft*,
Wing Area: 184.585 sq. ft.	32 670 ft.**
Weight Empty: 5 544 lb*, 5 478 lb**.	**Range:** 437 miles*, 396 miles**
Max. Take-off Weight: 6 692 lb*,	* Yak-7B/M-105PA and Yak-7B/M-
6 622 lb.**	105PF Prototype
Max. Speed: 362 mph. at 16 005 ft*.	** Yak-7B/M-105PF

miles plane to plane) but this was improved subsequently by putting all the elements inside the airframe and making sure it was properly insulated.

The specialists who tested Batch N°22 regretted the bad quality of Factory N°153's work (but also the sub-contracting) which meant that there were huge differences between the performances of individual planes. Thirteen examples built in 1943 were tested and revealed that with the MTOW at about three tonnes (with a tolerance of between 33 and 35 lb depending on whether or not the plane was fitted with an armoured windshield and a few production «technological deviations»), the top speed could vary from -5 1/2 mph to +7 1/2 mph (depending on altitude) between one machine and another because of the more or less well-adjusted settings and production standards; the performance of the superchargers suffered from the same variations for the same reasons.

But in the end, the GKO admitted that the Yak-7B/M-105PF corresponded more or less to what its directives (issued on 2 and 9 November 1942) specified. Two factories were allocated for the Yak-7B/M-105PF production programme: N°153 which built them up to December 1943 (batches N° 22 to N°50) and N°82 in Moscow which built batches N°1 to 28 until July 1944. The machines from this factory were generally heavier and slower than those from N°153. In all 5 120 Yak-7s with M-105PF engines were produced (a figure which is generally accepted). The model appeared for the first time in the skies over Stalingrad in August 1942.

Some batches were delivered to the PVO defence units and were quipped with an RPK-10 radio compass installed in the rear compartment which was now glazed again.

An FS-155 landing light was installed in the left wing as was an electric undercarriage position indicator. An average of about twenty of these machines was built every month and they were generally referenced as Yak-7B/MPVO or Yak-7PVO, depending on the sources.

YAKOVLEV

Yak-7-37/M-105PA Prototype and short production run (April and August 1942)

In 1940, Y.B. Yeskin, the manager of Factory N°301 had sent a document to A.I. Shakurin in which he explained that he thought that an axial 37-mm canon could be fitted onto the Yak-1. But studies carried out by the NKAP had shown that the fuselage had to be lengthened and the cockpit modified. Two years later, it was exactly what the Yakovlev OKB did when it made 22 machines designated Yak-7-37 with this modification. Although the fuselage was not lengthened, the cockpit was moved back 15 3/4 inches suppressing the rear compartment. This was to get sufficient space to install the cumbersome MPSh-37 canon (twenty 37-mm rounds) made by the armourer B.G. Shpitalny between the two rows of cylinders of the M-105PA engine, and the two heavy UBS machine guns and their rounds (260 on the left and 160 on the right) under the cowling. These weapons were fixed on a universal mounting so that several combinations were possible: VYa or ShVAK cannon, ShKAS or UBS machine guns. Moreover, six RS-82 rockets could be carried underwing (overload condition). The canon was fired electrically, it was loaded pneumatically (electro-pneumatically for the UBS).

The wingspan was reduced to 32 ft 2 in and the wing was fitted with automatic leading edge slats and a landing light; the wing tips were redesigned, the ventral tunnel was widened, the undercarriage doors were modified, the tail wheel tyre was bigger, the rear part of the canopy was bevelled, a radio antenna was installed on the rear decking of the fuselage and the fuel tanks filled with inert gases as they emptied of fuel. Moving the cockpit back did not spoil forward visibility in flight and improved it considerably to the rear. The presence of leading edge slats made the aircraft more stable and reduced its tendency to go into a spin inadvertently when flying at a big angle of attack or at slow speeds. Moving

Technical specifications

Wingspan: 32 ft. 2 in.
Length: 29 ft. 2 in.*
Wing Area: 184.585 sq. ft.
Weight Empty: 5 927 lb.
Max. Take-off Weight: 7 117 lb.

Max. Speed: 352 mph. at 15 609 ft.
Service Ceiling: 27 225 ft.
Range: 344 miles
* with the MPSh-37 barrel sticking out of the hub.

the CG did not however improve visibility for taking off and landing and using the brakes was delicate.

Factory N°153 finished the prototype Yak-7-37 on 10 April 1942. The machine did its factory and State tests from 15 April to 10 May at the hands of P.I. Fiodrovi but they were not finished because the mass had increased by some 440 lb compared with the Yak-7B, diminishing its overall performances (they were not all recorded), and because the MPSh-37 canon caused problems (several breech breakages) and the UBS were badly synchronised.

During firing tests, they damaged the propeller and Fiodrovi had to make an emergency landing.

These problems did not prevent 21 other machines from being built in August 1942. They were equipped with an NS-37 (Nudelman/Suranov) axial canon (theoretically more reliable) and did not have leading edge slats. To evaluate them operationally, they were delivered to Shinkarenko's 42.IAP who managed to increase, not without difficulty, the number of rounds to 32 for the axial canon. But the UBS cartridge belts got tangled up and were difficult to install anyway. During a demonstration in front of Marshal Vorochilov, four pilots took off aboard Yak-7-37s among whom Shikarenko. Two did not manage to raise their undercarriage and the cannon of the other two were quickly out of action. When they returned, Shikarenko's landing gear broke on landing.

Although the recoil from the canon was well absorbed by the airframe, in spite of several oil leaks near the reducer which were very quickly absorbed and although operations with these planes over the Demiansk salient turned out to be effective as far as fire-power was concerned (a 37-mm shell caused damage to more than a square yard, penetrated armour 2» thick and totally destroyed an adversary in the case of a direct hit) and although the 42.IAP shot down eight Bf 109s, one Fw 190 and one Hs 129 during twelve dogfights, the model was not put into mass-production. The Yakovlev OKB was already on the point of finishing the Yak-9T with the same type of reliable armament.

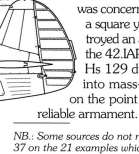

Yakovlev Yak-7-37.

NB.: Some sources do not mention the change of axial MPSH-37 canon for an NS-37 on the 21 examples which followed the prototype.

SUKHOI

I-135.2 Prototype or Su-3
(May 1942)

Technical specifications

Wingspan: 37 ft. 7 in.
Length: 27 ft. 10 in.
Wing Area: 193.734 sq. ft.
Weight Empty: 5 456 lb.

Max. Take-off Weight: 6 292 lb.
Max. Speed: 399 mph at 33 000 ft.
Service Ceiling: 39 270 ft.
Range: 438 miles

During the I-135.1 or Su-1 trials, a second prototype was being built at Kharkov under the supervision of P.D. Grushin with the same engine. It was at first designated I-135.2, then Su-3 (here again, the designation I-360 was often used because the resolution which authorised its construction was number «360»). The wingspan and the wing surface were reduced, its silhouette was different but all the modifications dictated by the Su-1 trials were progressively incorporated. In January 1941, the still unfinished prototype followed the Sukhoi OKB to Factory N°289 where it was in fact not finished because the programme was halted in April. It was only in 1942, when the VVS was again worried about German spy planes flying over Soviet sites,

Like the Su-1, this photo of the Su-3 has been touched up near the windshield. The canopy is missing as is the pressurisation system; and the TK-2 superchargers were not satisfactory during the trials. *(J. Marmain)*

This shot of the Su-3 shows the opening behind the cockpit which was used for getting rid of the gases from the superchargers (this feature also applied to the Su-1). *(J. Marmain)*

that the Su-3 prototype was finished (the story goes that elements were taken from the Su-1 to complete the Su-3) in order to undergo trials with the LII NKAP and the NII VVS during which it reached a speed of 398 mph and managed to climb to 39 270 feet. The machine behaved just as well as the Su-1 but its TK-2 superchargers were just as troublesome. Because of this, the programme was finally abandoned at the end of 1942.

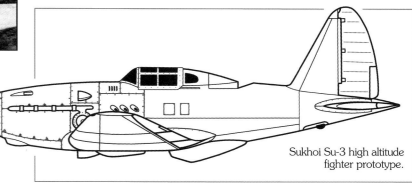

Sukhoi Su-3 high altitude fighter prototype.

The Yak-7-37 prototype was designed using the Yak-7B as a base, seen during its factory trials. Its designation has been painted on the tail fin and the long 37-mm canon barrel can be seen sticking out through the propeller boss. *(J. Marmain)*

LAVOCHKIN

La-7, «Type 37» (at the beginning LaG-5 and sometimes LaGG-5) (June 1942)

The success of the L-82, aka LaGG-3/M-82, programme enabled Lavochkin to take up his position of «Chief Manufacturer» once again and take over Factory N°21. The mass-production of the new model was immediately set up in order to respect the first delivery targets for June-July 1942. At the time, the LaG-5 reference appeared on most of the documents (some of which also attributed the designation LaGG-5 to the model). Although there has never been any official explanation, this designation was not fortuitous because when one compares the photographs and the plans of the first examples to come out of the factory and bearing in mind the fact that the model was also being built at Factory N°31 where Gorbunov was working, one can see that the way the LaGG-3/M-82 developed into the series model was very similar to the LaG-5 prototype built by Gorbunov… which does suggest that there was a certain element of cooperation between the Lavochkin and Gorbunov teams.

The first ten «LaG-5s» were completed in three weeks (June) and submitted for operational tests and various improvement programmes. All the airframes of the LaGG-3 being produced or ordered had to be brought up to the standards of the new model, but deliveries of the LaGG-3 only stopped officially at Factory N°21 in September. The

Technical specifications

Wingspan: 31 ft. 8 in.
Length: 28 ft. 9 in,
  28 ft. 8 in. (1942)
Wing Area: 186.953 sq. ft. (1941),
  185.877 sq. ft.,
  185.877 sq. ft. (1943).
Weight Empty: 5 898 lb. (1942),
  5 720 lb. (1943),

Max. Take-off Weight: 7 392 lb. (1942),
  7 040 lb (1943).
Max. Speed: 362 mph at 21 450 ft. (1942),
  375 mph at 21 450 ft. (1943)
Service Ceiling: 31 350 ft. (1942),
  31 845 ft. (1943)
Range: 409 miles (1942),
  562 miles (1943).

production rates were revised and increased so much that the first production series machines reached the units in the summer of 1942. But for all that, the model was not perfect. At 19 800 feet it was 25 to 30 mph slower than the prototype because it was heavier and because the fairing of the power plant fitted badly owing to the poor quality of the finish of the M-82 engine cowling panels. There was insufficient trim; the connections between the outer wing section and the central wing section were fragile; the propeller vibrated and raced on take-off or in a dive because it was not balanced properly. The canon mountings had to be redesigned to reduce the vibrations they made when they were fired. There were continual oil leaks which covered the windshield and at low rpm the oil pressure fell (the small size of the oil tank came in for a lot of criticism). The plane did not manoeuvre as well and the joystick was too hard, especially as there were no leading edge slats. It was too hot in the cockpit which did not have any ventilation system; and it was difficult to climb in and out of it. Landings usually involved several bounces. The range was too short because the tanks in the wing outer sections could only be filled in overload conditions and the drop tanks could only be used to the detriment of good handling.

All these defects were gradually remedied or reduced. From August 1942 every third example was equipped with an RSI-4 radio and an RPK-10 radio compass. The others received what was available. In September, the authorities gave the model the definitive designation of La-5. Various experiments were carried out. Thus La-5 ser. N°8-71 was equipped with a long air intake fitted on the top of the engine cowling and a different cooling system and a few other changes which were to be found again on the La-5FN version. After November 1942, all the La-5s could fly at 343 mph at ground level thanks to draconian technical testing and quality control set up at the end of the production lines. But apart from its oil leaks, the M-82A engine did not allow the plane to reach its estimated performances mainly because the performance of its two-stage centrifugal supercharger was not good enough. Armament comprised two synchronised ShVAK cannon but the La-5s built in 1943 were equipped with a UBS and a ShVAK.

In spite of all this and while waiting for a more powerful and more reliable engine to become available, the La-5s took part in the fighting on the Stalingrad front in November 1942 where the German Bf-109Fs and Gs soon caught on to their weaknesses: acceleration, rate of climb and manoeuvrability in the vertical plane. The Lavochkin

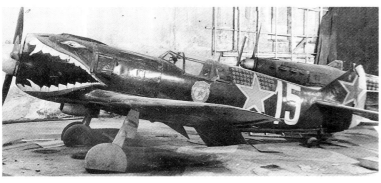

Left, from top to bottom.
An operational La-5 ready for take-off. Note the metal plate prolonging the exhaust. *(J. Marmain)*

An La-5 from the last 1942 production batches. Compared with the examples from the beginning of production, two half-moon undercarriage doors have been installed under the fuselage, the rear frame of the sliding canopy is thicker and the tail wheel doors are not rounded. *(G. Gorokhoff)*

The «Shark's Teeth» La-5 belonging to the Soviet ace G.D. Kostylev exhibited at the Leningrad Defence Museum in 1945. Its back has been decorated with 38 stars representing his kills. *(H. Leonard)*

OKB did its utmost to improve these characteristics with the following versions: the La-5F and La-5N. Some of the modifications carried out to lighten these two versions and make them perform better were applied retroactively to other La-5s in 1943.

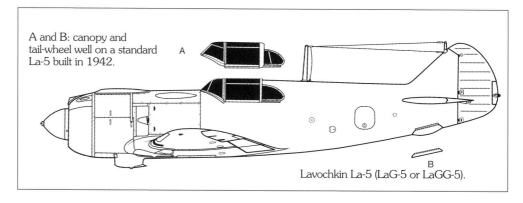

A and B: canopy and tail-wheel well on a standard La-5 built in 1942.

Lavochkin La-5 (LaG-5 or LaGG-5).

NB: Gudkov was the first to develop a prototype uniting a LaGG-3 airframe with an M-82 engine: the Gu-82 (see below). Lavochkin did not take kindly to its success even though this was only relative and, with the help of his friends within the NKAP, did what he could to block the development of the model's mass production (by which the VVS set so much store) to the advantage of his own model.

POLIKARPOV

I-185/M-71 «1942-standards» prototype, or I-186 (Fourth airframe) (June 1942)

Technical specifications

Wingspan: 32 ft. 4 in.
Length: 26 ft. 6 in.
Wing Area: 167.149 sq. ft.
Weight Empty: 5 929 lb.
Max. Take-off Weight: 8 067 lb.

Max. Speed: 425 mph at 22 440 ft. (442 mph with engine overrevving).
Service Ceiling: 36 300 ft.
Range: 500 to 705 miles

The fourth airframe of the I-185 programme was identical to that of the I-185/M-82A prototype, including fixed armament and equipment, except for the engine compartment into which an M-71 engine was installed in 1942. Its large 4 ft 7 in diameter meant Polikarpov had to design a very streamlined fairing to create as little drag as possible. Designated as the «1942- standards» I-185/M-71, this prototype was often referenced as «I-186» so as not to confuse it with the other I-185s powered by M-71s. It flew for the first time on 10 June 1942 and carried out its factory then State tests at the NII VVS from 18 November to January 1943. It was the test pilot, P. Loginov, who tested the machine from June to October, and then Stefanovski and Fiodrovi took over. During these trials, the prototype reached speeds of 360 mph near the ground, 416 mph at 20 130 ft and climbed to 16 500 feet in 4.7 minutes. On 15 December 1942 during a trial, it reached the speed of 442 mph with an overrevving engine, but the M-71 broke and Stefanovski was obliged to make a forced landing. The engine was changed on 26 December 1942 and Stefanovski flew again with an overrevving engine and tried once more to reach 442 mph which was a speed that no other fighter, including for what it's worth, German operational types, had yet reached. But the engine broke up again obliging the pilot to make another emergency landing. All in all the I-186 was only able to stay air borne for 5 hours and 13 minutes during its trials, both factory and State.

The model had an exceptional rate of climb. Stefanovski and Fiodrovi thought that it could still be improved on by installing a reliable engine and lightening the airframe, thus improving its flight characteristics. The proto-

The I-185/M-71 prototype. It's the third airframe of the I-185 programme which was intended originally for the M-71 engine tests. Its excellent performances were appreciated by the pilots of the 728.IAP who recommended mass-production... which never happened. *(J. Marmain)*

type was repaired at the NII VVS and taken in hand by V.A. Stepanshenok for another round of trials. On 5 April 1943, the engine stalled when he was in the landing approach stage. Stepanshenok was unable to avoid a hangar and was killed when the aircraft crashed into it. His death hastened the decision to end the whole I-185 programme in spite of the excellent reports from the test pilots who carried out both factory and State trials and operational evaluations on the front.

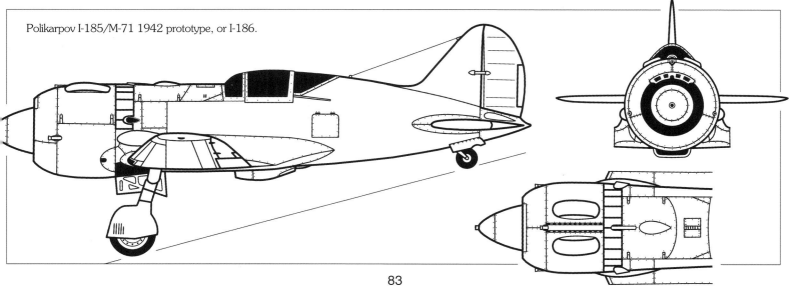

Polikarpov I-185/M-71 1942 prototype, or I-186.

YAKOVLEV

Yak-7D/M-105PA Prototype
(June 1942)

Below.
The Yak-7D as a single-seater for carrying freight or for long-distance reconnaissance; the rear cockpit canopy has been faired over with wood. Its designation has been painted onto the tail fin. *(J. Marmain)*

Bottom.
The Yak-7D as a two-seater for observation, reconnaissance or liaison. *(J. Marmain)*

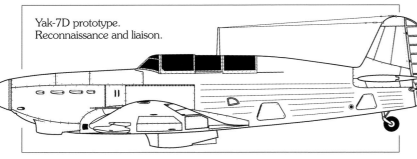

Yak-7D prototype.
Reconnaissance and liaison.

Technical specifications

Wingspan: 32 ft. 2 in.	**Max. Take-off Weight:** 6 897 lb.
Length: 27 ft. 11 1/2 in.	**Max. Speed:** 353 mph. at 16 500 ft.
Wing Area: 184.585 sq. ft.	**Service Ceiling:** 29 700 ft.
Weight Empty: 4 976 lb.	**Range:** 1 037 to 1 428 miles

The Yak-7D prototype marked the first step towards the creation of a new family of Yak-9 fighters (see below). Its wing was entirely redesigned: two spars and six metal ribs and the rest made of wood. The wingspan was reduced to 32 ft 2 in with more elliptical wing tips, but without any reduction in wing area. The skin was made of plywood. The joints for the ailerons and the flaps were redesigned also. The wing contained eight tanks, of which six were between the spars and two in the tips. Total capacity was 185 gallons. Two other tanks under the pilot's seat (only one according to different sources) containing 19 gallons and a distribution tank containing 1 1/3 gallons. These 205 gallons (1 518 lb) enabled the plane to cover a distance of 1 428 miles (6 1/2 hours' endurance at economical speed) since its primary functions were to carry out long-distance reconnaissance missions and carry mail or do liaison work.

A Yak-7D/M-105PA was chosen to be fitted with the new wing. It was an example with rear decking and a metal fairing covering the rear compartment. An AFA-B camera could be installed in there (or an AFA-IM, or an observer) capable of taking fifty shots up to a height of 26 400 ft. Its oil tank was enlarged (143 lb) but almost everything else was similar to the basic model, except for the enlarged ventral tunnel (identical to that of the Yak-7B with the frames at the rear of the fuselage reduced in size and an M-105PF engine) and only one axial canon with 60 rounds. The oxygen equipment enabled the pilot to stay for two hours at 26 400 ft. In spite of the increased mass (with the change from a wooden wing to one of mixed construction), the increase in fuel capacity took the weight up to 6 897 lb with an observer (two-seat lay-out), to 6 864 lb with a camera (single-seat lay-out). All its performances were reduced compared with the Yak-7B, except its range.

Yakovlev had not envisaged presenting this prototype for the State trials. Its principal defect was filling the tanks which could only be done through a single filler hole. The Yak-7D carried out its factory tests from 3 to 16 June 1942, both as a single-seater and a two-seater, then it returned to the factory for a schedule of modifications within the context of the Yak-7DI programme, the true prototype for the Yak-9.

YAKOVLEV

Yak-7DI/M105PF Prototype
(June 1942)

The experiment with the Yak-7D gave rise to another prototype: the Yak-7DI. The fuselage of the Yak-7B serial N° 23-36 (single-seat version, with reduced frames on the rear portion of the fuselage and an «all-round» visibility canopy) was married to a new wing of mixed

Technical specifications

Wingspan: 32 ft. 2 in.	**Max. Speed:** 356 mph. at 12 870 ft
Length: 27 ft. 11 1/2 in.	(353 mph. at 12 540 ft)
Wing Area: 184.585 sq. ft.	**Service Ceiling:** 34 320 ft (33 000ft)
Weight Empty: 5 192 lb.	**Range:** 375 miles (818 miles)
Max. Take-off Weight: 6 237 lb (6 677 lb)	*The figures in brackets refer to the «heavy» version.*

The Yak-7DI prototype (its designation has been painted on the tail fin) during its trials. The dorsal trapdoor for carrying miscellaneous loads or equipment can be seen clearly behind the cockpit. *(J. Marmain)*

The Yak-7DI with another camouflage scheme, no doubt being tested in its «heavy» configuration. The dorsal trapdoor swung over to the right to accommodate «even a man», or miscellaneous equipment. *(J. Marmain)*

construction similar to that of the Yak-7D, but only holding four tanks with a total capacity of 150 gallons (1 100 lb). They were interconnected and the distribution tank (1 1/3 gallons) ensured regular and automatic consumption. The tail was that of the Yak-7D and the engine was an M-105PF. All the rest was the same as the Yak-7B from batches N°22 to N°24. The armament however only comprised the axial canon with its 120 shells, and a UBS under the engine cowling with 200 rounds. In the overload condition, it could carry two 55 to 220-lb bombs. The space behind the cockpit was covered with a plywood fairing which swung over to the right and could carry a man (under very cramped conditions and without being able to see outside), or an extra tank, an AFA-IM or AFA-B camera or miscellaneous loads.

The Yak-7DI prototype was finished on 25 June 1942 and its factory tests started the following day lasting until 16 July. The 13 flights which were made by P.I. Fiodrovi were followed by the State trials, from 18 July to 15 August with K.A. Gruzdev. The model was intended to operate in two ways: «heavy» with full oil (110 lb) and fuel tanks, for long-range fighter, reconnaissance or patrol missions over 820 miles; or «light» with only 396 to 550 lb of fuel and 44 to 55 lb of oil for close-range fighter and infantry support missions over 375 miles. In its «heavy» version, the Yak-7DI performed almost as well as the Yak-7B, but the «light» version with only 78 gallons of fuel became very nimble and easy to pilot, and climbed better than the Bf 109.

The reports on the trials by the NII VVS noted that the Yak-7DI

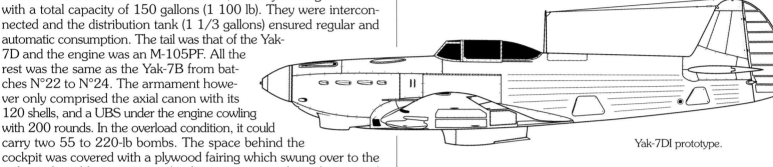

Yak-7DI prototype.

was without doubt the best Soviet fighter of the moment, because of its fighting capabilities, its overall performances, its range and its versatility (it could also be used for missions by night), but its landing and taking off distances were too long (625 feet on landing) and the risk of nosing over was very high (the pilots had to be careful when braking). With the beginning of the battle of Stalingrad, the VVS considered that they had to have Yak-7DI in their inventory. The model was immediately recommended for series production on condition that the defects which had been reported were corrected and in spite of the fact that the rocket launchers had not been tested. The production series armament had already been decided on: one ShVAK axial canon with 140 rounds and a UBS machine gun under the cowling with 240 rounds. But although only one Yak-7DI was built, it did give rise to the Yak-9 line.

YAKOVLEV

Yak-1/M-105PF (July 1942)

In July 1942, from the 10th example of the 79th batch (serial N° 10-79) onwards, the M-105PA was replaced by an M-105PF to power the Yak-1s. This engine came just at the right time to maintain the plane's original performances and counter the German Bf 109F effectively. It differed from the previous M-105PA in that the pistons were reinforced, the injection and the cooling system had been modified and above all, the admission pressure on the supercharger outlet had been raised to 1 050 mm Hg (compared with 950 on the PA). Thus its power rating was increased by 90 bhp at take-off and by 130 bhp at the second levelling-off height (8 910 ft).

This essential modification was made by the engineer, B.K. Nikitin who, with a team from Engine Factory N°26, was seconded in April 1942 to the 236.IAP (West Front). There, on his own initiative, he modified the

Technical specifications	
Wingspan: 33 ft.	**Max. Speed:** 356 mph (368 mph)
Length: 27 ft. 11 1/2 in.	**Service Ceiling:** 33 000ft (31 350 ft).
Wing Area: 184.585 sq. ft.	**Range:** 406 miles
Weight Empty: 5 306 lb (5 269 lb)	*The figures in brackets concern*
Max. Take-off Weight: 6 417 lb (6 380 lb)	*Yak-1/M-105PF with one cowling mounted UBS.*

admission pressure on the supercharger outlet on the M-105PA engines of seven Yak-1s and raised it to 1 050 mm Hg. The result was surprising because the flight characteristics improved greatly as did the speeds at the two levelling-out altitudes for the centrifugal supercharger: 2 310 ft and 8 910 ft (instead of 6 600 and 13 200 for the M-105PA). Encouraged to develop a new version of his engine on these bases, Klimov hesitated to do so because he considered that his team did not have time to waste developing a new engine whose working life expectancy would be definitely shortened, and because he also hoped to get the M-107 right (it was much more powerful than the M-105). But Yakovlev insisted and Klimov changed his mind. To his great surprise, Klimov noted that on the test bench, an M-105PA thus tuned managed to run for 203 hours before breaking up. He had proof that the power of a proven engine could be increased by such a simple modification without touching its basic technology.

However, the trials with the seven modified Yak-1s also revealed a well-known defect: overheating of the power plant, because the radiators were no longer adapted to the boosted centrifugal supercharger. It was therefore impossible to climb to any altitude without going through the levelling off heights, even with the flaps wide open. As a result, an OP-352 glycol radiator with a greater cooling capacity was installed near the engine, re-designated M-105PF which, apart from the modifications already mentioned, also had a fairing covering the oil radiator, itself of greater dimensions. All these modifications only increased the MTOW very slightly, to around 5 027 lb. The rate of climb and turn, and the level flight speeds were improved as was the landing speed. But the engine speeds had still to be limited when climbing to avoid the risk of the power plant seizing up because it still suffered from oil leakages.

This information was noted during Yak-1's (serial N°29-85) State trials in August 1942, but also on a Yak-7A (serial N°1411 and a Yak-7B (serial N°1423) and two Yak-1s seconded from 236.IAP to the NII VVS (serial N° 15-40 and 16-43). Consequently, nine other Yak-1s from various batches were tested in 1943 with M-105PFs at the NII VVS which all confir-

med the engine's ineffective cooling system. Moreover the brakes always had to be used with care. But the danger caused by the arrival in the USSR of the Bf 109F, meant that the authorities did not hesitate for very long. In spite of the fact that it had to limit its top speeds - which cancelled out the benefit of the increased power - the M-105PF was mass-produced at Factory N°26, instead of the M-105PA from 1 May 1942. Following a decree issued by the GKO dated 29 May, Factory N°292 was ordered to produce the Yak-1/M-105PF from 4 June 1942 onwards. The first batches were armed with an axial ShVAK canon and two synchronised ShKAS machine guns. The others, except for the «light» batches, had one UBS in place of the ShKAS under the cowling.

Out of a total of 5 672 Yak-1/M-105PF produced, including all versions (out of 8 670 Yak-1s built), 4 461 benefited from «aerodynamic improvements» applied from batch N°111 in December 1942. The modifications carried out on the recommendations of the TsAGI and the LII concerned: the tail wheel which was retractable again; the fuselage with insulated bulkheads; the elimination of the grill over the glycol air intake; the faired ejector effect exhaust pipes; the integrated propeller boss; the seals were made more hermetic; the oil radiator tunnel was redesigned; the engine cowling panels fitted better; better skin finishing, etc. All these changes were tested on the Yak-1/M-105PF serial N° 16-99 in October 1942 then on serial N°23-148 in September-October 1943 for comparison. Between these two periods, they were applied to all machines in the production series until production ceased.

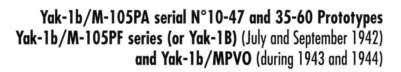

YAKOVLEV

Yak-1b/M-105PA serial N°10-47 and 35-60 Prototypes
Yak-1b/M-105PF series (or Yak-1B) (July and September 1942)
and Yak-1b/MPVO (during 1943 and 1944)

Out of the 8 670 Yak-1s powered by M-105P, PA or PF engines produced, 4 188 were designated as Yak-1bs (or Yak-1B, see Note). The addition of this suffix meant that a host of modifications were applied as soon as the M-105PF-powered Yak-1 production started. At the same time as production of the Yak-1/M-105PF with rear decking started, the Yakovlev team adopted the wind tunnel discoveries made by A.I. Silman at the TsAGI in July 1942 regarding the aerodynamic improvements (already described with the Yak-1/M-105PF). But the team went further in its attempt to lighten the airframe. To do this, it took into account several of the complaints made by the military authorities and reduced the size of the frames on the rear portion of the fuselage and installed an «all-round» visibility canopy, and tested this on serial N° 10-47 then on serial N° 35-60 produced at the Saratov factory in June. In fact, these two modifications were «fiddled privately» first on a Yak-7B/M-105PF (and not on a Yak-1 as too many sources affirm) by the maintenance and repair team of Major Shinkarenko who wanted

Technical specifications

Wingspan: 33 ft.
Length: 27 ft. 11 1/2 in.
Wing Area: 184.585 sq. ft.
Weight Empty: 5 095 lb.

Max. Take-off Weight: 6 345 lb.
Max. Speed: 370 mph. at 13 350 ft.
Service Ceiling: 33 165 ft.
Range: 437 miles

Below left and right.
Yak-1b serial N°04111 during its trials at the NII VVS. Its camouflage scheme was «theoretically» white, but it has been almost completely spattered with oil from the M-105PF engine which leaked very badly. *(J. Marmain)*

Yak-1b serial N° 35-60 considered as the «Standard» for the new 1942 version of the Yak-1. The rear frames of the fuselage have been reduced, an «all-round» visibility canopy has been installed and the radiator is the same as that of the Yak-7, since the engine was to be an M-105PF (it was still only an M-105PA). *(J. Marmain)*

to fly a machine with greatly improved rear visibility. These «repairs» were taken up by the Yakovlev OKB and were standardised on the new machines, designated Yak-1b/M-105PA.

Moreover, the glazing of the new canopy was flat, the pilot had a mirror fitted in the cockpit, and an armoured console on the left. Firepower was increased by replacing the two ShKAS machine guns with a UBS with 200 rounds. The axial ShVAK canon had 120 rounds (from 1943, these weapons had 230 and 140 rounds respectively). The feeding and firing systems were electric for the canon and electro-pneumatic for the UBS. The OPB sights were replaced by a VV-1. The joystick was copied from the Bf 109's which enabled the pilot to handle the plane and fire with the right hand whilst controlling the throttle with the left which was impossible beforehand. The tail wheel retracted and the oil and glycol radiator intakes were redesigned.

With all these modifications, the «35-60» was finished on 1 July 1943 and tested at the NII from 4 to 14 July by A.G. Proshakov so as to be used as a «standard». The report noted

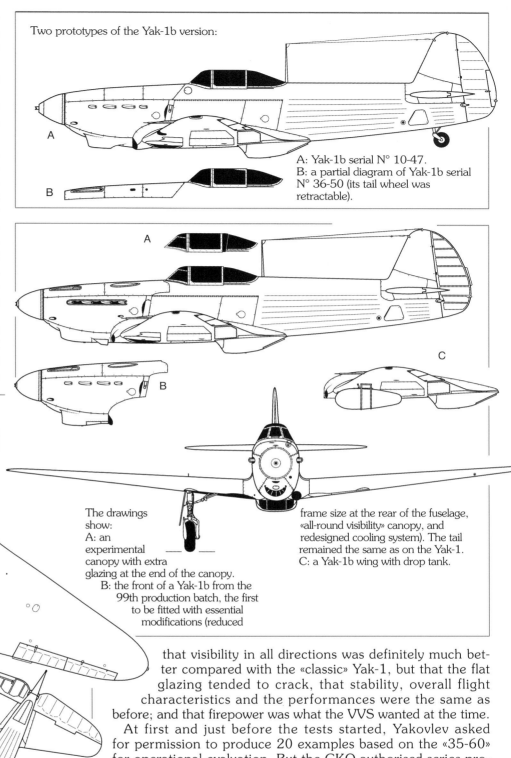

Two prototypes of the Yak-1b version:

A: Yak-1b serial N° 10-47.
B: a partial diagram of Yak-1b serial N° 36-50 (its tail wheel was retractable).

Standard Yakovlev Yak-1b from production batch N°110 onwards.

The drawings show:
A: an experimental canopy with extra glazing at the end of the canopy.
B: the front of a Yak-1b from the 99th production batch, the first to be fitted with essential modifications (reduced frame size at the rear of the fuselage, «all-round visibility» canopy, and redesigned cooling system). The tail remained the same as on the Yak-1. C: a Yak-1b wing with drop tank.

that visibility in all directions was definitely much better compared with the «classic» Yak-1, but that the flat glazing tended to crack, that stability, overall flight characteristics and the performances were the same as before; and that firepower was what the VVS wanted at the time.

At first and just before the tests started, Yakovlev asked for permission to produce 20 examples based on the «35-60» for operational evaluation. But the GKO authorised series production of the Yak-1b/M-105PF with ViSH-105SV-01 from 11 August 1942. Ten examples were made in September and from October, all Yak-1s were produced in the model of the Yak-1b. All the improvements were not introduced at once: the tail wheel was retractable from Batch N°87 onwards; a small flap preventing oil spraying onto the windshield was only installed with Batch N°89; the reduction in the size of the rear fuselage frames was only introduced from Batch N°99. Finally, all the modifications mentioned were standardised definitively until the end of Yak-1 production with Batch N°111 in December 1942. The Yak-1bs appeared on the Kalinin front (32.IAP) and

NB.: The suffix «b» (very often replaced by a B in the West) added to «Yak-1» was ignored outside the USSR for a long time. Until the beginning of the 80s, most of the articles dealing with the Yak-1 (and sometimes in the Eastern block countries also) used an «M» suffix («M» for modified) applied to this version of the Yak-1 in order not to confuse it with the others. In fact, the «M» was only applied officially to the two Yak-3 prototypes and meant «Moskit» (mosquito).

A Yak-1b at the front. This was the machine belonging to the French volunteer, Yves Biziern, from the «Normandie-Niemen» squadron. The inscription on the fuselage meant «To the defenders of the Stalingrad front on behalf of the workers from the Saratov District». Note that the upper propeller blade has been damaged. *(J. Marmain)*

at Stalingrad (176.IAP) in December 1942 and in January 1943 when their pilots obviously appreciated the improvements made during the operational evaluations.

During the 669 missions made by the 58 machines, 25 enemy machines were shot down for the loss of only six Yak-1bs.

In 1943 and 1944, 385 Yak-1bs were delivered to the PVO defence units and referenced Yak-1/MPVO.

Although their characteristics and performances were the same, they were equipped with instruments for bad weather flying, including an FS-155 landing light, a VR-2 speed indicator, an RPK-10 radio-compass, an AG-5 artificial horizon.

Their mass was slightly higher than that of the standard Yakovlev Yak-1.

LAVOCHKIN

LaGG-3/2VRD-1 or LaGG-3PVRD
Prototype (August 1942)

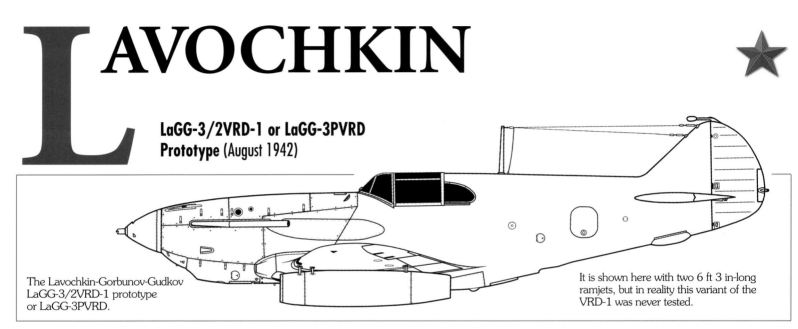

The Lavochkin-Gorbunov-Gudkov LaGG-3/2VRD-1 prototype or LaGG-3PVRD.

It is shown here with two 6 ft 3 in-long ramjets, but in reality this variant of the VRD-1 was never tested.

In August 1942, LaGG-3 serial N° 31213173 was equipped with two VDR-1 ramjets. They were designed by M.M. Bondaryuk, the head of OKB-3 at the NII GVF. They were attached to the underside of the wing by means of faired pylons on the second rib of each wing section, outboard of the undercarriage legs. They used the same fuel as the main M-105PF engine and were supplied with kerosene by means of a BNK-10 pump. The air under pressure enabling the fuel to be injected into each combustion chamber came from the centrifugal supercharger. The programme had to evaluate the operational worth of the design, its reliability and its true effectiveness. Two variants of the VRD-1 were developed: the first was 7 feet long, with a opening at the front measuring 5 1/2 inches and a mass of 35.2 lb; the second was supercharged, measured only 6 ft 3 in long with an opening at the front of 6 3/4 inches, but with the same mass. The theoretical calculations forecast that the speed would be increased by 10 to 14 mph at 4 950 ft and 13 200 ft with the first variant and 25 to 30 mph with the second respectively at the same altitudes.

Designated LaGG-3/2VRD (or LaGG-3PVRD depending on the sources, the PVRD indicating that it used ramjets), this prototype was first fitted with two VRD-1s of the first type. Before testing them in flight, two ignition tests were made on the ground. These revealed that the BNK-10 pump was not properly adjusted: its distributor supplied kerosene to the two ramjets irregularly. The first flight was made by Mischenko on 5 August 1942 and only served to test the VRD-1s' pylons. Up to 14 August, six flights were used to test the ignition, consumption and operation of the VRD-1s at different speeds and heights. They were followed by seven other flights to measure the per-

This LaGG-3 powered by an M-105PF served as a prototype for trying out two 7-ft long Bondariuk VRD-1 ramjets attached under the outer wing surfaces. Designated LaGG-3/2VRD (sometimes LaGG-3PVRD), its trials were both encouraging and disappointing. Another 6 ft 3 in version of the VRD-1 should also have been tested but wasn't.
(RART)

formances with and without the VRD-1s, the solidity of the fixations and whether they were correctly positioned. Unfortunately the lack of precision of the distributor of the BNK-10 pump only allowed an increase of 7 1/2 to 9 mph at 4 950 feet. On the other hand the ramjets slowed the prototype down by 22 to 25 mph when they were not used because they caused too much drag.

The report on the trials concluded that it was necessary to improve the air-kerosene mixture distributor control for the ramjets and also the ramjet attachment fairings. Although they were disappointing, the results were thought to be sufficiently interesting to justify continuing the trials with more powerful ramjets. On the other hand, the second variant of the VRD-1 was not tried out.

Technical specifications

Wingspan: 32 ft. 4 in.	**Max. Speed:** 253 mph. at 4 950 ft without VRD-1, 262 mph at 4 950 ft with VRD-1.
Length: 29 ft.	
Wing Area: 189.644 sq. ft.	**Service Ceiling:**
W. E.: M.T.-o. W.:	**Range:**

MIKOYAN -GUREVICH

I-230 Prototype and Pre-series (or MiG-3U, or MiG-3D) («D» Programme)
(August 1942 and during 1943)

As the end of production of the MiG-3 did not mean the demise of the Mikoyan-Gurevich OKB, they developed a new programme to take its place: the «D» programme (D for Dalnostnyi, or long-range), or the I-230. The aim was to produce a new fighter which «was faster at all altitudes» in the same conditions as the MiG-3, using the same production lines, without interruption, without slowing down the production rates, and with the same tooling. With this in mind, the OKB could not really deviate from its original technological base and also had to take the complaints from the pilots at the front into account. The fuselage was streamlined and extended by 14 1/2 inches, the undercarriage was fitted with better and more reliable shock absorbers; the cockpit was considerably improved, the air intakes for the engine cooling system were redesigned. The ventral tunnel was placed further forward and was more streamlined; the tail surfaces were revised and the armament «at last» comprised two ShVAK cannon under the upper part of the engine cowling (150 rounds per canon). Moreover, although the whole of the airframe was still made of wood (except for the engine mounting) the wing, fitted with automatic leading edges slats, was built around a single metal main spar.

But the idea of «long-range» was a mistake in that fuel capacity did not really increase compared with that of the standard MiG-3. The four original metal tanks were replaced by a single self-sealing one, installed in the fuselage with a capacity of 98 gallons. Although all these modifications did not present any particular problems, Mikoyan and Gurevich did not have any engine at their disposal for their new programme, referenced as MiG-3U in some documents (U for Ushluchennyi, or improved), or MiG-3D in others. The Am-35A was no longer built, the Am-39 which had been envisaged for a while was not yet ready and the other engines were simply too heavy, too big (see I-210 and I-211) or not available. The OKB had no other solution but to use an AM-35A, patched up and put into service by the factory's maintenance workshops. It weighed 88 lb more than a new engine.

When trials started on 11 August 1942, the I-230/MiG-3U prototype's finish was very well cared for. Its «thoroughbred appearance» suggested it would perform very well. This was the case because it reached 410 mph at 19 800 feet, but almost a year later during the State trials from 28 July to 6 August 1943 at the hands of V. Khomiakov. At the time, the engine factories were moving again and the

The first I-230 prototype, or MiG-3U. It was never mass-produced because there were no engines for it, despite its excellent performances. *(J. Marmain)*

question of putting the Am-35A back into production was no longer under consideration which put paid to the hope of starting series production of the «new model MiG-3». However, five other models were built, all with reconditioned AM-35A engines and AV-5L propellers (the second, N°02, was fitted experimentally with a larger wingspan and wing surface, and an AV-5A propeller with better performances at high altitude).

The I-230 N°02 prototype as shown on the fuselage, designed by Mikoyan and Gurevich in an attempt to start MiG-3 production up again. The model was sometimes referenced as MiG-3U or MiG-3D without these designations ever having been made official. Unlike the first prototype, N°02 was equipped with a radio transmission system. *(J. Marmain)*

Technical specifications

Wingspan: 33 ft. 7 1/2 in. (N°1), 36 ft 4 in. (N°2)
Length: 28 ft. 5 in.
Wing Area: 187.706 sq. ft. (N°1), 193.734 sq. ft. (N°2)

Weight Empty: 5 746 lb.
M. Take-off Weight: 7 227 lb.
M. Speed: 410 mph. at 19 800 ft.
Service Ceiling: 39 600 ft. (N°1 and N°2) **Range:** 843 miles

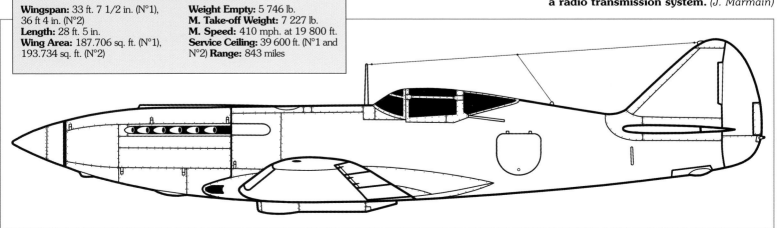

YAKOVLEV

Prototype Yak-7PD/M-105PD
(September 1942)

Like Pavel Sukhoi, Semyon Lavochkin, Mikoyan and Gurevich, Yakovlev designed a high-altitude fighter for the Defence (PVO) units entrusted with intercepting the German Junkers Ju-86R spy-planes flying at around 43 000 feet in all impunity: the Yak-7PD. Yak-7B serial number 22-02 was equipped with an M-105PD engine with a Dollejal supercharger and had to be brought up to «model B» standards with smaller frames at the rear of the fuselage. Its canopy gave «total visibility» but had a windshield with flat, armoured panes. The radio antenna was located behind the cockpit but no means of transmission was installed aboard (no generator). In order to avoid a weight increase, the two ShKAS were removed, to the great disappointment of the military who considered that a single axial canon and its 120 shells was not sufficient to shoot down a Junkers Ju-86R, considering that at the altitudes it flew at, only one fly-past was possible because the engine would inevitably overheat after the fast climb,

which forced the pilot to bring the plane down to a more reasonable altitude to cool the engine down properly.

The trials on the Yak-7PD/M-105PD prototype were carried out at the NII VVS from 17 to 23 September 1942. During the 11 flights, the pilot A.G. Proshakov noticed that the aircraft flew well and much faster than the MiG-3 below 16 500 feet but that it was slower above 19 800. He noted also that there were continual oil pressure problems (no automatic control on the supercharger, making piloting very complicated), that the M-105PD was not very reliable and vibrated too much. The report by the NII VVS turned the machine down saying that it could be put into service with the PVOs when all the problems had been sorted out and its firepower increased (at least one canon and one UBS). Earlier, ten Yak-7PD/M-105PDs had been ordered for operational evaluation and for engine improvements. But they were not built because the Luftwaffe no longer sent its Ju-86Rs over Moscow or other Soviet targets very often and because Yakovlev preferred to develop a new high-altitude version based on the Yak-9 (see below), after the Yak-7D had undergone a 50-hour test programme at LII NKAP where 27 flights were carried out (with more success than the others).

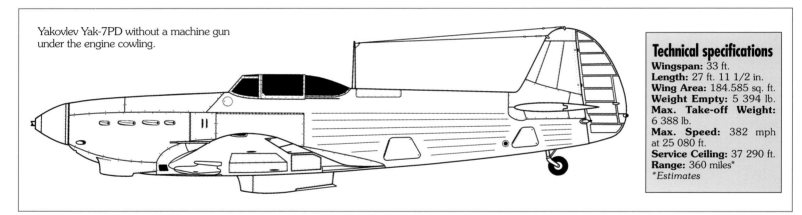

Yakovlev Yak-7PD without a machine gun under the engine cowling.

Technical specifications
Wingspan: 33 ft.
Length: 27 ft. 11 1/2 in.
Wing Area: 184.585 sq. ft.
Weight Empty: 5 394 lb.
Max. Take-off Weight: 6 388 lb.
Max. Speed: 382 mph at 25 080 ft.
Service Ceiling: 37 290 ft.
Range: 360 miles*
*Estimates

YAKOVLEV

Yak-9/M-105PF
(October 1942)

The Yak-9 was the third major variant of the Yakovlev «front» fighter family. It was the model which was produced in the largest numbers and used by the VVS from the Battle of Stalingrad onwards: 16 769 examples were produced, of all versions and prototypes, including 611 two-seaters, by three factories from 1942 to 1948: N°153 at Novosibirsk, N°166 at Omsk and N°82 at Moscow. The versatility of the basic conception, its excellent flight characteristics, its performances, the lack of major vices and its easy maintenance enabled the VVS to use it for a variety of roles (depending on the versions): «front» fighter (heavy and light armament), escort fighter, high-altitude fighter; for bombing, photographic reconnaissance, training and fast liaison.

The Yak-9/M-105PF (with VISh-61P propeller) was the version used

The Yak-9 during its factory and LII trials, at the end of 1942. The gill in the root of the left wing is closed. Note the two little tail wheel well doors, the faired exhaust pipes and the absence of radio antenna.
(J. Marmain)

Standard Yakovlev
Yak-9.

A

Drawing A shows the lower front part of
the engine cowling of an example from
the beginning of production,
with a different oil radiator fairing.

Technical specifications

Wingspan: 32 ft. 2 in.
Length: 28 ft.
Wing Area: 184 585 sq. ft.
Weight Empty: 5 009 lb.

M. Take-off Weight: 6 314 lb.
M. Speed: 374 mph at 14 190 ft.
Service Ceiling: 36 660 ft.
Range: 412 miles

for the production series based on the prototype Yak-7DI, with the same mixed construction wing. But when it appeared (autumn 1942), the VVS above all needed close-range fighters. It was different because of the quantity of fuel carried (only 506 lb in two wing tanks); the quantity of oil reduced to 57 lb - 66 lb; there were no bomb-launchers. On the other hand, the armament was the same: one axial ShVAK canon with 120 rounds and one UBS under the cowling with 200 rounds. In spite of the reduction of the oil and fuel capacity, the Yak-P weighed as much as the Yak-7DI no doubt because the production standards were not rigorous enough. It manoeuvred very well horizontally and vertically; there were no piloting problems and there was no major vice.

During production, the radiator tunnel was revised and a thick armoured pane was mounted behind the pilot's back.

The Yak-9/M-105PF was mass-produced by Factory N°153 from October 1942 to February 1943 (batches N°1 to N°3, 195 machines) and by Factory N°166 from January to August 1943 (batches N°1 to N°6, 264 machines). These two factories then faced difficulties producing them because the building techniques for the new mixed construction wing had not been mastered properly by the workers. The Yak-9 entered service during the Soviet counter-offensive at Stalingrad (second half of December 1942), but in June 1943, during the Kursk tank battle, the fragility of the skin on the wings became obvious, caused by the bad quality of the basic raw material. There were some fatal losses which caused Yakovlev and Stalin to have a stormy interview. This defect was rectified by special teams hurried to the units and it subsequently disappeared during the production series.

A line-up of Yak-9s straight from the factory. Their inscription means «from the little theatre for the front». (G. Gorokhoff)

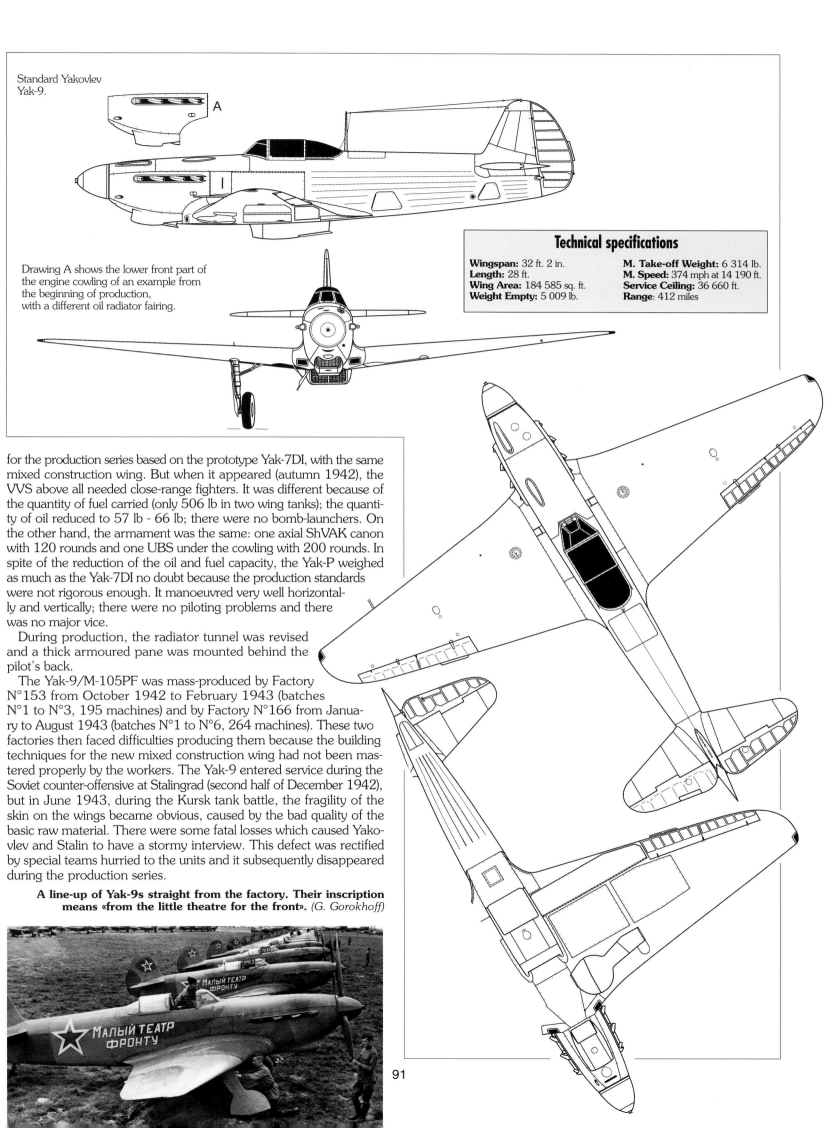

91

YAKOVLEV

Yak-9/M106-1sk Prototype
(October 1942)

During the battle for Stalingrad, the Soviet pilots encountered the new German Bf 109Gs. They were outclassed and very quickly the VVS felt the need to improve the performances of its machines. A first attempt at increasing the power of the basic Yak-9 was made by installing an M-106-1sk, a practical solution because it was the same size as the M-105PF, could be mounted on the same frame and needed no particular modifications to the fuselage or engine cowling structure. It was Yak-7B serial N° 23-91 which was the first to use this engine in October 1942 as part of the programme to help the Yak-9 production series and under-

went some further modifications: redesigning the cooling tunnels with an increase in the frontal surfaces of the oil and glycol radiators (respectively by 76% and 86%); modifications to the flaps, lowered and retracted; reduction of the rear frame of the fuselage and a better finishing on the articulations of the moving tail surfaces; installation of an all-round visibility canopy, with armoured windshield and glazed partition behind the pilot's back; improved general finish and of the skin in particular; revised exhaust pipes; etc.

Although the prototype did not have a specific designation, the majority of the documents refer to it as the Yak-9/M106-1sk. Its factory trials took place from 17 November 1942 to 20 January 1943, followed by the State ones from 17 January to 11 February 1943. Compared to the Yak-7/M-105PF which underwent similar improvements, it flew faster, climbed better and higher, manoeuvred better at medium and high-altitudes, took off and landed better. During a simulated combat against a captured Bf 109G-2 (the five-gun version), the Yak-9/M106-1sk slightly outclassed it in dog-fights below 9 900 feet, but lost its advantages over 16 500 feet.

Unfortunately the M106-1sk was not always operational. It vibrated and lost as much oil as the M-105, gave off large clouds of smoke, caused the plane to yaw, wore the spark plugs out too quickly, etc. The government stopped production at the same time as it stopped the development programme for a Yak-9 with this engine.

A single Yak-9 prototype was equipped with an M-106-1sk engine (Yak-9/M-106-1sk) because it was so unreliable that no mass-production could be envisaged. *(J. Marmain)*

LAVOCHKIN

La-5F Type 37»
(November 1942)

An La-5F from 18.GvIAP (Guards Regiment) no doubt in the summer of 1943. The La-5s and La-5Fs appeared in great numbers during the battle of Stalingrad. *(J. Marmain)*

After being ordered to come a first time to Moscow by Stalin and Malenko to explain why the performances of the La-5 had dropped compared with the prototype, Lavochkin had to go there a second time to explain why their range was so limited. He was forced to tell Stalin that with the way the airframe was designed, it was impossible to increase the La-5's range. But Stalin asked him to «try again». The request together with complaints coming from the front made him redesign the La-5: the airframe was streamlined and lightened; the engine cowling fitted better; the number of fuel tanks was reduced without a reduction in capacity; moving surface trim and visibility from the cockpit were improved; and above all the engine was modernised. A joint research programme was undertaken with four La-5s at the end of 1942 by the Ts AGI, the LII, the TsIAM and the Lavochkin OKB. The results gave rise first to the La-5F «Type 37» (then the La-5FN Type 39, see below) designated in this way because it was equipped with a supercharged M-82F engine enabling the power rating of 1 700 bhp to be maintained from take-off to levelling-off altitude. At the same time, Shvetsov succeeded in making the engine more reliable by increasing the quality of the spark plugs (they used to give up the ghost after only five to ten hours flying time), increasing the outlet of the oil pump and suppressing the tendency of the exhaust pipes to burn (they were individual pipes), thus increasing its life expectancy to 100 -150 hours.

Although the La-5F only appeared in January 1943 with an M-82F engine, the model benefited from another important modification, which was carried out in November 1942 from the 9th production batch: the frame at the rear of the fuselage was made smaller, and an armoured all-round visibility canopy was fitted (only the windshield was still not armoured). Pilot protection was increased by adding armoured plates for his head and shoulders.

Moreover, the joystick was like that of the Bf 109, the movable surfaces were reduced in size (improved trim) and the split flaps were increased in size, noticeably increasing the La-5F's handling and manœuvrability. Many examples had a fixed tail wheel which simplified production. In order to lighten the aircraft, Lavochkin and his team used all the means at their disposal since they did not have spars and other elements made out of light alloys.

The central section of the wing, the landing gear, the shock absorbers and the engine compartment were redesigned and lightened without the airframe suffering. All the instruments and equipment which were not indispensable were removed.

On the other hand, nothing could be done regarding the weight of the tanks for range to be increased (this was only done with the La-5FN).

Armament comprised two synchronised ShVAK cannon, but as with the La-5 built in 1943, some models had only one, with an UBS. As before, 440 lb of bombs could be carried underwing or four to six RS-82 rockets.

This La-5F was the 14th example from the 8th production batch. It was tested intensively at the LII and in the TsAGI wing tunnel in March 1943, and its airframe was lightened and streamlined during the final preparation stages and this model already has the characteristic duct on the engine cowling. The rear fuselage frames were only reduced in size from the 9th production batch onwards. *(J. Marmain)*

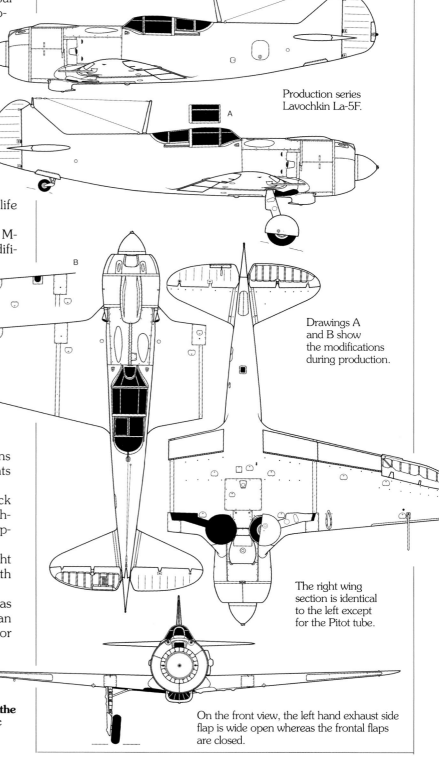

Production series Lavochkin La-5F.

A

B

Drawings A and B show the modifications during production.

The right wing section is identical to the left except for the Pitot tube.

On the front view, the left hand exhaust side flap is wide open whereas the frontal flaps are closed.

La-5F serial N° 39270101 (a modified La-5 airframe) used for equipment testing (windshield, very long antenna, internal equipment, etc). *(RR)*

Above from left to right. **La-5 serial N° 37210514 was a machine used as a test bed for both the La-5F version and the following one (La-5FN). A host of modifications were carried out on the orders of the TsAGI, the LLII and the Lavochkin OKB, such as the long air intake on the engine cowling. Its undercarriage well doors were different and the windshield was that of an LaGG-3.**

An La-5F from the beginning of production undergoing a whole series of tests right in the middle of winter to *«get it right».* **(J. Marmain)**

LAVOCHKIN

La-5FN Prototype
(End of 1942)

At the end of 1942 Shvetsov, the engine maker, supplied a new version of his M-82 air-cooled engine: the supercharged M-82FNV, with direct injection, rated at 1 850 bhp at take-off. An airframe was adapted to take the engine and incorporated all the modifications described for the La-5F and some others, like the long air intake on the cowling for the centrifugal supercharger and the protective side panels for the exhaust. The prototype was designated La-5FNV and flew at 386 mph at 18 480 feet. The M-82FNV was recommended for the production series under the designation M-82FN (Forsirovany-Nyeprosredstcenno, « directly boosted »). A new schedule of research by the TsAGI, the LII and the Lavochkin OKB enabled more weight to be saved and above all, to redesign the fuel distribution system. Thanks to the work of L.A. Zaks and A.I. Mindrov, the plane now only had three self-sealing tanks instead of five, concentrated in the wing central section for the same capacity of 103 gallons.

Some 352 lb had thus been saved on the overall weight of the airframe, making the model almost exactly what the GKO wanted, bringing it down to 6 820 lb.

The first «real» «Type 39» La-5FN prototype (beginning of 1943), sometimes designated as La-5FNV because its engine was an M-82FNV (re-designated M-82FN when mass-produced). The model was better streamlined and equipped with a long air intake on the engine cowling which spoilt the pilot's forward visibility. *(J. Marmain)*

Technical specifications

Wingspan: 32 ft. 4 in.	**Max. Speed:** 386 mph. at 18 480 ft.
Length: 28 ft. 9 in.	
Wing Area: 186.953 sq. ft.	*No other figures are available.*

La-5FN and La-5 «Double» (Type 39)
(December 1942 and March 1943)

In December, a prototype which brought together all the modifications and improvements carried out for the La-5F and the La-5FNV prototype was tested at the NII VVS and the LII in December 1942 and January 1943). Another was only tested in the TsAGI wind tunnel. Without any specific designation, these two machines with M-82FN engines can be considered as the precursors of the La-5FN version. The mass had been reduced to 7 040 lb in flying order and one of the two ShVAK cannon had been replaced by an UBS. The results of the prototype trials were surprising: 347 mph at sea level at full speed, 375 mph at 20 790 feet. 382 mph at 19 140 ft was reached by increasing the admission pressure at the supercharger outlet. The machine was very fast in a tight turn, climbed fast and manoeuvred marvellously in the vertical plane. But the trials were not followed through to the end because of supercharger problems (the only criticism voiced by the pilot, Kubishkin, together with the apparent lack of structural strength due to too much weight saving).

In March 1943, the Lavochkin OKB brought out the true first prototype of the La-5FN series: the La-5 «Double», or «Type 39» for Facto-

Technical specifications

Wingspan: 32 ft. 4 in.	**Max. Take-off Weight:** 6 969 lb.
Length: 28 ft. 7 in.	**Max. Speed:** 405 mph. at 20 790 ft.
Wing Area: 185.877 sq. ft.	**Service Ceiling:** 36 960 ft.
Weight Empty: 5 680 lb.	**Range:** 300 miles

ry N°21. It was the same as the previous prototype but its wings were built around two metal spars, its wingspan was slightly reduced and its armament comprised the two ShVAK cannon under the engine cowling. Its streamlining was improved and its finish very cared for. The airframe was lighter and now only weighed 6 969 lb. The trials were undertaken by A. Nikashin, a close friend and Lavochkin's «perfector», ever since the launching of the I-301 prototype... but for the last time. He was killed while taking off in the Gudkov Gu-1 prototype. Beforehand he had reached 405 mph at 20 790 feet aboard the La-5 «Double» (371 mph at sea level). The climb to 16 500 ft only lasted 4.7 minutes and the tight turns were done in 18.5 seconds. Without any possible doubt, the efforts of Shvetsov and the OKB finally bore fruit: the «Double» was a «thoroughbred» and the government was not mistaken when it ordered production to start immediately under the designation La-5FN.

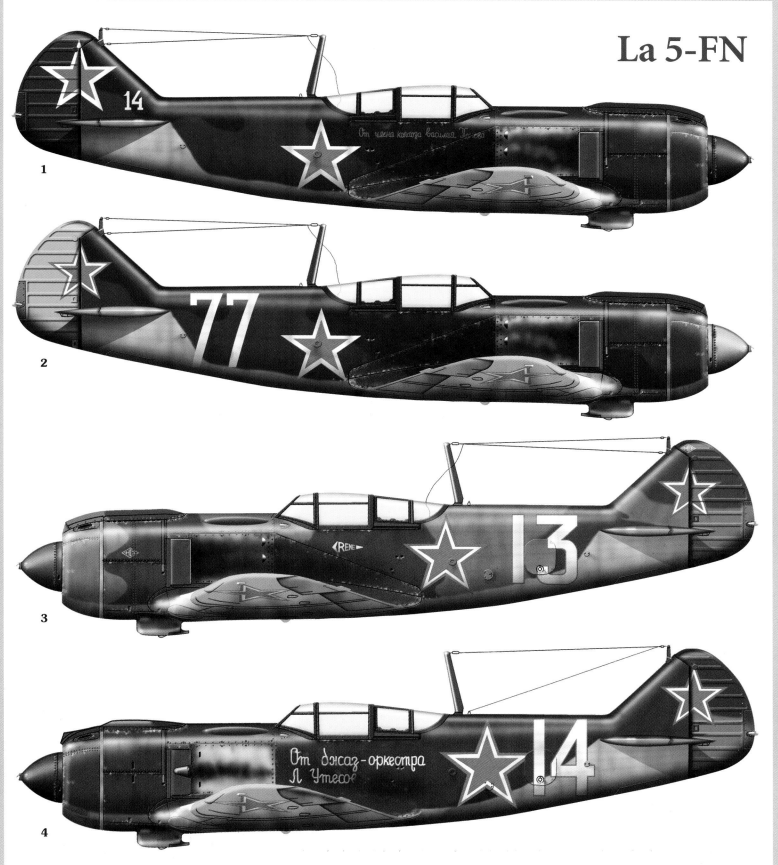

La 5-FN

1

2

3

4

1. Lavochkin La-5FN flown by Lieutenant Ivan N. Kojedub, when he was in command of the 240th Fighter Regiment (IAP), in May 1944.

2. Lavochkin La-5FN from an unknown unit operating from Moscow-Kubinka airfield in 1943. The brown and dark green-based camouflage was worn by the first machines of this type to go into action.

3. Lavochkin La-5FN flown by Sub-Lieutenant Pavel Kocfelda from the 1st Czechoslovak Fighter Regiment damaged during a forced landing in Slovakia on 11 October 1944. The abbreviation «FN» was painted both on the engine cowling and on the top of the tail and the Christian name «Renée» painted below the canopy was the name of the pilot's English fiancée whom he had met whilst serving in the RAF.

4. Lavochkin La-5FN belonging to Major Alexander A. Aleliukhin, 9th Guards Fighter Regiment, Berlin region, May 1945. The fuselage inscription means «on behalf of the L. Utesov Jazz Band», the musical ensemble which had financed the machine.

YAKOVLEV

Yak-1/M-106-1sk Prototypes and short run
(December 1942, January and February 1943)

Originally the «K» programme for a «front» fighter planned to use the very promising M-106 engine, but the technological difficulties encountered while it was being developed delayed its availability for aircraft builders until 1942 and it was only between 27 October and 9 November that this engine managed to satisfy the «hundred hour bench» test. It was the same size and mass as the M-105, boosted by a single-stage supercharger designed by V.A. Dollejal with an admission pressure at the outlet of 1 175 mm Hg, a compression rate reduced from 7.5 to 6.0, improved oil pumps, reinforced reducer pinions, etc. This system had the advantage of giving the engine steadily increasing power for the whole of the climb to altitude, theoretically without jolts, swerves or sudden changes of speed.

Yak-1 serial N°50-85 was equipped with an M-105-1sk (VISh-61P propeller) in December 1942 for the first tests carried out at the end of January 1943 at the LII NKAP by the test pilot A.I. Kokin. This machine, armed with an axial ShVAK cannon and a UBS under the engine cowling, originally with rear decking and M-105PF engine was transformed gradually into a Yak-1b as a result of the various modifications carried out by the Yakovlev OKB subsidiary at Factory N°153 in Novosibirsk. Designated Yak-1/M-106-1sk, this prototype enabled comparative tests to be made between the performances of the M-105PF and M-106-1sk with a horizontal speed of 381 mph at 12 375 ft and 378 mph 16 500 ft with the latter engine (MTOW of 6 006 lb) which was some 8.75 mph faster with the rate of climb to that altitude reduced by 0.6 minutes. Unfortunately the M-106-1sk was even more difficult to cool than the M-105PF, confirmed by Yak-1 serial N°01-111 equipped with the same engine and factory-tested. In these circumstances, putting into service a new version whose engine cooling system was not improved by at least 15% was out of the question for the VVS. However on 10 January 1943, the GKO ordered 47 Yak-1/M-106-1sk, banking on the fact that the engineers would succeed in solving the power plant's overheating problems. These machines were finished at Factory N°292 in February and received their engines, but only 19 of them were accepted and delivered to the VVS for evaluation. Meanwhile, in January 1943,

(J. Marmain)

Yak-1 serial N° 32-99 was also fitted with an M-106-1sk engine, was lightened and modified slightly: metal wing spars and tail surfaces «à la Yak-7», glycol radiator intake repositioned further forward under the belly, installation of cylindrical oil radiators (9 in. diameter) in the wing roots. This prototype was similar externally to Serial N° 50-85 and was also tested with the M-105PF engine just for the comparison. But although the performance climbed to 393 mph at 11 220 ft with the M-106-1sk, the recurrent engine defects persisted: overheating, oil leaking and spraying. Moreover, the engine gave off a lot of smoke, vibrated and caused the plane to swerve, the spark plugs unscrewed themselves or burnt out quickly, the exhaust smoke seeped in everywhere, etc. Nothing could be solved without an intensive power plant research programme and without considerably increasing the cooling capacity of the radiators. Faced with such a huge task, it was decided purely and simply to abandon the M-106-1sk. The 300 aircraft which had already been built were refitted with M-105PFs. However, engine factory N°26 continued to use a Yak-1/M-106-1sk until it crashed in October 1943.

Technical specifications

Wingspan: 33 ft.
Length: 27 ft. 11 1/2 in.
Wing Area: 184.585 sq. ft.
Weight Empty: 4 965 lb.
Max. Take-off Weight: 6 065 lb.

Max. Speed: 393.75 mph. at 11 220 ft.
Service Ceiling:
Range:
These figures concern Yak-1/M-106-1sk serial N° 32-99.

SUKHOI

Su-7 Prototype
based on Su-6 (A) (End 1942)

In 1942, the Peoples' Defence Commissariat drew up a new specification for a heavy low and medium altitude armoured fighter. Sukhoi responded but brought out a high altitude fighter version of his armoured ground attack bomber, the Su-6 (A). The engine chosen was the M-71F, boosted by two TK-3 superchargers (M-71/2TK-3). The *semi-monocoque* fuselage was made of wood covered with thick plywood. Highly heat-resistant steel plates covered all the front part of the fuselage up to the rear of the cockpit which had a rearwards sliding canopy extending into the rear decking. The central section of the low cantilever wing, the spars and the elevators were entirely made of metal. The two outer wing sections and the tailfin were made of wood covered with plywood. The leading edges had automatic slots and the trailing edges had ailerons and split flaps. The two single undercarriage legs retracted rearwards turning through 90°, and lodged in

(J. Marmain)

The Su-7 prototype powered by an M-82FN engine in 1943 before the project was abandoned «for inadequate performance».

the central section of the wing. The armour and the bomb bay belonging to the Su-6 (A) were suppressed and the armament comprised two wing-mounted ShVAK cannon.

Designated Su-7, the prototype underwent satisfactory factory trials at the end of 1942. But in 1943 when the engine's lifespan had reached its limit and there were no others available because production had been abandoned in the meantime, Sukhoi had to turn to an M-82FN specially prepared for the Su-7 by Shvetsov, but without superchargers. Unfortunately this engine did not correspond to the specifications for a heavy fighter. As a result, the prototype turned out to be underpowered and its performances were disappointing, causing the programme to be stopped.

1943

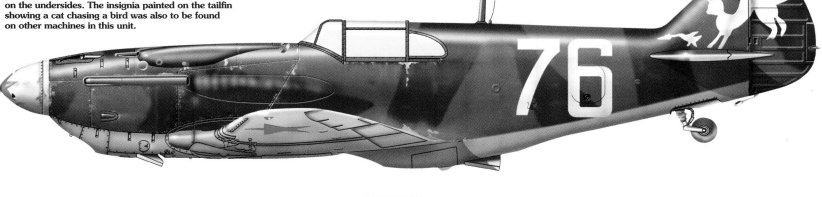

LaGG-3 Type 1 piloted by Leonard Galtchenko, 145th Guards Fighter Regiment, Karelia Front, autumn 1944. this aircraft which bears the old form of camouflage (dark green and black), the red stars were only painted on the undersides. The insignia painted on the tailfin showing a cat chasing a bird was also to be found on other machines in this unit.

GLOSSARY

The «Standard» model of the Yak-9T
(serial N°01-08) armed with the very
destructive axial 37-mm canon. (J. Marmain)

YAKOVLEV

Yak-9T/M-105PF (or Yak-9-37)
(January 1943)

During the first phase of the battle of Stalingrad, for the embattled Soviet authorities there was one thing which stuck out a mile: they had to shoot down all the German transport planes supplying German troops in Stalingrad. At best the Russian fighters only had a 20-mm axial canon and a 12.7-mm UBS with which to damage the enemy planes which were often well-armoured. Ever since the first weeks of the German invasion, the military had highlighted the need to arm the fighters more heavily. This had given rise to specific programmes developed by Gudkov (K-37) and Lavochkin (LaGG-3-37) fitted out with a 37-mm axial canon, or Gudkov (Gu-1, a totally failed copy of the Bell P-39 «Airacobra»). But the airframes were not suitable for these weapons which were far from perfect themselves and whose recoil was more or less well absorbed by the airframes.

In 1941, the OKB-16 of the armourers, Nudelman and Suranov, developed the 11P-37 model, a 37-mm canon which was much more reliable than Shpitalny's MPSh-37 and which was finally approved and accepted by the VVS on 12 December 1942 under the designation NS-37. Yakovlev's first attempt at adapting the canon onto the airframe of one of his fighters (Yak-7-37) at the beginning of 1942 ended in a «half-success» for the same reasons. With the appearance of the Yak-9D, the OKB started again knowing that installing such a canon, which weighed close to 330 lb and was 11 ft 3 in long, meant a host of modifications which would naturally increase the mass and thus reduce performance.

The development of the programme did not give rise to a prototype, but a «standards» plane, or one from the very beginning of the production run, designated Yak-9T (serial N°01-08 or Yak-3-37) which was finished in January 1943. In order to find the space for the canon and its 30-32 rounds without changing the centring too much, the cockpit

Technical specifications

Wingspan: 32 ft. 2 in.	**Max. Take-off Weight:** 6 655 lb.
Length: 28 ft. 6 in. to 28 ft 6 1/2 in*.	**Max. Speed:** 373 mph. at 12 969 ft.
Wing Area: 184.585 sq. ft.	**Service Ceiling:** 33 000 ft.
Weight Empty: 5 055 lb.	**Range:** 387 miles

was moved back by 15 3/4 inches (as with the Yak-7-37), the structure of the whole of the front part of the plane was reinforced to absorb the recoil movement and the standards of finish were particularly cared for. Although the directive dated 18 February 1943 from the GKO ordered all Yak-9s and Yak-9Ts to be equipped with tanks so as to be able to hold a total of 1 056 lb of fuel, the Yak-9T was only designed to carry 726 lb in order to limit its MTOW to 6 655 lb, so that during the trials from 10 to 12 February 1943 at the NIPAV, then those from 15 February to 24 March at the NII VVS, the plane performed like the standard Yak-9, except manœuvrability in the vertical plane (Pilot: V.I. Khomiakov). But its firepower was very clearly better than that of all the Soviet and foreign fighters present in the skies, including the redoubtable Bf 109G-2 with five guns.

During simulated dogfights between Yak-9T and the Bf 109G-2, the former outclassed the latter up to 15 180 ft except in rate of climb. But above 16 500 ft, the German outclassed the Russian in spite of a slightly longer turning time. No major flaw was reported by the NKAP or the NII VVS and the model was put into production immediately at Factory N°153 from March 1943 until June 1945. During this period, 2 748 examples were built and delivered to the VVS who used them as fighters and interceptors against incoming enemy formations, for «tank busting», infantry ground support and against enemy boats out in the Black Sea. Operational evaluation was carried out with 34 machines between 5 July and 6 August 1943 by 80 pilots from 273.IAD, 6.IAK and the 1.GvIAD «Stalingrad». During the 150 sorties made by the Yak-9Ts, 49 German planes were shot down for the loss of only 12 Yak-9Ts.

The German pilots got a nasty surprise when the Yak-9T appeared on the front; they avoided head-on attacks. The presence of the 37-mm axial canon enabled the machine to fire further: between 330 and 1 320 feet for a fighter, 1 650 to 1 980 ft for a bomber or a transport. With disintegration shells intended to disperse the enemy formations it was

Yak-9T serial N° 01-21 during trials in the winter of 1943. Note the length of the barrel of the NS-37 axial canon with its muzzle brake. This machine was used to prepare for the Yak-7K series equipped with the same axial canon. (J. Marmain)

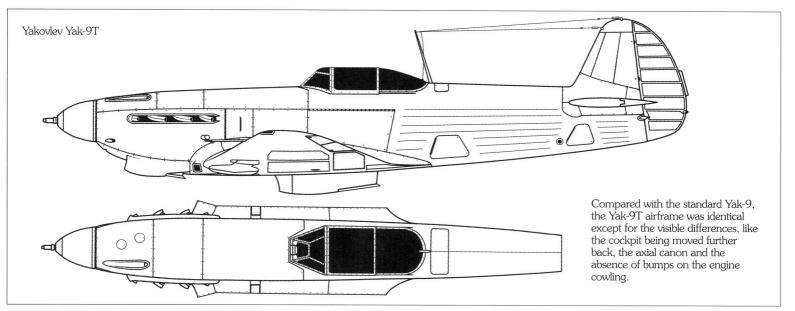

Yakovlev Yak-9T

Compared with the standard Yak-9, the Yak-9T airframe was identical except for the visible differences, like the cockpit being moved further back, the axial canon and the absence of bumps on the engine cowling.

possible to open up from 3 300 feet. The canon was «assisted» by a UBS (200-220 rounds) which was very often fitted with tracer bullets to help aiming because the VV-1 sights (a circle fixed on the instrument panel and a spoke in front of the windshield) were after all very rudimentary. In order to aim better at ground targets, marks were made on the leading edges of the wings. The report on the operational evaluations insisted on the effectiveness of the Yak-9T, particularly against enemy bombers and fighters, its popularity with the pilots and the fact that 30-50% of the fighter regiments had to be equipped with Yak-9s and 50-70% with Yak-9Ts, whilst nevertheless recommending that the Yak-9Ts only be entrusted to the most experienced pilots because only they could destroy an enemy with one or two shells (the NS-37 could pierce armour 1 1/8 in thick). The development of the Yak-9T contributed greatly to the Soviets regaining air superiority.

A Yak-9T, or Yak-9-37 as indicated on the rudder. The barrel of the axial 37-mm canon has not yet been fitted with a muzzle brake. *(J. Marmain)*

Y★AKOVLEV

Yak-9D/M-105PF
(January 1943)

To respond to the demands of the GKO requesting the Yak-9s to be able transport 145 gallons (1 056 lb) of fuel, the Yakovlev OKB developed the Yak-9D at the same time as the Yak-9T. This model was the only one which really fitted the appellation «standard escort fighter». The need for such a machine had been forecast early enough for it to be present at the front when the Soviet troops went over to the attack launching their huge counter-offensives against the Germans in 1943. In this context, the progression and the in-depth penetration over German lines needed air support which the standard Russian fighters ris-

Technical specifications

Wingspan: 32 ft. 2 in.	**Max. Take-off Weight:** 6 857 lb.
Length: 28 ft.	**Max. Speed:** 373 mph. at 12 045 ft.
Wing Area: 184.585 sq. ft.	**Service Ceiling:** 30 030 ft.
Weight Empty: 5 170 lb.	**Range:** 850 miles

Below from left to right.
Yak-9D serial N° 01-04, one of the very first examples of this version which was no doubt the most versatile of the Yak-9 family. Its wing held four fuel tanks giving it a very long range.

Yak-9D serial N° 01-04, one of the very first examples of this version which was no doubt the most versatile of the Yak-9 family. Its wing held four fuel tanks giving it a very long range.

(J. Marmain)

(J. Marmain)

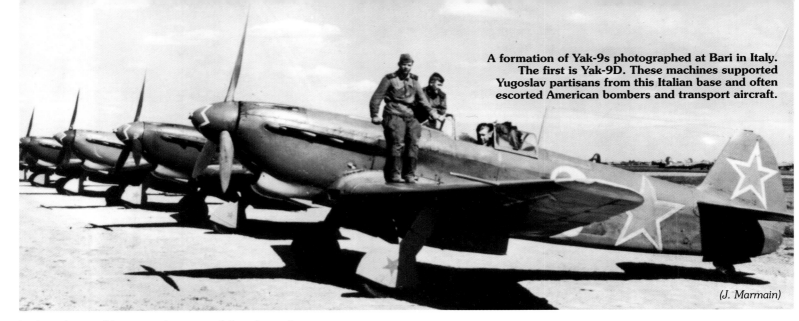

A formation of Yak-9s photographed at Bari in Italy. The first is Yak-9D. These machines supported Yugoslav partisans from this Italian base and often escorted American bombers and transport aircraft.

(J. Marmain)

ked not being able to give because of their limited range.

The Yak-9D differed from the Yak-9T for two reasons: the cockpit was not moved back by 15 3/4 inches because the armament only comprised one axial ShVAK canon (120 rounds) and a UBS under the engine cowling with 200 rounds; the fuel was contained in four tanks fitted between the metal spars of the wing sections with a total capacity of 145 gallons: one holding 46 gallons in the wing roots, another holding 26 gallons in the outer wing sections (according to some sources, the figures were, respectively 149, 48 and 26 gallons). A 1 1/3-gallon distribution tank ensured regular consumption (the first example did not have one). The oil tank held 105 lb.

The State trials for the first machine were held between 14 January and 26 February 1943 at the NII VVS by V.E. Golofastov. Although it was heavier than the Yak-9T, the model was 14 mph faster at the second levelling-off height thanks to the recommendations of the TsAGI (filling in of unneeded openings, more carefully sealed joints, better finish for the wings and the fuselage, etc.). The Yak-9D suffered from the absence of some items of equipment which handicapped the pilot for long-distance escort missions: no artificial horizon, no receiver and «too short» transmitter (with a range of only 37 miles). The MTOW of the Yak-9D was higher than that of the Yak-9 but in the units, most of the pilots did not fill their tanks completely firstly because most of the missions did not require full tanks and then because they wanted an effective fighter with which to face the enemy fighters (most reports state that only 54 gallons were carried on average). It was only when the Yak-9D had burnt up half its total fuel capacity that it had the same performances as the Yak-9, whe-

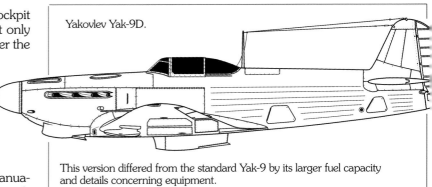

Yakovlev Yak-9D.

This version differed from the standard Yak-9 by its larger fuel capacity and details concerning equipment.

re both performance and manœuvrability were concerned.

The reports from the trials were so favourable that the Yak-9D was immediately put into production from March 1943 onwards. Until June 1946, 3 058 examples came off the production lines. Operational evaluations were carried out by three Yak-9Ds in the 18.GvIAP from 17 August to 18 September 1943. The pilots reported that it was able to carry out a variety of roles: bomber escort (with full tank), fighter, interceptor, reconnaissance, airfield protection, bad weather flying, etc. (with half a tank). The airframe was able to take a hammering and most of the time the Yak-9Ds flew with the Yak-9s and the Yak-9Ts. At the end of 1944, after the Bulgarians had turned against their erstwhile German allies, a few Yak-9Ds were supplied to their air force.

YAKOVLEV

Yak-9/M-107Z Prototype
(January 1943)

Technical specifications

Wingspan: 32 ft. 2 in.	**Max. Speed:** 425 mph. at 19 140 ft.
Length: 28 ft.	
Wing Area: 184.585 sq. ft.	*There were no other figures.*

In 1942, the M-107A engine, long-awaited by the aircraft manufacturers and the fighters, finally succeeded in passing the 50-hour bench test. In December, the Klimov OKB confirmed that it was possible to mass-produce it, stating that it was not reasonable to mass produce it. In January 1943, ten examples were ready to be tested on airframes.

One of them was installed on a Yak-9 which, given the tests carried out, turned out to be faster than the Bf 109G and the Fw 190A. A letter from Major-General Fiodrovi to A.I. Shakurin on 2 March 1943, recommended that 15 machines be produced for operatio-

nal evaluation, insisting on the flying characteristics and the performances obtained.

The prototype, referenced Yak-9/M-107A had reached 425 mph at 19 140 feet. Oil and water temperatures had remained within acceptable limits, manœuvrability was excellent, particularly in the vertical plane and taxiing presented no problems.

But this letter was written too soon, for before the aircraft could be presented for its State trials, it crashed. The NKAP forbade any further installation of the M-107A engine on any airframe whatsoever before it was ready.

SUKHOI

Preliminary study for a fighter, without designation with a Diesel engine and two ramjets
(January/February 1943)

In January and February 1943, Sukhoi designed a preliminary project of a heavy fighter-interceptor with a mixed power plant. It was a monoplane entirely made of metal, with a Charomski M-30B Diesel engine in the nose driving an 11 ft 3 in diameter three-blade variable pitch propeller, and two ramjets under the low cantilever wing, itself built around two spars. Its trailing edge was occupied by ailerons and slotted wing flaps. The tail was classic. A small cross-section intake was fitted under the nose to cool the radiators for the oil and the glycol. The exhaust was directed towards the ramjets to increase their compression rate. The single-seat cockpit was enclosed by a canopy followed by dorsal decking which was an integral part of the rear fuselage. The standard undercarriage retracted inwards towards the fuselage into the thickness of the central wing section. Armament consisted of two machine guns under the engine cowling. No details are known about the history of this preliminary study, except that it was not pursued.

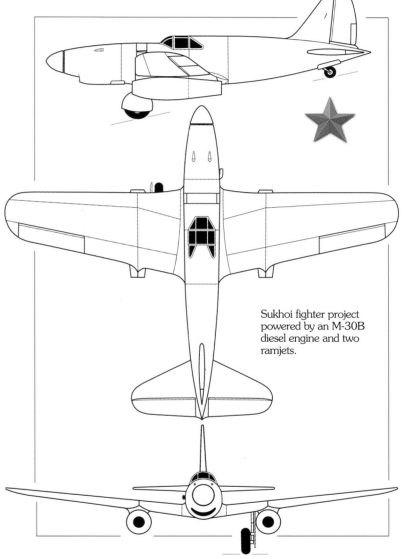

Sukhoi fighter project powered by an M-30B diesel engine and two ramjets.

Technical specifications

Wingspan: 39 ft. 11 in.	**Max. Take-off Weight:** 12 760 lb.
Length: 37 ft. 2 1/2 in.	**Max. Speed:** 481 mph. at 26 400 ft
Wing Area: 322.890 sq. ft.	**Range:**
Weight Empty: 9 240 lb.	*These figures are estimates*

YAKOVLEV

Yak-1M/M-106-1sk (then M-105PF and M-107A) and Yak-1M/M-105PF-2 «Double» Prototypes («Moskit», Yak-3 Prototypes)
(February, March and September 1943)

On 15 February 1943, the Yakovlev OKB finished the Yak-1M/M-106-1sk (M for «Moskit», or Mosquito), the first prototype for the future Yak-3 series and «fourth offspring of the Yakovlev fighter family». In its design, this prototype incorporated two years of experience. Its engineers only kept the «best» of the technology developed for the Yak-1 and Yak-9 and thought up various innovations to be applied to the Yak-3, the most brilliant of all because it was finer, lighter, faster, more manoeuvrable and more reliable because it was equipped with the well-tried M-105PF. In fact the prototype was originally reequipped with and M-106-1sk engine but after the first trial, its lack of reliability was totally unacceptable and it was replaced by an M-105PF in March (Yak-1M/M-105PF).

The design of the Yak-1M's wing was the same as that of the Yak-9 with two metal spars making a box and its two Dural ribs (N°1 and N°7), the rest being made of wood with smooth fabric-covered plywood skin. But

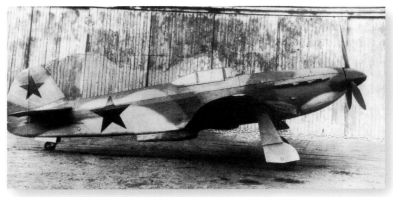

After wind tunnel tests, the Yak-1M/M-105 N°1 was modified, like this air intake under the nose. The exhaust pipes are of the ejector-effect type and the propeller has very wide blades.
(J. Marmain)

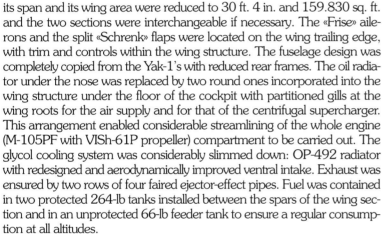

Left from top to bottom.
The first «Moskit» prototype, or Yak-1M/M-105PF, the prototype for the future Yak-3 series, during its factory trials and at the NII VVS. The whole of the front of the machine has been refined thanks to the cooling systems being redesigned; its dimensions have been slightly reduced.
(J. Marmain)

its span and its wing area were reduced to 30 ft. 4 in. and 159.830 sq. ft. and the two sections were interchangeable if necessary. The «Frise» ailerons and the split «Schrenk» flaps were located on the wing trailing edge, with trim and controls within the wing structure. The fuselage design was completely copied from the Yak-1's with reduced rear frames. The oil radiator under the nose was replaced by two round ones incorporated into the wing structure under the floor of the cockpit with partitioned gills at the wing roots for the air supply and for that of the centrifugal supercharger. This arrangement enabled considerable streamlining of the whole engine (M-105PF with VISh-61P propeller) compartment to be carried out. The glycol cooling system was considerably slimmed down: OP-492 radiator with redesigned and aerodynamically improved ventral intake. Exhaust was ensured by two rows of four faired ejector-effect pipes. Fuel was contained in two protected 264-lb tanks installed between the spars of the wing section and in an unprotected 66-lb feeder tank to ensure a regular consumption at all altitudes.

The shock absorbers on the two single strut undercarriage legs were increased by 4 inches and their cantilever was increased by 7 1/8 inches. The undercarriage doors comprised three parts. The tail wheel, steered from the joystick was semi-automatic. The tail surfaces were like those of the Yak-1 but smaller. Armament consisted of an axial ShVAK canon with 120 rounds and a synchronised UBS under the upper part of the engine cowling with 200 rounds. The pilot was protected by armoured glazing behind him and his seat was armoured too. The canopy consisted of three elements moulded from one piece: the rounded non-armoured windshield, the sliding central part and the rear part which covered the antenna cable for the radio which was installed behind the pilot, as was the battery). All this weight reduction and slimming down reduced the mass of the Yak-1M to 5 841 lb, i.e. 616 lb less than the standard Yak-1 being built at the same time.

Yak-1M/M-105PF prototype underwent factory trials at the hands of Fiodrovi from 28 February to 7 June 1943 (first with the M-106-1sk, then with the M-105PF) from March onwards. They were followed by the State trials carried out in two phases by A.G. Prosharov from 7 June to 4 July, then on 21 and 22 July. This second phase was for the supercharger whose intake pressure after the two stages was increased. The final report on the trials concluded that the intake pressure after the first stage of the compressor could be raised to 1 100 mm Hg but that the quality of the fuel used did not permit this to be done for the second stage. However, it stressed the fact that this increase would have a great operational effect on the condition that the M-105PF remained reliable (it was subsequently re-designated M-105PF-2) and that its «boosting» be automatic. Moreover, the prototype was faster at low altitudes than any other fighter in service, both Soviet or foreign: 37 1/2 to 40 1/2 mph faster at 8 250 feet than the

Fw 190, and 13 3/4 mph faster than the Bf 109G-2 up to 14 850 feet. Beyond that the Messerschmitt was better again. But without any doubt the main advantage of the Yak-1M was its rate of climb, which was clearly better compared with German fighters. Moreover it handling was excellent as were its spinning characteristics. The controls were efficient, manœuvrability in all planes outdid all other fighters and landing and take-off characteristics (in terms of visibility and braking) were praised by the pilots who tested it (A.G. Proshakov, A. G Kochetkov and I.A. Antipov). But the prototype also had a few black points: the oil overheated when the engine was flat out during the climb phase and when flying level; there were oil leaks, mainly because of the increase in the intake pressure to the supercharger, spraying on to the windshield; the radio range was too short (only 22 to 25 miles) because of the lack of a mast and bad airframe insulation. The prototype underwent wind tunnel trials at the TsAGI which recommended a few modifications, among which an extra very well streamlined air intake under the nose to cool the oil and fitting the machine with a propeller with longer blades. Finally, within the context of the trials being carried out on the M-107A (VK-107A) engine for the Yak-3/M-107A version, the prototype was fitted out with one (Yak-1M/M-107A). The top of the engine cowling was given an extra intake, the air intake for the oil cooler disappeared and exhaust was by means of two rows of seven pipes (like all the Yak-3 with this engine).

The Yakovlev team tried to solve most of the defects and other problems by producing a second prototype while the first's trials were going on. The Yak-1M/M-105PF-2 «Double» was finished on 9 September 1943. Its aerodynamic silhouette was further improved; the M-105PF-2 engine drove a VISh-105SV-01 propeller with a rounder boss and included two rows of six ejector-effect pipes; the fuel tanks were separated from the fuselage by sealed bulkheads, filling up with inert gases taken from the exhaust and their protection was reduced. Capacity was increased to 605 lb (22 lb for the distribution tank). The skin fabric for the fuselage was replaced by 1/8-inch plywood. The canopy could be discarded. The undercarriage doors were redesigned. The counterweights on the elevators were embedded. The diameter of the shock absorbers was reduced. Pilot protection was reinforced for the head and shoulders.

The oil and glycol radiators were enlarged (OP-555 and OP-554) and an ART-41 temperature regulator was fitted. A RSI-4 radio, a VR-30 variometer and a mirror were part of the equipment. The semi-automatic mechanism for the tail wheel was linked to the elevator mechanism. Armament comprised an axial Sh-A-20M (or B-20M) canon with 110 rounds and two UBSs under the engine cowling, with 150 rounds each. These changes only increased the mass of the aircraft very slightly because the OKB made all the necessary readjustments at the same time to prevent any risk of gaining weight. The factory trials for the «Double» took place from 20 to 30 September 1943 at the hands of Fiodrovi then the State trials were from 6 to 15 October, done by Proshakov. The plane was still faster than the first prototype: 10 1/2 to 12 1/2 mph faster from 0 to 16 500 feet, outclassed the Yak-9 at all altitudes by 31 1/4 to 33 mph and turned out to be faster than the Fw-190A-4 and the Bf 109G-2 up to 29 700 feet and 19 800 feet respectively.

The «Double» was unequalled in handling and manoeuvrability in all planes. The oil and glycol temperatures no longer presented any problems thanks to the redesigned radiator intakes and piping, the best performance being obtained at 2 700 rpm. Range was increased to 509 miles (365 for the first prototype).

On the other hand, although it had been improved, the radio range was still on the «short side». The evaluation reports warmly recommended the model for series production with the M-105PF-2 engine. On 26 October the GKO approved, giving it the Yak-3 series designation.

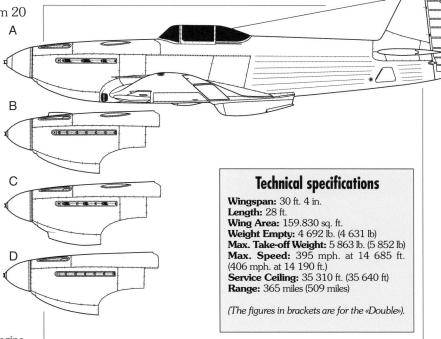

A: the first M-105PF powered prototype
B: the first prototype powered this time by an M-107A engine.
C: the first prototype with an M-105PF again and equipped with an extra oil cooling air intake the oil under the nose.
D: the second prototype «Double» with an M-105PF-2 engine.

Technical specifications

Wingspan: 30 ft. 4 in.
Length: 28 ft.
Wing Area: 159.830 sq. ft.
Weight Empty: 4 692 lb. (4 631 lb)
Max. Take-off Weight: 5 863 lb. (5 852 lb)
Max. Speed: 395 mph. at 14 685 ft. (406 mph. at 14 190 ft.)
Service Ceiling: 35 310 ft. (35 640 ft)
Range: 365 miles (509 miles)

(The figures in brackets are for the «Double»).

YAKOVLEV

Study by the TsAGI for Yak-9 with VRDK (or Yak-9VRDK) (February 1943)

In February 1943, the TsAGi studied the feasibility of installing a VRDK supercharger (see Note) aboard a Yak-9 fighter. The classic engine was the M-105REN which was similar to the M-105F but fitted with a special gear box and reduction gear producing an extra 250 bhp. This type of engine had been conceived beforehand to power the twin-engined Petlyakov Pe-2 ordinary bomber and dive-bomber, modified by the engineer A.D. Nadiradze within the context of the development of air cushion landing gear system. The relative failure of this experimental programme left the M-105REN unused.

In 1943, V.A. Kuznetsov, V. Fedulov and V. Cherenko thought of using it together with a VRDK supercharger installed in the tail of a Yak-9, referenced as Yak-9VRDK for the occasion. The study did not mean greatly modifying the structure of the fighter's fuselage, but did not include a number of the armament components. The VRDK combustion chamber was fed air by means of a 2-foot diameter three-stage supercharger, itself dri-

ven by a system including shafts and intermediate gearboxes. Initially, the cooling radiator for the M-105REN was installed in front of the supercharger, but the three men very quickly realised that this arrangement was not suitable and moved the radiator behind the supercharger. The VRDK's combustion chamber measured almost 2 feet across. The ejection nozzle was mounted on a hinged frame enabling it to be raised by 7° on landing so as not to touch the ground. In flight it was brought back to a normal position.

The gearbox for the M-105REN (VISh-61P propeller) engine did not enable an axial canon to be installed which reduced the fighter's firepower quite substantially. The 253 lb of extra weight caused by the installation of this type of mixed power plant reduced manoeuvrability in the vertical plane all the more so as the M-105REN only delivered 1 100 bhp (instead of the 1 250 bhp of the M-105PF used on the Yak-9). As a result, the estimated performances only forecast an increase of 50 mph (410 mph at 13 200 feet, with an MTOW of 6 677 lb). Kuznetsov, Fedulov and Cherenko admitted that the association of the M-105REN/VRDK would only be effective if a new, specific airframe was built and as a result abandoned the idea without submitting it to the authorities. There are no other details.

Note: For the description of the «VRDK» see the Mikoyan-Gurevich I-250 mixed power plant fighter.

SUKHOI

Su-6GK Preliminary Study (February 1943)

In February 1943, Sukhoi presented a new preliminary study based on the Su-6 ground attack aircraft: the Su-6GK, high altitude fighter-interceptor with pressurised cockpit, whose development had been requested because German spy planes were again flying over the battlefields. The engine was an M-71 fed by two TK-3 (M-

Technical specifications

Wingspan:	**Max. Speed:** 396 mph. at 27 390 ft.
Length: 30 ft. 6 in.	**Service Ceiling:** 39 600 ft.
Wing Area: 279.838 sq. ft.	**Range:** 687 to 937 miles
Max. Take-off Weight: 9 952 lb.	*These figures are estimates.*

71/2TK-3) superchargers. Although the preceding TK-1 and TK-2s had been relative failures when applied to fighter aircraft, the development of the TK-3 designed by the TsIAM and improved by

Mikulin turned out to be more reliable during the trials on other types of machines.

The Su-6GK preliminary study was destined for intercepting bombers and reconnaissance aircraft flying between 29 700 and 33 000 feet and even above.

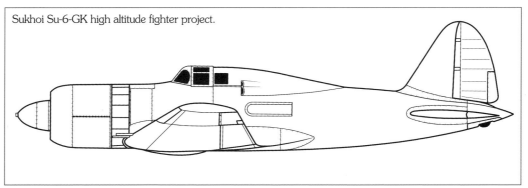

Sukhoi Su-6-GK high altitude fighter project.

structure. The two TK-3 superchargers were installed on either side of the fuselage, a long way back from the engine which itself drove a four-blade, variable-pitch, 10 ft. 6 in.-diameter AV-9-118 propeller.

Pressurisation was by compressed regeneration of the air. But once again, Sukhoi's work was not rewarded by success: the preliminary study was turned down because the military considered that the mass of the aircraft was too high, the theoretical performances were not high enough, the wingspan ought to be reduced and the ammunition carried should be increased to 300 rounds for each canon and to 350 rounds for each machine gun.

Its armament comprised two 20-mm ShVAK cannon (110 rounds) and two 12.7-mm UBS machine guns (260 rounds). The armour weighed 235 lb. The airframe was similar to that of the preliminary study for the previous interceptor, itself based on the Su-6 ground-attack aircraft. The monocoque fuselage was made of wood, the wing had two spars and the tail surfaces were made of metal. The ailerons and the moving surfaces had a fabric-covered metal

POLIKARPOV ★

I-187/M-71 and I-187/M-71F prototypes
(February 1943)

Before the I-185 programme was buried and Polikarpov undeservedly disgraced, his OKB brought out a two-part project designated I-187. It was derived directly from the I-185 programme, whose plans were finished in February 1943. It differed mainly in the rear part of the fuselage which had smaller frames, by its all-round vision sliding canopy, its average-chord engine cowling, and its ejector effect exhaust pipes grouped together behind two side flaps which acted together with the louvers on a cone extending from the AV5-118AD propeller

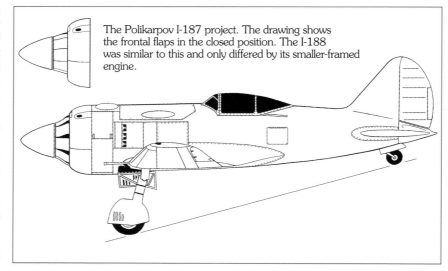

The Polikarpov I-187 project. The drawing shows the frontal flaps in the closed position. The I-188 was similar to this and only differed by its smaller-framed engine.

boss and regulating the flow of cooling air; and by its armament: two synchronised ShVAK cannon under the upper part of the engine cowling (200 rounds per gun) and two other ShVAK in the wings (120 rounds). Two 550-lb bombs or eight unguided RS-82 rockets could be carried underwing.

The two parts of the project concerned the power plant: an M-71 with improved reduction (I-187/M-71) and M-71F (I-187/M-71F). But the death of the pilot, Stepanchenok aboard the I-186 put paid to Polikarpov's work on this programme.

POLIKARPOV ★

I-188/M-90 and I-188/M695 Prototypes
(February 1943)

Technical specifications

W.: 32 ft. 4 in. **L.:** 26 ft. 6 in.	**Max. Speed:** 500 mph. at ft.
Wing Area: 167.149 sq. ft.	**Service Ceiling:** 36 960 ft.
Weight Empty: 4 950 lb.	**Range:**
Max. Take-off Weight: 7 678 lb.	*These figures are estimates.*

At the same time as he was working on the I-187 project he also drew up plans for the I-188 project, also in two parts: I-188/M-90 and I-188/M-95. It was a pure fighter-interceptor without the possibility of carrying any external loads, with the same fixed armament. The rare documents concerning the two parts of the I-188 show that it had the same configuration as that of the I-187, and only the slightly smaller diameter caused by the M-90 and M-95 engines differentiated them. However an artist's impression in the Russian newspapers showed an I-188 which very closely resembled the I-185/M-71 with, apparently the same armament. But the caption says that this was the I-188 with M-90 engine. Like the I-187 project, the I-188 was buried with the official rejection of the I-185 programme.

Technical specifications

Wingspan: 32 ft. 4 in.	**Max. Speed:** 448 mph. at 20
Length: 26 ft. 6 in.	625 ft. (M-71), 443 mph
Wing Area: 167.149 sq. ft.	13 200 ft (M-71F).
Weight Empty: 5 478 lb.	**Service Ceiling:** 38 445 ft.
Max. Take-off Weight: 7 550 lb.	**Range:**

Artist's impression of the I-187
with its ring of inlet flaps for cooling
the M-71 engine and its «all-round»
visibility canopy. (RR)

(RR)

A BRAMOVICH (TsAGI)

S-1 VRDK-1 Study
(March 1943)

In March 1943, G.N. Abramovich presented a memorandum based on his studies to the TsAGI, entitled «Concerning the use of jet engines in airplanes». It included the description of «an experimental single-seat patrol fighter-interceptor» designated S-1VRDK with all the specifications. The machine was made entirely of metal with a low cantilever wing with square wing tips but without dihedral angle. It had tricycle retractable undercarriage; the nose wheel retracted rearwards into the lower part of the fuselage.

The main undercarriage members retracted into wells in the wings between the two wing spars.

The classic engine was the Shvetsov M-82 installed in the fuselage. It did not drive any propellers but an axial flow three-stage VRDK supercharger with a diameter of 4 ft. 3 1/2 in. by means of a co-axial reducer. It had a frontal air intake with axial fairing enclosing a ShVAK canon with 60 rounds. This supplied air to the VRDK whose combustion chamber was installed in the rear part of the fuselage. This had a diameter of 4 ft. 11 in. and a length of 13 ft. 10 in. The air first cooled the engine, then was compressed, mixed up with hot air from the exhaust, pushed through side conduits to the combustion chamber and mixed with fuel. All this was ignited by spark plugs and the gases were accelerated by a nozzle at the end of the fuselage. The combustion chamber was made up of two concentric cylinders between which the compressed air was fed. The temperature of the mixture of ignited air and fuel was estimated at 1 500°C (calculated by D.A. Frank-Kamenyets-

ki). The thrust was regulated by controlling the flow of fuel, by the M-82 throttle and by moving an axial cone in the exhaust nozzle.

In order to reach the 512 mph at 25 080 feet with a mass of 14 960 lb calculated by Abramovich, a TsAGI 1V-10 wing profile was chosen in preference to a NACA one as in theory it caused less drag. The twin tails were literally «sitting» on the fuselage, mounted on a special, very rigid pylon in order not to interfere with the exhaust of the VRDKs (some sources say that project had twin boom and twin tail, whereas others describe it as it is here, although Professor Kuznetzov estimated that such an arrangement would be less efficient because of the absence of air flow normally caused by a propeller). The main tank had a capacity of 267 gallons. It was placed between the M-82 engine and the cockpit. Two other 67-gallon tanks were installed in the central part of the wing and two other 45-gallon tanks in the wing sections.

Fuel consumption was estimated at 2.42 lb per second with an endurance of 15-20 minutes at full throttle and 3 1/2 hours using the VRDK at its lowest speed. But the project did not get anywhere and only served to iron out certain theoretical aspects of «jet» propulsion. Considering all the parameters the military decided that the S-1VRDK-1 was less manoeuvrable than a standard Lavochkin La-5 (the wing loading was too high), even if its climb rate was very clearly better. Moreover its performances were spread over far too wide an operational field (the La-5 reached its optimum at 21 450 feet) and its armament was definitely below what was required by the VVS.

POLIKARPOV

Unfinished VP (K) study and prototype
(March 1943)

The 1942 programme for a high-altitude fighter which incited Polikarpov to transform his IPT airframe into an M-2 and to compete with the Mikoyan-Gurevich OKB was completed a short while later by an addition which gave rise to a new specification recommending the use of a supercharged engine and a pressurised cockpit for the pilot. Polikarpov and MiG were given the task of building such a machine and the machines which were designed respectively bore the designations «Samlovet K», or VP (K) and «Samlovet A», or I-220 (A), or MiG-11 (see below).

The preliminary studies for the VP (K) (VP for Vysotnyi Perekhvachik, or high-altitude interceptor) started in March 1943. The specification asked for an M-71 power plant with two TK-300 superchargers and an armament of two synchronised ShVAK cannon. As he often did, Polikarpov placed the cockpit (pressurised this time) a long way behind the low cantilever wing, almost at the base of the tail, incorporated into the all-metal monocoque fuselage. But forewarned by the difficulties encountered in using the M-71 engines, Polikarpov finally chose two other power plants: an AM-39A and an M-32B with two TK-300A superchargers driving a three-blade variable-pitch metal propeller. Three large air intakes surrounded the front of the tight-fitting engine cowling for the oil cooling

(J Marmain)

Photograph of the VP (K) model. The prototype with the M-39B engine was not finished because Polikarpov died in July 1944.

Technical specifications

W.: 36 ft. 4 in. **L.:** 30 ft. 4 in.	**Max. Speed:** 446 mph. at 43 725 ft. (AM-39A)
Wing Area: 174.360 sq. ft.	441 mph. at 23 100 ft. (AM-39B)
Weight Empty: 6 000 lb.	**Service Ceiling:** 48 675 ft. (39A)
Max. Take-off Weight: 7 304 lb.	47 850 ft. (39B)
Range:	*These figures are estimates*

system, the TK-300A air supply and the carburization. The intakes for cooling the engine were installed in the leading edges of the long aspect ratio metal wing with a large «Karman» fairing. The retractable undercarriage was standard. The VP (K) was armed with two 23-mm VYa or NS-23 cannon.

The estimates were encouraging. With the AM-39A and its superchargers, the model could fly at 312 mph at sea-level and 446 mph at 43 725 feet. With an AM-39B, the speeds were different, i.e. 366 mph at 0ft and 441 mph at 23 100 feet. But when building of the prototype had reached an advanced stage, Polikarpov suddenly died on 30 July 1944. Work was immediately halted. His close friend, D.L. Tomashevich stood in until a decision was reached in high places concerning the future of the OKB. This was taken quickly, condemning the OKB to closure. All the programmes under development were cancelled and abandoned and the VP (K) remained unfinished.

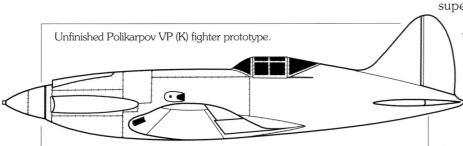

Unfinished Polikarpov VP (K) fighter prototype.

GUDKOV

Gu-1 project and prototype
(September 1940 and March 1943)
and Gu-2 project (March 1943)

Before being separated from his colleagues Lavochkin and Gorbunov with whom he had collaborated on the I-301/LaGG-1 project, Gudkov had established the first working drawings of a fighter of his own design and submitted them to the authorities as early as September 1940: the Gu-1 which was strongly influenced by the American Bell P-39 fighter, of which several thousand examples were supplied to the Russians during the war. But it was bigger. Approved at the end of October when Gudkov stayed in Moscow after the evacuations, the project was fitted with an engine installed in the fuselage, near the CG, just behind the single-seat cockpit which itself was equipped with all-round visibility rear-wards sliding cano-

Technical specifications

Wingspan: 33 ft.	**Max. Speed:** 421 mph. at 24 750 ft.* (437 mph*)
Length: 32 ft. 3 in.	
Wing Area: 215.260 sq. ft.	**Service Ceiling:** 33 000 ft.*
Weight Empty: 8 234 lb.	**Range:** 625 miles*
Max. Take-off Weight: 10 142 lb.	**Estimates.*

py.

The Gu-1 was of mixed construction. The structure of the front and central parts of the fuselage was made of welded steel tubes covered with duralumin sheet. The rest of the fuselage was made of wood, as were the tail surfaces, whose moving parts had a fabric-covered metal structure. The low cantilever wing was very similar to the P-39's configuration, but it did not have a laminar profile (1V-10 Type 12 profile). It comprised a central section incorporating partially closing wheel wells for the inwardly retracting undercarria-

LaGG-3

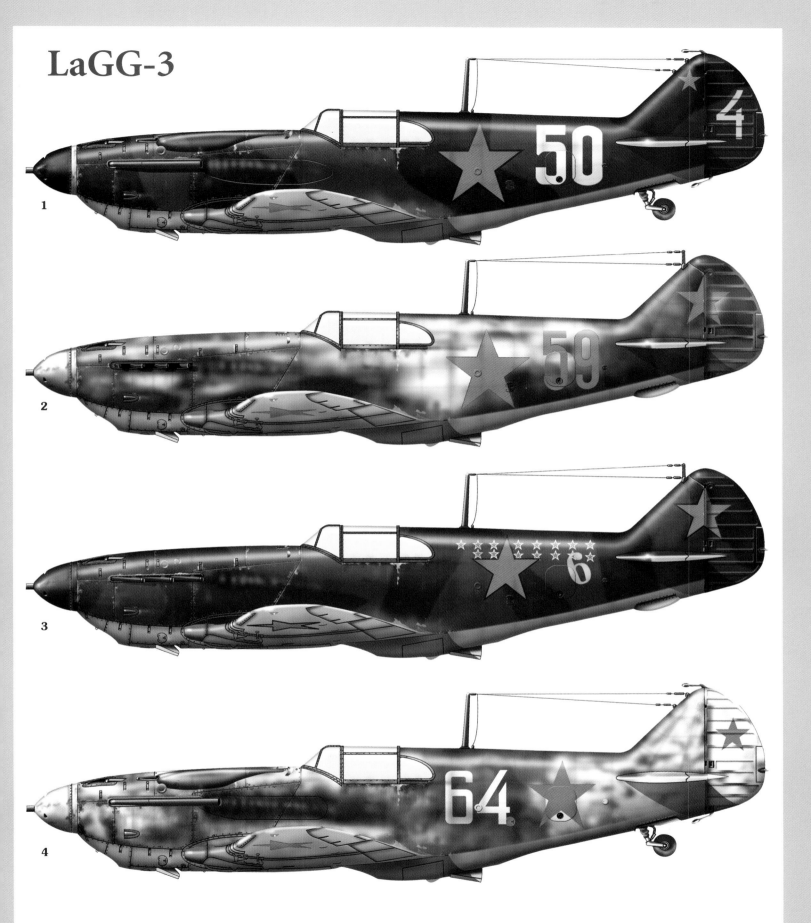

1. LaGG-3 Type 4, from an unidentified unit operating on the Caucasus Front. The main particularity of this fighter is the presence of two individual numbers, no doubt the result of successive assignments.

2. LaGG-3 Type 35, from the 3rd Guards Fighter Regiment (GvIAP) operating in the Lake Lagoda region during the winter of 1942-43.

3. LaGG-3 Type 35, piloted by Captain Gerasim Grigoriev, 178th Fighter Regiment (IAP). The kills this ace obtained have been painted on the rear of the fuselage and partly cover the individual number.

4. LaGG-3 from the 3rd Guards Fighter Regiment (GvIAP), Baltic Fleet Air Force, «Order of the Red Flag», Lake Lagoda region, January 1943.
The original green and black camouflage has started to show underneath the temporary white paint. Note that the size of the red star is different on the tail and that it has changed places.

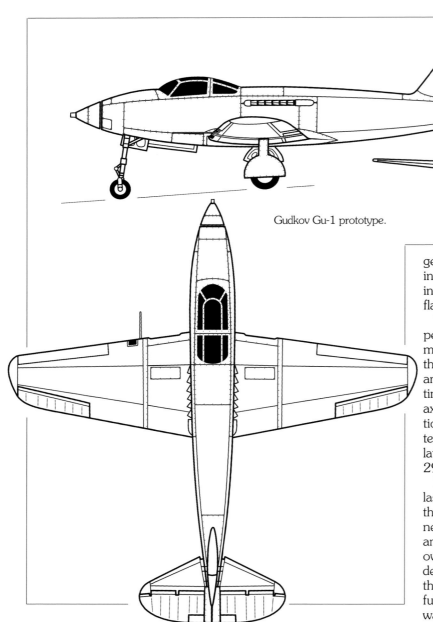

Gudkov Gu-1 prototype.

ge; the intakes for the oil and engine cooling system were installed in the wing roots. Two outer wing sections were attached to this and included leading edge slats and the ailerons and the trailing edge split flaps.

The engine was a Mikulin AM-37UV driving a three-blade propeller by means of a long 4 3/4 inch diameter shaft. An axial 23-mm canon was fitted between the cylinders banks of the V and fire through the propeller hub (according to certain sources, two ShKAS and two BSs were to be fitted in the wing and in the fuselage). Getting the experimental power plant, the long propeller shaft and the axial canon ready was so delicate a job that it delayed the completion of the prototype until 1943. It was only of 18 March that the test pilot A.I. Nakshin carried out the first three taxiing trials. A month later a fourth was carried out, with small «flea» jumps, then a fifth on 29 May.

It was only on 12 June that Nikashin took off for the first… and last time. The prototype had barely reached 660 feet after a lengthy 2 640 foot take-off run when Nikashin lost control of the machine. It dived, side-slipped and crashed to the ground killing the pilot and Gudkov's hopes of setting himself up as an aircraft builder in his own right forever. The inquest found that there was a defect in the design of the wing, which was too small and too heavily loaded. Also the air supply to the engine cooling system caused too much harmful drag. Gudkov's design team was disbanded immediately afterwards and the Gu-2, of similar design, disappeared with it.

YAKOVLEV

Yak-9PD/M-105PD and Yak-9PV/M-106PV (or Yak-9/M-106PV) prototypes (April and August 1943)

In 1942, after having noticed that German spy planes were still over-flying Moscow with impunity at 39 600-42 900 feet, Stalin ranted against the NKAP bosses who had not been able to produce a reliable high altitude fighter capable of countering them. In September the Yakovlev OKB produced the Yak-7PD but the trials were unsuccessful because of the power plant, an M-105PD with Dollejal superchargers (see below). On 12 November, the GKO ordered the Yakovlev OKB to deliver five Yak-9s powered by the same engine by 15 January 1943 (the Mikoyan-Gurevich and Lavochkin OKBs had been given the same task). But it was only in April that these machines were built because of the M-105PD engine not being available within the time limit.

Based on the Yak-9D and designated Yak-9PD/M-105PD, these machines differed in their armament (consisting of and axial ShVAK canon with 120 rounds), several structural details concerning the engine compartment, the exhaust (individual pipes) and of course the engine. The five prototypes were sent straight to the 12.GvIAP where they

Technical specifications

W.: 35 ft. 4 1/2 in. **L.:** 28 ft. 5 1/2 in.
Wing Area: 191.581 sq. ft.
Weight Empty: 5 082 lb.
Max. Take-off Weight: 6 259 lb.
Max. Speed: 384 mph. at 26 400 ft.

Service Ceiling: 43 230 ft.
Range: 359 miles*
*estimated. All these figures correspond to the Yak-9PD/M-105PD) before the modifications.

were evaluated from 16 April to 25 June 1943. During the 69 flights carried out, the usual defects of the M-105 appeared: oil leaks, excessive engine vibration at high altitudes, glycol and oil overheating preventing a steady climb rate to service ceiling (estimated at more than 39 600 feet). To reach this altitude, the pilots were obliged to go up through successive levelling out heights in order for the engine to cool down sufficiently, thus limiting the model's operational possibilities. During the trials Yakovlev visited the 12.GvIAP and had the size of the gills for the supercharger incorporated in the wing roots increased.

Yak-9PD serial N° 01-29, one of the five examples built for high-altitude interception. The radiator duct under the nose has been widened. The propeller boss has not yet been cut down to improve power plant cooling.
(J. Marmain)

The only attempt at interception occurred in 6 June 1943 when the pilot, L.A. Sholokhov, was alerted by the control tower at Khodinka that a Ju-86R was arriving from south of Moscow. He succeeded in climbing to 40 293 feet (the altimeter only indicated 38 445 feet) aboard his Yak-9PD, serial N° 01-29, only to find that the enemy was flying some 3 300 to 4 950 feet higher. He was unable to climb to that height, all the more so as at that very moment the fuel pressure plummeted. Obliged to return to 35 640 feet, Sholokhov tried once again to get near the enemy. But the power plant started to overheat again, the canopy iced over and, anyway, the enemy had already disappeared.

Six days later, a GKO directive ordered Yakovlev to supply a Yak-9PD with pressurised cockpit on 1 August which would at last be capable of reaching 42 900 feet. This, the Yak-9PD serial N° 01-29, underwent a host of modifications: experimental M-105PD engine with the supercharger compression ratio increased to 9.72 instead of 8.48; new oil and glycol radiators (Op-229 and OP-300) with a bigger cooling capacity; increase in the size of the intake conduits for the radiators and installation of an oil tank; spark plug cooling; pump and filter maintenance; number of rounds reduced to 110; and above all the wing span was increased by three feet and its surface by 7 sq. ft. and the aileron trim was modified. The tip of the propeller hub was cut to help the engine cooling system. All this saved some 600 lb off the MTOW compared with the Yak-9D. The cockpit pressurisation equipment was not installed because it was not ready at the time.

This prototype was tested at the LII NKAP from 3 August to 18 October 1943 by G.M. Shiyanov and V.I. Yuganov. The reports noted that although the experimental M-105PD worked perfectly well up to the first levelling height out during the climb, the oil and the glycol overheated beyond this. The supercharger worked irregularly at high altitudes and the engine misfired from 37 950 feet upwards. The M-105PD was powerful but its performance was too unreliable to hope to reach the height required (42 900 feet). Moreover the prototype did not fly above 41 250 feet on the ninth flight and the climb rate to this altitude was far too long (nearly 33 minutes).

With a Dollejal E-100 supercharged M-106PV installed and tuned to reach even higher altitudes, and an enormous tunnel under the nose, aircraft serial N°01-29 was unofficially redesigned Yak-9PV/M-106PV (according to the documents). Four test flights were carried out from 15 to 18 October 1943 during which an altitude of 43 320 feet was reached (on the second flight). However, the same recurrent defects remained, making the plane unusable operationally and putting an end to the programme.

Yak-9PD serial N° 01-29, one of the five examples built for high-altitude interception. The radiator duct under the nose has been widened. The propeller boss has not yet been cut down to improve power plant cooling. *(J. Marmain)*

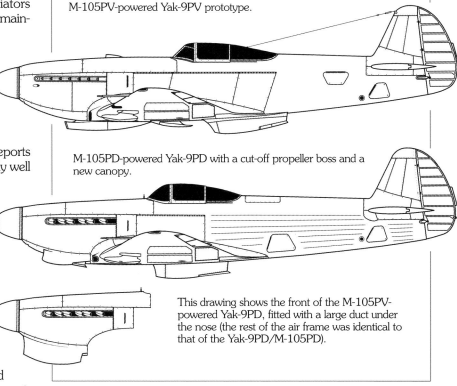

M-105PV-powered Yak-9PV prototype.

M-105PD-powered Yak-9PD with a cut-off propeller boss and a new canopy.

This drawing shows the front of the M-105PV-powered Yak-9PD, fitted with a large duct under the nose (the rest of the air frame was identical to that of the Yak-9PD/M-105PD).

NB: According to some sources, the serial N° 01-29 prototype was not equipped with an M-106PV, but was modified as stated above, its designation remaining Yak-9PD/M-106PD.

LAVOCHKIN

«Type 39» and «Type 41» La-5FN «1944 Standard» (Spring 1943 and May 1944)

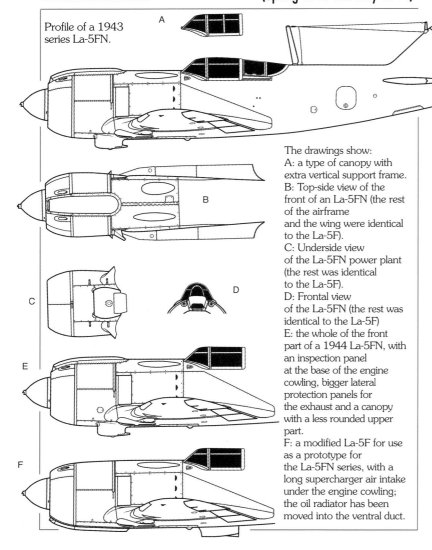

Profile of a 1943 series La-5FN.

A

B

C

D

E

F

The drawings show:
A: a type of canopy with extra vertical support frame.
B: Top-side view of the front of an La-5FN (the rest of the airframe and the wing were identical to the La-5F).
C: Underside view of the La-5FN power plant (the rest was identical to the La-5F).
D: Frontal view of the La-5FN (the rest was identical to the La-5F)
E: the whole of the front part of a 1944 La-5FN, with an inspection panel at the base of the engine cowling, bigger lateral protection panels for the exhaust and a canopy with a less rounded upper part.
F: a modified La-5F for use as a prototype for the La-5FN series, with a long supercharger air intake under the engine cowling; the oil radiator has been moved into the ventral duct.

La-5F, the leading edge slats were automatic and the trim had been improved and standardised, and certain other planned improvements could not be incorporated into the machines. The mass remained high and the performance suffered as a result. During tests with an La-5FN, the fabric of the tail surfaces tore and some manufacturing defects were revealed: e.g. difficulties in aiming because of the presence of the long supercharger air intake fairing and the sights being

(J. Marmain).

The first (serial N° 37210514) of the four prototypes of the «FN» series. It was still an La-5 airframe, improved according to the instructions of the TsAGI, the LII and the TsIAM, including the long air intake on the engine cowling.

placed too high up on the instrument panel; overheating inside the cockpit through insufficient ventilation with exhaust gases seeping in; inadequate radio communication; etc.… Despite these defects and the tendency for Soviet pilots to fly with the canopy open, the La-5FN was a formidable opponent for the German fighters as far as speed and vertical and horizontal manœuvrability were concerned.

The fact that there were not enough M-82 FN (10 ft. 3 in VISh-105V propeller) engines prevented mass production of the La-5F before the autumn of 1943 (the factories continued making the La-5FN). But their role was essential if air supremacy was to be regained. In May 1944, the «Type 41» La-5FN, the «1944 standard» appeared; this differed from the «Type 39» by its slightly shorter wingspan and by the two metal spars around which the wings were built. Some 220 lb were saved on the structural weight and the fuel capacity was increased to 125 gallons. These improvements enabled performance to be improved to the point where the German pilots refused frontal attacks, both against the La-5FNs and the La-5Fs which they were unable to tell apart in the air. In all 1 500 «Type 39s» and «Type 41s» were built before the La-7 fitted with the same wings with a metal spar replaced them on the production lines.

By authorising the mass production of the «Type 39» La-5FN, the government insisted on the fact that the performances of the La-5 «Double» prototype had to be those of the production series. This «insistence» could not be respected however. The lack of light alloys meant that wings with metal spars could not be made for the 1943 production batches. The wingspan had increased compared with the

GORBUNOV

«Type G-43» or «Gorbunov-43» Prototype (April 1943)

Despite the failure of his «light» LaGG-3 programme, Gorbunov returned to the attack by producing his «Type-43». The modifications concerned the aircraft's streamlining: the tail wheel retracted, the

radio antenna was removed (the cable was enclosed inside the fuselage), the bomb-launchers were removed, as were the aileron counterweights; the wheel well doors were revised. The underside flaps were in one piece on each wing section (there were two elements on the LaGG-3) and their surface was increased). This prototype was tested in April 1943 and justified the modifications which had been made and which brought it up to LaGG-3 standards. Some of these

A unit of «Type 41» La-5FNs during a parade or an inspection.

(J. Marmain).

A «Type 41» La-5FN waiting on paved tarmac

(G. Gorokhoff)

(G. Gorokhoff)

Right, from top to bottom.

A line-up of La-FNs from different production batches: the nearest to the pilots was made in 1944 whereas the others are no doubt models from the 1943 batches. The difference lies in the little «tear drop» inspection panel which can just be seen in front of the wing root on the nearest aircraft and not on the others.

The second La-5FN «Type 39», produced at the beginning of 1943 (serial N° 39210102). The air intake on the engine cowling is still that of an La-5F because the first examples were fitted with M-82F engines while still waiting for production supply of the M-82FN to start.

A «Type 41» La-5FN in mid-winter. The glazed section just behind the sliding part of the canopy opened to the right for access to the equipment inside.

An La-5FN from the first production series batches in 1943. The triangle painted on the cowling is the emblem of Shvetsov, the engine designer.

Below. The fourth La-FN produced (serial N° 39210104), equipped with an M-82FNV engine and re-designated M-82FN subsequently, with its long air intake on the engine cowling, already tested earlier on two other examples. *(J. Marmain)*

(J. Marmain

(V. Koulikov)

Technical specifications

W.: 32 ft. 4 in. **L.:** 28 ft. 7 in. (1943), 28 ft. 4 1/2 in. (1944).	**Max. Speed:** 387 mph. at 20 295 ft. (1943), 425 mph at 19 800 ft.* (1944).
Wing Area: 189.321 sq. ft.	**Service Ceiling:** 35 310 ft. (1943),
Weight Empty: 5 891 lb. (1943) 5 731 lb. (1944).	35 475 ft. (1944).
Max. Take-off Weight: 7 308 lb. (1943), 7 183 lb. (1944)	**Range:** 362 miles (1943), 493 miles (1944). ** «1944 Standard»*

(G. Gorokhoff)

NB.: According to certain sources the «G-43» designation was another designation for Gorbunov's «105» programme (see below).

modifications were made to the production series machines.

Reports coming back from the «front» noted the speed of Gorbunov's «light» fighters. It is not known however whether or not a small production series of a specific version was made, or whether the designation «light» in these reports was meant for the LaGG-3 built in 1943 with the modifications required by the «G-43» programme.

YAKOVLEV

Yak-9P/M-105PF Prototype
(The first with this name, April 1943)

With mass production of the Yak-9T starting, the Yakovlev OKB studied the question of reinforcing the Yak-9 armament by installing a synchronised SP-20 canon (with 175 rounds) in place of the UBS under the cowling, but keeping the axial ShVAK and its 120 shells. The change needed no particular modification, only very slightly increased the mass, and did not reduce performance or flight characteristics; but it did increase firepower by 25% compared with a standard Yak-9. Designated Yak-9P/M-105PF, this

The Yak-9P prototype -the first to bear the name-tested in 1943 with a short-barrelled SP-20 canon under the cowling, instead of the usual UBS. *(J. Marmain)*

prototype underwent trials at the NII VVS from 17 to 23 April 1943. The SP-20 worked perfectly well in all conditions and aiming was only affected when the pilot fired long bursts with both cannon simultaneously. In spite of satisfactory tests, this model was not mass produced because the military preferred the Yak-9 to be armed with bigger calibre cannon. The trials of the «Yak-9P» gave rise to the Yak-9K (see below).

1943 Yakovlev Yak-9P with an axial ShVAK canon and an SP-20 canon under the engine cowling.

LAVOCHKIN

La-5/M-71 Prototype
(April 1943)

In 1943, the Lavochkin OKB developed a prototype based on the La-5F equipped with the most powerful double-row air-cooled radial of the time, the M-71, «still» being perfected. It was rated theoretically at 2 200 bhp at take off, but the example supplied to Lavochkin only offered 1 670 bhp. The supercharger air intake was moved under the cowling and the exhaust manifold system was redesigned (double and triple pipes). The oil radiator was moved into a ventral intake directly under the centre of gravity and some modifications were made to the fuselage structure. The dimensions of the M-71 which were smaller than the M-82FN, reduced the prototype's length by nearly eight inches.

Designated La-5/M-71 and armed with two synchronised ShVAK

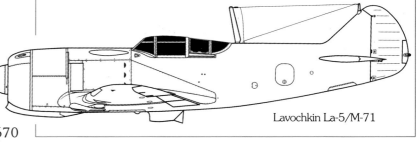

Lavochkin La-5/M-71

cannon, it underwent its trials with G. Mischenko from the end of April to the beginning of June 1943. He made 20 flights and declared that its longitudinal stability was not as good as the La-5's, that it was very sensitive to joystick and rudder bar movement, but that it was pleasant to handle and marvellously manoeuvrable. The LII specialists thoroughly tested it in the autumn and managed to reach 428 mph at 18 150 ft. The TsAGI theoreticians even forecast a

(V. Koulikov).

speed of 453 mph with an M-71 which really did develop its 2 200 bhp. But it was still not reliable enough for mass-production, thus condemning the Lavochkin attempt to failure. Except for the fact that the La-5/M-71 fuselage was 8 inches shorter than the La-5F, no other dimensions were mentioned in the period documents and the only figures which have come down to us are the following.

Above left and right
The La-5/M-71 prototype just before its tests at the end of April 1943. Its cowling has not yet been painted.

The La-5/M-71 prototype in the TsAGI wind tunnel. The supercharger intake has been moved to under the M-71 engine cowling. *(J. Marmain)*

GORBUNOV

«105-1» and «105-2 Double» Prototypes
(May 1943 and February 1944)

In May 1943, Gorbunov presented a new «light» prototype based on the LaGG-3: the «105-1» with a greatly modified silhouette. The cooling and carburization systems for the M-105PF engine were installed under the belly and the oil was cooled by radiators installed in the wings (gills were set in the roots of the wing sections). This suppressed the one under the nose of the LaGG-3 and enabled the front part of the fuselage to be really streamlined. The cross-section frames at the rear were reduced and an all-round-visibility canopy was fitted over the cockpit. The wing had redesigned ailerons, the leading edge slats were made inoperative and the landing gear hydraulic system was replaced by a pneumatic one. The tail wheel retracted and the radio antenna was lost in the fuselage. Armament comprised only an axial ShVAK canon and a synchronised UBS under the engine cowling. The bomb launchers were removed. All these modifications enabled Gorbunov to save some 660 lb off the aircraft's weight. Tested in May 1943 by the test pilot, S. Pligunov from Factory N°31, the «105-1» improved its top speed by 15.6 mph compared with the standard LaGG-3 of the time. It climbed faster and turned better and was actually faster and more manoeuvrable. The pilot Shevelev, belonging to a fighter regiment from the 4th Air Army who evaluated the prototype declared that the «105-1» was better than all the Messerschmitt Bf 109 present over the USSR.

A second prototype was already being built at the time the «105-1» was being tested. It was designated «105-2», or «Double» (sometimes «LaGG-3 Double») and benefited from the same treatment as its predecessor, except that its engine was an M-105PF, its propeller had wide blades which widened out at the base, the engine cowling was slightly revised and its armament comprised a 23-mm axial VYa canon and a synchronised UBS. As a result it was heavier but Gorbunov's estimates had set high standards as far as its performances were concerned.

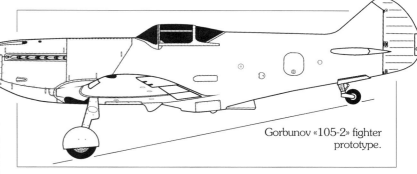

Gorbunov «105-2» fighter prototype.

The «105-1» prototype was a modification of the basic LaGG-3, lightened, refined and fitted with an «all-round» visibility canopy. The photograph is dated 27 January 1944, but the machine underwent its trials some while before. *(J. Marmain)*

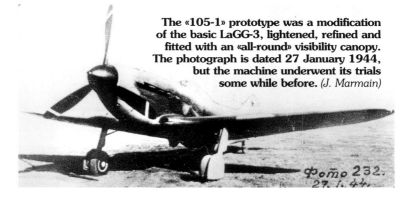

NB.: *According to some sources, the rear section of the first «105» was not reduced and the aircraft was not fitted with an «all-round» visibility canopy. The only known photograph of the «105-1» taken from three-quarters front and widely publicised shows exactly the opposite. However, on closer examination, one can see that the rear part of the fuselage and the canopy are «blurred» and «could have been touched up». Perhaps Soviet propaganda had wanted to make the first prototype resemble the second. Or were the two prototypes similar? Maybe!*

The «105-2» prototype (the number 02 has been painted on the rudder). Its spite of being lighter and more refined aerodynamically, the model was disappointing and was not mass-produced. *(J. Marmain)*

It appeared in February 1944 and its trials at the NII VVS from May to June 1944 unfortunately revealed the opposite. The engine overheated and maximum revs could only be maintained for three or four minutes. Moreover its competitors (La-5 and Yak-1M) outclassed it. The model was refused by the military authorities and Factory N°31 was reconverted in 1944 to produce Yak-3s.

Technical specifications

Wingspan: 32 ft. 4 in.
Length: 29 ft. 1 1/4 in.
Wing Area: 188.460 sq. ft.
Weight Empty: 4 914 lb (1), 5 027 lb (2).
Range: 335 miles (2)

Max. Take-off Weight: 6 199 lb (1), 6 325 lb (2).
Max. Speed: 382.5 mph. at 11 220 ft. (1), 386 mph. at 11 220 ft. (2)
Service Ceiling: 33 825 ft. (1), 35 475 ft. (2)

M★IKOYAN-GUREVICH

I-220, or MiG-11, Prototypes («A» Programme) (June 1943 and July 1944)

The first Mikoyan-Gurevich I-220 prototype (A). It is only equipped with its two guns under the upper engine cowling (the two side guns are not installed). The dotted lines show where the radio was installed in the second prototype, which was itself armed with the four fixed guns.

Towards the end of 1942, the Mikoyan-Gurevich OKB took up the studies for a high-altitude fighter-interceptor in answer to a new specification, «VP» (Vysotsnyi Pyerekhvachik, or high altitude interceptor) issued in 1941 (an up date of the one which gave rise to the MiG-3). The programme was coded «A», referenced I-220 and the designation MiG-11 was reserved for a possible production series. This time the preliminary study no longer resembled the MiG-3. It was of mixed construction and had a new wing made of two trapezoidal sections with leading edge slats and holding four guns, two of which were in the wing root. But in the end the wing was

built around a metal main spar, comprised a Dural D16 central section and two outer sections made of wood with an increased sweep. Its span was increased by some 31 1/2 inches; it had metal leading edge slats and it had a TsAGI laminar profile; the cockpit was moved further forward, just in front of the two self-sealing tanks (there were four others in the wings), and could be equipped with a pressurisation system (eventually not fitted); all the air intakes concerning the engine cooling and the carburization system were grouped together on the leading edge of the wing central section where the radiators were set. Armament comprised two SP-20 ShVAK cannon (total 300 rounds) grouped together above the engine, but two others on the side were planned (their ports were not filled in). The aerodynamic finesse of the fuselage whose rear part and tail consisted of a welded steel tube structure was entirely redesigned. The undercarriage cantilever was designed with a new suspension system with an equalising bar for the wheels, fitted with 650x200 mm tyres (350x125 mm for the tail wheel).

Originally Mikoyan and Gurevich had banked on the AM-39 engine for the prototype. But this was unavailable and moreover was not very reliable. Other types of engines were considered, but in the end, an AM-38F was chosen even though it was not optimised for high altitudes, because only a minimum of structural modifications were required for it to be fitted onto the front of the airframe. It drove an 11 ft 10 in-diameter AV-5A propeller. Exhaust was by means of two rows of six pipes.

I-220 N°01 left the factory in June 1943 and underwent its trials at the hands of A.P. Yakimov, I.I. Shellets and P.A. Juralev from July to the end of August. Its behaviour in flight was considered to be excellent because it was light, but its engine did not allow it to reach high speeds at high altitudes (the top speed was only 393.75 mph at 23 100 feet). The engine was changed to a non-approved AM-39 in January 1944 with which it carried on with tests until August.

Meanwhile a second prototype was built, the I-220 N°02. It left the factory in July 1943 with another non-approved AM-39 engine. It did its factory trials in the same month and in August at the hands of I.I. Shellets. The State trials were carried out at the NII VVs from 14 to 24 July 1944 and it was on board this machine that a top speed of 435 mph was reached at 23 100 feet. But the plane never managed to climb to 46 200 ft as required by the authorities. It differed from the N°01 by its armament which consisted of four SP-20 ShVAK cannon grouped together around the engine and its «whiplash» antenna for the radio transmitter. The engine broke up during the trials and obliged the OKB to replace it with an AM-37 which was not satisfactory and this completely buried the programme once and for all in spite of the fact that at 23 100 ft it outclassed the La-5 by 31 to 59 mph (depending on the versions)

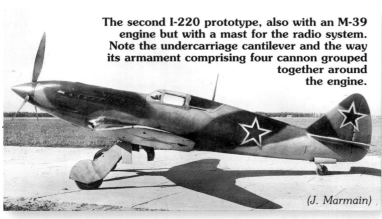

The first I-220 prototype with M-39 engine during its trials in the summer of 1944. Note the position of the antenna cable on the back of the fuselage.

(J. Marmain)

The second I-220 prototype, also with an M-39 engine but with a mast for the radio system. Note the undercarriage cantilever and the way its armament comprising four cannon grouped together around the engine.

(J. Marmain)

Technical specifications

Wingspan: 36 ft. 4 in.
Length: 31 ft. 7 1/2 in.
Wing Area: 219.349 sq. ft.
Weight Empty: 6 459 lb (AM-38F), 6 628 lb (AM-39).
Max. Take-off Weight: 7 862 lb (AM-38F), 8 437 lb. (AM-39).
Max. Speed: 393 mph. at 23 100 ft (AM-38F). 417 mph. at 23 100 ft. (AM-39).

Service Ceiling: 31 350 ft (AM-38F), 36 300 ft. (AM-39).
Range: 600 miles (AM-38F), 412 miles (AM-39).

These figures correspond to the first prototype with the AM-38F engine and the second with the AM-39 engine.

ILYUSHIN

Il-2i, or Il-2iB Prototype
(July 1943)

During the winter of 1942, the Ilyushin Il-2 Shturmovik crews from the 33rd Regiment of the Guards assault aviation, were the first to be committed against the concentrations of Luftwaffe aircraft who supplied the German ground troops encircled in the Demainsk pocket. During the battle for Stalingrad, the Il-2s turned themselves into improvised bomber interceptors and attacked German Ju-87 Stukas or Ju-52 transport aircraft. Considering the reports from these pilots, the National Defence Committee asked for an armoured heavy fighter-interceptor version of the Il-2 to be made.

Ilyushin took a first generation two-seat Il-2M airframe, transformed the cockpit for a single pilot (single-seat 1942 version canopy), removed all the armour from the second crew member's compartment, reinforced the wooden structure of the wing, removed the ShKAS machine guns, the rocket launchers and the bomb bay in the wings, thus saving some 1 672 lb on the aircraft's mass. Designated Il-2i (or Il-2iB, I for istrebityel, B for Bombardirovshchik, or bomber hunter), the prototype was armed with two wing-mounted VYa cannon and it was powered by an AM-38F. Optionally, it could carry two 550 bombs under the wing central section.

Flight tests were carried out at The NII VVS in July-August 1943 by A. Dolgov. But they were not very convincing since the prototype did not exceed 259 mph at 4 290 feet, a speed which was considered to be just about fast enough to intercept enemy bombers and transports. But its mass and its generally weak performances made it an easy prey for the much faster German fighters. As a result, the programme was very quickly abandoned.

Ilyushin Il-2i armoured fighter prototype.

The Il-2i (or Il-2iB) heavy fighter derived from the Il-2M «Shturmovik» ground attack aircraft, during its trials at the NII VVS during the summer of 1943. Because its weight made it vulnerable to enemy fighters, no mass-production was envisaged.

Technical specifications

W: 48 ft. 1 1/2 in. **L:** 38 ft. 5 3/4 in.   **Max. Take-off Weight:** 11 842 lb.
Wing Area: 414.375 sq. ft.   **Max. Speed:** 259 mph. at 4 290 ft.
Weight Empty: 9 673 lb.   **S. C.:** 21 450 ft. **Range:** 406 miles

LAVOCHKIN

La-5F/2TK-3 or La-5TK Prototypes
(Summer 1943)

At the same time as Alexeyev's team succeeded in grafting an M-82 engine onto the LaGG-3 airframe, the Lavochkin OKB was studying the development of a high altitude interceptor version, but its realisation was put off until 1943. An La-5F airframe from the beginning of production (with rear decking) was used as a prototype without the OKB needing to change its installations since only the power plant was revised. Its M-82F was fitted with two TK-3 superchargers designed by S. Treskin, but the cockpit was not equipped with a pressurisation system. Designated La-5F/2TK-3 in period documents, the prototype appeared in the summer of 1943 and competed with the Yakovlev Yak-9PD which was of the same type. As with the latter machine the tests were disappointing, all the more so as the La-5/2TK-3 weighed half a tonne less.

The programme was quickly abandoned without the performances being registered (the dimensions were those of the La-5F but the wing area was very slightly reduced to 188.998 sq ft), and the authorities decided that the development of planes intended for intercepting intruders at the higher altitudes would be reserved for Mikoyan and Gurevich, and possibly Yakovlev.

NB.: Many foreign and Soviet historians note that three «La-5TK» prototypes were built, one testing the power plant, another tried out the cockpit pressurisation system, whereas nothing is said about the third. But according to the known Lavochkin OKB documents, only a single La-5F/2TK-3 was built.

Two shots of the La-5TK high-altitude fighter prototype, whose M-82F engine was boosted by two TK-3 superchargers. The airframe was that of an La-5F from the beginning of production series (before the 9th Batch). Note the highly heat-resistant metal plate which protects the exhaust further away.

YAKOVLEV

Yak-9R/M-105PF
Short- and long-range versions
(September 1943)

On 5 June 1943, the NKAP ordered the Yakovlev OKB to build the Yak-9R model, a photographic reconnaissance version based on the Yak-9. In fact, the Yakovlev OKB studied two variants: one for short-range missions and another for long-range ones. The first was based on the Yak-9 whereas the second came from the Yak-9D. Both were equipped with M-105PF engines driving ViSH-61P propellers and differed from one another by their fuel capacity and the cameras carried.

The machine at the beginning of the production series was Yak-9 serial N°05-15, built by Factory N°166 at Omsk on 16 June 1943 and modified by Factory N° 301 in September. The space available behind the cockpit was equipped with a sort of tub in which an AFA-1M camera for vertical shots was installed; a panel opened in the floor controlled by the pilot by means of a cable. The shots could be taken between 1 000 and 10 000 feet. Its State evaluations took place at the NII VVS from 21 September to 10 October 1943 by A. G Prochakov. The modifications needed to change the Yak-9 into a Yak-9R were so simple that the plans were sent directly to the unit maintenance workshops where they were put into effect. As a result, it is nowadays impossible to determine the exact number of Yak-9s that were brought up to R standard.

As for the Yak-9Rs based on the «D» version, they were made exclusively by Factory N°166 where 35 examples were thus adapted up to 13 August 1943. They covered the greatest distances (some 875 miles thanks to their four tanks), but their installation for the photographic material was the same except that the camera used was an AFA-3S/50 with a focal length of 50 mm. Moreover they were equipped with a RPK-10 radio-goniometer, an AG-2 artificial horizon and an RSI-4 radio which enabled them to fly around in bad weather. Certain examples kept their original armament (axial ShVAK canon and one UBS under the engine cowling), but the others did not have any UBS machine gun. This long-range version did not undergo any trials but five examples were evaluated in a VGK (VVS Headquarters) air regiment at Steppe, on the Osnova front, in the Kharkov sector from 23 September to 12 October 1942.

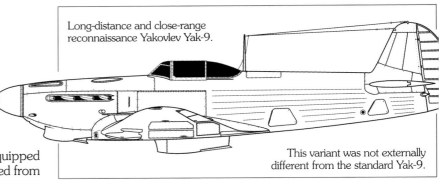

Long-distance and close-range reconnaissance Yakovlev Yak-9.

This variant was not externally different from the standard Yak-9.

Technical specifications

Wingspan: 34 ft. 1 1/2 in.
Length: 28 ft.
Wing Area: 184.585 sq. ft.
Weight Empty: 5,031lb*, 5 165 lb**, 5,181 lb***.
Max. Take-off Weight: 6,358 lb *, 6 780 lb **, 6 903 lb***.
Max. Speed: 373 mph. at 14 025 ft.

Service Ceiling: 25 475 ft.*, 31 680 ft.**
Range: 360-412 miles*, 875 miles**

* Yak-9R, short-range version
** Yak-9R, long-range version without cowling UBS
*** Yak-9R, Long-range version with cowling UBS

Most of the missions were carried out at 10 000 feet for the Yak-9R (short-range missions) and at 26 400 feet for the Yak-9R (long-range missions). But in bad weather conditions, they operated at 1 000 feet at the risk of being hit by ground fire because at that height they were obliged to fly past more slowly. In spite of its performances which enabled it to operate over well-defended sites, the Yak-9R was not an ideal reconnaissance plane and did not replace the Pe-2 which was adapted for the same tasks. This was for two reasons: downwards visibility was not the best for aiming at the targets to be photographed; and the three-man crew in a Pe-2 were better at collecting «visual» information. Moreover the shots brought back by the Yak-9Rs were not always of good enough quality. In fact the Yak-9R and the Pe-2 were very often complementary No document has been discovered to this day indicating that production went beyond the 35 examples of the long-range version supplied by Factory N°166.

MIKOYAN -GUREVICH

I-231 or MiG-3DD
prototype («2D» programme)
(Summer of 1943)

The relative failure of the I-230 programme did not discourage the Mikoyan-Gurevich OKB, all the more so since an AM-39 engine was

(J. Marmain)

(J. Marmain)

The I-231 during its trials. Although it performed very well, its AM-39 engine was very unreliable and condemned it t o be forgotten. Note the lay-out of the various air intakes for the power plant under the fuselage and the wing roots.

Yak-3

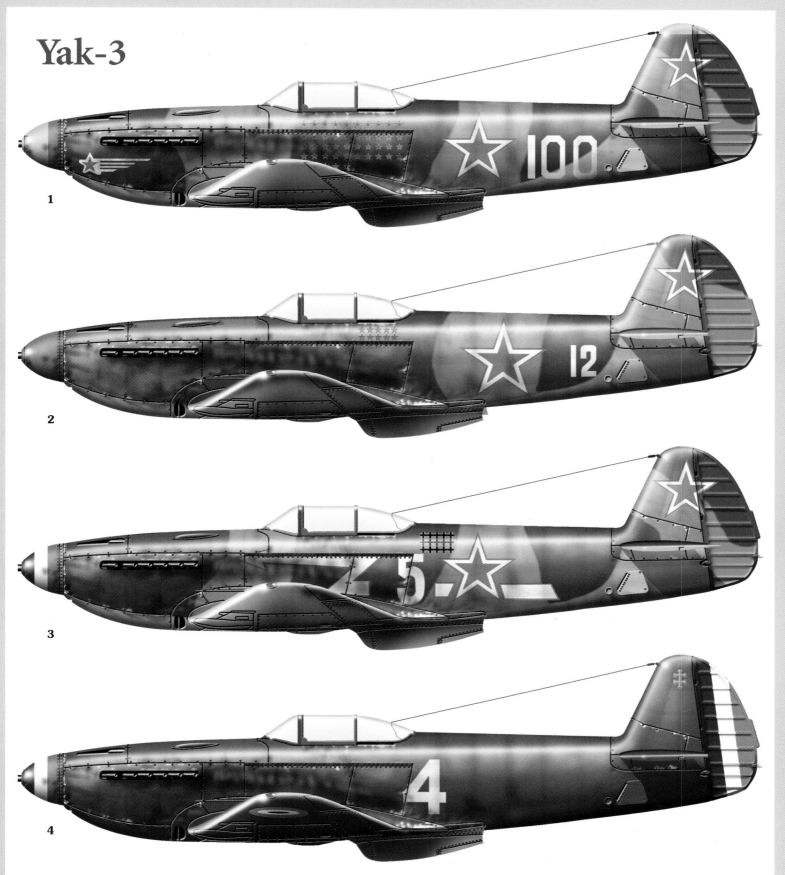

1. Yakovlev Yak-3 piloted by Ivan V. Fedorov, from the 812th Fighter Regiment (IAP). The tally (36 confirmed kills) of this ace, a Hero of the Soviet Union, has been painted on the left-hand side of his machine in the form of little red stars, a very widespread practice in the VVS (Soviet Air Forces).

2. Yakovlev Yak-3 belonging to Lieutenant Vladimir A. Orekhov in the 32nd Guards Fighter Regiment (GvIAP). The main feature of this plane is the fact that the front part of the fuselage has been entirely painted red, no doubt to facilitate identification.

3. Yakovlev Yak-3 piloted by officer cadet Roger Sauvage from the «Normandie-Niemen» Regiment, Eylau, spring 1945. Although he only joined this famous unit in January 1944, Sauvage nevertheless obtained 16 confirmed kills and one probable which, unlike the Soviets who used little red stars for their tallies, were represented by black crosses painted below the canopy.

4. Yakovlev Yak-3 from the «Normandie-Niemen» Regiment, France end of 1945. The pilots in this unit were allowed to return to France with their Yak-3s, given to them as a present by Stalin. The planes gradually had their Soviet markings replaced by French roundels, with a Croix de Lorraine added to the tail.

put at its disposal. The team mounted it on an airframe which was similar to the I-230, with an AV-5L propeller, the same armament (160 rounds per canon), but with extra refinements (very well fitting and sealed cowling and canopy, and slightly larger frames for the rear part of the fuselage, a redesigned ventral intake, lowered horizontal tail surfaces) and an entirely metal *semi-monocoque* fuselage which reduced the plane's weight. The fuel capacity was reduced as was that of the oil.

The prototype, designated I-231 (programme «2D»), or MiG-3DD (an unofficial but nevertheless erroneous designation) was probably tested in the summer of 1943 (the exact completion dates and dates of the trials at the NII VVS remain unknown) by I.A. Antipov and P.M. Stefanowski who incidentally crashed the machine when landing it. Beforehand Antipov reached a speed of 441 mph at 23 430 feet which theoretically meant that production of the «new MiG-3» would start up again. It did not because the Am-39 engine remained imperfect and anyway was not mass-produced because at the time no factory was available to make the I-231, the Lavochkin and Yakovlev fighters having «top priority».

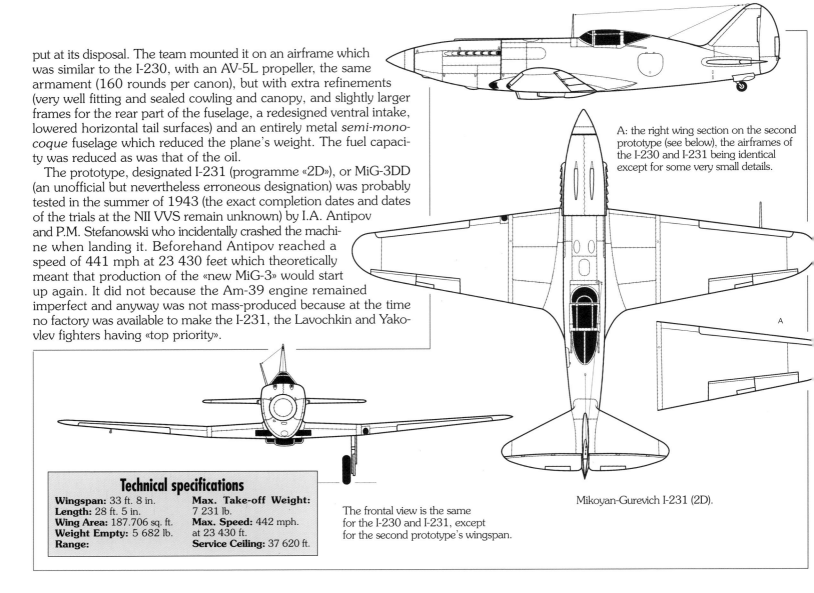

A: the right wing section on the second prototype (see below), the airframes of the I-230 and I-231 being identical except for some very small details.

Mikoyan-Gurevich I-231 (2D).

The frontal view is the same for the I-230 and I-231, except for the second prototype's wingspan.

Technical specifications

Wingspan: 33 ft. 8 in.
Length: 28 ft. 5 in.
Wing Area: 187.706 sq. ft.
Weight Empty: 5 682 lb.
Range:

Max. Take-off Weight: 7 231 lb.
Max. Speed: 442 mph. at 23 430 ft.
Service Ceiling: 37 620 ft.

MIKOYAN-GUREVICH

I-211 prototypes and pre-series Or I-211 (E) or MiG-9 («E» programme) (August 1943)

The I-210's wind tunnel tests at the TsAGI dictated the modifications which were to be applied to the model. But they also enabled Mikoyan and Gurevich to try and fit an M-82 engine onto the MiG-3 airframe. The new programme was referenced «E» (for «experimental») and I-211 or I-211 (E). At the time, the engine builder, Shvetsov, had developed a boosted version of his double-row radial engine to power in particular the Lavochkin fighters: the M-82F. Theoretically, this power plant enabled the plane to fly and climb faster. The Mikoyan-Gurevich OKB installed it onto a completely new airframe in December 1942 (with a ViSH-105V propeller) but work only finished in August 1943. The frames of the front of the fuselage were revised to fit perfectly around the engine. The cowling was designed particularly well so that it was sealed much more hermetically. The exhaust was placed under two adjustable flaps on the side of the fuselage «à la La-5». The air intakes for the two oil radiators were set into the wing roots, on either side of the fuselage. The engineers did a great deal of research work to save a maximum of weight.

The new model was shorter and for centring reasons, the cockpit was moved 9 3/4 inches further back whereas the leading edge

The I-211 (E) prototype with a double row M-82F radial engine and with a very well streamlined and sealed fuselage, seen during its trials in the summer of 1943. But the appearance of the La-5FN the same year put paid to this machine. *(J. Marmain)*

of the tail fin was moved forwards, with an increased surface for better stability while yawing. The leading edges did not have slats and the armament was completely redesigned: two ShVAK can-

This shot of the I-211 prototype gives a good view of the two ShVAK canon ports under the engine cowling. Ten examples were sent to the front for operational evaluations, but the model was not mass-produced.
(J. Marmain)

Technical specifications

Wingspan: 33 ft. 7 in.	**Max. Take-off Weight:** 6 820 lb.
Length: 26 ft. 3 in.	**Max. Speed:** 418 mph. at 23 100 ft.
Wing Area: 187.706 sq. ft.	**Service Ceiling:** 37 290 ft.
Weight Empty: 5 561 lb.	**Range:** 712 miles

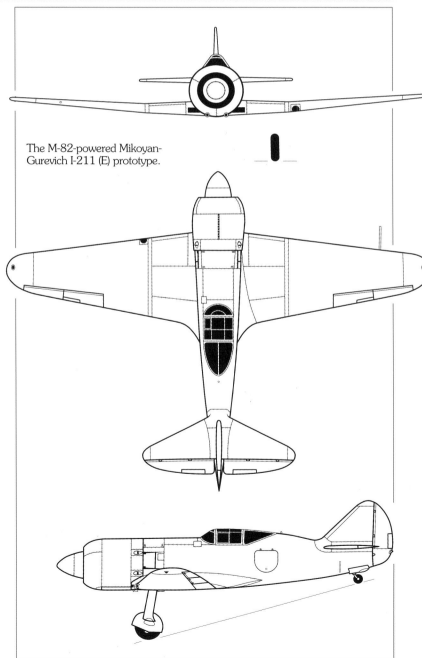

The M-82-powered Mikoyan-Gurevich I-211 (E) prototype.

non installed in the central wing section (150 rounds each), the barrels protruding through the lower part of the cowling, near the plane's axis. The canopy did not slide but swung over to the right.

Savkin, the factory test pilot carried out the first flight in August 1943. Meanwhile, a second prototype was built, together with eight pre-series machines. The trials took place very quickly up to the end of August at the hands of Golofastov and showed that the I-211 (E) was definitely better than the fighters then in service, both in speed (25 to 41 mph faster than a 1942 La-5, 40 to 45 mph faster than a Yak-9 of the same year) and rate of climb. Its range was greater also. The ten machines were sent to the front, to the north-west of Kalinin where the pilots reported that the performances were only just slightly better than those of the new La-5FN which had entered series production.

However, the in-flight behaviour of the I-211 (E) was very much appreciated as was its armament. But at the time, the GKO decided not to launch production because the La-5FN had made its appearance during the summer.

In some documents, the MiG-9 designation was used for the second time.

NB.: Mikoyan and Gurevich were the first to adopt this type of very well sealed engine cowling, the way the engine compartment was installed with the exhausts. On the orders of the NKAP, the technical innovations were transmitted to Lavochkin so that they could be applied to the La-5FN, including the leading edge slats. But historians of the Lavochkin OKB maintain that the realisation of their LaGG-3/M-82 had help from nobody, except perhaps that of Shvetsov, the engine builder, and his team; and that the leading edge slat technology for that prototype was transmitted to MiG who applied them to his fighters. Concerning the date of the I-231's first flight, the period documents are very incomplete. Some mention 18 December 1942, others February 1943, other again situated it in August 1943, this last date being taken up by a lot of sources. Finally some of them mention the production of ten pre-series machines although this is not confirmed in the official sources.

Technical specifications

W.: 31 ft. 7 in.	**Max. Speed:**
Length: 28 ft. 9 in.	375 mph. at 7 590 ft.
Wing Area:	**Service Ceiling:**
186.953 sq. ft.	**Range:**
Weight Empty:	*These figures cor-*
5 667 lb.	*respond to the La-*
Max. Take-off	*5UTI developed by*
Weight: 7 062 lb.	*Lavochkin.*

LAVOCHKIN

La-5UTI (UTI-La-5 or ULa-5) (August 1943)

In order to familiarise pilots in handling the La-5 and to enable them to train, front-line maintenance teams modified certain machines, transforming them into two-seaters, not without success (this carried on until the end of the war). Lavochkin was informed of this and decided to develop a «real training version» based on the La-5. A second cockpit for the instructor with dual controls was fitted out behind the original. The right-hand canon, the armoured glazing, the radio, the oxygen, the inert gas filling system for the fuel tanks and the bomb launchers were all removed since they were not considered indispensable for training. The prototype, designated La-5UTI was built in August 1943 but did not have a canopy for the rear cockpit. It was tested at the NII VVS in September by the test pilots Kubichin and Antipov, who liked it a lot and recommended it immediately for use

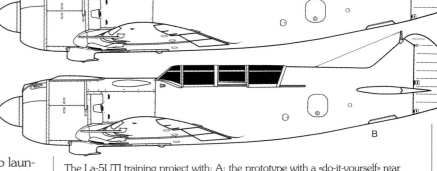

The La-5UTI training project with: A: the prototype with a «do-it-yourself» rear cockpit and without a canopy. B: the standard La-5UTI based on an La-5F airframe. Some La-5UTIs were equipped with an engine cowling which was identical to that of the La-5FN even though they were powered by an M-82F.

in the flying schools and the reserve regiments since its flying characteristics were the same as those of the single-seat La-5.

But only 28 examples, based on La-5 airframes were built by the Gorki factory and delivered to the VVS which sometimes used them for fast liaison flights and close-quarters reconnaissance. This was because beforehand, Yakovlev had developed the two-seat Yak-7V trainer which was already being mass-produced and was doing the same job and becoming the main training machine for fighter pilots during the second half of the war against the Germans. Some La-5UTIs were equipped with an engine cowling «à la La-5FN» (long air intake on the top) although all the machines had been equipped with an M-82F engine, probably because at the time deliveries of M-82FN engines were not regular enough and reserved anyway for the La-5FN.

This La-5UTI is an La-5 airframe converted into a two-seater by the maintenance teams in the 1st Air Depot, in Leningrad, 1945.
(J. Marmain)

NB.: According to the documents and writings published some time ago, the two-seaters based on the La-5 and La-5F which were modified within the units had the designations ULa-5, UTI-La-5 or La-5UTI, without there being any official document to corroborate the first two designations. Generally these machines had their right-hand cannon removed, keeping only the synchronised UBS machine gun.

Two shots of the La-5UTI prototype designed by the Lavochkin OKB and built at Gorki in August 1943. The rear compartment does not have a canopy. The frame was that of a modified La-5F and the inscription on the fuselage means «Present to the Front from the League of the Union's Young Communists on the occasion of the 25th anniversary».

MIKOYAN
-GUREVICH

MiG-3 prototype with six propeller blades (September 1943)

In September 1943, a MiG-3 was equipped with an experimental very large diameter six-blade propeller. No details of this test programme however have come down to us, neither for any other programme this prototype may have been equipped in this manner.

The six blade propeller was fitted on a MiG-3 airframe as an experiment. The photograph is dated 18 September 1941. *(RR)*

YAKOVLEV

Yak-9TK/M-105PF Prototype
(October 1943)

In October 1943, the Yakovlev OKB designed and tested the Yak-9TK/M-105PF prototype. It was a Yak-9T equipped with a universal mounting for its axial gun, able to take four different types of cannon: 20-mm ShVAK, 23-mm VYa37, NS-37 and 45-mm NS-45. This arrangement meant a cheap solution for developing a single fighter capable of carrying out a great variety of missions in answer to requests coming from the front. In the units one or another of the cannon could be mounted between the cylinders of the M-105PF depending on the job to be done. This mounting went hand in hand with other modifications: revising the exhaust installation; fitting the ammunition supply according to the type of cannon used; collecting the empty shell cases.

The prototype Yak-9TK underwent State trials at the NII VVS in October 1943 by V.I. Khomiakov. Although the Yakovlev OKB's idea was thought to be valid, the same could not be said about the cannon. The ShVAK and the VYa were not a problem, their recoil being similar and well absorbed by the airframe; but that of the NS-37 and NS-45 cannon was very heavy and affected their accuracy. It was recommended not to fire more than one shell at a time since a burst would have no effect. However, these shells got through very thick armour and with

> ## Technical specifications
> **W:** 32 ft. 2 in. **L:** 29 ft. 3 in. **Service Ceiling:** 32 101 ft.
> **Wing Area:** 184.585 sq. ft. **Range:** 603 miles
> **Weight Empty:** 5 156 lb. *These figures correspond to a Yak-9TK*
> **Max. Take-off Weight:** 7 141 lb. *tested with an axial NS-45 canon and a*
> **Max. Speed:** 358 mph. at 12 870 ft. *UBS machine gun under the cowling.*

the help of tracer shells by day or night, accuracy was increased as the tracers were visible for about four or five seconds.

In spite of successful tests, no mass-production was undertaken because the armaments industry could not supply enough weapons. Moreover, the NS-45 was still not perfect and the Vya was unpopular with the VVS as a fighter weapon. Subsequently the scheme was applied to the Yak-PU (see below).

The only Yak-9TK prototype, a «T» equipped with a universal engine mounting which was adapted to take several types of axial canon of different calibres from 20 to 45-mm (the markings on its tail indicate that here it was equipped with a 20-mm axial canon).

(J. Marmain)

TsAGI ★

Two studies without any designations with «VRDK» (October 1943)

In parallel with Abramovitch's «S-1VRDK-1» study, another was being carried out at the TsAGi with an AM-39F engine rated at 1 620 bhp driving a propeller installed in the nose of an airframe and a VRDK compressor in the fuselage. The characteristics which had been worked out were theoretically better at higher altitudes (compared with the M-82) but unlike the Abramovitch study, the exhaust gases were not directed to the combustion chamber but were ejected through pipes. The calculations by the TsAgI specialists suggested that an increase in the speed

Technical specifications	
Max. Take-off Weight: 12 100 lb. (2nd).	**Endurance:** 1 1/2 hours (1st) and 2 1/2 hours (2nd).
Max. Speed: 531 mph. at 28 050 ft. (1st), 506 mph at 26 400 ft (2nd).	*These figures are estimates.*

of a fighter-interceptor of something in the order of 75 to 94 mph was possible taking into account the fact that 30% of the power from the engine was used for the motor-compressor. This could be closed down and could only be started up and brought into action by the pilot. With the AM-39F and the VRDK in action, the machine was supposed to fly at 506 mph. However, the MTOW of a fighter equipped with this kind of power plant would have increased by almost a tonne. A study for a second all-metal interceptor was made with the same engine but without a propeller, a VRDK, armament consisting of two ShVAK cannon and two UBS machine guns. The calculated speed was in the region of 531 mph at 28 050 feet. The two studies were dated October 1943. There are no other details and the study was not followed up.

Y★AKOVLEV

Photographic reconnaissance Yak-7B/M-105PF (or Yak-7R) (October 1942)

In October 1943, the Yak-7B/M-105PF, serial N°14-10 produced by Factory N°82 was tested with an AFA-IM camera (with a focal distance of 135 x 135 mm) installed between the third and fourth frames to the right of the rear compartment. It was intended for low-altitude close-quarters reconnaissance missions from 990 to 1 320 feet and up to 9 900 feet) over a zone of 1.158 sq. miles. This installation was made following a specification drawn up by the NII VVS's special services in September. The success of the trials gave rise to the pro-

Technical specifications	
W.: 33 ft. **L.:** 28 ft.	**Wing Area:** 184.585 sq. ft.

duction of 350 examples of the photographic reconnaissance Yak-7B/M-105PF sometimes referenced as the Yak-7R (for the second time) by factories N°82 and N°153. Not all the machines however were equipped with cameras as the type of installation was not suitable and was only considered as «temporary». In fact during the whole of the war, the VVS never had a specific reconnaissance plane, the reconnaissance version of the twin-engined Petlyakov Pe-2 being the only model to give the best results in this role.

YAKOVLEV

Yak-7/M-105PF Prototype (November 1943)

On 4 November 1943, on the orders of the NII VVS's Chief Engineer, A.K. Repine, a new prototype was accepted at the NII VVS to be tested there until 13 December: the Yak-7 P (P meaning that it was fitted with cannon); it was the result of studies by P.A. Nevitski (Chief Engineer of the 1st Air Force Army) concerning the increase in firepower for the Yakovlev fighters. The plane was a real «composite» as its fuselage was that of the Yak-7B, serial N° 46-13 produced by Factory N°13 in June 1943 (two-seat, rear decking), an example which had had an accident and was brought to the 281.SAM (Independent repair workshops); its wing came from another damaged Yak-7B; its engine was a revised M-10PF; and all the equipment had been taken from damaged Yaks. Moreover its armament comprised a ShVAK axial canon plus two others instead of the UBSs (the mountings came from an La-5 and a Hawker Hurricane) whose barrels stuck out much further from the ports.

The performances of the Yak-7P were not officially registered since the airframe and the engine had been repaired (the dimensions were those of a Yak-7B). The pilot V.A. Modestov noted however that the flight characteristics and the performances of the machine remained unchanged compared to a new Yak-7B, that its firepower deserved «to be noted in high places», but that the

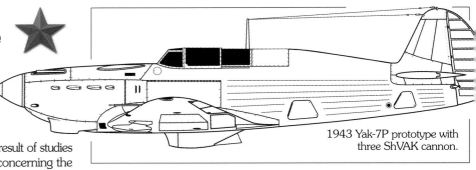

1943 Yak-7P prototype with three ShVAK cannon.

Technical specifications
Dimensions as for the Yak-7B. No other figures available.

loading and supply to the cannon was not very good; that the synchronisation of the guns under the cowling was not perfect and that the shell cases which were ejected to the rear damaged the leading edge of the wing. Yakovlev himself came to inspect this hybrid prototype during its trials. But although the machine remains unique and although the idea of equipping a Yak-7B with synchronised B-20 cannon under the engine cowling did not get anywhere, Yakovlev used the information he got from the prototype to install this type of equipment on the Yak-3UTI and Yak-3P versions, in 1944 and 1945 respectively. As for the Yak-7P, it returned to the workshops, underwent some modifications and a series of operational trials in a unit of the 1st Air Force Army.

YAKOVLEV ★

Yak-9U/M-105PF-2 Prototype («1944 model» Yak-9, or Yak-9-23) (November 1943)

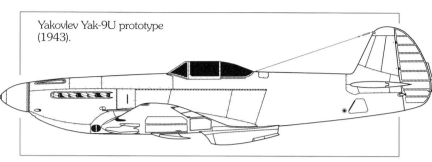

Yakovlev Yak-9U prototype (1943).

The Yak-9U/M-105PF-2 model represented a development of the Yak-7/Yak-9 family which was just as important as that of the Yak-3 for the Yak-1. At first, the Yakovlev OKB had put its hopes in the M-107A engine as the power plant but this was not reliable enough and in the end it was the M-105PF-2 which was chosen. The airframe was extensively modified, like the Yak-3 which the Yak-9U resembled a lot (U for «improved»). The prototype was built by the OKB in November 1943 under the official designation of «1944 Model Yak-9» (sometimes also referenced as Yak-9-23). The wing roots were redesigned with a view to installing two circular oil radiators in the central section, removing the intake under the nose and enabling this part of the machine to be better streamlined. The landing gear bolts were incorporated into the wing structure. The aileron counterweights were removed and the joints were better designed. The undercarriage doors were redesigned and the leading edge was carefully polished and varnished. The canvas which covered the rear part of the fuselage was replaced by 1/8 in thick plywood. The ventral intake for the glycol radiator was moved further back, redesigned and its surface area increased. All the unneeded openings were filled. The protection for the pilot consisted of an armoured windshield, the back of the seat (it was not so high but it enveloped the pilot, like a «sarcophagus»), glazing to the rear and the left part of the cockpit where the pilot's arm rested handling the throttle.

The propeller was a VISh-105V-01 which had more efficient blades and the exhaust piping comprised two rows of individual pipes. Fuel capacity was reduced to 95 gallons (704 lb) and the oil to 55 lb. Armament consisted of an axial VYa-23 canon with 60 shells and two UBS under the cowling with a total of 341 rounds. The VYa was replaced by a B-20 or an NS-37. In the latter case, the right-hand UBS had to be removed. But it was the first lay-out which was more convenient despite the VYa's unpopularity (hence the designation Yak-9-23 in certain Soviet

Technical specifications

Wingspan: 32 ft. 1 1/2 in.	**Max. Take-off Weight:** 6 380 lb.
Length: 28 ft.	**Max. Speed:** 387 mph. at 12 705 ft.
Wing Area: 184.585 sq. ft.	**Service Ceiling:** 34 320 ft.
Weight Empty: 4 936 lb.	**Range:** 531 miles

documents, these figures being painted on the tail fin of the prototype).

At the same time as these modifications, the airframe was lightened and now weighed 6 380 lb on take-off. As a result, the Yak-9U/M-105PF-2 prototype became the member of the Yak-9 family with the best performances during its factory trials, which took place in December 1943. The State ones took place at the NII VVS from 2 to 11 March 1944 at the hands of V. I Khomialov. The plane was fast, very stable and manoeuvrable, climbed easily and higher, was easy to fly and did not have any quirks. It was almost the equal of the light Yak-3 and outdid the Yak-9Ts, Yak-9Ms and Yak-1/M-105PFs. Piloting it was made easier by a system for regulating the power plant's cooling air intakes automatically, and by modifications to the tail wheel controls. Its only real defect was in its range: only 531 miles instead of the 875 specified in the GKO directive of 26 October 1943 which was applied to all future Yaks. In spite of this, the trial reports all recommended mass-production of the model. This was not carried out because the armament scheme retained was not applicable because the cannon selected was not available in large numbers and because the range was too short (the range asked for was never obtained by any of the Yak-9 versions to come).

LAVOCHKIN ★

La-5FN serial N°39210206 Prototype, or La-5 «206» or «206» (November/December 1943)

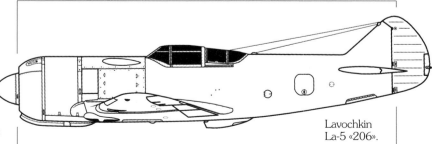

Lavochkin La-5 «206».

With the improvements made to the La-5FN, A.K. Martinov and L.A. Zaks (TsAGI) took La-5FN serial N° 39210206 in November 1944 off the production line and subjected it to a series of modifications dictated by wind tunnel research at the TsAGI. These concerned the question of sealing the whole power plant, the change in the cooling and exhaust systems and the redesign of the centre section of the wing with completely enclosed undercarriage wheel wells. The work was very carefully carried out with models of the components made of clay and plywood, delivered to the workers so that they could make them themselves. In this way, these elements were

built exactly as the wind tunnel trials recommended and were applied to the plane gradually in order to perfect its aerodynamic envelope.

The prototype was designated La-5 «206» (an abbreviation of its serial N°39210206), or «206». Externally, compared to the La-5FN were very obvious: the air intake for the supercharger was repositioned under the engi-

Above and right.

La-5FN serial N°39210206, or La-5 «206» in a hangar at the TsAGI. This machine has been refined aerodynamically and structurally. A long air intake has been added under the engine cowling. The excellent improvements which were carried out gave rise to the La-7 series (the two photographs are dated 8 December 1943).

ne cowling, the oil radiator was lodged in a small very well streamlined intake under the belly; the engine cowling was very finely adjusted around the power plant ensemble; the Dural metal skin on both sides of the fuselage were removed directly under the cockpit; the antenna mast was removed. On the other hand the armament of two ShVAK cannon under the cowling was kept.

For a period of preparation in the T-104 wind tunnel, the aircraft was entrusted to the care of N. Adamovich and V. Molochayev (LII) who tested it from 14 December 1943 to 10 February 1944. The tests revealed that the «206» was 40 mph faster than an La-5FN (even though its was 330 lb heavier), 22 1/2 mph faster than the «Type 39 Double» and that it outclassed its contemporaries with M-71 engines up to 14 190 ft, even though they were more powerful. These figures were confirmed again on 11 February 1944 by the flight tests carried out by the pilot A.V. Chelasov. When the report was read, the authorities ordered a new even more refined prototype to be made, the prelude to the La-7.

Close-up of the series of six left-hand side exhaust pipes on the La-5 «206» prototype. *(J. Marmain)*

Technical specifications

W.: 32 ft. 4 in. **L.:** 26 ft. 7 in.	**Max. Take-off Weight:** 7 579 lb.
Wing Area: 189.621 sq. ft.	**Max. Speed:** 427 mph. at 20 295 ft.
Weight Empty:	**Service Ceiling: Range:**

YAKOVLEV

Yak-9U/M-107A Prototype, Short series Yak-9/M-105PF-2 And Yak-9U/VK-107A series (December 1943 and April 1944)

The Soviet authorities did not authorise the mass-production of the Yak-9/M-105PF-2 only because its range was insufficient but also because the version of the Yak-9U with the more powerful M-107A engine was being tested at the same time. In December 1943, it seemed possible to install this engine on a new airframe from the Yak-9U programme. The prototype was built the same month and factory trials took place from 28 December 1943 to 12 January 1944. Its engine mounting was new, the fuselage structure and the wing were made of metal; the whole aircraft was covered with a plywood skin (the wing was bakelised). As

Technical specifications

W.: 32 ft. 1 1/2 in. **L.** 28 ft.	(proto), 7 049 lb. (series).
Wing Area: 184.585 sq. ft.	**Max. Speed:** 437 mph. at 18 150 ft.
Weight Empty: 5 449 lb. (proto),	(proto), 420 mph at 16 500 ft. (series)
5 526 lb. (series)	**Service Ceiling:** 35 145 ft. (series)
Max. Take-off Weight: 6 930 lb.	**Range:** 421 miles (series)

with its predecessors, the tail surfaces were made of Dural. In order to have a good cooling system for the glycol and the oil, the radiators were respectively an OP-555 and an OP-554 with a larger frontal surface. The motor had individual faired exhaust pipes. A cooling intake for the spark plugs, the exhaust and the GS-15-500 generator were installed among the plane's axis, over the engine cowling, between the two gun ports. Fuel capacity was increased to 106 gallons (781 lb) and the oil to

(J. Marmain)

The «1944-model» Yak-9U prototype, also designated as Yak-9-23 because it was equipped with a 23-mm canon as shown by the figures painted on the tail fin. This was a very significant development in the Yak-9 line. *(J. Marmain)*

Right, from top to bottom.
The Yak-9U/M-107A with its ventral radiator moved further back. It almost resembles the Yak-3. The windshield glass is flat and the intake on the cowling is missing. The aircraft was damaged on 23 February 1944 when the engine caught fire in flight; everything was repaired afterwards.

(J. Marmain)

A production series Yak-9U/VK-107A with an air intake on the cowling and the definitive rounded windshield, seen here during trials at the NII VVS.

Yak-9U/VK-105PF-2 serial N°03-16 during its evaluation at the NII VVS. The windshield was curved and moulded from a single piece.

77 lb. In order to re-centre the model, the wing was repositioned 4 inches further forward and in order to soften the hard joystick, the horizontal tail surfaces were reduced slightly. The rear part of the canopy was lengthened and the antenna cable was put inside it. As usual, armament was the same axial ShVAK canon with its 120 rounds and the same two UBSs with 170 rounds each. All these changes pushed take-off weight of the Yak-9U/M-107A prototype up to 6 930 lb, 550 lb more than its predecessor powered by the M-105PF-2.

The State trials took place at the NII VVS from 18 January to 20 April 1944 at the hands of A.G. Prochakov. They revealed a very exceptional machine, with a very clear superiority in top speed over all the other fighters in service in the USSR, both on the Soviet and the German side, including the Yak-3 «Double», and up to 19 800 feet. The machine was very simple to fly and its stability would enable it to be put into the hands of competent pilots. Unfortunately, the inherent defects of the M-107A and moreover all the M-105 variants from which it derived, persisted: power plant overheating (the Yakovlev OKB engineers were never able to cool the Klimov engines properly); oil leaks (the Klimov OKB engineers were never unable to suppress them) and the loss of pressure when climbing; the intense vibrations of the M-107A with bad centrifugal supercharger performance; fast burning out of the spark plugs and above all, the short (not more than 25 hours) engine life. Subsequently for production machines, the pilots were ordered not to use the engine at combat speeds since this tended to reduce its life to two or three flights only. Moreover, the positioning of the two exhaust manifolds leading to the pipes made maintenance very difficult. In these conditions, using the engine to its fullest capability was impossible, meaning that maximum speed for the production machines was limited. Anyway, the prototype had an accident on 23 February 1944 after a fire started in the engine compartment.

In spite of all theses engine defects, considering the performance which it offered, the Yak-9U/VK-107A (ex-M-107A) was ordered into production by the government in April 1944. Until December 1944, 1 134 examples were produced but the first models were all equipped with VK-105PF-2 engines (Yak-9U/VK-105PF-2). Operational evaluation was carried out by 32 aircraft in the 163.IAP between 25 October and

(J. Marmain)

25 December 1944. In the course of 398 sorties, 27 Fw 190As and one Bf 109G-2 were shot down for the loss of two Yak-9U/VK-107As in dogfights; one was lost to AA fire and four through accidents. The appearance of the Yak-9U/VK-107A in the Russian sky during the summer of 1944 very largely contributed to the Russians winning air superiority, to the extent that the Germans avoided crossing swords with the Yaks «without antenna masts».

From December 1944, new improvements and changes increased its performances further. The oil and glycol radiators were replaced by OP-728s and OP-736s, the intakes were more spacious enabling the engine to be used at all speeds without the fear of overheating. Production standards were made higher at all stages of the design. The undercarriage locking system ensured that the landing gear was really solid, and closing up the wells was far better now. The thickness of the fuselage plywood skin was increased to 1/4 in and the finish for the wing was very much more careful (polishing and varnishing). The Yak-9U was even more manoeuvrable in all planes and was kind with pilot error. Maintenance was made easier and the armament corresponded to the VVS'S wishes. All pilots were happy flying this fighter-interceptor which was feared so much by their German counterparts. From April 1944 to August 1945, 3 941 aircraft of this type were produced.

Standard Yakovlev Yak-9U, with VK-105PF engine from the first production batches.
A: canopy with an unarmoured curved windshield.
B: front section of a Yak-9U with VK-107A engine.
C: camera installed on the outside of some Yak-9Us.

The first production series Yak-9U built by Factory N°166 at Omsk (serial N°2516621, VK-107A engine). (RR)

M★IKOYAN-GUREVICH

I-221, or MiG-7
Prototype (Programme «2A»)
(December 1943)

(J. Marmain)

The second project which came under the classification «A» for high-altitude fighter-interceptor was coded «2A» by the OKB and referenced as I-221 by the NKAP. It differed from the I-220 by its totally redesigned wing, with a NACA-234 profile, metal structure for the outer wing sections and a wingspan increased to 42 feet 11 inches; its Dural structure for the rear part of the fuselage; its pressurized cockpit; the reappearance of a ventral air intake for cooling (heat exchanger) connected to the air conditioning system according to a sequential (pressurisation) cycle developed by A. Y. Shcherbakov. It was powered by an AM-39A boosted by two TK-2B (AM-39A/2TK-2B) superchargers so that it could reach at least 42 900 feet (see NB). It was Mikoyan himself who entrusted a young engineer by the name of R. Beliakov with the task of designing the supercharging of the AM-39A (he became the head of OKB in 1970). The glycol radiators were included in the central section of the wing and the available documents show that the fuel capacity was increased (no details available). To make up for the increase in mass caused by the power plant, the armament was reduced to two ShVAK cannon on the side (150 shells per canon).

The test programme was undertaken by P.I. Juralev who made the first flight of the I-221 on 2 December 1943 and by A.P. Yakimov of the LII VVS. But from the outset, there were problems with the power plant and

Left, from top to bottom.
The I-221 prototype, the second attempt at making a high-altitude fighter within the «A» programme. The aircraft was very fast, but its accidental end started a controversy.
(J. Marmain)

The streamlining of the I-221 prototype and the arrangement of the cooling air intakes for the AM-39A power plant boosted theoretically by two superchargers (only one according to MiG documents). *(J. Marmain)*

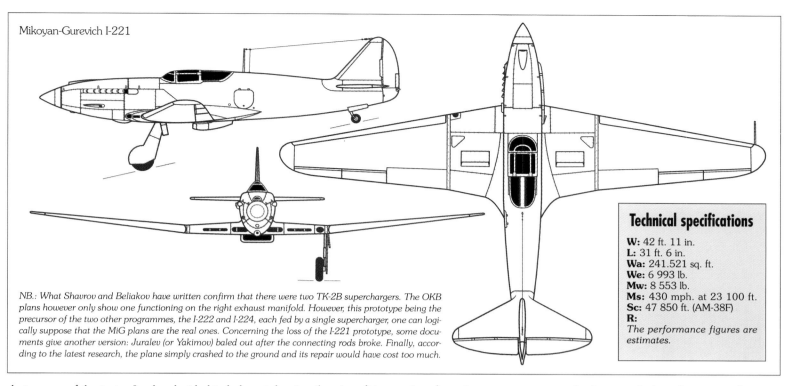

Mikoyan-Gurevich I-221

NB.: What Shavrov and Beliakov have written confirm that there were two TK-2B superchargers. The OKB plans however only show one functioning on the right exhaust manifold. However, this prototype being the precursor of the two other programmes, the I-222 and I-224, each fed by a single supercharger, one can logically suppose that the MiG plans are the real ones. Concerning the loss of the I-221 prototype, some documents give another version: Juralev (or Yakimov) baled out after the connecting rods broke. Finally, according to the latest research, the plane simply crashed to the ground and its repair would have cost too much.

Technical specifications
W: 42 ft. 11 in.
L: 31 ft. 6 in.
Wa: 241.521 sq. ft.
We: 6 993 lb.
Mw: 8 553 lb.
Ms: 430 mph. at 23 100 ft.
Sc: 47 850 ft. (AM-38F)
R:
The performance figures are estimates.

during one of the tests, Juralev decided to bale out, leaving the aircraft to crash. His action was due to a misunderstanding. He was new to the test pilot circuit and nobody had told him that flames coming from the exhaust pipes from time to time were perfectly normal when the power plant was working with superchargers. Thinking that the plane had caught fire, he left the plane to its sorry fate.

M★IKOYAN-GUREVICH

"Lightened" (or "improved") MiG-3 Prototype (During 1943)

On 16 February 1943, a meeting between Stalin, Beria, Molotov and Malenkov decided upon a last attempt to improve the MiG-3 for intercepting German spy planes. Thus the Mikoyan-Gurevich OKB was ordered to make six prototypes based on the MiG-3 to reach a height of 44 550 feet. These machines, simply referred to as «lightened» or «improved» MiG-3s, were produced during the year and benefited from a number of innovations intended to reduce their weight: the fuselage was of wooden monocoque construction; the tail fin could be removed; the wing spars were made of metal; the cockpit was enlarged; the two cylindrical oil radiators were replaced by a single one under the central

wing section and a single fuel tank holding 98 gallons was placed between the fire proof bulkhead of the engine and the cockpit (instead of four, holding some 110 gallons previously). In spite of these modifications, the MiG-3 airframe offered no further advantages than it had done before and this sealed the fate of the model once and for all, because during the evaluations by the 12.IAP pilots, landings turned out to be difficult and chaotic, the controls were heavy, low-speed engine vibrations were legion and the performance not really convincing. Moreover it could not fly higher than 39 270 feet. The head of NII VVS informed the higher authorities of these reports: «The performances obtained from the «improved» MiG-3/AM-35A and the defects that were noted during the evaluation do not argue in favour of starting mass-production of this aircraft again.» There are no other details or figures.

NB.: According to certain sources, it was not six examples which were thus modified, but only two «from which everything that could be removed was removed to gain weight». Some 411 lb were saved for an MTOW of 6 815 lb.

Y★AKOVLEV

Yak-7GK Prototypes (During 1943 and 1944)

Within the context of the development of Yak fighters intended for high altitudes, LII tested two Yak-7Bs with rear decking equipped with different pressurised cockpits designed by Shcherbakov and made of aluminium, functioning according to the principle of air regeneration by means of a compressor driven by the engine. Referenced as the Yak-7GK, the first (serial N°08-05, beginning of pro-

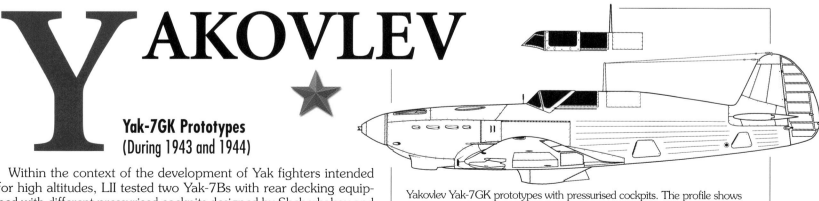

Yakovlev Yak-7GK prototypes with pressurised cockpits. The profile shows the first prototype which came from a Yak-7B airframe from the beginning of production. The drawing shows the pressurised cockpit of the second prototype which came from the airframe of a Yak-7b at the end of the production series.

Yak-7GK tested at LII (based on a Yak-7B with rear decking) with a pressurised cabin designed by Shcherbakov, tested at the LII in 1943.

(V. Koulikov)

The second Yak-7GK was also a Yak-7B airframe with modified rear decking, tested at the LII in 1944. Its canopy was more standard than the first Yak-7GK.

duction) carried out its trials in 1943. Its canopy was made of very thick glass cut on the cross. The second was equipped with a more classic sliding canopy in 1944 (a Yak-7B airframe from the last production batches) but just as thick with fairly wide supports. The cockpits of these two prototypes were sealed by inflatable rubber seals. There are no other details.

YAKOVLEV

Yak-7B/M-105PF with cut down rear fuselage and all round visibility canopy (During 1943)

The modifications to the Yak-7B ordered by Major Shinkarenko (cutting down the rear of the fuselage and installation of an «all-round» visibility canopy) carried out by personnel in his unit (42.IAP) and giving rise to the Yak-1b (see below), were also applied to the Yak-7B/M-105PF. But the very angular glazing of the Shikarenko canopy was more rounded on the production machines and the rear part of the fuselage was cut down even further. The aerodynamic form of the oil intake under the nose was better designed. It was in 1943 that aircraft serial N° 31-01 was tested with these changes and with a radio transmission system entirely enclosed within the fuselage; the wing and tail leading edges were smooth and polished; two kinds of exhaust were tested: with eight pipes (OKB) and with 12 (NII VVS); the retractable tail wheel was totally redesigned; all «unneeded» openings were completely covered over. This machine flew at 382 mph at 13 200 feet and climbed a bit faster, outdoing the Bf 109G-2 by 10 to 14 mph at low altitudes. But over 16 500 feet, the German fighter had the advantage again. On the other hand the radio system did not give the expected results and did not perform as well, so the radio antenna was kept for the production series machines... until further notice.

Technical specifications

W: 33 ft. **L:** 28 ft.	**Service Ceiling:** 33 000 ft.
W A: 184.585 sq. ft. **W E:** 5 561 lb.	**Range:** 687 miles
M T-o W: 6 705 lb.	*The service ceiling and the range are estimates.*
M S: 382 mph. at 13 200 ft.	

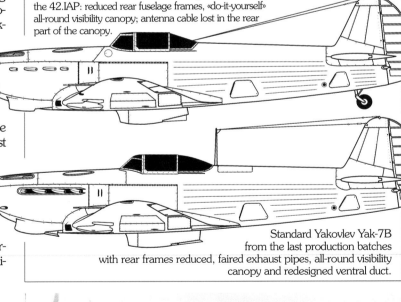

Yakovlev Yak-7B from an intermediate production batch, modified while at the 42.IAP: reduced rear fuselage frames, «do-it-yourself» all-round visibility canopy; antenna cable lost in the rear part of the canopy.

Standard Yakovlev Yak-7B from the last production batches with rear frames reduced, faired exhaust pipes, all-round visibility canopy and redesigned ventral duct.

(J. Marmain)

Yak-7B/M-105PF serial N° 41-01 built in Moscow (1st batch, 41st machine). The rear of the fuselage has been cut down, there is an «all-round» visibility canopy and the four exhaust pipes on both sides of the fuselage are faired.

A Yak-7BM/-105PF with the reduced rear frames and an «all-round» visibility canopy built at Novosibirsk. Compared with serial N° 41-14 from Moscow, the ventral duct is slightly different and the pipes are not faired.

LAVOCHKIN

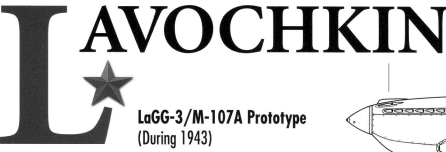

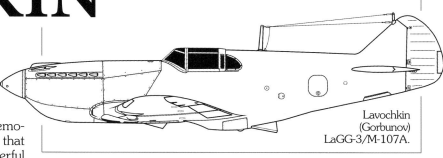

Lavochkin
(Gorbunov)
LaGG-3/M-107A.

LaGG-3/M-107A Prototype
(During 1943)

When it was announced that the LaGG-3 was going to be removed from the production planning in 1943, Lavochkin realised that the only way he could «save» his fighter was to use a more powerful engine. The only model which enabled this to be done without modifying the airframe too much was the M-107A which was still being perfected. The first bench trials showed that it was rated at 1 400 bhp (1 300 bhp at 16 500 feet), some 25% more than the M-105PF. The documents available do not agree as to the realisation of this programme. According to some, it was the Lavochkin OKB which undertook to build the LaGG-3/M-107A in 1942. But other sources give the Gorbunov OKB as taking charge installing a pre-series M-107A engine onto a LaGG-3 airframe at Factory N°31 in 1943. Neither refers to a precise period for the prototype's trials.

It is more likely that the LaGG-3/M-107A was developed by Gorbunov at the end of 1942 since the airframe was that of a machine from the end of production, with a revised canopy and the front of the fuselage without the oil radiator intake, like Gorbunov's «105» (see below) making it more streamlined. The M-107A did not complicate the structure of the LaGG-3 as only the mounting and the

Technical specifications

The dimensions were the same as for the LaGG-3. There are no other figures or details.

cowling were redesigned, and an intake appeared on the cowling for the carburization. The trials took place «in 1943» at the hands of G. Mischenko. The 33 flights ended with as many emergency landings, as the engine overheated constantly. To remedy this, a programme with an M-82 was studied and developed giving rise to the LaG-5 still under the leadership of Gorbunov, with better results to boot, but which was replaced by Lavochkin's La-5. (see below)

NB.: Gorbunov also envisaged converting a LaGG-3 airframe with an M-107 engine without however undertaking a serious study, nor designing a preliminary one, preferring to concentrate his efforts on the development of the Gu-82 programme, a LaGG-3 with an M-32 engine.

POLIKARPOV

Polikarpov I-185 mixed power plant project.

Studies for I-185 with a mixed
power plant (During 1943)

Before the end of the I-185 programme was announced, Polikarpov studied a version with a mixed power plant. Until now, no document has ever been published describing the exact method of propulsion for this study, except for a fairly precise artist's impression showing an I-185 with a wide-bodied fuselage and a tail ending with a large diameter nozzle. The machine was very similar to the I-185/M-82A, the armament too, but the exhaust pipes were grouped together on either side of the fuselage under a flap and the oil radiator intake was incorporated under the engine. The bevelled glazing at the rear of the cockpit no longer was no longer present. The rear part of the fuselage enclosed either a pulse jet or a ram jet, or «VRDK» compressor (the rare, very fragmentary indications that have appeared would tend to suggest the pulse jet). In all three cases, the air was supplied by means of a ventral intake installed under

the cockpit. The elevators were lower compared with the I-185 prototypes. No further details concerning this study have been published up to now, but another profile which appeared in «Polikarpov's I-16 fighter» (Yefim Gordon and Keith Dexter, Midland Publishing, 2001) is very similar to the artist's impression described here and suggests that there was another means of jet propulsion apart from the VRDK, a ram jet or a pulse jet.

Artist's impression of an I-185 with mixed power plants. The normal engine seems to be an M-82A (rather than an M-71). The size of the rear fuselage frames and the exhaust nozzle in the tail show that either a VRDK motor compressor, a ramjet or a pulse-jet has been installed (no details).
(RR)

(RR)

KOCHERIGIN

Non-designated project
(During 1943)

In 1943, Kocherigin clearly got his inspiration from the Curtiss P-40 when he studied a model designed around the Mikulin AM-39 engine, intended for high altitude.

The preliminary study was for a low wing cantilever monoplane with a cockpit enclosed under a rearwards sliding canopy.

A large faired intake under the nose and two gills at the wing roots contributed to the cooling of the engine. The classic undercarriage retracted into the wing.

The wing was designed around a main spar and another auxiliary one and enclosed four fuel tanks. The leading edges had ailerons and large split flaps.

The machine was armed with four guns (the type is unspecified) under the engine cowling. There are no other details.

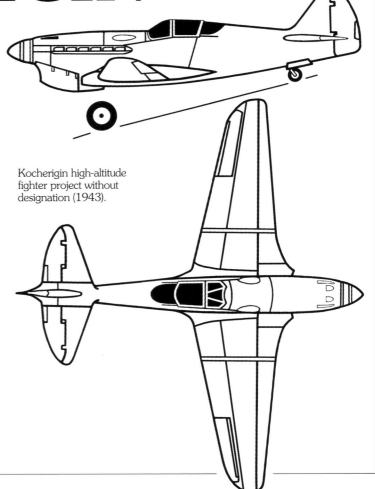

Kocherigin high-altitude fighter project without designation (1943).

PELENBERG (MiG OKB)

VTOL fighter project
(Without designation)
(During 1943)

★

With the arrival of monoplanes during the 1930s, the personnel of operational units were confronted with new problems which were just as much technological as logistical: the increase in maximum take-off and landing weights, and as a corollary, the increased take-off and landing distances. While the army engineers did their utmost to lengthen the strips, a number of aeronautical engineers worked on developing innovatory lift increasing devices to reduce these lengths and reduce the speeds (various flaps and special leading edge slats, split wings, etc.). The aircraft builders were not to be outdone, thinking up all sorts of more or less futuristic models, some of which reached the prototype stage, like Nikitin and Shevchenko's IS-1 and IS-2, two sesquiplane fighters which could change into high-wing monoplanes after taking off; or Bakchayev's «RK», a monoplane with a telescopic wing. But in spite of all these efforts, none of these solutions was entirely satisfactory in any significant way.

In 1943, on his own initiative, Konstantin V. Pelenberg studied an STOL fighter within the Mikoyan-Gurevich design team of which he had been a member since it was set up. The various builders had nonetheless been recommended to study the development of such a machine since the beginning of the «Great Patriotic War», so that they could be used in the front line units very near the battlefields

and whose airstrips were likely to be damaged by enemy forces. But instead of insisting on working on the wing concepts, Pelenberg concentrated on the power plant; at the same time imagining variable geometry wing and tail surfaces.

After several analyses in 1942 and 1943, Pelenberg designed a low-wing monoplane, with twin boom and tail lay-out, a central nacelle whose rear section was taken up by a pusher engine. It had retractable tricycle undercarriage, the two main half-fork legs retracting into wells in the booms and the nose wheel backwards into the front part of the nacelle, where the armament was concentrated, comprising one to four cannon (the original text only stipulates «one to four cannon» whereas the accompanying drawing shows two on either side).

Installed behind the single-seat cockpit equipped with an «all-round visibility» canopy was the engine (inline according to the plans) which drove a couple of three-blade co-axial contra-rotating propellers by means of two reduction gears and two drive shafts (in order to cancel out the effect of the torque). So that all the conditions were united for the project to take off and land in a short distance, Pelenberg designed a new mechanism which enabled the propeller to be turned downwards through 90° on a horizontal axis thanks to a suita-

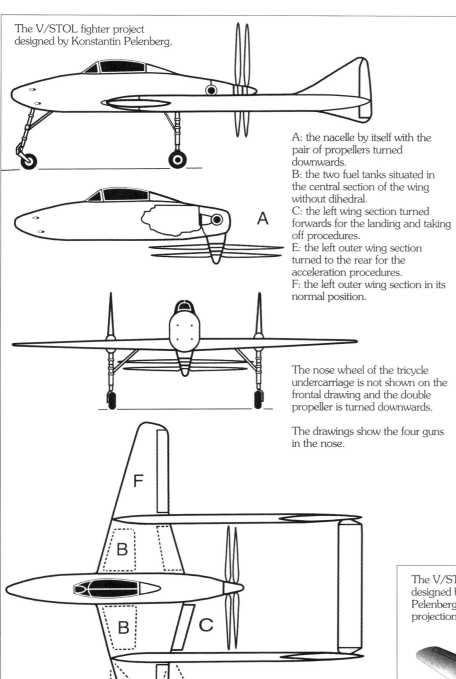

The V/STOL fighter project designed by Konstantin Pelenberg.

A: the nacelle by itself with the pair of propellers turned downwards.
B: the two fuel tanks situated in the central section of the wing without dihedral.
C: the left wing section turned forwards for the landing and taking off procedures.
E: the left outer wing section turned to the rear for the acceleration procedures.
F: the left outer wing section in its normal position.

The nose wheel of the tricycle undercarriage is not shown on the frontal drawing and the double propeller is turned downwards.

The drawings show the four guns in the nose.

ble hydraulic system which would cause a vertical, propulsive flow of air. To this was added the possibility of changing the incidence of the horizontal tail surfaces bracing the booms downwards or upwards and by deploying the underside flaps towards the rear. Thus, considering that part of the airflow caused by the propellers was spread over the underside of the wing, the whole system contributed to create an air cushion pushing the machine upwards on take-off and substantially reducing the run-in on touch-down. Moreover to make up for the negative aerodynamic aspect of this type of arrangement, the two wing sections outboard of the booms could pivot forwards to create extra lift. After taking off up to a safe height, the pilot brought the propellers and the outer wing sections back to their normal positions. In ordinary flight, these could pivot backwards to gather speed.

Pelenberg's project was able in theory to take off almost vertically but it needed a great deal of power. Unfortunately at the time there was no Soviet engine capable of providing the necessary power and only a twin-engine lay-out could have enabled the machine to take off under these conditions. As a result the project never got beyond of the drawing board although it did show how far ahead of their time and very unusual for the period these arrangements really were. After the war, Pelenberg developed other VTOL models, one of which was powered by a jet with three directional nozzles thrusting out from under the belly (the main one) and on the sides.

———————

NB.: Since the middle of the 1930s several teams from the MAI had designed STOL aircraft projects, one of which had a circular wing, a study which was later supported by a group within the Polikarpov design team under the designation «Koltseplan» during the war (see below) although they came to nothing apart from a few static or flying smaller-scale models.

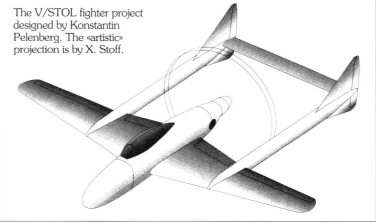

The V/STOL fighter project designed by Konstantin Pelenberg. The «artistic» projection is by X. Stoff.

SUKHANOV

«Koltseplan» Study (During 1943)

Technical specifications

Wingspan (diameter of the wing): 10 ft.	**Max. Speed**: 400 mph. at 9 900 ft.
Wing Area: 113.011 sq. ft.	(462 mph absolute speed).
Max. Take-off Weight: 5 500 lb.	*No other figures; the speeds are estimates.*

In 1943 Konstantin Pelenberg was not the only person to be interested in STOL aircraft (see below). M.V. Sukhanov had been working on a type of V/STOL machine while he was studying at the MAI. It was designed with an 800-bhp Hispano-Suiza engine and 10-foot circular wing surrounding the fuselage. In theory the experimental model should

have flown at 375 mph and given rise to a fighter. But it was only in 1940 that the study «reached the ears of the VVS High Command» which asked the TsAGI to examine it. Unfortunately for Sukhanov, the beginning of war between Germany and the USSR put an end to the venture, at least for the time being. In 1942 however, several models

were produced at Novosibirsk under the generic name «Koltseplan». Very interested by the work of Sukhanov, Polikarpov assigned a study group to him which built a flying model equipped with an engine driving a couple of contra-rotating propellers and the original annular wing. After undergoing a series of convincing tests under the supervision of Professor V.P. Vetchinkin, Polikarpov sent Sukhanov to present his project in Moscow to the TsAGI. The engine selected was the M-82A driving a faired propeller incorporating a fan; the fuselage and the single-seat cockpit were the result of studies and designs connected with the I-185 programme (they were very similar to the I-185/M-90), the tail surfaces were elliptical, the circular wing was set very far out in front of the fuselage to which it was joined by two fixed wing sections with a negative dihedral and on whose trailing edge were located the ailerons. The undercarriage was standard. Armament comprised four guns (two above the engine, two underneath). After examining the project it was decided to evaluate different variants in the MAI wind tunnel. But this work was stopped once again in 1943 for reasons which remain obscure to this day; the project was totally buried. There are no other details.

Artist's impression of the very strange «Koltesplan» project, taken from a book on the MAI. It had a fuselage which was very similar to the M-90-powered I-185, a faired propeller with incorporated fan, a circular wing and four nose-mounted guns. *(RR)*

POLIKARPOV

«VP» studies, or I-185-P (1943) (End of 1943)

At the end of 1943, the authorities asked Polikarpov to study a high altitude fighter-interceptor. The recommended engine was the M-71 with two TK-3 superchargers. The cockpit was to be pressurised and the armament was to comprise two 23-mm VYa cannon. This was modified afterwards, the engine being replaced by an AM-39B boosted by two TK-300Bs. Polikarpov referenced his general study as «VP» (VP for Vysotsnyi Pyerekhvaychik, high altitude interceptor) or I-185/VP but nothing is known of how it evolved afterwards.

POLIKARPOV

Twin-boom fighter without designation with a pusher engine (End of 1943)

At the end of 1943, Polikarpov studied a design for a twin-boom monoplane fighter with a pusher engine at the rear of central fuselage-nacelle.

It had tricycle undercarriage, the elevators stiffened the two booms whereas the fins were incorporated into the wing tips. But the project did not get beyond the preliminary studies and sketches, as the first estimates suggested only mediocre performances.

The study was abandoned so quickly that it did not have time to be given a specific designation.

There is no other information.

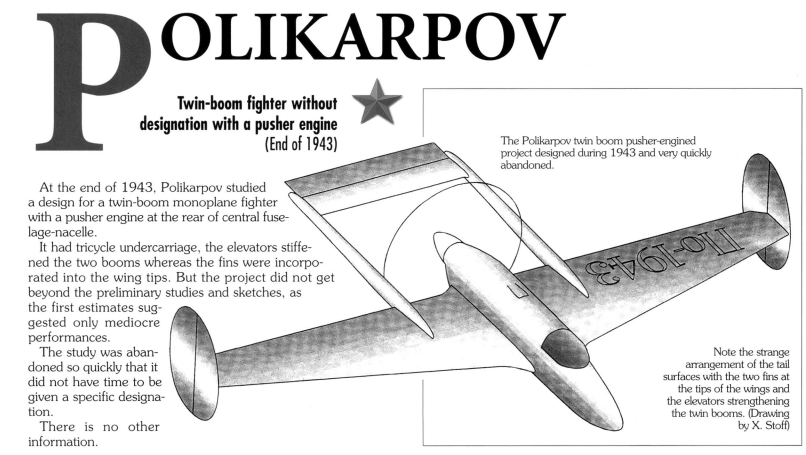

The Polikarpov twin boom pusher-engined project designed during 1943 and very quickly abandoned.

Note the strange arrangement of the tail surfaces with the two fins at the tips of the wings and the elevators strengthening the twin booms. (Drawing by X. Stoff)

1944

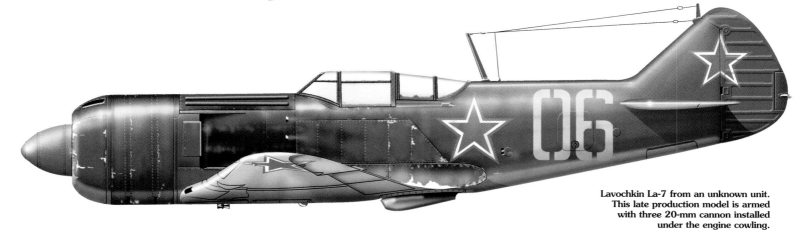

Lavochkin La-7 from an unknown unit. This late production model is armed with three 20-mm cannon installed under the engine cowling.

GLOSSARY

YAKOVLEV

Yak-9K/VK-105PF or Yak-9-45
(January 1944)

Technical specifications

Wingspan: 32 ft. 1 1/2 in.	**Max. Take-off Weight:** 6 661 lb.
Length: 29 ft. 3 in.	**Max. Speed:** 358 mph. at 12 870 ft.
Wing Area: 184.585 sq. ft.	**Service Ceiling:** 33 000 ft.
Weight Empty: 5 040 lb.	**Range:** 375 miles

With the success of the Yak-9T armed with a 37-mm axial canon, Yakovlev developed a new version designated Yak-9K (or Yak-9K-45) fitted with an even heavier canon, the 45-mm NS-45, even though it was not quite ready. Its installation between the cylinders of the VK-105PF engine (former M-105PF) was reinforced and keeping the barrel along the correct axis was done by means of a special mechanism fitted under the ViSH-61P propeller boss. The only outside difference with the Yak-9T was this barrel, equipped with a muzzle brake to absorb 85% of the recoil, which stuck out through the boss by 10 5/8 inches. A UBS machine gun was lodged under the engine cowling (200 rounds); the HS-45 could fire 29 rounds. The belts and the empty cases were collected and the pilot had an ammunition supply indicator in the cockpit; he could fire each weapon separately (PBP-1a sights).

The difference with the Yak-9T was its ability to carry more fuel: four wing tanks for a total capacity of 145 gallons. The distribution tank was replaced by a valve system enabling the pilot to go from one set of tanks to another, which rather complicated his job. The pilot was protected by an armoured windshield and a thick bullet-proof pane behind his back. The tail wheel locking system was manual, as was the power plant cooling flap control. The first Yak-9K was built at the end of 1943 and did its State trials at the NII VVS on 8 April 1944 at the hands of Golofastov. In April and in June, 53 others were built for operational evaluation. But only 44 of them underwent the trials, in two stages, with the 278.IAP and the 274.IAP: from 13 August to 18 September 1944 and from 15 January to 15 February 1945 in White Russia (3rd and 1st Fronts). These machines had two of their tanks removed in order not to spoil their overall performances, their heavy weight changing them into underpowered fighters.

Under the supervision of a commission chaired by General E. I Savitski, these machines carried out a total of 340 sorties. Twelve enemy figh-

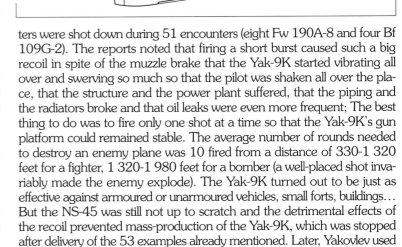
Yakovlev Yak-9K

ters were shot down during 51 encounters (eight Fw 190A-8 and four Bf 109G-2). The reports noted that firing a short burst caused such a big recoil in spite of the muzzle brake that the Yak-9K started vibrating all over and swerving so much so that the pilot was shaken all over the place, that the structure and the power plant suffered, that the piping and the radiators broke and that oil leaks were even more frequent; The best thing to do was to fire only one shot at a time so that the Yak-9K's gun platform could remained stable. The average number of rounds needed to destroy an enemy plane was 10 fired from a distance of 330-1 320 feet for a fighter, 1 320-1 980 feet for a bomber (a well-placed shot invariably made the enemy explode). The Yak-9K turned out to be just as effective against armoured or unarmoured vehicles, small forts, buildings… But the NS-45 was still not up to scratch and the detrimental effects of the recoil prevented mass-production of the Yak-9K, which was stopped after delivery of the 53 examples already mentioned. Later, Yakovlev used Nudelman's N-45 model which was lighter and more reliable to produce his Yak-9UT.

The Yak-9K prototype (a modified Yak-9T) with its 45-mm canon quite clearly sticking out through the tip of the propeller spinner.

(J. Marmain)

(J. Marmain)

The emblem painted on the cowling of this Yak-9K is that of 3.IAP. The NS-45 45-mm canon caused too much recoil in spite of the large muzzle brake, so the production series was reduced to only 53 machines which were intended for operational evaluation.

YAKOVLEV ★

Yak-3/VK-107A and Yak-3/VK-107A «Double» Prototypes
(January 1944)

As with other builders, Yakovlev decided to test the new powerful VK-107A engine on his fighters. The Yak-3 was no exception and two special prototypes were built in January 1944: the Yak-3/VK-107A N°1 intended for factory trials and the Yak-3/VK-107A N°2 «Double» intended for military evaluations. Although the fitting of the VK-107A did not

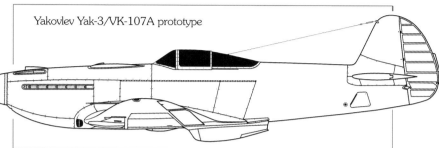

pose any particular problems (with its ViSH-107LO), several modifications were nevertheless necessary: engine mounting redesigned (extending the front by 2 inches); moving the cockpit back by 15 3/4 inches; reinforcing the undercarriage shock absorbers; increasing the fuel capacity to 115 gallons (858 lb, the VK-107A being greedier than the VK-105PF-2) spread out between four wing tanks and one distribution tank; oil capacity increased to 13 1/2 gallons; installing a spark plug cooling system; moving the air scoop for the supercharger onto the nose; getting rid of the axial canon, armament being reduced to two B-20S cannon under the engine cowling with 120 rounds per gun.

The Yak-3/VK-107A N°1 was finished on 6 January 1944 and undertook its first factory tests on 15 April without armament in order to save on weight. The test pilot Fiodrovi carried out 32 flights up to 20 November; they were all given over to getting the engine to function correctly. It overheated considerably and had to be changed three times. As of the 25th flight, this time with armament, the performances could at last be recorded. In spite of a high MTOW (6 564 lb), the prototype showed how good its flight characteristics were, both manœuvrability and handling; it reached 441 mph at 16 500 ft, then 450 mph at 18 975 ft - when the VK-107A did not cause too many problems. But the landing and take-off runs were longer than a standard Yak-3, as were the speeds; the installation of the left canon broke after firing 329 rounds (the guns were installed on the UBS mountings); the airframe was insufficiently rigid and the ground angle was not adequate. Moreover the on-board equipment only allowed the plane to fly by day in good weather. On the other hand, the radio satisfied the specifications (62.5 to 65.6 miles range with the ground).

As for the VK-107A, its sump and cylinders were fragile, the vibrations it caused were violent, the radiators leaked, the oil spread over the exhaust manifolds and the pipes with the attendant fire risk, and sprays onto the

Yakovlev Yak-3/VK-107A prototype

windshield; the supercharger functioned badly during the climb and the fuel and oil pressures fell below 26 400 feet. It was imperfect and the VK-107A could not be exploited operationally in the state it was in.

These defects were corrected with the «Double» prototype which was finished on 22 January 1944. It did its factory trials from 25 to 29 January with Fiodorov at the controls then it was delivered to the NII VVS to undergo its State trials which took place in two stages: 7 February to 15 May and from 13 July to 29 August. Between the two periods, a large number of modifications were carried out both at the factory and at the NII VVS and showed that the Yak-3 airframe was incompatible with this engine, which was still problematic. Despite excellent performances, the airframe had to be redesigned before the model could be approved for operational use.

Technical specifications

W: 30 ft. 4 in. **L:** 28 ft. 4 1/2 in. **Max. Take-off Weight:** 6 564 lb.
Wing Area: 159.830 sq. ft. **Max. Speed:** 450 mph. at 18 975 ft.
Weight Empty: 5 161 lb. **Sc:** 38 940 ft.. **Range:** 662 miles

LAVOCHKIN

«Object 120» or La-120 Prototypes («1944 standard La-5»)
(January and March 1944)

Lavochkin took notice of the TsAGI and LII reports made on the La-5 «206» programme and designed a new model, «Object 120» or La-120, referenced as «La-5, 1944 standard» which with the government's agreement benefited from the modifications carried out on the «206», but also from those developed by the Lavochkin OKB. Led by Alexeyev, the «120» incorporated the metal spars already designed for the last batches of the La-5FN with improved attachments to the fuselage and a laminar profile; the new faired ventral intake for the oil radiator; the individual exhaust pipes; engine cowling made up of less Dural panels and better sealing for the power plant; 8 3/4-inch shock absorbers for the landing gear, lengthening each member by 3 1/8 inch; a new VISh-105V-4 propeller with a wider boss (as with the 206); a roll bar in the cockpit to protect the pilot in case the plane overturned (not applied to

(J. Marmain)

The «120» with its flaps closed, its laminar wing and its very small air intakes for cooling the engine.

The Yak-9B prototype (or Yak-9L) during trials in 1944. It was a Yak-9D which was fitted out as a bomber. The rear part of the canopy has been clearly lengthened to allow access to the bombs. *(J. Marmain)*

A Yak-9B from a Guards unit (insignia on the nose) in the 130th Bomber Division.
(J. Marmain).

luation of performances and spin trials. Before they were completed, 108 other examples were built for operational evaluations which took place from 18 December 1944 to 20 February 1945 by the 130.IAD. The reports noted that the «Yak-9B was a good fighter and a good bomber», but that it was not to be put into the «hands of just anybody». For the Yak-9B was very heavy with its 880 lb of bombs and lacked stability along all its axes as long as it was carrying them, so that only the most experienced pilots were allowed to fly them fully laden with offensive loads (in general, this was reduced to two bombs or two little boxes). Once the bombs were released the fighter recovered its fighter's qualities and could be used as such.

The bombs or the boxes were dropped in pairs or all together thanks to two types of controls: electric on the joystick and manually in case of emergency. The aiming system was out-of-date and differed depending on the type of attack. While flying level, the pilot lined up the target on the ground with the nose of the plane (a line was painted along the axis of the cowling), counted up to three after the target disappeared and then dropped the bombs. Markings were painted on the windshield, the cowling and the wings to make aiming easier when level and if diving but only slightly because the security standards did not allow the plane to attack in a pronounced dive.

The versatility of the Yak-9 airframe was shown with this version because with the same VK-105PF engine, with two bombs and an overload weight on take-off of 7 383 lb, the Yak-9B's speed only dropped by 3 to 4 1/2 mph compared with the Yak-9D at top speed. But its climb rate dropped, taking off was difficult and the take-off distances were clearly longer.

During the operational evaluations, the Yak-9Bs carried out 2 494 sorties, dropped 51 057 bombs of all sorts (356.5 tonnes) and destroyed 25 enemy aircraft (of which 20 Fw 190 and two Bf 109) during 53 dogfights. Four Yak-9Bs were lost and four others damaged. The imminent end of the war meant that no

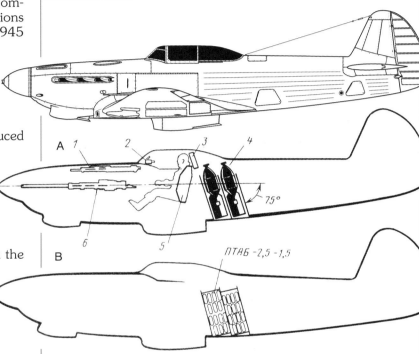

The A and B profiles are original drawings showing the bay for the FAB-100 bombs or the PTAB-2.5-1.5 boxes.
1. 12.7-mm UBS machine gun.
2. PBP-1A sights.

3. Armoured head-rest.
4. FAB bombs (two to four).
5. «Sarcophagus»-type armoured seat.
6. 20-mm MPSh-20 axial canon (ShVAK).

other Yak-9B production was started; they were used very little because of their instability, their very uncertain aiming system and the complicated way of «bombing up».

Two poor shots of Yak-9Bs dropping a 220-lb bomb or boxes of little bombs. Only the most experienced pilots were allowed to fly them, the offensive load usually carried being 440 lb.
(J. Marmain)

YAKOVLEV

Yak-7B/2DM-4S or Yak-7PVRD
(or Yak67B/M-105PF/2DM-4S)
(March 1944)

Declared as «ready for service» at the beginning of 1942, the Merkulov DM-4S ramjets were only mass-produced two years later because of the evacuation of the factories and the offices after the German invasion and their re-establishment on other sites. Their trials on a Yak fighter only took place in 1944 (they were tested on the UTI-26-2 prototype in 1942 (see below) when the LII NKAP decided to attach two examples under the wings of a Yak-7B/M-105PF with rear decking. Designated Yak-7B/2DM-4S or Yak-7PVRD (or sometimes Yak67B/M-105PF/2DM-4S), the machine was only considered as a flying test bench. The Yak-7B was chosen for its speed, its stability and its manœuvrability but also because the rear cockpit could accommodate a flight test engineer. As a result, this second cockpit was covered with a fairing made of Dural with three little rectangular panes on each side.

The programme started on 24 March and the trials took place on 15 May (first flight, pilot S.N. Anokhin from the LII NKAP) until the 12 December 1944. But as was the case beforehand with the other types of ramjets (Bondariuk's DM-2, DM-4 and VRD-1) tested on Polikarpov and Lavochkin fighters, the results turned out to be «mitigated». If the two DM-4S increased momentarily the prototype's speed by some 33 mph, if they suggest that a top speed of more than 375 mph, they caused so much drag when they were not used that the flight characteristics and performances were greatly reduced. Moreover such a top speed was only obtained at the cost of a huge consumption (48 to 66 lb per minute for each ramjet) so that using them was

only possible for a maximum of ten minutes.

The installation of the two DM-4S ramjets was so simple that it could be carried out in the fighter units. The VVS adopted them as a reserve measure in case this system was developed on a larger scale and built up a stock of DM-4S available at any moment. But the trials did not extend beyond 12 December, Yakovlev preferring to bank on the development of the new generations of «fighters powered by turbojets»

NB.: The majority of the Soviet documents do not mention any particular designation for these flying test beds and only refer to those of the models chosen (UTI-26.2 and Yak-7B) mentioning also the ramjets.

Technical specifications

Wingspan: 33 ft.	**Max. Take-off Weight:** 6 670 lb.
Length: 27 ft. 11 1/2 in.	**Max. Speed:** 362 mph. at 24 090 ft.
Wing Area: 184.585 sq. ft.	**Service Ceiling:** 32 175 ft.
Weight Empty: 5 742 lb.	**Range:** 375 miles

Yakovlev Yak-7B/2DM-4S or Yak-7PVRD.
The rear cockpit was occupied
by a flight test engineer.

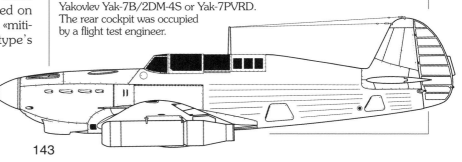

YAKOVLEV

Yak-3PD/VK-105PV or Yak-3PV
preliminary study and prototype
(April and September 1944)

In April 1944, the Yakovlev OKB presented a preliminary study for a highly manoeuvrable high altitude fighter-interceptor equipped with a VK-105PV engine with Follejal E-100 two-stage supercharger and armed with a ShVAK axial canon and another synchronised one installed under the top part of the engine cowling. The engineers estimated its MTOW at 5 830 lb, its operational ceiling at 42 570 feet and its top speed at 446 mph at 35 640 ft. In autumn, the studies for this project enabled the mass to be reduced to 5 676 lb and the service ceiling to be put at 41 250 ft without the top speed changing. This work gave rise to two programmes: Yak-3PD/VK-105PV which started in September, and the Yak-3PD/VK-105PD which was finalised in February 1945 (see below).

Yak-3 serial N° 44-19 was equipped with an M-105PV driving a

ViSH-105TL-2 and its structure was lightened. The programme took place between 29 September and 7 October 1944 at the hands of the pilot, V.L. Rastorguyev. During the six flights carried out between the 3 and 7 October, the programme concentrated on the reliability of the engine and its Dollejal E-100 supercharger as well as the flight parameters up to 21 450 feet and more. Meanwhile the propeller was replaced for a ViSH-105SV-01 but the frequent power plant failures did not allow the plane to fly faster than 410 mph at 18 232 ft. The prototype, sometimes unofficially designated Yak-3P in rare sources was delivered to the LII where its specialists had a close look at it. There are no other details.

YAKOVLEV

Yak-9PD/M-106PV
And short-run Yak-9PV
(April 1944)

In 1944, Yakovlev once again tried to develop a new high-altitude interceptor knowing full well that it would only be successful if the airframe was drastically lightened and if the engine was sufficiently powerful and reliable. A Yak-9U/VK-107A built by Factory N°166 was modified to take the M-106PV engine with the compression rate of the supercharger increased to 9.72 (at 31 350 ft). It drove a ViSH-105TI with broad blades and 9 ft 3 in diameter. A water-methanol injection system was fitted to improve the cooling of the supercharger air. The radiators were enlarged and an extra air intake was installed under the engine; the pumps were redesigned; the split flaps, the aileron counterweights, and those on the joystick too, were reviewed. The oil and fuel capacities were reduced to 66 lb and 528 lb respectively; the single axial ShVAK canon now only had 60 rounds. All these modifications reduced the MTOW to 5 500 lb and enabled the M-106PV engine with water-methanol injection to work perfectly well at a nominal speed without misfiring. The service ceiling was estimated at 43 230 ft.

This undesignated prototype was finished on 20 April 1944. It was often unofficially designated Yak-9PD/M-106PV and obtained excellent performances as far as speed and rate of climb were concerned, during its factory tests from 27 to 30 April by V.I.Yuganov, who allowed himself a little trip up to 44 550 feet. Unfortunately the absence of pressurisation greatly reduced its operational value because the pilot was only equipped with a simple oxygen mask which did not allow him to stay at such high altitudes for a very long time. Only three test flights were carried out, and then the plane was delivered to the 12.GvIAP where it remained until the end of the war.

At the time, spy planes did not operate over the vital Soviet sites which rather made this type of interceptor redundant. However, Factory N°301 transformed 30 other Yak-9Us into Yak-9PD/M-106PVs, or Yak-0PVs (the unofficial designation). They were assigned to the PVOs, but were not used operationally (according to certain sources, these machines were refitted with M-105PD engines during their stay in the units).

YAKOVLEV

Yak69DD/VK-105PF (or YAK-9Yu)
(April 1944)

In 1944, the Russian front reached from Norway down to Yugoslavia. There was a need for a very long-range fighter to escort bomber forma-

tions well over into enemy territory. In April 1944, in reply to a directive from GKO on 20 February, the Yakovlev OKB extrapolated the Yak69DD/VK-105PF (or YAK-9Yu for the OKB) based on a Yak-9D airframe, but taking into account its principal defect: the unending filling of the eight wing tanks. This time, all had their own filler which enable the plane to be refilled in twenty minutes. Except for the two little tanks in the

La-5, La-7

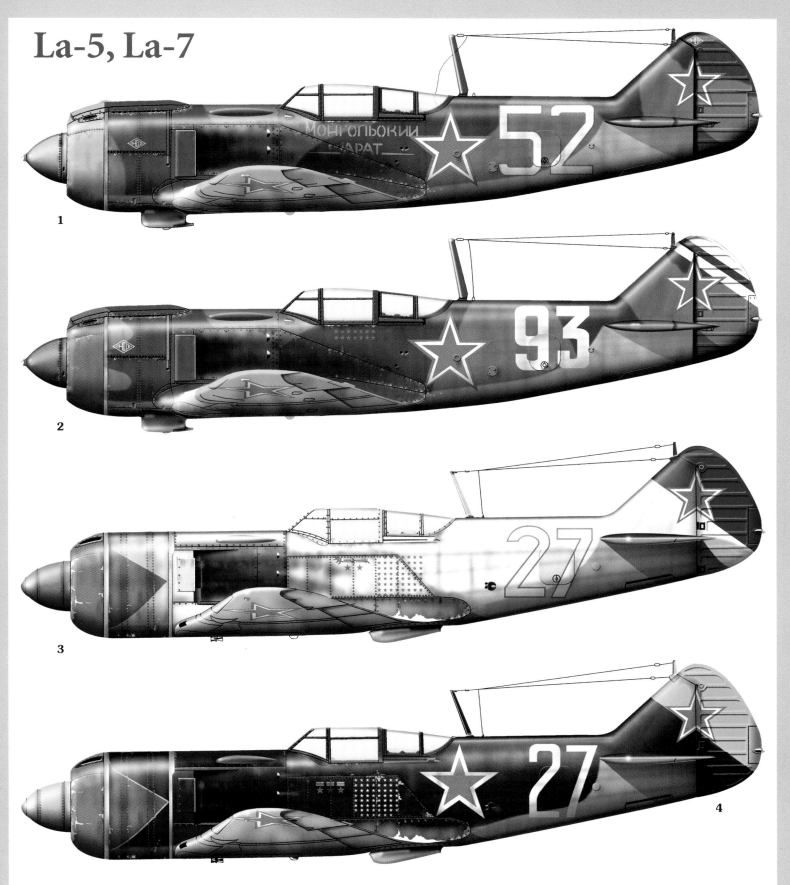

1. Lavochkin La-5FN from the 2nd Guards Fighter Regiment (GvIAP). This machine was financed thanks to donations from the People's Republic of Mongolia and bears the inscription «Mongolskii Arat».

2. Lavochkin La-5FN flown by Lieutenant Vladimir A. Orekhov from the 434th Fighter Regiment (IAP) during the Battle of Kursk, July 1943.

3. Lavochkin La-7 belonging to Captain Ivan N. Kojedub, commanding the 176th Guards Fighter Regiment, winter 1944-1945. Despite the temporary white camouflage, the tally and the decorations have been kept on the plane's fuselage.

4. Lavochkin La-7 flown by Ivan N. Kojedub, commanding the 176th Guards Fighter Regiment, spring 1945. This plane was the last flown by the Soviet ace of aces (63 confirmed kills, the highest score of all the Allied pilots) at the very end of the Great Patriotic War and bears the pilot's tally and the Hero of the Soviet Union's three stars on the fuselage sides.

The Yak-9D long-distance escort fighter prototype (serial N° 09-89) during its trials at the NII VVS. *(J. Marmain)*

One of the 229 Yak-9DDs produced, during its evaluations in the spring of 1944. *(J. Marmain)*

wing tips, all the others were protected by 1/4-5/8th inch thick Dural sheets and filled up with inert gases when they emptied. The total capacity was 188 gallons (1 386 lb) and a little distribution tank enabled the flow to be regulated steadily. The oil tank contained 15 1/2 gallons. In order to carry such a quantity of fuel, the structure of the wing was reinforced.

The model was essentially intended for long-distance escort duties, armament was reduced to a single axial ShVAk canon with its 120 rounds (some production series were subsequently fitted out with a UBS under the engine cowling). The position of the cockpit was the same as that of the Yak-9T (15 3/4 inches further back). Particular care was taken with the on board instrumentation and especially to the radio. But in order to have a good radio system, the Soviets were obliged to use Allied technology by installing an SCR-147N with two BTs-454A and BTs-455A receivers and two BTs-474 and BTs-459A transmitters with a longer antenna mast. An RPK-10M/DF radiogoniometer was fitted as was an AG-2 artificial horizon, a powerful battery and generator, as well as a 2-gallon oxygen bottle. All these changes and installations increased the Yak-9DD's MTOW to almost 7 480 lb to the detriment of its performances and flight characteristics. But they were the same as those of the Yak-9D once half the fuel was burned up. The 188 gallons enabled the plane to cover 843 miles at low altitude at 90% of its maximum power and 1 428 miles at optimum cruising speed.

Although the production series Yak-9DD trials were not undertaken by the NII VVS until the summer of 1944 (from 24 July to 2 August by Stefanovski and Antipov), series production started as soon as May. 299 examples were made up to September. Operational evaluation took place in the 368.IAP between 9 March and 25 April 1945 using 40 machines from production batches N°1 and N°2. They were given the unflattering nickname of «flying fuel tank» and were not particularly liked by the pilots for several reasons: underpowered when fully-laden; inconstant consumption; lack of manoeuvrability and stability; rate of climb to slow; unreliability of the tyres and the tail wheel because of the higher mass, etc. It turned out that the Yak-9DDs fulfilled their role well when escorting the Petliya-

Technical specifications

Wingspan: 32 ft. 2 in.	**Max. Take-off Weight:** 7 451 lb.
Length: 28 ft.	**Max. Speed:** 365 mph. at 12 870 ft.
Wing Area: 184.585 sq. ft.	**Service Ceiling:** 31 020 ft.
Weight Empty: 5 161 lb.	**Range:** 828 to 1 428 miles

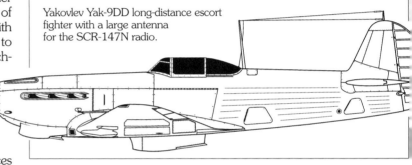

Yakovlev Yak-9DD long-distance escort fighter with a large antenna for the SCR-147N radio.

kov Pe-2 twin-engined bombers but were incapable of doing the same with the much faster Tupolev twin-engined bombers. They lacked that reserve of power needed to protect them, particularly when escaping from a zone which they had just bombed. This did not prevent the Yak-9DDs from fulfilling most of their missions satisfactorily. The most famous were accomplished by a dozen or so of them from August 1944. Commanded by Major I.I. Ovcharenko, they flew 812 miles from Baltsi to Bari in Italy to take part in the support for the Yugoslav Liberation Army (NAO). They carried out 155 escort missions for Douglas C-47s supplying the NAO over the Adriatic and landing on hastily made landing strips high up in the mountains. There were no technical malfunctions. The Yak-9DDs took part in escorting allied four-engined bombers (B-17s and B-24s) operating «shuttle missions» between Poltava in the Ukraine and Bari in Italy to bomb Rumanian targets.

M IKOYAN-GUREVICH

I-222 Prototype or MiG-7 («3A» Programme) (April 1944)

Technical specifications

Wingspan: 42 ft. 11 in.	**Max. Take-off Weight:** 8 338 lb.
Length: 31 ft. 8 in.	**Max. Speed:** 431 mph. at 41 250 ft.
Wing Area: 241.521 sq. ft.	**Service Ceiling:** 47 850 ft.
Weight Empty: 6 967 lb.	**Range:** 437 miles

The loss of the I-221 prototype did not mean the end of the Mikoyan-Gurevich OKB's researches into a high-altitude fighter-interceptor. A new programme coded «3A» (OKB) and referenced I-222 (NKAP) resembled the previous one. The frames of the fuselage's *semi-monocoque* rear section made of wood were lowered to give better visibility to the rear from the pressurised cockpit which had a redesigned canopy. The plane was of mixed construction: the front of the fuse-

lage, the central wing section, the moving surfaces and the flaps were made of metal and the rest was made of wood. Cooling for the oil and the water was by means of gills set in the leading edge and the radiator was situated in an intake installed under the rear part of the engine. This was an AM-39B boosted by an experimental TK-300B

The I-222 high-altitude fighter prototype when it came out of the factory. It has not been painted yet and it has a three-blade propeller. Note the fitting of the supercharger, mounted onto the exhaust (there was another one on the right-hand side). *(J. Marmain)*

supercharger developed at the TsAGI; the propeller was a three blade AV-5A but this was very quickly replaced by a four blade AV-9L-26 with variable pitch after the first trials. The centrifugal supercharger had direct controls (PTsN). The soft fuel tanks were installed in the central wing section; the oil tank was installed in its leading edge.

The surfaces of the fixed part of the tail were increased in size. The landing gear was fitted with 650x200 mm tyres (350x125 mm for the tail wheel). The pilot's seat was armoured as was the windshield (2 5/8 inches thick) and the rear part. Armament consisted of two ShVAK cannon on either side of the power plant with a total of 160 rounds.

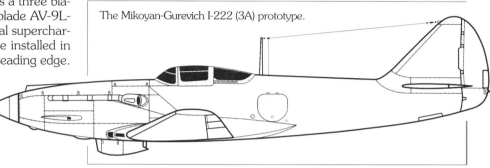

The Mikoyan-Gurevich I-222 (3A) prototype.

(J. Marmain)

The I-222 high-altitude fighter prototype when it came out of the factory. It has not been painted yet and it has a three-blade propeller. Note the fitting of the supercharger, mounted onto the exhaust.

The I-222 prototype left the factory on 23 April 1944 and made its first flight on 7 May at the hands of A.I.Jukov. Its performances were exceptional, but the pressurisation system did not function properly and the canopy glass covered misted over (it was not very transpa-

(J. Marmain)

rent to begin with) and the pressure was very difficult to keep up. In spite of all that, the plane reached 47 850 feet and flew at 431 mph at 41 250 ft. Unfortunately, the task for which all the class «A» category prototypes were built was no longer needed at the time since German spy planes no longer risked themselves over Soviet sites. As a result, producing the model under the designation MiG-7 was not considered timely.

MIKOYAN-GUREVICH

I-240 Project (April 1944)

In April 1944, the Mikoyan-Gurevich OKB received a new request from the VVS for a single-seat high-altitude fighter-interceptor. This time the engine had to be an AM-43 boosted by a supercharger. The specifications stipulated that the service ceiling had to be 39 600 feet and its top speed 437 mph at 26 400 ft. The Mikoyan-Gurevich team «developed the I-240 project with M-43 engine whose top speed was estimated between 437 and 468 mph with armament of one fixed 45-mm canon and two 20-mm ones» But no official trace of this project having been realised has been found up to now. It can be supposed that the I-240 project was replaced by the I-250 mixed power plant fighter programme (see below). Or that the designation was perhaps used for the second I-225 prototype which appeared in 1945 for which an AM-43 engine was intended.

NB.: The supposed existence of this I-240 project was revealed in an article on A. Mikulin by L. Berne and V. Perov which appeared in the magazine «Dvigatel» (N°2 and N°3 of 2001)

ILYUSHIN

Il-AM-42, or Il-1
(May 1944)

Technical specifications

W: 44 ft. 3 in. **L:** 36 ft. 7 in. **Max. Take-off Weight:** 11 704 lb.
Wing Area: 322.890 sq. ft. **Max. Speed:** 362 mph. at 10 758 ft.
Weight Empty: 9 427 lb. **S C:** 28 380 ft. **Range:** 625 miles

At the end of 1943, Ilyushin responded for the second time to the specifications issued by the Defence Commissariat for an armoured heavy single-seat fighter to operate at low and medium altitude. Its speed had to be at least 375 mph so that the plane could at least «fight on equal terms» with the German Messerschmitt Bf 109G-2 fighter. The programme was designated Il-AM-42 and incorporated in its design 67% of the elements from its big brother, the two-seat Il-2 Type 3M «Shturmovik».

The low cantilever wing was new and entirely made of metal. The wing span and the surface area were reduced compared with the Il-2

Ilyushin Il-1 armoured fighter prototype.

With 67% of its components coming from the Il-2 Type 3M ground attack aircraft, the Il-1 (or Il-AM-2) heavy fighter prototype was easy to produce. It was much more refined and smaller than the Il-2. But the trials showed that its performances were lower than those of the latest Lavochkin and Yakovlev fighters which were much lighter (it weighed more than five tonnes) and the programme was abandoned.

(J. Marmain)

(J. Marmain)

and the profile was different. The central section without dihedral angle incorporated the two undercarriage members which retracted to the rear pivoting through 86° to lie flush in the thickness of the wing. The two outer sections with dihedral angle were each fitted with a VYa canon with 150 rounds. Two 220-lb bombs could be carried under the central section for secondary ground support missions. The tail wheel half retracted. The fuselage was shortened and included the armoured compartment typical of the Il-2, protecting the all the vital parts of the aircraft. The Am-42 engine (metal three blade AV-51-24 propeller with a diameter of 11 ft 10 in) was contained inside it as was the single seat cockpit. The windshield and most of the canopy (swing-over to the right) were armoured. The engine was cooled by means of two radiators (oil and glycol) supplied with air through two gills in the wing roots. This installation made streamlining all the front of the all metal fuselage easier. It also simplified production. The rear was made of wood and incorporated a DAG-10 grenade launcher for lower rear defence. The tail surfaces were made of metal.

The wind tunnel tests at the TsAGi confirmed how good Ilyushin's new concept was. It was officially designated Il-1. The test pilot, Kokkinaki, took off for the first time on 19 May 1944. His reports were very satisfactory, but the prototype did not reach the 375 mph at 10 725 feet mark with an MTOW of a little over five tons. This speed was however higher than the Focke-Wulf Fw 190-A at the same altitude. Piloting it was easy and the Il-1 could do all the acrobatic figures. But at a time when the Luftwaffe was running out of breath and that German troops were being overrun on all fronts, there was no longer any need for such a machine, even more so as the latest versions of the Lavochkin and Yakovlev fighters could fly faster. So the Il-1 was not presented to its State trials and the programme was abandoned.

YAKOVLEV

Yak-9M/VK-105PF, Yak-9M/VK-105PF-2
and Yak-9M/PVO/VK-105PF and PF-2
(May and October 1944)

In 1944, the Yak-9Ts and Yak-9Ds were produced in the same factory, N°153. In order to standardise production, the Yakovlev OKB developed the Yak-9M/VK-105PF (VISh-105-V-01 propeller) which in itself brought out nothing new from a technological point of view. But its make-up gathered together «three formulae in one», enabling

a desired version to be built according to the orders received. The fuselage was that of a Yak-9T with its cockpit placed 15 3/4 inches further back, the wing and the armament were those of a Yak-9D whose axial ShVAK canon could be replaced if needs be by another 37-mm one. Following on Stalin's criticisms in 1943 concerning the wing skin which tended to come unstuck or to tear in flight («the pilots were frightened of flying Yaks»), this was now made of bakelised plywood and the fabric was glued better than before (the plywood on the wings of all the Yaks was fabric-covered). Other modifications were incorporated into the Yak-9M: installing a canopy ejection system, of a ART-1

Technical specifications

Wingspan: 32 ft. 2 in.	361 mph. at 12 705 ft (PVO) ft.
Length: 28 ft.	**Service Ceiling:** 31 350 ft.
Wing Area: 184.585 sq. ft.	31 020 ft (PVO)
Weight Empty: 5 341 lb.	**Range:** 593 miles,
5,192lb (PVO)	458 miles (PVO)*
Max. Take-off Weight: 6 809 lb.	*The figures correspond to the Yak-*
6 855 lb (PVO)	*9M/VK-105PF and its PVO variant.*
Max. Speed: 358 mph. at 12 375 ft.	*estimate

(J. Marmain)

cooling regulator for the glycol, a more appropriate communication system, dust filters on the power plant air intakes, pneumatic weapon loading, shortened radio antenna cables, etc.

The first Yak-9M did its State trials at the NII VVS from 17 to 27 December 1944 at the hands of the pilot, V.G. Ivanov. The production series had started ever since May and only finished in June 1945 after the 4239th example rolled off the production line. In October 1944, the VK-105PF-2 engine replaced the previous one on the assembly lines (Yak-9M/VK-105PF-2). From 1 August 1943, every tenth Yakovlev fighter was equipped according to the demands of the units entrusted with defence (PVO). Thus the Yak-9M/VK-105PF then Yak-9M/VK-105PF-2 were equipped with night-flying and bad weather instruments: FS-155 light; VR-2 variometer; RPF-10/DF radio-goniometer, RSI-4M radio transmission with RSI-6MU receiver, RSI-transmitter, STSH-3/IFF transponder… The weight of fuel and oil were only 924 lb and 66 lb respectively (instead of 1 056 and 99 lb) and the armoured glazing behind the pilot's back was removed saving 35 lb. The deliveries of Yak-9M/PVO were made until all the PVO units were reconverted to this model, then according to the needs of the VVS and the NKAP.

A brand-new Yak-9M. It was mix of Yak-9T (fuselage) and Yak-9D (wings), intended to simplify mass-production. The machine could be fitted with a 20-mm (most of them) or a 37-mm axial canon.

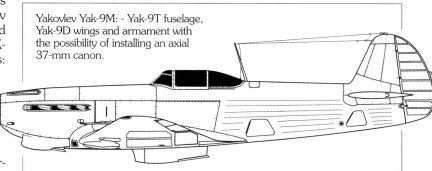

Yakovlev Yak-9M: - Yak-9T fuselage, Yak-9D wings and armament with the possibility of installing an axial 37-mm canon.

DeuTwo Yak-9Ms from the 976.IAP on the 1st Baltic Front. In front of them a Petlyakov Pe-2 bomber. *(J. Marmain)*

(J. Marmain)

As with the «T» version, the cockpit on the Yak-9M was 15 3/4 inches further back. This example was tested in the winter of 1944/45.

L AVOCHKIN

La-7 «Type 45» (May 1944)

The excellent characteristics and performances of the «206» and «120» prototypes hastened the start of the new La-7 «Type 45» model production. The authorities had recommended that ventilation in the cockpit be improved and also the demisting of the glass, that the hardness of the rudder bar be softened, that the cylinder cooling system of the M-82FN engine be improved and that the emergency bale out system be simplified. Moreover the engine, propeller, supercharger and radiator flap controls had to be synchronised to ease the pilot's job. Of all the recommendations, only one was applied immediately to the series: the automatic synchronisation of the propeller pitch. All the other modifications were only made later after the trials for the La-7 serial N° 38101356 (24 flights from 20 March

An La-7 built before the end of the war. As with the La-5FN, the rear part of the canopy swung over to the right.
(G. Gorokhoff)

Technical specifications

W: 32 ft. 4 in. L: 28 ft. 7 in.
Wing Area: 189.321 sq. ft.
Weight Empty: 5 731 lb.
Max. Take-off Weight:
7 128 lb, 7 293 lb.*

Max. Speed: 411 mph. at
19 470 ft. 413 mph 19 800 ft.*
Service Ceiling: 37 290 ft,
34 485 ft.* Range: 415 miles
* with three B-20s.

The «Standard» of the 57 first La-7s
built in May 1944. These machines
were armed with two 20-mm cannon
under the engine cowling.
(V. Koulikov)

An La-7 equipped with a windshield moulded from one piece as an experiment and a double Pitot tube under the right wing section.
(H. Léonard)

The La-7 kept in the Monino Museum exhibited in public at Domodedovo Airport in September 1967. It bears the colours of the most famous Russian ace, Ivan Kojedub, triple Hero of the Soviet Union; his 62 kills have been painted on the fuselage.
(H. Léonard)

Factory N°21 produced the first 57 La-7s in May 1944. At the end of the year, 1 782 machines left the assembly lines because Factory N°99 at Ulan-Ude and N°381 in Moscow also produced them. The first La-7 reached their units from June onwards, but as was often the case in the USSR, the State approval trials for the La-7 were only carried out much later: from 15 September to 15 October 1944 by the 63.GvIAP under Major Gorbatov. The pilots reported that the air intakes for the supercharger and the oil radiators of the thirty La-7s supplied sucked in a lot of dirt and caused the engine to seize up. La-7 serial N°38102668 was fitted out with filters which were not totally satisfactory. Indeed, this machine was tested only after the war (it came from a batch made in May 1945) and the filters were fitted only on subsequent models.

The La-7s from the series were slower than the prototypes by 25 mph. The bad finish of the Ash-82FN (ex M-82FN), the inadequate sealing of the power plant and of the fuselage itself and the badly made propeller blades were the main reasons for this. As it turned out, the La-7 was scarcely faster than the La-5FN. But the engineers got down to making the necessary rectifications and applied them to an La-7 which reached 421 mph at 19 800 ft. In spite of this and because the State trials only took place «just too late», the La-7 only flew at 411 mph at 3 750 ft. However the La-7 was equal to the latest Bf 109 fighters and manoeuvred just as well if not better, obliging them to change their system of attack completely.

The armament was only tested in July 1944. But the empty cartridge cases from the two B-20 cannon finally chosen were ejected in the direction of the elevators and often damaged them. Moreover the B-20 canon was not very reliable which did not prevent the government from authorising its mass-production and equipping VVS fighters with it, among which the La-7. Originally, there were to have been three cannon but the numbers available did not allow this and only 368 examples were built with three cannon, by Factory N°381. These were distinguishable from the two-cannon La-

NB.:
According to some sources, the production of La-7s by Factory N°21 was only 4 357 examples (1 558 in 1944 and 2 799 in 1945) which only brings the total to 5 905 examples. A La-7 was tested at the end of 1944 with an NS-23 canon and a UBS-20. But the latter was not made to do its firing tests.

to 8 April 1945) fitted with a regulator and *thermo-regulators* acting automatically and a system for channelling part of the cooling air towards the cockpit (under the instrument panel) for ventilation and demisting.

Two of the 368 La-7s with three 20-mm cannon mounted under the engine cowling. They were built by Factory N° 381 and differed from the others by their long slender fairings on the top of the engine cowling.
(G. Gorokhoff and H. Léonard)

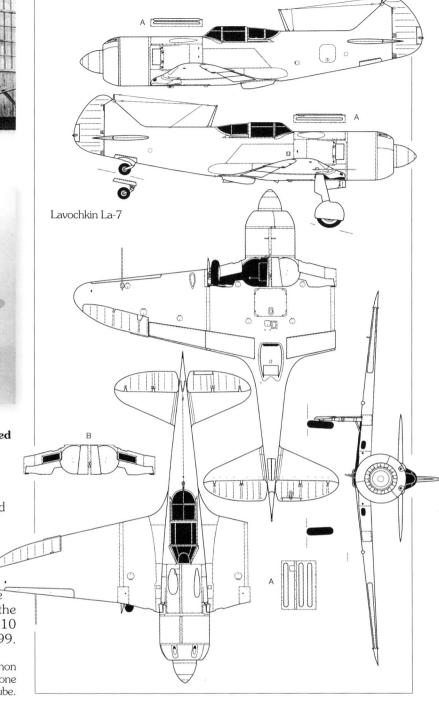

Lavochkin La-7

7 by the long bumps on the top of the engine cowling. The second prototype «120» was fitted with two 23-mm NS-23 cannon (Nudelman-Sudonov). The trials took place from 20 to 31 July 1944 and turned out to be fraught with problems since the NS-23 were not ready. Subsequently, a new set of trials was carried out with revised NS-23s, whose performance was rather better. They were mass-produced but were not fitted to La-7s. Production ceased at the end of 1945 after the 6 158th example came off the production lines, of which 4 610 came from Factory N°21, 1 298 from N°381 and 250 from N°99.

The detailed drawings A, B and C show the differences shown by the three-canon version of the La-7. The left outer wing section was identical to the right one except for the Pitot tube.

MIKOYAN-GUREVICH

I-225 N° 01 and N°02 prototypes (Programme «5A») (June 1944 and March 1945)

Fifth and last programme for a fighter in the «A» class, the «5A», or I-225, was the heaviest and most powerful of the series. However, the change in specifications enabled the service ceiling to be lowered by 6 600 ft for the model to perform better. As a result the I-225 was no longer a machine intended for higher altitudes. Two examples were built under the management of A.G.Brunov. They were the same size and had the same wing surface area as the I-200 prototype, but kept the rear of the fuselage which were typical of the I-222 and I-224 models (see below). The overall structure was

Technical specifications

Wingspan: 36 ft. 4 in.
Length: 31 ft. 4 in. 31 ft 7 in. according to some sources.
Wing Area: 219.349 sq. ft.
Weight Empty: 6 622 lb.
Max. Take-off Weight: 8 580 lb.

Max. Speed: 450 mph. at 28 050 ft (N°1), 453 mph at 33 000ft (N°2)
Service Ceiling: 41 580 ft.
Range: 812 miles
These figures concern the second prototype.

reinforced, the outer wing sections were made of metal and the cockpit was pressurised. The first was powered by an AM-42B whereas the second was powered by an AM-42FB, both boosted by TK-300B supercharger working off the right hand side manifold. They drove an AV-5A-22V three blade propeller with a diameter of 11 ft 10 1/2 in. The temperature exchan-

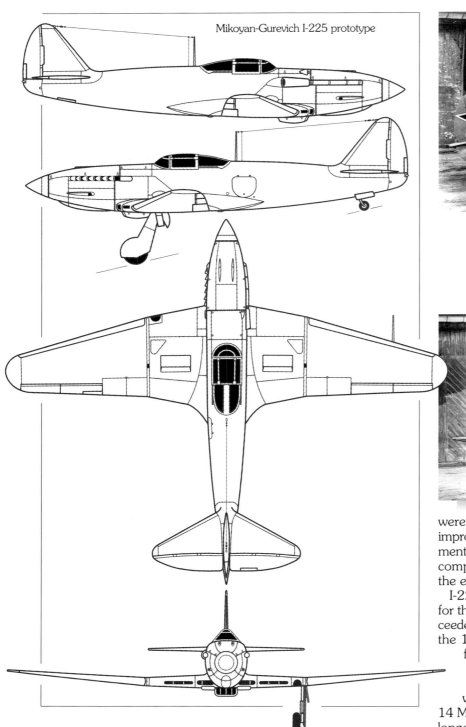

Mikoyan-Gurevich I-225 prototype

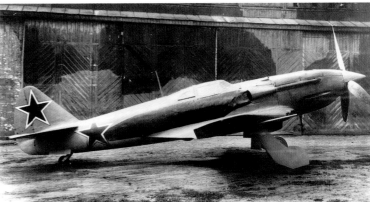

The first I-225 prototype powered by an AM-42B and TK-300B supercharger. The machine came from the I-220 and the second prototype (I-225 N°02) managed to reach a speed of 450 mph during its trials (AM-42FB and TK-300B supercharger).
(J. Marmain)

were armoured (1/4 in) and the cockpit pressurisation was greatly improved. On board equipment was complete enough to allow instrument flying and a short-wave radio set was also installed. Armament comprised four ShVAK cannon with 1o0 rounds each: two above the engine, two on the side.

I-225 N°1 derived from the I-220 directly in June 1944 and flew for the first time on 21 July flown by Yakimov. On 7 August, he succeeded in reaching 441 mph at 28 050 ft. But two days later during the 15th flight, it crashed to the ground — engine breakdown — from 50 feet. The prototype was beyond repair and it was only at that moment that Brunov undertook to finish prototype I-225 N°2. It was identical to N°1 except for the cockpit which was roomier and its canopy improved. It started its tests on 14 March 1945 and flew at 450 mph. But at the time the USSR no longer feared anything from anybody and the development of piston engines fighters for high altitudes was no longer necessary. All the more so as the military authorities were now interested in the new generation of jet-powered combat aircraft, and the work on Class «A» stopped there.

ger took up less space than those of the I-222 and I-224 prototypes and was placed under the wing central section. The windshield and the rear part of the canopy were 2 1/2 inches thick. The pilot's seats

YAKOVLEV

Yak-9/VK-105PF-2 «Kouriersky» (July 1944)

This was the only model in the Yak-9 family not to be armed, the Yak-9/VK-105PF-2 «Kouriersky» was a hybrid plane intended as a rapid VIP and senior officer transport plane at the front or to the

front. The prototype was made up of a Yak-9V fuselage and engine with the wing from a Yak-9DD. With its 188 gallons of fuel (1 386 lb) held in its eight tanks (plus the distribution tank) it could cover a range of 1 125 miles and its VK-105PF-2 engine enabled it to fear no enemy interception and to be able to fly without escort. As a result «Kouriersky» flew scarcely slower than a Bf 109G-2 or an Fw-190A. The two cockpits were covered with a canopy with sliding sections for each compartment. The rear cockpit did not have anything mili-

La-7

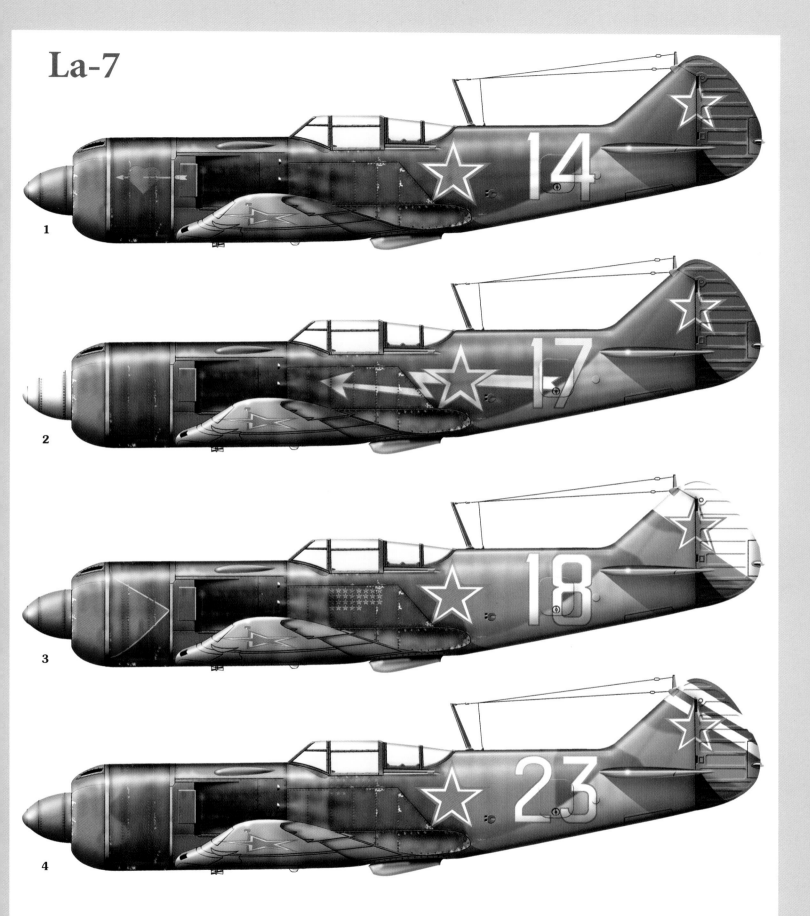

1. Lavochkin La-7 belonging to Major Alexander A. Aleliukhin from the 9th Guards Fighter Regiment. Although this pilot is not well known he did score 40 confirmed kills.

2. Lavochkin La-7 belonging to Major Vladimir D. Lavrinyenkov, the 9th Guards Fighter Regiment, Eastern Prussia, winter 1944-1945. The colour of the propeller boss has only been guessed at as it could be light blue or bare metal. Likewise some sources give an entirely red fuselage arrow.

3. Lavochkin La-7 belonging to Alexander S. Kumanishkin, 176th Guards Fighter Regiment, winter 1944-1945. This ace finished the war with 31 kills to his credit and added an extra one in Korea.

4. Lavochkin La-7 belonging to Major Vladimir A. Orekhov, 32nd Guards Fighter Regiment, Lithuanian Front, 1944.

Technical specifications

W: 32 ft. 2 in. **L:** 28 ft.
W A: 184.585 sq. ft.
W E: 4 972 lb.
M T-o W: 6 820 lb.
M S: 352 mph. at 12 540 ft.
S C: 31 350 ft. **R:** 1 125 miles

(J. Marmain)

Two shots of the «Kouriersky» two seat liaison aircraft based on the Yak-9V (fuselage) and Yak-9D (wings) for carrying VIPs to the front. The single prototype was not followed up by any production series.

tary and for piloting, but the instrument panel remained carefully lit so that the passenger could follow the pilot's manoeuvres; its floor was made of wood and the sides were lined with carpet with storage space for maps and other objects. A. Stepaniets' memoirs revealed that the two cockpits were equipped with «urinals» (no doubt a simple rubber pipe).

At the same time as these «luxurious fittings» intended to increase passenger comfort, the front cockpit was equipped with all the instruments deemed necessary including artificial horizon. A landing light was fitted on the leading edge for night flights. The two canopies were jettisonable in flight. A 16 gallon oil tank replaced the previous one and the brakes were improved because all the changes had increased the weight and moved the CG back to 26.4% of the MAC, making the machine a bit less stable and 6 to 10 mph slower than a Yak-9DD.

Produced at Factory N°153 in July 1944, the «Kouriersky» was tested in August and September at the hands of A.E. Pashkevich. But the machine was unique no doubt because its radio system, installed between the two cockpits was not effective enough (it only had a range of 37 to 62 miles). After the factory tests, the prototype did not fly any more and was not presented for its State trials.

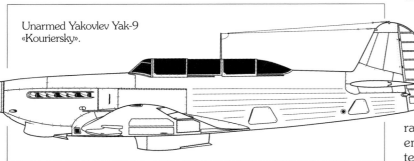

Unarmed Yakovlev Yak-9 «Kouriersky».

LAVOCHKIN ★

La-7TK preliminary study and prototype or La-7/ASh-82FN/2TK-3 (July 1944) and prototype La-7TK (or La-7/ASh-71/2TK-3) La-7/Ash-7& or La-7/M-71 (Summer of 1944)

The La-7TK prototype differed from the standard La-7 by the absence of weapons, by the two TK-3 superchargers installed on either side of the engine.

In 1943, the Mikoyan-Gurevich, Yakovlev and Lavochkin OKBs received specifications for designing the umpteenth high altitude fighter to intercept German spy planes from the «Rowhel» group which had resumed their activities above Moscow. In the eyes of the engineers and the government, the La-7 was an excellent platform for developing experimental versions. Lavochkin assigned this task to Alexeyev, who produced the La-7TK prototype, or La-7/ASh-82FN/2TK-3.

Based on one of the first La-7 air frames, the machine appeared in July 1944. It was powered by an Ash-82FN boosted by two Tres-

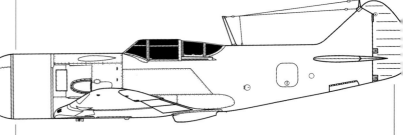

Close-up of the burning exhaust gases from the left-hand TK-3 supercharger on the La-7TK prototype. Although the prototype was lost, the VVS accepted 10 machines of this type, each armed with only a single canon under the engine cowling for defending Moscow, although there was actually no real need.
(J. Marmain)

Below, from left to right
The La-7TK prototype whose AsH-82FN (ex-M-82FN) engine was boosted by two TK-3 superchargers.

(J. Marmain)

(J. Marmain)

Technical specifications	
E: 9,8 m; **L:** 8,67 m	**Md:** 3 280 kg (82FN),
Sa: 17,59 m²	3 505 kg (71)
Mv: 2 711 kg (ACh-82FN),	**Vm:** 676 km/h à 8 000m
2 849 kg (ACh-71)	**Pp:** 11 800 m; **Df:**

kin TK-3 superchargers (Ash-82FN/2TK-3 with ViSH-105V propeller). In spite of the prototype being lost as a result of one of the two TK-3s disintegrating in flight, the test programme seemed to have been convincing since it reached a speed of 422 mph at 26 400 ft and climbed to 38 940 ft faster than a standard La-7.

But at the time, the VVS had already won air superiority and the German spy planes no longer ventured over Moscow except very occasionally. As a result, the programme was abandoned but not without ten examples, armed with a single ShVAK canon under the

cowling, having been built in the summer of 1944 and assigned to a regiment of the Moscow defence. Alexeyev did not develop just the La-7TK with ASh-82FN/2TK-3 engine. Another part was added to the programme with a double row eighteen-cylinder air-cooled ASh-71 engine boosted by two TK-3 superchargers. This engine was supposed to develop 2 027 bhp but still caused a lot of technological problems. Information concerning this programme also designated La-7TK or La-7/ASh-71/2TK-3) is very rare. It is only known that during the prototype trials for the two 20-mm cannon (in the summer of 1944?), *«the performance reported for this type of engine did not live up to expectations.»* They were not recorded and were not known.

NB: The few sources that tell of the existence of this prototype do not all mention the use of two TK-3 superchargers. Some speak of the Ash-71 engine only and designate the prototype as La-7/Ash-71 or even sometimes La-7/M-71.

SUKHOI

Preliminary study for a high altitude fighter (without designation) (July 1944)

In July A.S. Yakovlev sent Sukhoi a memorandum asking him to study a new high altitude fighter-interceptor. This request was made by the presence of pressurised machines in the Allied air forces, operating at higher altitudes like the strategic bomber, B-29 and the figh-

ter, Supermarine «Spitfire» HF Mk. VII. But the VVS did not have any of this kind of machine. The memorandum was accompanied by technical specifications: an operational altitude of 46 200 ft with a service ceiling of 49 500 ft, 1 1/2 hours' endurance; a top speed of 418 mph at 39 600 to 46 200 ft; armament was to consist of two 20-mm cannon with 120 rounds each. But Sukhoi did not develop the project further because of the supposedly rapidly approaching end of the war (there are no historical or technological details known concerning the realisation of any project connected to Yakovlev's memo).

(J. Marmain)

YAKOVLEV

The Yak-7L prototype with its strange
laminar tapered airfoil designed
at the TsAGI, photographed in front
of a hangar at the LII
(no doubt on 17 August 1944).

Yak-7L Prototype
(August 1944)

A Yak-7/M-105Pf was equipped with a so-called laminar wing, «knocked together» rather than designed by the TsAGI engineer G.P. Svishchov, probably in August 1944. little is known about this prototype referenced Yak-7L and only one photograph taken from the front, in front of a hangar at the LII NKAP has been

published up until now (it seems to have been dated 17 August 1944). The profile of the wing was almost symmetrical and the thickest part was about 40% of its chord. This profile «plunged» on the leading edge at the root of each wing section. This flying test bed was first tested in a wind tunnel, but no detail has come down to us of its final evaluation, or any dates or figures, except possibly that the tests seem to have made the aircraft gain 9 - 12 1/2 mph in pure speed.

ABRAMOVICH (LAVOCHKIN)

Study for La-5VRDK
(Summer 1944)

After doing a number of studies at the TsAGI on planes equipped with back-up engines among which the VRDK motor compressors, G.N. Abramovich left the institute in the summer of 1944 to head as assistant manager a new establishment based on the defunct RNII: the Scientific Research Establishment for jet propelled planes, or NII-1. His task was to organise it and he remained there until 1948.

Then he was transferred to the TsIAM.

Just before he left the TsAGI, he started a last attempt to improve the performances of a fighter using a VRDK motor compressor with an La-5 airframe as a base. In this case the classic engine chosen (the version of the La-5 chosen was not known) was planned to have a fan fitted. But its first flights revealed that this arrangement was even less auspicious than the preceding projects he had developed (see below) and the first sketches of an La-5VRDK were abandoned. There are no other details or figures.

LAVOCHKIN

La-7UTI «Type 45» or UTI-La-7
(Prototype in Autumn 1944,
production series in Spring 1946)

In autumn 1944, the Lavochkin OKB started a programme for a two-seat La-7UTI (Type 45) in order to make pilot conversion to

La-7 and training easier. The La-7 serial N° 0305 was used as a basis for this programme. A second cockpit with dual controls was installed for the instructor behind the original one used for the pupil and the canopy was lengthened and fitted with two sliding sections, causing the engineers to heighten the frames at the rear of the fuselage. Although no other important structural modification was made, some weight had to be saved: the right-hand canon, the armoured

(J. Marmain)

(H. Léonard)

**An La-7UTI in mid-winter, 1945-46. The oil radiator
is still supplied air by a ventral fairing.**

**An La-7UTI with oil radiator under the nose.
This machine apparently landed in Tunisia where its crew «sought
refuge». Note the position of the antenna mast.**

Technical specifications

Wingspan: 32 ft. 4 in.
Length: 28 ft. 6 in.
Wing Area: 189.321 sq. ft.
Weight Empty: 5 992 lb.

Max. Take-off Weight: 7 418 lb.
Max. Speed: 405 mph. at 9 900 ft.
Service Ceiling:
Range: 359 miles

glazed partition behind the front seat and its armour were removed
as was the mechanism to retract the tail wheel which was then fixed
in order simplify production. The radio antenna was installed obli-
quely on the right side, directly below the rear of the front cockpit.

The development of the La-7UTI was rather long and the trials
were undertaken only in August 1945. They immediately revealed that there was a totally unacceptable defect in a training aircraft: the CG had moved and made the aircraft difficult to control.
The schedule of modifications undertaken to eradicate this defect
was partly unsuccessful and only slightly improved the flight
characteristics. Thus the oil radiator was moved several times
during the production series and ended up under the nose
in April 1946, like the La-5 which re-established the CG in
a better position. The performances were sacrificed on the
«altar of the changes and the MTOW of almost 7 480 lb». In spite of the end of standard La-7 production, the government authorised production of the two seat version to continue. 584 examples were built up to 1,947in spire of the fact that the military
had already decided in August 1945 that it was obsolete because
of its lack of on-board equipment, compared to what was necessary for the adequate training of the future pilots of jet-propelled fighters.

*NB.: In certain period documents, the two-seat version was described as
having two 20-mm cannon under the designation UTI-La-7.*

Profile and partial view showing a standard La-7UTI. The missing elements
are the same as the single-seater La-7. Drawing "A" shows the prototype's oil
radiator and some rare examples from the beginning of the production
series, for the huge majority of the 584 examples built had the oil radiator
placed under the nose.

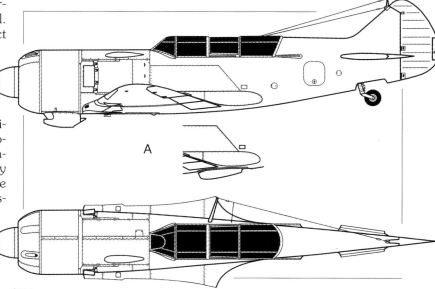

A

MIKOYAN-GUREVICH

I-224 Prototype or MiG-7 («4A» programme) (September 1944)

The Mikoyan-Gurevich I-224 (4A) prototype. The drawing shows the installation of the supercharger exhaust outlet.

The «4A» programme, or I-224, was the fourth to come from the «A» class for the development of high-altitude fighter-interceptors. It resembled the I-222 like a brother, both in its outline and its structure, but its heat exchanger under the nose was bulkier. Its air-conditioned cockpit was pressurised and made of welded aluminium alloy. The sealing of the moving part of the canopy was ensured by inflatable rubber tubes. The cooling air for the power plant was ejected on the upper surfaces of the wings by means of four «chimneys» or «slats». Armament consisted of two synchronised lateral ShVAK cannon on either side of the engine cowling (100 rounds each). The engine was an AM-39B-1 boosted by a Tk-300B supercharger (this engine was sometimes designated as AM-39FB) working from the right exhaust manifold. The propeller was a four blade AV-9L-22B with variable pitch and a diameter of 10 ft 6 in. It was specially designed for high altitudes (width of blades 15 3/4 in).

The prototype I-224 (4A) came out of the factory in September 1944 and made its first flight on 20 October piloted by A.P. Yakimov. The trials were carried out by him and Igor Shelest. The machine behaved well in flight, but was disappointing as far as performance was concerned. Its range was 250 miles shorter than planned in spite of the increase in fuel capacity (94 to 149 gallons (there was no

Technical specifications

Wingspan: 42 ft. 11 in.	(normal), 8 626 lb (overload).
Length: 31 ft. 4 1/2 in.	**Max. Speed:** 358 to 375 mph
Wing Area: 241.521 sq. ft.	depending on the mass.
Weight Empty: 6 831 lb.	**Service Ceiling:** 46 530 ft.
Max. Take-off Weight: 8 316 lb	**Range:** 625 miles

explanation) and its service ceiling was 1 320 feet lower than the previous I-222. The programme finished abruptly with the prototype being lost through an engine fire caused by the supercharger breaking up, forcing Yakomov to bale out. Once again the designation MiG-7 had been reserved in case the machine was mass-produced.

For its cooling and its carburization, the AM-39B-1 on the I-224 was supplied with air from a series of gills on the wing leading edges and by an enormous ventral tunnel. Note the width of the propeller blades.

The I-224 high-altitude fighter was tested in October 1944. It was lost after its supercharger disintegrated in mid-flight. Note the «chimneys» on the wing central section, ensuring that the cooling air flowed out from the engine.

(J. Marmain)

The I-224 prototype was powered by an AM-39B-1 boosted by a TK-300B operating off the right-hand exhaust manifold. The cockpit was pressurised.
(J. Marmain)

LAVOCHKIN

La-7R-1 and La-7R-2 prototypes
(October 1944 and January 1945)

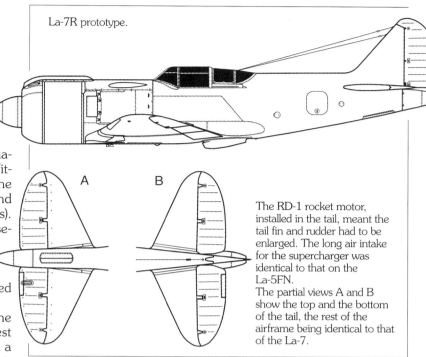

La-7R prototype.

The RD-1 rocket motor, installed in the tail, meant the tail fin and rudder had to be enlarged. The long air intake for the supercharger was identical to that on the La-5FN.
The partial views A and B show the top and the bottom of the tail, the rest of the airframe being identical to that of the La-7.

In March 1944, Lavochkin entrusted his assistant, S.M. Alexeyev with the task of installing a rocket motor in the tail of an La-7 taken from the beginning of the production series. The team set itself up on the premises of Factory N°381 (this section was pompously called «Experimental Factory N°81) and converted an La-7/Ash-82FN in October. Re-designated La-7R (a second example was planned), this prototype was fitted with a Glushko RD-1 rocket motor with electric ignition in the rear part of the fuselage whose structure had been revised and separated from the rest of the airframe (welded stainless steel tubes). The special fuel (374 lb of nitric acid) tank was installed in the fuselage instead of the central tank containing kerosene and the fuel tank (132 lb of kerosene) was placed in the right wing section. The capacity of fuel for the Ash-82FN was reduced from 740 lb to 462 lb. A long «à la La-5FN» intake was placed over the engine cowling.

In order to avoid corrosion, all the elements in contact with the nitric acid were made of stainless steel and aluminium in its purest form. The combustion chamber of the Rd-1 was supplied with a mixture of fuel and comburent by means of pumps driven by a drive shaft linked to a special reduction gear revolving at 26 000 rpm, and linked to the classic ASh-82FN engine. The base of the rudder was cut back to allow the gas exhaust nozzle to protrude from the tail of the fuselage. Combustion was controlled automatically thanks to a push button installed on the throttle of the normal engine.

The La-7R-1 started its programme of factory trials on 27 October 1944. The first two flights were made without igniting the RD-1. After a bit of tuning, they were followed by three ignition trials with a gradual thrust from the RD-1 at 9 900 to 10 560 feet. After 2 to 2 1/2 minutes, excessive vibration was reported on the exhaust nozzle and the pressure in the combustion chambers dropped from 23 to 8 atmospheres. During the 3rd flight with the RD-1 running, there was a 53 mph increase in speed at 9 900 ft. The factory test programme ended on 24 February 1945 then the La-7R-1 underwent a maintenance schedule. The test pilots G.M. Shianov and A.V. Davidov made 15 flights, of which five were with the RD-1 running. The motor was ignited fifty times on the ground and six others in flight, most of them very brief.

This prototype was followed by a second, better developed and designed, designated La-7R-2, converted in January 1945 by the Aleyev team at Experimental Factory N°81. This prototype was designed on the basis of an La-7 coming from production batch

N°51 (metal spars) with new aerodynamic refinements and an RD-1 rocket motor in the tail, following the same technological criteria as the La-7R-1. Its test programme was carried out between 26 January and 27 March 1945 during which the RD-1 was ignited 39 times on the ground and six times during the 19 flights carried out by Shianov and Davidov.

On 1 March 1945, the top speed of the La-7R-2 increased by 50 mph during the brief run of the RD-1 (1 1/2 minutes) but it had to be stopped because of the vibrations generated by the combustion chamber). On 10 March, 59 mph more were registered at 8 910 feet. But it was clear that the ignition system did not work properly during this test period: the RD-1 refused to work fifteen times. On 27 March, the tests were interrupted by the combustion chamber exploding at 9 900 feet. This seriously damaged the tail surfaces. Shianov managed nevertheless to bring the plane down in spite of a very clear loss of stability and the cockpit filing with nitric acid fumes.

The necessary repairs and some slight modifications delayed the resumption of the trials to 14 March 1945. But the Rd-1 refused to ignite between 16 500 and 19 800 feet. As a result, the Factory N°16 (engines) design team decided to replace the electrical ignition system with another system, chemical this time, reference «KhZ». The new RD-1KhZ rocket motor was installed in the tail

(J. Marmain)

(J. Marmain)

Two shots of the La-7R-1 prototype. The exhaust nozzle for the RD-1 rocket motor can be seen clearly on the tail. The airframe was one taken from the beginning of the production series, fitted out with a long air intake on the engine cowling «à la La-5FN».

The La-7R-1 during its trials at the end of 1944. *(J. Marmain)*

of the La-7R-2 on 29 April. The fuel used was of the «B23-75» type (a mixture of petrol and semi-synthetic rubber) mixed with nitric acid. But ignition was not improved for all that and on 12 May the combustion chamber exploded again but on the ground this time.

After laboratory studies which showed that the pressure was too brutal when the valves injected the fuel and the comburent into the combustion chamber, a new RD-1 was delivered. It was equipped with a special new chemical starter associated with an sequential injection system for the fuel/comburent, substantially increasing the spray effect and ensuring a «soft» ignition. The new RD-1KhZ was installed in the tail of the La-7R-2 on 25 July 1945. Until 16 September, the motor was ignited 49 times of which eight were during the 14 test flights. But the RD-1KhZ refused to start 23 times and the combustion chamber and the piping had to be changed four times and twice respectively. In spite of all these problems, the scheduled test programme was completed before being abandoned, and after the La-7R-2 had reached the extraordinary speed of for the time of 496 mph at 20 790 feet.

NB.: Some documents say that the fuel and the fuel for the RD-1 were not separated in the same way. According to them, the kerosene was placed behind the cockpit (20 gallons) and the nitric acid was situated in the wing central section (38 gallons).

Technical specifications

La-7R-1	La-7R-2
W: 32 ft. 4 in. **L:** 28 ft. 5 in.	**W:** 32 ft. 4 in. **L:** 28 ft. 5 in.
Wing Area: 189.321 sq. ft.	**Wing Area:** 189.321 sq. ft.
Weight Empty: 5 964 lb.	**Weight Empty:**
Max. Take-off Weight: 7 700 lb.	**Max. Take-off Weight:** 7 776 lb.
Total Fuel Weight: 1 328 lb.	**Total Fuel Weight:** 1 199 lb.
Max. Speed: 470 mph. at 19 800 ft. (with RD-1)	**Max. Speed:** 410 mph. at sea-level without RD-1KhZ, 473 mph at 9 900 ft., and 496 mph at 20 790 ft with RD-1KhZ.
Service Ceiling: 42 900 ft.	**Service Ceiling: Range:**
Range:	

YAKOVLEV ★

Yak-3/VK-108 Prototypes
(October 1944 and August 1945)

On 1 October 1944, a new prototype based on the Yak-3 appeared. It was built in the experimental workshop of the Yakovlev OKB under the leadership of the engineer, A. Kanukov. It differed from the standard Yak-3 by its VK-108 engine which was purely experimental, driving a ViSH-107LT-5 propeller. Its mounting was slightly different; the oil and glycol radiators were an Op-622 and OP-624 respectively, the latter supplied air through a deepened (by almost two feet) duct inside the structure of the fuselage itself; the exhaust was made up of four rows of six pipes, of which two were on the top of the engine cowling; a faired air intake for carburization was placed under the nose, immediately below the wing roots; the fuel capacity was reduced to 770 lb; oil capacity was raised to 110 lb; the canopy was copied from that of the Yak-3/VK-107 «Double» (the rear portion was lengthened); the insulation and proofing of the fuselage was very carefully done; the ailerons were

Technical specifications

W: 30 ft. 4 in. **L:** 28 ft. 2 1/2 in.	**Max. Speed:** 465 mph. at 20 790 ft.
Wing Area: 159.830 sq. ft.	
Weight Empty:	**Service Ceiling:** 34 320 ft.
Max. Take-off Weight: 6 371 lb.	**Range:**

covered with sheets of Dural; the pilot was protected only by his armoured seat, taken from the Yak-1.

Because there were two rows of exhaust pipes on the engine cowling, armament could only consist of one NS-23 axial canon with 60 rounds. But this was not fitted and fuel capacity was reduced for the prototype's factory trials. It was referenced Yak-3/VK-108. They took place on the ground from 7 October 1944, and then the pilot V.L. Rastorgonov took it up for the first time on 19 December. In spite of his enthusiasm for the performances (top speed of 465 mph), the VK-108 had exactly the same defects as the VK-107: excessive vibrations and overheating; giving off clouds of smoke and swerving; frequent cut-outs; oil leaks, etc. On 21 December 1944, the engine had to be changed and the

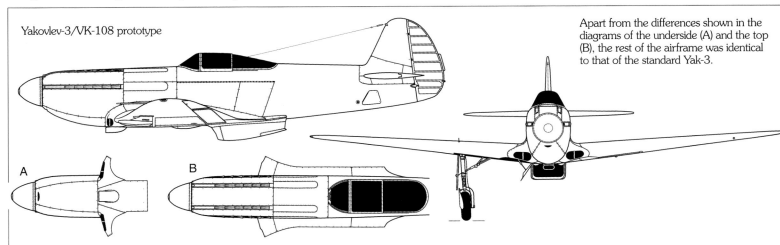

Yakovlev-3/VK-108 prototype

A B

Apart from the differences shown in the diagrams of the underside (A) and the top (B), the rest of the airframe was identical to that of the standard Yak-3.

One of the two Yak-3/VK-108 prototypes during its trials. There were four rows of exhaust pipes, of which two were on the engine cowling. Each row was prolonged by a highly-heat resistant metal plate. Note the extra air intake under the cowling and the depth of the ventral duct. In spite of its breath-taking performances, the VK-108 caused too many problems for the authorities to envisage any production series.
(J. Marmain)

trials only resumed on 8 March 1945. But at the end of that day's flight, the programme was stopped because the VK-108 was totally unreliable.

Between 1 August and 1 November 1945, the engineer, V.G. Grigorev from Yakovlev's OKB fitted out another Yak-3 with a VK-108 engine. This new prototype was armed with B-20S cannon under the engine cowling with 120 rounds each. But this failure was just as resounding as the first. As a result the programme was totally buried with its engine in spite of a directive being distributed by the Ministry of Aircraft Production (MAPn ex NKAP) dated 28 May 1946, asking for the production of three new Yak-3/VK-108 prototypes by Factory N°31, to be delivered on 1 September, 1 October and 1 November. But the request came to nothing.

LAVOCHKIN

La-7/Ash-83 (ex La-120 N°2) Prototype (December 1944)

At the end of 1944, the «120 N°2» prototype was equipped with an Ash-83 engine rated at 1 900 bhp (double row 14 cylinder air-cooled) and a laminar profile wing. The two NS-23 cannon which it had previously tested were still used and the airframe comprised a larger percentage of metal elements. It was finished in December 1944 and was tested until September 1945 It flew at 453 mph at 24 420 feet, but its programme was not developed because the military autho-

Technical specifications	
W: 32 ft. 4 in. **L:** 28 ft. 7 in.	**Max. Take-off Weight:** 6 908 lb.
Wing Area: 189.321 sq. ft.	**Max. Speed:** 453 mph. at 24 420 ft.
Weight Empty: 5 548 lb.	**S C:** 38 280 ft. **Range:** 500 miles

rities did not think a plane of this sort was needed because of the end of the war, including against the Japanese, particular bearing in mind the new generation of jet-powered combat planes. In some documents, this prototype was designated La-7/Ash-83.

YAKOVLEV

Yak-3RD (or Yak-3/RD-1) Prototype (December 1944)

As with the Lavochkin and Sukhoi OKBs, the Yakovlev OKB responded in 1944 to the government's demands for a fighter with mixed power units by designing the experimental prototype Yak-3RD (or Yak-3/RD-1). Entrusted with the project, the engineer, B.S. Motorin, chose Yak-3 serial N°18-20 in December, modified its tail and installed a Glushko RD-1 (serial number 009) rocket motor onto a special faired, easily removable mounting, incorporated into the rear of the machine. This «accelerator» gave a static thrust of 660 lb at 21 450 ft and burnt a mixture of kerosene (fuel) and nitric acid (comburent). In order to find the necessary space for the RD-1 and its exhaust nozzle, Motorin cut the lower part of the fin, compensa-

Technical specifications	
W: 30 ft. 4 in. **L:** 28 ft.	**Max. Take-off Weight:** 6 556 lb.
Wing Area: 159.830 sq. ft.	**Max. Speed:** 488 mph. at 25 740 ft
Weight Empty: 5 240 lb.	with the RD-1.

ted the loss of surface are by increasing its chord and covered the tail with metal heat-resistant panels. The elevators were scalloped at the roots and were covered with Dural, as were the moving surfaces. The VK-105PF engine was equipped with a linkage system to the nitric acid pump. The fuel capacity was 572 lb (four wing tanks plus 26 lb held in the distribution tank) of which 110 lb were intended for mixing with the 440 lb of comburent (a special steel tank was fitted in the fuselage). The oil and glycol radiators were placed in the same ventral tunnel and the left gill in the wing root supplied

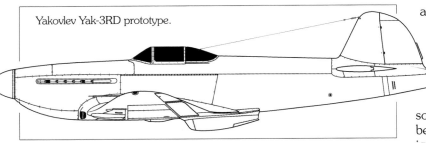

Yakovlev Yak-3RD prototype.

(G. Gorokhoff)

The Yak-3RD prototype (or Yak-3/RD-1) painted entirely cherry-red. Its tail fin had been enlarged because the rudder was shortened at its base. The RD-1 rocket motor was installed in the tail. A fairing protected it when it was not in use.
The machine was lost on 15 August 1945, killing its famous pilot, V.L. Rastoguyev. The inquest was unable to determine the causes of the accident and the programme was immediately stopped.

air to the carburization and the supercharger for the VK-105PF-2 (the other was stopped). Armament was reduced to a single axial NS-23 canon with 60 rounds. Igniting the RD-1 was done electrically and the volume of fuel and comburent enabled it to operate for three minutes at full speed.

The factory trials took place from 22 December 1944 at the hands of V.L. Rastorguyev. The RD-1 was ignited forty or so times, of which eight were during eight of the 21 flights made between the 22 January and 14 May. During the trials, the electric ignition system turned out to be unreliable and caused a number of stoppages and incidents. Glushko even designed a chemical ignition system (the reference «KhZ» was added to the RD-1's designation). One model (serial N°018) was installed in the tail of the Yak-3RD to continue the trials until 14 May. On that day the RD-1KhZ exploded in the air, very seriously damaging the prototype's tail. Beforehand, Rastorguyev had managed to reach 488 mph at 25 740 ft, 113 mph more than a standard Yak-3 at the same height.

The Yak-3 RD was repaired, the rocket motor was replaced, the airframe was inspected from top to bottom and the defects which were found were corrected. The trial flights resumed on 14 August 1945 because the prototype had to take part in the annual VVS Air Show four days later. On the 15th, after The RD-1KhZ ignited perfectly, the power and pressure dropped suddenly after fifteen seconds and the fuel sprayed into the cockpit, Rastorguyev cut the RD-1KhZ and returned to make an emergency landing at Moscow Central. The engineers found that one of the pipes had burst under pressure from the fuel. The following day, Rastroguyev took the Yak-3RD up again with the rocket motor working. Then he put it out and reached a height of 8 250 ft, levelled out then, watched by everybody, dived to the ground and crashed without anybody understanding why. Rastorguyev was killed and the exact causes of the accident were never discovered. The death of this celebrated pilot put an end to the Yak-3RD programme. Apparently Yakovlev forbade any more experiments of this type with any of his aircraft.

Close-up of the RD-1KhZ rocket motor installed in the tail of the Yak-3RD prototype (the protective fairing has been removed for the trials).
(J. Marmain)

KOROLEV (LAVOCHKIN)

La-5VI studies
(December 1944)

At the end of December (or June according to different sources), S.P. Kororlev signed a document which gave an account of two years of research, experiments and projects mounting Glushko RD-1 and RD-3 rocket motors using combustible liquids on standard combat planes. The document included «Scheme IV» together with a rather crude artist's view of a production series La-5 in flight, rechristened La-5VI for the occasion, powered by a normal engine and three RD-1 rocket motors with 660 lb thrust.

According to the study, installing three RD-1s aboard the La-5VI only caused minor structural modifications. The wing area was raised to 263.786 square feet for a wingspan of 36 ft 11 1/2 in (compared with 189.644 sq ft and 32 ft 4 in), the wing profile retained was a NACA 230, the planned armament comprised four heavy 12.7-mm machine guns and only the back of the pilot's seat was armoured. It was powered by an M-82FNV boosted by two TK-3 superchargers for the high altitudes (Korolev started his studies at the time when the M-82FNV made its appearance (it was mass-produced under the designation M-82FN). It drove a 10 ft 6 in-diameter 3SMV-14 three-bla-

de variable-pitch propeller (the study and the estimates were made with this propeller) or a four-blade 4F-1 propeller of the same size.

The machine was 29 ft 2 in long (28 ft 7 in on the standard La-5) because of the power plant being repositioned a few inches further forward and the RD-1 being installed in the tail of the fuselage.

The other two were fitted in faired nacelles under the wings. Fuel supply for the two systems depended on the type and the number of rocket-motors which were planned (Korolev had also studied the possibility of installing a single Rd-1 or a 1 980-lb thrust RD-3 in the tail of an La-5VI). In this case, the capacity of the two tanks of kerosene was reduced to 440 lb (in the fuselage and central wing section) in order to add a ton of nitric acid in the wing tanks or faired underwing tanks without increasing the mass of the aircraft too much. This last solution seemed to have been the one used by Korolev in his study since it meant better weight distribution and allowed more room for fuel in the production machines. He noted that the increase in frontal resistance of the plane was increased only slightly thanks to the «excellent streamlining of the engine nacelles and the tanks, both being well fitted into the wing» and that the speed reduction in level flight at all altitudes was only 3% in absolute terms, i.e. a loss of 9 to 15 mph compared with normal standards. The M-82FNV/2TK-3 engine drove a turbo-pump which brought the nitric acid/kerosene mixture to the combustion chambers of the three RD-1s. The unloaded weight of the La-5VI with a full load of kerosene and oil, but without the rocket-motor parts, turbo-pump, nitric acid, etc., was estimated at 7 040 lb.

Korolev's study comprised several plans for carrying nitric acid quantities ranging from 1 364 lb to 2 640 lb. The La-5VI was meant to fly at all the different altitude levels - high (hence the presence of the two TK-3s), medium and low. The use of the RD-1s (or the RD-3) was temporary. The normal engine was used for taking off, for normal flying, and for landing. The rocket motors were only used for the combat phases or when needed to increase speed and power to meet all dangers. According to these new flight data, Korolev noted that with the RD-1s or the RD-3, «the La-5VI (or any other fighter similarly equipped) outclassed all the other propeller driven planes, opening up wide,

new tactical applications at altitudes». These altitudes increased by between 4 620 feet 5 280 feet and the maximum speeds calculated for level flight were in the region of 365 mph at sea-level with the three RD-1s, 427 mph with the FD-3, and 512 mph (RD-1) and 625 mph (RD-3) at 46 200 feet. On the other hand the prototype's speed dropped by about 37 mph on average when the rocket-motors were not used. The height of 36 300 ft could be reached in five minutes (service ceiling was at 59 070 feet).

Presented on 19 December 1944, Korolev's study was not used in any serious way. The La-5VI remained at the project stage because the end of the WWII was imminent; a new class of jet fighters which were much more promising was beginning to appear and there were new objectives for developing rockets in the USSR. Work on this project was not continued after the war.

LAVOCHKIN

La-7L Prototype
(End of 1944)

Towards the end of 1944, an La-7 was equipped with a laminar section wing. Re-designated La-7L, it was a test bench for use only in the T-101 wind tunnel at the TsAGI until 2 February 1945 in the context of the La-9 programme which was planned with the same wings. No other details.

SUKHOI

Su67R (ex-Su-7) Prototype
(End of 1944)

In 1944, Sukhoi brought his Su-7/M-82FN up to date by adding a Glushko RD-1 electrically-ignited liquid-fuelled (nitric acid and kerosene) rocket motor giving 660-lb thrust installed in the tail. The metal skin on the sides was prolonged. Re-designated Su-7R, the prototype tested the rocket motor eighteen times on the ground from 31 January to 10 February 1945. The 66 flight tests which followed (pilot G. Komarov) were constantly interrupted or put off because the rocket motor was not reliable and getting it operational caused a lot of problems. In the summer, the RD-1 was replaced by an RD-1KhZ with chemical ignition. With this, the trials took place from 28 August till 19 December 1945. But Komarov noted only a slight increase in speed (46 to 56 mph depending on the trials) when the RD-1KhZ was operational, a parameter which was considered as negligible in relation to the technology used, particularly when the rocket motor was only used for periods of a little more than four minutes. Clearly the Glushko' family of «RDs» was not ready and they were not mass- produced, particularly as the new generation of jet engines seemed much more promising. The programme was stopped at the end of 1945.

The Su-7R prototype during its trials in the summer of 1945. It was equipped with an RD-1KhZ rocket motor, covered here by its protective fairing. The end of the metal plate on the fuselage side has become elliptical. The performances were thought to be disappointing and the programme was abandoned at the end of December 1945.
(H. Léonard)

Technical specifications	
Wingspan: 44 ft. 6 in.	without Rd-1. 353 mph at 7 590 ft with
Length:	RD-1 (Sukhoi's original estimate:
Wing Area: 279.838 sq. ft.	440 mph at 39 600 ft.)
Weight Empty: 7 071 lb.	**Service Ceiling:** 42 075 ft.*
Max. Take-off Weight: 9 592 lb.	**Range:** 775 miles*
Max. Speed: 320 mph at 18 480 ft	*estimates

(H. Léonard)

The Su-7R with its RD-1 rocket motor, «bare» in the tail of the aircraft, photographed in January or February 1945 during its first set of trials. A long metal plate has been fixed on the fuselage skin up to directly under the end of the rear decking.

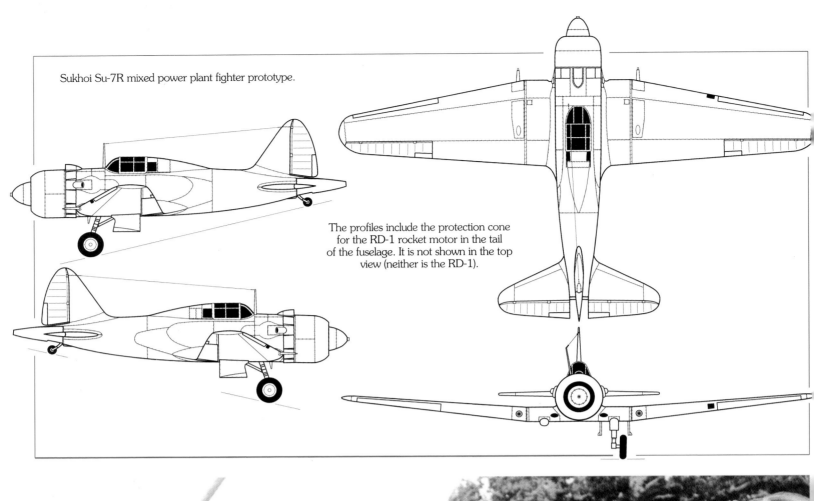

Sukhoi Su-7R mixed power plant fighter prototype.

The profiles include the protection cone for the RD-1 rocket motor in the tail of the fuselage. It is not shown in the top view (neither is the RD-1).

1942: a group of pilots poses in front of one of the best fighters of the time: the Yak-1. It was faster than the Spitfire and well-armed, with its 20-mm canon in the nose. The pilots wore their leatherjackets even when flying in summer. *(RR)*

1945

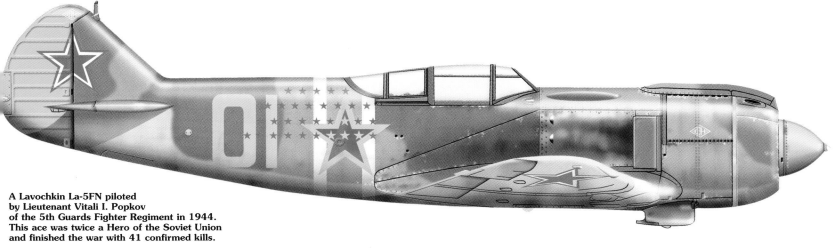

A Lavochkin La-5FN piloted
by Lieutenant Vitali I. Popkov
of the 5th Guards Fighter Regiment in 1944.
This ace was twice a Hero of the Soviet Union
and finished the war with 41 confirmed kills.

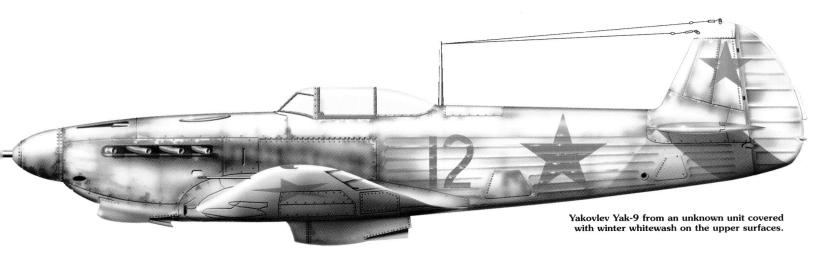

Yakovlev Yak-9 from an unknown unit covered
with winter whitewash on the upper surfaces.

GLOSSARY

LAVOCHKIN

La-7 Project with RD-2M-3V rocket. (or La-7/RD-2M-3V) (Beginning of 1945)

At the beginning of 1945 within the framework of the experimental programme for stand-by engines, A.I. Shakhurin asked Lavochkin to prepare an La-7 fighter airframe to receive an RD-2M-3V rocket motor with two tons thrust, designed by

Dushkin and Bibikov. The plan was to have the La-7/RD-2M-3V ready for trials on 25 July 1945.

But this project was not carried out because the RD-2M-3V was far from being ready. It was only bench-tested in 1947-48 at a time when the authorities had already decided to rely thenceforth on jet engines only to power the VVS's combat aircraft.

No figures or other details.

YAKOVLEV

Yak-3T/VK-105PF-2 Prototype (or Yak-3T-37 and Yak-3K/T-45) (January 1945)

On 29 December 1944, GKO issued a directive asking for the firepower of the Yak-3 to be increased. The Yakovlev OKB answered in January by extrapolating an anti-tank version from airframe serial N°36-20, designated Yak-3T/VK-105PF-2. The new version was armed with an N-37 axial canon with 25 rounds (its barrel was shorter by 6 inches than that of the NS-37 and it was lighter) and two B-20S cannon under the engine cowling with 100 rounds each, for which there long bumps just in front of the windshield. The muzzle brake of the N-37 absorbed 75% of the recoil and stuck out nearly 16 inches beyond the tip of the propeller spinner. The cockpit was moved back by 16 inches, the volume of fuel was reduced to 80 gallons (355 litres), the OP-554 glycol radiator was replaced by an OP-662 which was more efficient, the system of filing the tanks by means of neutral gases was removed and a host of minor alterations changed the movement of the flaps, the leading edges of the wings and the tail (perfectly polished), the wheel well doors, the compressed air bottles, the rear part of the canopy (extended), etc. the VICh-105L-28 propeller was experimental and the take-off weight rose to 6 063 lb.

The prototype, sometimes referenced as Yak-3T-37, was delivered to the LIS on 9 January 1945 where three flights were made between the 10th and the 30th. It was transferred to the NII VVS on the 31st and its State tests were carried out between the 17 and 27 April by L.M. Kuvshinov. During the 44 flights, the prototype did not exceed 393 mph at 13 350 ft and climbed less quickly than a standard Yak-3. However its flying qualities and its behaviour had hardly changed considering its mass and its reduced forward visibility due to the cockpit being moved further back. Its armament

Technical specifications

Wingspan: 30 ft. 4 in.
Length: 28 ft.
Wing Area: 159.830 sq. ft.
Weight Empty: 4 686 lb.

Max. Take-off Weight: 6 063 lb.
Max. Speed: 393 mph at 13 530 ft.
Service Ceiling: 34 320 ft.
Range: 372 miles.

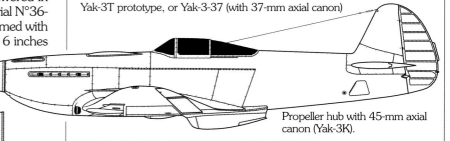

Yak-3T prototype, or Yak-3-37 (with 37-mm axial canon)

Propeller hub with 45-mm axial canon (Yak-3K).

was effective against airborne and ground targets, recoil being well absorbed by the airframe and enabling 4 to 5 rounds salvoes to be fired with the N-37 canon. But the evaluations also revealed a host of defects: increased oil consumption limiting flights to 15 minutes, with a drop in the oil pressure and leaks spraying onto the windshield; the temperature limits for the oil and glycol were exceeded; the B-20S cannon were not attached firmly enough; there was no protection for the pilot's head and shoulders; the plane's range was too short and the system for filling the tanks with inert gases was omitted; the wheel well doors were deformed (this had already been noticed on the standard Yak-3s); the radio range was limited; etc.

The plane was taken back by the Yakovlev OKB where from 12 to 24 May, it was subjected a whole series of modifications: the armament chassis was reinforced; the engine cowling was refined; the skin was finished better; the undercarriage wells were rectified; the airframe was sealed better; the air intakes for the power plant were revised (oil radiator, OP-554U); the Yak-9U/VK-107A canopy was adopted; the ailerons were perfected; a VICH-105SV-01 propeller replaced the previous one and its boss was modified, etc. Up till 2 July M.I. Ivanov carried out twelve flights: they showed that the oil and glycol temperatures were still too high which caused the pilot to reduce the rated engine speed to 2 500 rpm (instead of 2 700), that the engine vibrated, gave off smoke and caused the plane to swerve, the spark plugs burned out and that the fuel was subjected to large variations in pressure. Because of all this and because of the end of the war in Europe, the Yak-3T was not put into production and the programme stopped there.

The only Yak-3T/M-105PF-2, or Yak-7-37 prototype with its 37-mm canon sticking out of the propeller boss. The trials were not crowned with success and the programme was abandoned in the summer of 1945. (G. Gorokhoff)

NB: A source of Polish origin suggests (with a profile drawing as evidence) that this prototype was tried out with a heavy 45-mm axial canon (T-45, NS-45 or N-45) and that in that weapon configuration it would have had the designation Yak-3K (or Yak-3K/T-45). But nothing written up till now by the Russian specialists in the matter mentions anything about this designation, or even about trials for a canon of that type aboard this prototype.

Yak-9

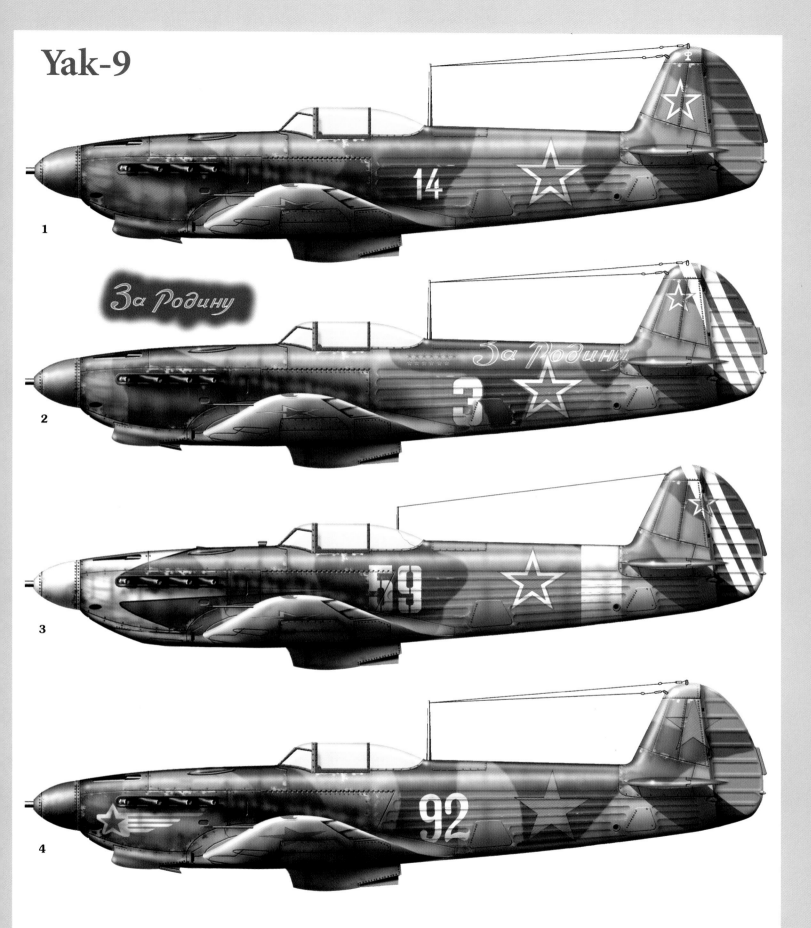

За Родину

1. Yakovlev Yak-9 piloted by Lieutenant Marcel Lefèvre, commanding the "*Normandie-Niemen*" Regiment. The letter U painted on the top of the tail meant "*Frantzus*" (French).

2. Yakovlev Yak-9 belonging to Lieutenant Nikolai Denshik, second-in-command of the 1st Squadron of the "Alexander Nevski" Regiment, 4th Guards Fighter Division (GvIAD), Baltic Front, winter 1943-44. The slogan "for the Motherland" has been painted behind the pilot's tally on the rear of the fuselage.

3. Yakovlev Yak-9 from the 4th Squadron of the "Order of Suvarov" Regiment, 4th Fighter Division of the Guard, Germany 1946. The white fuselage stripe was a special mark used during exercises in 1946.

4. Yakovlev Yak-9T from the 3rd Fighter Air Corps, end of 1944.

The Yak-9UT prototype (serial N°40166022) during its operational evaluations in the summer of 1945. It was equipped with a 37-mm axial canon and gave rise to a production series of the model. *(J. Marmain)*

YAKOVLEV ★

Yak-9UT/VK-107A
(February 1945)

At the beginning of 1945, the Yakovlev OKB took up the idea again of a standard armament frame for all its fighters. In February, in answer to the directive from the GKO date 29 December 1944, the Yak-9U/VK-107A serial N° 39-083 from Factory N° 166 was taken and transformed into a Yak 9U/VK-107A (with a VICh-107LO propeller). It was fitted with an N-37 axial canon and two B-20S cannon under the engine cowling. These weapons were lighter and less massive than the previous ones. The plan developed by the OKB included replacing the N-37 canon with a B-20M, an NS-23 or and NS-45. In the latter case, the B-20S canon on the right had to be removed. All of them could be installed without major modifications to the airframe but, in theory, it should be done only in the factory. However, «*there must be a certain flexibility in allowing this to be carried out in the units*». For each armament scheme there were different parameters concerning take-off weight, centring and performances. But as a general rule, flight characteristics for the Yak-9UT did not differ from those of the Yak-9U.

State trials were done between 8 and 29 March 1945 at the hands of A.A. Manucharov and the operational evaluations for the model took place from 17 March to 9 July with the NII VVS. The reports show that ground and flight characteristics were similar to those of the Yak-9U/VK-107A and its performances very close. But although the controls were hard, the oil and glycol temperature levels were within acceptable limits. Gunnery tests were highly appreciated, both with the N-37 canon and the NS-45, against both airborne and ground targets. At all altitudes and in all flying conditions, the Yak-9UT's armament was more effective than that of the Yak-9T and Yak-9K because the recoil of the N-37 was much lighter and better absorbed by

A Yak-9UT with 37-mm axial canon. Its windshield had flat glass. *(J. Marmain)*

Yak-9UT serial N° 40166074 undergoing its firing tests with a 57-mm axial canon whose tube does not stick out beyond the propeller boss. *(J. Marmain)*

Yak-9UT serial N°40166074 equipped with a 37-mm canon without muzzle brake. *(J. Marmain)*

Technical specifications

Wingspan: 32 ft. 2 in.
Length: 28 ft. 2 1/2 in.
Wing Area: 184.582 sq. ft.
Weight Empty: 5 471 lb.

Max. Take-off Weight: 7 172 lb.
Max. Speed: 419 mph at 16 170 ft.
Service Ceiling: 35 310 ft.
Range: 431 miles.

the airframe. A 4- or 5-round salvo affected target aiming only very slightly.

After the trials at the NII VVS, the Yak-9UT/VK-107A was warmly recommended for mass-production, the reason given being that with that armament «the model was needed by the VVS». In fact, production had already started in February and March 1945; 282 examples were built. However, the armament which was fitted only comprised one NS-23 (an NS-37, depending on the sources) instead of the N-37, plus the two B-20S cannon under the engine cowling. A single Yak-9UT-equipped unit took part in the final phase of the war against Germany and in 19 dogfights, its pilots managed to shoot down 27 Fw 190s and one Bf-109G-6 for the loss of only two Yak-9UTs.

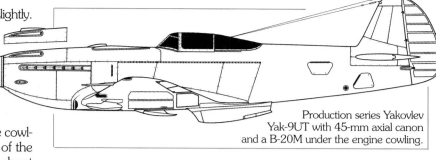

Production series Yakovlev Yak-9UT with 45-mm axial canon and a B-20M under the engine cowling.

The partial view shows the front upper part of the prototype's engine cowling with an extra intake.

YAKOVLEV

Yak6-PD/VK-105PD, then Yak-3PD/VK-105PV aka Yak-3PV
(January and June 1945)

At the end of January 1945, the Yakovlev OKB presented a new high-altitude fighter-interceptor powered by a VK-105PD engine with an E-100 Dollejal two-stage supercharger: the Yak-3PD/VK-105PD designed according to a project date April 1944. Its top speed at 35 640 ft and with a take-off weight of 5 830 lb, was 447 mph. In January 1945 the Yak-3 serial N° 36-20 was taken and fitted with the new engine and underwent a series of modifications concerning: increasing the wing area by 5.38 sq. ft., and its wingspan by 2 ft; installing a 10 foot diameter experimental VICh-105-2 propeller, optimised for high altitudes; the addition of a faired air intake in front of the ventral duct; mounting an NS-23 axial canon with 60 shells. The engine supplied by Factory N°466 was inspected by the LII specialists who had a water/methanol injection system installed and a scoop fitted on the top of the engine cowling, just behind the propeller to improve the power plant's cooling. With a take-off weight of 5 755 lb, the prototype made

Technical specifications

Wingspan: 32 ft. 4 in.
Length: 28 ft
Wing Area: 165.212 sq. ft.
Weight Empty: 4 776 lb.
Max. Take-off Weight: 5 755 lb (5 843 lb **).
Range: 437 miles*.

Max. Speed: 432 mph at 35 640 ft (36 300**).
Service Ceiling: 37 950 ft (43 890 ft**).
* Estimates
** Figures given in brackets refer to the prototype with VK-105PV engine

The prototype was delivered to the LII NKAP where it was refitted with a VK-105PV engine with the same Dollejal E-100 supercharger (Yak-3PV/VK-105PV). The tests were carried out by I.I. Shunenko in June and July 1945 mainly to determine the performance at high altitude and the service ceiling.

At the suggestion of the pilot, the plane was equipped with a system to expel part of the compressor airflow directly into the atmosphere so that it would perform better and hope to reach the 42 900 ft without changing the engine. The prototype carried 594 lb of fuel, 66 lb of oil and 55 lb of water-methanol mixture. Insulation and sealing of the wing and tail bulkheads was improved. On 25 June, Shunenko reached 443 mph at 36 300 ft and on 6 July, he reached a height of 43 890 ft after undergoing special training for climbing so high - the prototype was not pressurised - and Shunenko only had an oxygen mask. Stability was good, even in tight manoeuvring at more than 36 300 ft.

This success did not however give rise to series production of the model (sometimes designated Yak-3PV by the rarer sources) but the lessons learnt were noted in a report which was submitted to the authorities in March 1947, particularly concerning the cooling system for the power plant.

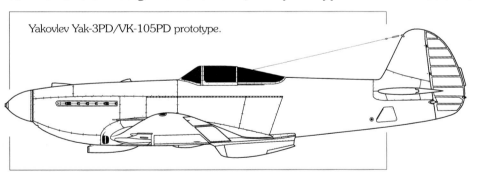

Yakovlev Yak-3PD/VK-105PD prototype.

18 trial flights at the hands of S.N. Anokhin from 23 February to 3 May 1945, during which the engine was changed because the oil leaked continually and the supercharger broke.

The maximum ceiling reached was only 37 650 ft where the OKB had forecast 42 900 ft and the top speed recorded was only 432 mph instead of the calculated 446 mph. The engine's shortcomings and the impossibility of determining the exact causes of its rather uncertain performance (particularly the supercharger) caused the programme to be stopped on 14 May 1945.

The Yak-3PD/VK-105PD during its factory trials. Note the air intake under the engine cowling. (J. Marmain)

YAKOVLEV

Yak-3P/VK-105PF-2 (March 1945)

Technical specifications

Wingspan: 30 ft. 4 in.	**Max. Take-off Weight:** 5 957 lb.
Length: 28 ft.	**Max. Speed:** 404 mph at 12 870 ft.
Wing Area: 159.830 sq. ft.	**Service Ceiling:** 33 165 ft.
Weight Empty: 4 730 lb.	**Range:** 381 miles

On 29 December 1944 following the certification of the B-20 canon on the preceding 10 October, the GKO asked Yakovlev to design two Yak-3s armed with three of these cannon, which were lighter than the earlier ChVAK and present them in January 1945 so that series production could start in February. In itself modifying the Yak-3 airframe to take an axial B-20M (120 rounds) and two B-20S under the engine cowling (130 rounds each) all loaded and fired by a pneumatic system was not complicated. Only a few minor modifications had to be made: reinforcing the structure of the central section of the wing; reviewing the undercarriage doors; making the warning lights for the fuel gauges more visible and the installation of an RSI-6M radio.

The Yak-3P prototype with its three 20-mm cannon during its State trials in the spring of 1945. The production series examples were only equipped with this armament once production had got under way, from 1 August 1945. *(J. Marmain)*

The new model was designated Yak-3P (P for canon) and the first machine made its State trials at the NII VVS from 23 March to 9 April flown by V.G. Ivanov. The 37 flights carried out with a take-off weight of 5 957 lb showed that the machine was an excellent gun platform, that the guns fired perfectly, that they did not alter the machine's performance in any way and that the recoil was well absorbed by the airframe. On the other hand, the attachments of the weapons broke easily; the undercarriage doors did not close properly and deformed the nearby skin; and the brakes were to be used with care. In spite of all this, the Yak-3P was produced by Factories N° 292 and 31 from April 1945

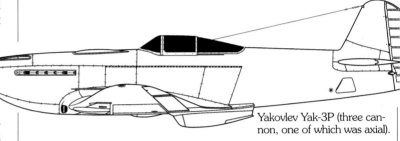

Yakovlev Yak-3P (three cannon, one of which was axial).

YAKOVLEV

Yak-3/VK-107A
(Factory N° 31) (April 1945)
(made entirely of metal)

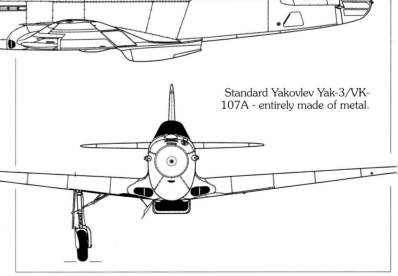

Standard Yakovlev Yak-3/VK-107A - entirely made of metal.

On 29 December 1944, the GKO issued a directive asking for the development of the Yak-3 with VK-107A engine to be continued in spite of the failure of the first two prototypes which had been tested in the previous May. Because of this, the following spring, the NKAP asked Factory N° 31 at Tbilissi to get to work, relying on the fact that the standard Yak-3s which were being produced were better from the point of view of quality than those built by factory N°292. But the latter factory was not forgotten because a short while later it was also included in this programme (see below).

To do this, Factory N° 31 kept airframe Yak-3 serial N°70-03, equipped it with the latest VK-107A engine driving a VICh-107LO propeller and carried out the following modifications: moving the cockpit 16 inches further to the rear; replacing the stressed skin on the rear portion of the fuselage with Dural panels; replacing the canvas on the tail moving surfaces with «Elektron» (a magnesium alloy); installing an entirely metal wing; lightening all the linkages and the master cylinder for all the controls; recasting the aileron articulations; fitting a «boosted» pump and reducing the volume of the oil tank to 70 lb (instead of 88); modifying the compression rate of the supercharger (1 080 mm Hg); changing the oil radiator with a larger frontal surface (OP-662 then OP-700); reducing the fuel capacity from 115 to 104 gallons (770 lb), then to 94 gallons

Technical specifications

Wingspan: 30 ft. 4 in.	**Max. Take-off Weight:** 6 457 lb.
Length: 28 ft. 2 in.	**Max. Speed:** 441 mph at 19 470 ft.
Wing Area: 159.830 sq. ft.	**Service Ceiling:** 36 465 ft.
Weight Empty: 5 152 lb.	**Range:** 485 miles

A VK-107A-powered Yak-3 entirely made of metal by Factory N°31 at Tbilissi. The machine was no doubt used for various tests, which explains its «metal» colour scheme and the red paint.

(704 lb) and suppression of the distribution tank. Moreover, armament consisted of a B-20M axial canon and a B-20S (120 rounds) housed under the left part of the engine cowling. All these modifications reduced the take-off weight very slightly to 6 457 lb.

The «entirely metal» prototype which did not have any specific designation but which was simply referenced as Yak-3/VK-107A, made 13 test flights from 14 April to 10 May 1945 flown by M.I. Ivanov. The recorded speeds were lower than those of the prototypes tested after May 1944 because of the poor quality of the general finish due to a lack of experience in the design of «entirely metal» planes (riveting in particular was badly thought out) and the general performances did not correspond to what the GKO wanted in December 1944. Moreover, the usual defects in the Klimov engines (oil leaks, overheating) had not disappeared, the well doors did not close properly and got out of shape, but braking was improved. The motor did not vibrate too much, there were no problems diving and the propeller did not tend to race; handling was still excellent, the controls were «tame» and the plane's manœuvrability did not disappoint anyone. Finally the new pump maintained a good pressure level during climbs and the supercharger worked well. On the other hand, the elimination of the distribution tank required a lot of attention from the pilot and reduced the reliability of the fuel supply to the engine. Armament, in spite of its being less effective compared with that of the standard Yak-3 and Yak-9U/VK-107As functioned well but the canon attachment was still fragile. Radio was satisfactory (RSI-3MI instead of RSI-3 radios with a range of 35 to 45 miles with another aircraft).

On 11 May 1945, the prototype was presented to the NII VVS for its State trials which were carried out from 35 May to 9 June by Antipov and a few other famous pilots, among whom Proshakov and Kochekov; they noted that although at the time the overall performances corresponded to the VVS requirements, the major defects concerning the power plant were still present. The NII VVS turning down the model did not prevent 40 aircraft from being produced by factory N°31 in 1945, followed by eight others the next year so that they could be evaluated and the faults corrected. But at the end of 1946, all work was halted, the authorities having decided that the Yak-9U corresponded better to the use of VK-107A engine.

An entirely metal Yak-3 used by the LII as a flying test bed. It was equipped with a camera fixed on the windshield frame.

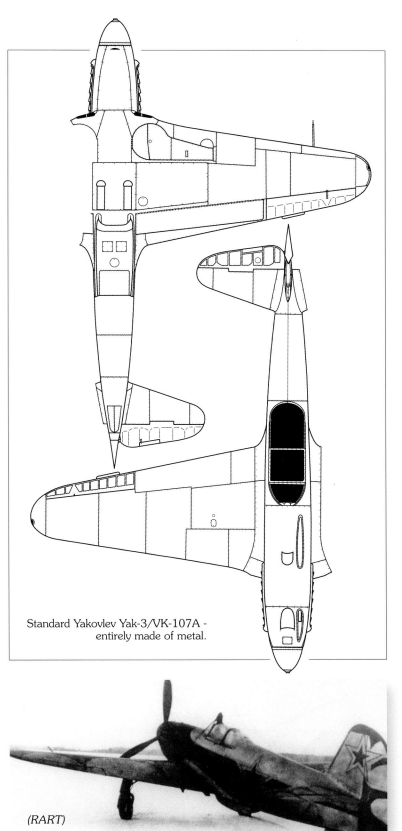

Standard Yakovlev Yak-3/VK-107A - entirely made of metal.

(RART)

YAKOVLEV ★

Technical specifications		
Wingspan: 31 ft.		**Max. Speed:** 426 mph.
Length: 26 ft. 11 in.		at 19 800 ft.
Wing Area:		**Service Ceiling:** 37 125 ft.
184.585 sq. ft.		**Range:** 486 miles
Weight Empty: 5,000lb.		**Max. Take-off Weight:** 6 142 lb.

Yak-3U/ACh-82FN Prototype (April 1945)

At the end of the war, the double-row Shvetsov Ach-82FN radial engine was a well proven model very widely used by the Lavochkin La-5 and La-7. In response to a GKO directive, the Yakovlev OKB tried once again to adapt this big power plant on to a Yak-3 airframe at Novosibirsk from 20 January (the plane was finished on 23 April) with the double aim of developing a powerful version with another engine rather than the very troublesome VK-107A and of putting a fighter which was far better than all the models powered by V-engines into service. With this in mind, the Yak-3 airframe had to be lightened and modified considerably. Apart from the increase in frame size for the whole of the front part of the fuselage in order to install a new mounting for the ASh-82FN, the fairing, exhaust system and the oil radiator, the other modifications were: the wing was positioned 8 1/2 inches further forward with a 6-in increase in the wingspan and a return to a wing area of 184.585 sq. ft.; replacing the metal tanks with others made of flexible materials; a redesigned shape for the fuselage central section with the cockpit raised by 2 1/2 inches to give a better field of vision in all directions; replacing the plywood skin of the fuselage and fabric of the ailerons with Dural; building metal tails surfaces; redesigning the controls and linkage systems; reinforcing the undercarriage doors; installing two B-20S cannon under the upper part of the engine cowling with 120 rounds each.

These changes reduced the mass of the aircraft by some 422 lb and 1 040 lb respectively compared with the Yak-3/V-107A and the La-7/Ash-82FN. The lighter weight thus obtained and the radical modification of the airframe's streamlining should have enabled the plane to reach 440 mph at 20 130 ft thanks to the 1 850 bhp given by the ASh-82FN. During the 19 test flights from 29 April to 9 June 1945 by Fiodrovi, the prototype, reference Yak-3U/ACh-82FN, only managed however to reach 426 mph at 19 800 feet but its rate of climb was excellent. The main defect was the very clear tendency to nose-over when landing caused by the position of the wing which was now further forward. The aircraft returned to the workshop where the wing was replaced by an entirely metal one. Its elevators were redesigned, its undercarriage legs were lengthened by 2 1/2 inches and their inclination increased; the sealing of the fuselage was also improved again and some other small details were also modified. All this work was finished on 25 September 1945 and the few tests which followed revealed the need for the transformations. The plane was considered as «successful», but was not followed up as a fighter since the military were now only thinking of their air force in terms of jet-propelled planes. The Yak-3U was not presented for its State tests and remained eleven months in its workshop before being scrapped in the end. Its design was taken up subsequently for the development of an advanced training prototype designated Yak-U, powered by an ASh-21 radial engine which was referenced as Yak-11 in the production series.

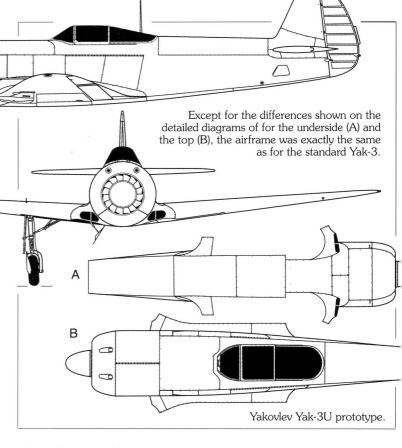

Except for the differences shown on the detailed diagrams of for the underside (A) and the top (B), the airframe was exactly the same as for the standard Yak-3.

Yakovlev Yak-3U prototype.

Three views of the ASh-82FN-powered Yak-3U prototype during its factory trials in the spring of 1945. After some modifications and a new set of trials in the autumn which were very satisfactory, the machine was set aside before being scrapped, since the VVS considered that they no longer needed this type of fighter.
(J. Marmain)

YAKOVLEV ★

Yak-9V/VK-105PF-2
(April 1945)

From 10 to 17 April 1945, a new two-seat conversion trainer started its trials at the NII VVS at the hands of V.G. Ivanov: the Yak-9V/VK-105PF-2. It was a blend of the Yak-9T and Yak-9M and was equipped with two cockpits with dual controls, the instructor sitting at the rear.

Technical specifications	
Wingspan: 32 ft. 1 1/2 in.	**Speed:** 352 mph. at 11 880 ft.
Length: 28 ft. **Wing Area:** 184.585 sq. ft. **Weight Empty:** 5 156 lb. **Max. Take-off Weight:** 6 835 lb. **Max.**	**Service Ceiling:** 32 670 ft. (production series) **Range:** 862 miles (production series)

Intended as much for flying schools as for the units, its VK-105PF-2 engine enabled the aircraft to be used in combat if needs be. The canopy common to both cockpits was in two sliding parts which could be ejected in flight. The backs of the seats were not armoured, the two cockpits being separated by glazing and most of the instruments were still there including an RSI-6MU radio, an RPK-10M/DF radio-compass and an AG-2 artificial horizon. The two men could communicate between themselves with an SPU intercom. The system for filling the tanks by means of inert gases was not used and the capacity of the oil tank was limited to 11 gallons. The machine was only armed with the axial ShVAK canon and an automatic PAU-22 camera on the leading edge of the right wing. There was no oxygen bottle as training and formation flights both by day and night were not planned for above 14 850 feet.

Adding a second cockpit and the suppression of the NS-37 axial canon caused the CG to slip to 26.5% of the MAC (21.85% on the Yak-9T). These changes only altered the Yak-9V's flight characteristics very slightly: with the canopies closed and the radiator flaps open, the top speed was only 2 1/2 mph slower than the Yak-9T at the service ceiling and the other parameters were practically identical except where longitudinal stability was concerned which made landing manoeuvres less easy. Between August 1945 and August 1947, 793 Yak-9V/VK-105PF-2 two-seaters were built of which 337 were Yak-9Ms reconverted as Yak-9Vs.

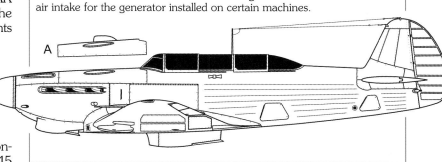

Yakovlev Yak-9V two-seat trainer. Partial diagram A shows the extra air intake for the generator installed on certain machines.

A Yak-9V two-seat trainer during its evaluations. The antenna mast has been fixed on the right-hand side of the fuselage.

This Yak-9V "40" is in fact a Yak-9D changed into a two-seater.

(J. Marmain)

(J. Marmain)

YAKOVLEV

Yakovlev Yak-9S prototype.

Yak-9S/VK-105PF-2 Prototype (May 1945)

After the «U» series of the Yak-9, the OKB modified two Yak-9M airframes in May 1945 in order to test new armament: an axial NS-23 canon with 60 rounds and two synchronised B-20S cannon under the cowling each with 120 rounds. The two prototypes (serial N°01-01 and 01-02) were referenced as Yak-9S/VK-105PF-2 (VISh-105V-01 propeller) by the OKB (the «S» had no particular meaning). Thus armed the aircraft answered the VVS specifications for 1945, the operation of the cannon in flight presenting no problems no matter what the conditions. The NS-23 could penetrate 20-mm armour at 660 feet.

The factory trials for this machine were carried out by Fiodrovi between 10 and 28 May 1945. The State trials took place with V.G. Ivanonv and A.A. Manucharov at the NII VVS from 28 August to 14 September. The reports noted the excellent armament, but were concerned by the loss in performance compared with the Yak-3 and Yak-9U/VK-107A (the latter had just gone through its trials and production had started in April); the top speed of the Yak-9S was respectively 42 and 55 mph slower and the climb rate was too slow. For these reasons the model was not mass-produced.

Technical specifications

Wingspan: 32 ft. 1 1/2 in.	**Max. Take-off Weight:** 6 886 lb.
Length: 28 ft.	**Max. Speed:** 364 mph. at 13 035 ft.
Wing Area: 184.585 sq. ft.	**Service Ceiling:** 32 175 ft.
Weight Empty: 5 163 lb.	**Range:** 581 miles

(J. Marmain)

The Yak-9S fitted with a 23-mm NS-23 axial canon and two UBS cannon under the engine cowling during its trials at the NII VVS. The airframe was that of a Yak-9M adapted for the new armament.

The Yak-9S during its trials in August and September 1945. The NS-23 canon is clearly visible sticking through the tip of the propeller boss (with the «Hucks» starter). *(J. Marmain)*

YAKOKLEV

Technical specifications

Wingspan: 32 ft. 2 in.
Length: 28 ft. 2 1/2 in.
Wing Area: 184.585 sq. ft.
Weight Empty: 5 511 lb.
Max. Take-off Weight: 6 881 lb.

Max. Speed: 389 mph.
at 18 150 ft. Service Ceiling:
37 290 ft. (production series)
Range: 406 miles (production series)

Yak-9UV/VK-107A Prototype
(June 1945)

The Yak-9 gave rise to a two-sweater conversion trainer: the Yak-9UV/VK-107A. Apart from the second seat and the canopy which was common to the original, the UV model was only very slightly different from the Yak-9U technologically. Its on-board equipment was less sophisticated but nevertheless permitted it to fly at night or in bad weather conditions. The armament only comprised the ShVAK axial canon with 100 rounds. The prototype was given the rather strange serial number 00-00. It was produced by Factory N°82 in June 1945 and the State trials at the NII VVS took place from 10 July to 12 October at the hands of L.M. Kuvshinov.

Despite the fitting of new radiators for the glycol and oil, the VK-107A engine still overheated especially during the frequent unavoidable landing and take-off procedures during training sessions. Because of this, the engine had to be limited to 2 800 rpm instead of 3 000, with the oil radiator flaps almost full open. There were no differences in in-flight characteristics or in performances compared to the single-sweater. On the other hand, the presence of two seats which weighed the aircraft down and the limits imposed on the engine's rpm caused the aircraft's speed to drop between 21 and 56 mph depending on the altitude. The NII VVS turned the Yak-9UV down and there was no series production, primarily because of the end of the war, as much in Europe as in the Pacific and because the VVS had officially decided that the future was for the jet plane. With this in mind, only a jet-powered two-seater was wanted, but this did not appear before 1948 with the building of the Yak-17UTI.

(J. Marmain)

The Yak-9UV prototype with the unusual serial N° 00-00. Its lack of performance because of the problematic VK-107A engine was why it was rejected by the VVS. The machine was only officially tested after the war.

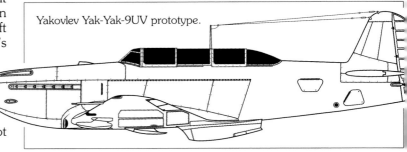

Yakovlev Yak-Yak-9UV prototype.

LAVOCHKIN

«Object 120R»
or La-120R Prototype
(July 1945)

After the two La-7R prototypes, Aleyev's team decided to fit one of the two «120» prototypes (forerunners of the La-7) with an RD-1-KhZ rocket motor made by Glushko at Experimental Factory N°81. The machine was equipped with the same pure aluminium and stainless steel elements as the La-7R (fuel tanks, rear fuselage structure, piping, etc.); the RD-1KhZ was installed in the tail and the ASh-83 was moved forward 2 3/4 inches. The streamlining of the fuselage was improved

(J. Marmain)

The "120R" with RD-1KhZ rocket motor in the tail. The tail is much bigger than a standard La-7. Note that the tail wheel has been retracted into the fuselage.

and the tail was redesigned. The central fuel tank contained nitric acid; another tank for the kerosene was installed in the right wing section and all the parts concerning the rocket motor, like the pumps, were

Igniting the La-120R's RD-1KhZ rocket motor on the ground. There is a thin wire around the rear part of the fuselage to prevent the prototype from moving under the thrust of the RD-1KhZ, which replaced the RD-1 after a first set of trials when it exploded, on 27 March 1945.

La-9, La-11

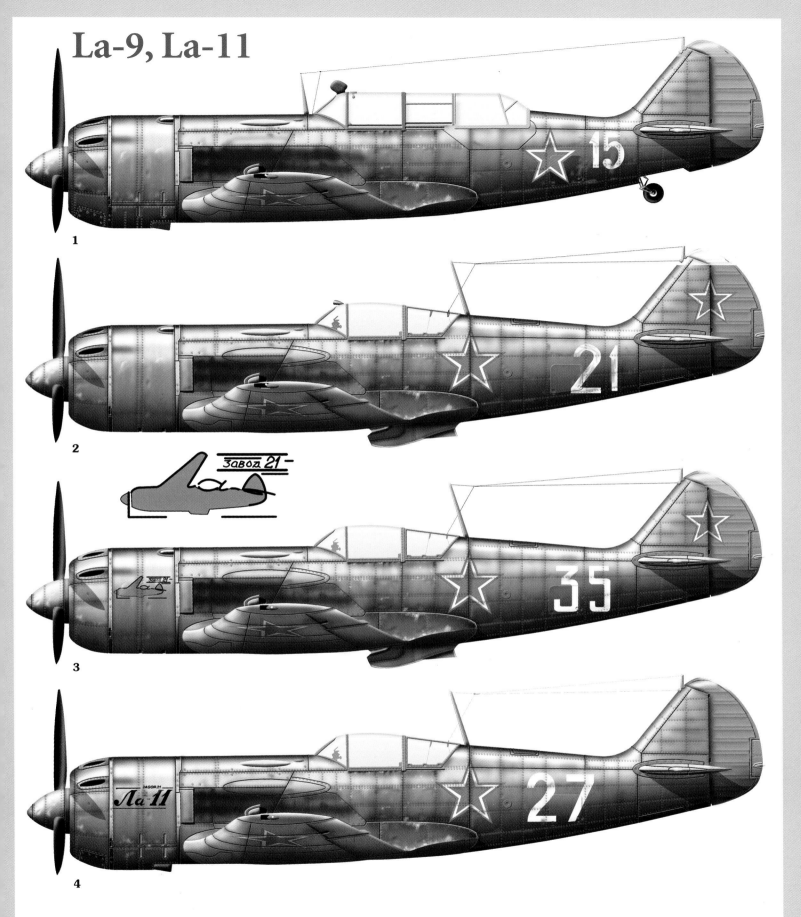

1. Lavochkin La-9UTI from the Yelsk Military Pilot Training School. This two-seater has had its engine exchanged for that of an La-11.

2. Lavochkin La-9 from the end of the production series belonging to an unknown unit. The camouflage is very simple, the whole plane being painted medium grey, the coloured tip of the tail being the unit marking.

3. Lavochkin La-9 from the beginning of production and from an unidentified unit. The insignia of the factory where the machine was made (Zavod 21) has been painted on the engine cowling.

4. Lavochkin La-11 from an unidentified unit but one which took part in escorting Tu-4 bombers over the North Pole in 1948.

175

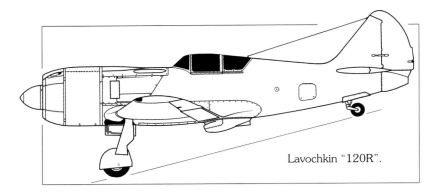

Lavochkin "120R".

the same as those of the La-7R-2. The oil system had a capacity of 110 lb (in fact, with all the leaks, this meant a real capacity of only 77 lb). Armament comprised an 80-round NS-23 axial canon and a 100-round synchronised B-20 under the engine cowling.

Re-designated «Object 120R» (or La-120R), its trials programme started on 2 July 1945. There were only two flights (12 July and 25 September) during which the whole oil system failed causing the ASh-83 to overheat. The prototype was transferred to Factory N°301 for a series of modifications and was not ready to start trials before 12 April 1946. But the NKAP only allowed it to do a few routine tests using the ASh-83 and some short flights using the ignited RD-1KhZ rocket engine until 1 July (in all 21 ignitions including seven failures) for a total duration of 8 minutes and 20 seconds.

Very rare picture of the La-120R in flight with its rocket motor in action. Unfortunately the photograph is very blurred. Note the bigger tail fin.

(J. Marmain)

Soon after the first flight on 10 August 1946 after the NKAP had lifted its veto, the combustion chamber had to be changed. Although ignition was normal, the motor started to vibrate. In all the RD-1KhZ was ignited twenty times, five in flight, for a total time of 11 minutes and 55 seconds. The combustion chamber had to be replaced four times for the same reasons: the injectors and the nozzle showed signs of cracks and flaws. A stainless steel combustion chamber was installed on 1 October. On the test bench it resisted «everything», after being ignited four times and undergoing three very thorough tests, for a total time of 50 minutes.

Before that, on 18 August 1946 A.V. Davidov flew over Tushino airfield using the RD-1KhZ, on the occasion of the anniversary of the creation of the VVS. Before the trials were stopped on Yakovlev's orders, the «120R» carried out 16 flights, of which seven were with the RD-1KhZ running. Four of them took place at 9 900, 6 600, 2 640 and 230 feet but the top speed was only recorded once: 453 mph at 7 095 feet (388 mph without the rocket motor). With the ASh-83 reaching the «end of its life» however, no more trials were undertaken, especially as the nitric acid fumes had finished by corroding part of the airframe.

During the whole period of the trials, five combustion chambers were tried out, for a total operating time of 28 minutes and 19 seconds. There were several reasons for Yakovlev cancelling the programme: the war had ended a year earlier; rocket motors (like ramjets and pulse-jets) had no real operational future because they lacked endurance (an average of three minutes); ground crews who had to be expert in the handling of nitric acid had to be trained; and the very promising generation of combat aircraft powered by jet engines was about to enter operational service.

Technical specifications

Wingspan: 32 ft. 4 in. **Length:** 28 ft. 6 in. **Wing Area:** 189.321 sq. ft. **Weight** Empty **Max. Take-off Weight:** 7 772 lb.

Total weight of fuel: 968 lb **Max. Speed:** 388 mph at 7 095 ft without RD-1KhZ, 453 mph at 7 095 ft. **Service Ceiling:** ? **Range:**

LAVOCHKIN

La-7PuVRD (or La-7D, La-7/2D-10 sometimes La-7PVRD) Prototype
(November 1945)

In 1942, the engine builder and chief designer at Factory N°51, V.N. Tchelomeyi started bench tests on a pulse-jet of his own design. In November 1945, two of these stand-by jets, designated D-10, producing 440 lb of static thrust, were fitted under the wing of an La-7 armed with three cannon. The front part of the D-10 was made of aluminium and the rest of the body was made of steel. It used the same fuel used as the La-7's standard engine (ASh-82FN). It was fed to the pulse-jet injectors and ignited electrically. Each pulse-jet was fitted to the wing by means of a faired pylon (two fixation points at the front and one at the rear). The airframe itself underwent only slight modifications, except for those to the split flaps (their surface area was reduced), and instruments for the pulse-jets were installed.

(J. Marmain)

The La-7PuVRD (sometimes the La-7PVRD) with its two Chelomeyi D-10 pulse-jets under the wings. In spite of its excellent performances in 1946 with the D-10 working, the VVS abandoned the programme, preferring the new generation of turbojets to power their aircraft.

The prototype was called La-7PuVRD (or La-7D, La-7/2D-10 sometimes incorrectly La-7PVRD depending on the sources), the initials "PuVRD" indicating that pulse-jets were fitted, according to the Soviet nomenclature. The trials started at the end of the summer of 1946 at the hands of N.V. Gavrilov from Factory N°51 and they surprised everybody taking part in the programme because, at first, the increase in speed was of the order 75 mph (18 mph faster than the estimates), then it went up to 120 mph at 2 640 feet at full power.

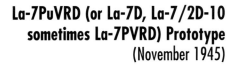

Lavochkin La-7PuVRD

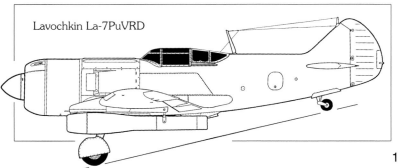

The authorities however limited the top speed to 393.75 mph with the pulse-jets working, which meant that the complete scale of performances could not be fully explored; neither could the real potential of the D-10 be fully exploited. There were several reasons for their decision to limit the speed: the D-10 was unpopular with some of the pilots (three La-7UTIs had also been fitted with pulse-jets — see below) after they had tested it because of the very strong vibrations that were transmitted to the wings and the airframe, the significant reduction in performance when the jets were not being used (their mass and the drag they caused), and the lack of manoeuvrability due to their size. On 15 October 1946, a report from the mainte-

nance team declared the plane to be "unfit to continue the tests" and no other flights were made with an La-7 airframe fitted with pulse-jets.

LAVOTCHKIN

«Object 126» prototype or La-126 (entirely metal" La-7) (End of 1945)

The problems perfecting the ASh-83 engine, which was to be used on the production series of the new model, itself developed from the «120 N°2» (tested in 1944) and using the same engine (or La-7/ASh-83), a laminar wing, and a lighter airframe (by 330 lb, thanks to the substitution of wooden parts for metal ones) put paid to this lay-out. OKB-301 concentrated its efforts on another programme, «Object 126», armed with four NS-23 cannon (200 rounds) grouped together around the ASh-82FN engine. Sometimes designated La-126, the prototype had a redesigned cockpit canopy, an entirely metal fuselage with elements made of «Elektron» and stressed skin; its laminar profile wing with an extra 2° dihedral compared to the La-7, was positioned slightly further forward along the fuselage, but was still covered with a plywood skin.

The «126's» trials took place from the end of 1945 until April 1946 at the hands of the pilots Davidov, Fiodorov, and A.A. Popov. Although they did not give rise to a production series - no doubt

(J. Marmain)

The La-126 prototype, the forerunner of the La-9, which it resembles already except for the wooden wing (the fuselage was made of metal). The ASh-82FN is surrounded by four 23-mm NS-23 cannon.

because of certain obsolete aspects of the aircraft's structure - the lessons learnt were retained for the development of the first prototype of the La-9 series. In their documents, the NKAP and the GKO often referred to it as the «entirely metal La-7», in spite of its plywood wing. The La-126 was subsequently equipped with two VRD-430 pulse-jets (see below).

YAKOVLEV

Yak-3UTI or Yak-UTI, Yak-11 series (Le-10 then C-II) and Yak-11U (C-11U) (End of 1945, autumn 1946, and 1951)

In 1945, the Yakovlev OKB responded to a request by the VVS and the A-VMF dating from the middle of the preceding year for a new «post-war» trainer design based on the Yak-3. The experience gained with the Yak-3U was used to advantage to develop the Yak-3UTI prototype, or Yak-UTI. Elements common to both the Yak-3U and the standard Yak-3, especially the former's 31-foot wingspan, were retained and married to an ASh-21 (seven-cylinder air-cooled radial) driving a 10-foot two-blade ViSH-111V-20 propeller. The machine was made entirely of metal, was armed with an UBS (100 rounds) and could carry two 220-lb FAB -100 bombs. A long canopy covered both cockpits. The trials were carried out at the end of 1945 by G.M. Klimushkin and were satisfactory, but there was no production series of the aircraft in this form.

The model nevertheless gave rise to the Yak-11 in the autumn of 1946. This was an improved version which had an engine cowling with a deeper chord. The fuselage was covered with

plywood at the front and fabric at the rear. Its structure consisted of steel tubes and its back was made of plywood. The two cockpits each had a sliding canopy and both pilots had a complete set of instruments. The wing was built around two metal spars (Clark YH profile) and had a 5° dihedral; the skin was made of 2-mm thick Dural panels from the leading edge to the first spar, after that it was 1-mm thick. The tail, the ailerons and all the moving surfaces were also made of Dural. The ASh-21 engine was fitted to a mounting equipped with a

A line-up of Yak-11s of which some are ready to take off. Note the two sliding canopies of the second machine in the near distance and the air flow regulating cooling flaps in the closed position on the first machine in the foreground.
(J. Marmain)

(RART)

(RART)

Top, from left to right.

The Yak-11u with retractable tricycle undercarriage. The front of the fuselage has been lengthened and the two-blade propeller has had its boss removed.

The Yak-3UTI with its ASh-21 engine and its two-seat cockpit. The whole of the airframe was that of a Yak-3.

(V. Koulikov)

rubber antivibration system and used the same propeller. The 8 1/2-gallon oil radiator was cooled by gills in the wing roots. Fuel was housed in two 38 1/2-gallon wing tanks and a small 3-gallon distribution tank ensured that the flow was steady. The retractable undercarriage was fitted with 600x180-mm tyres (255x110-mm for the tail wheel). A UBS was installed under the upper left-hand side of the engine cowling with 100 rounds. A PA-22 camera gun was installed on one of the canopy supports.

After Klimushkin's factory trials, the machine was presented

to the NII VVS where it was tested in October 1946 and fulfilled the specification. There were no vices and it was very agile. Mass-production was ordered in Leningrad and at Saratov, the first deliveries being made in the middle of the following year. The Yak-11 was fitted out with a complete set of instruments and an RS-3M/4M radio with antenna masts fitted behind the second cockpit and under the fuselage. The tail wheel was fixed and the UBS was often replaced by a ShKAS; there was a landing light on the leading edge of the left wing, a mirror was installed on the windshield mounting and the propeller was often replaced by a ViSH-111D-15. In all 3 859 examples of this plane were produced in the USSR plus another 707 armed with a ShKAS under licence in Czechoslovakia where they were designated Le-10, then C-11. The model was exported to 18 countries where it remained in service for many years.

In 1951 the Yakovlev OKB produced the Yak-11U variant with an ASh-21 engine without the propeller boss and equipped with retractable tricycle undercarriage; the nose wheel rose rearwards into a well under the engine of which the flow of cooling air was regulated by an adjustable frontal ring of flaps. The model was intended for training jet pilots. According to certain documents, the Yak-11U replaced the Yak-11 on the production lines from 1951 onwards and a certain number of examples were produced in Czechoslovakia under the designation C-11U. But the most recent sources report only a small number of Yak-11Us being produced, with reduced fuel capacity because of the tricycle undercarriage.

NB.: according to certain documents the 707 examples made in Czechoslovakia are included in the total figure of 3 859 machines produced.

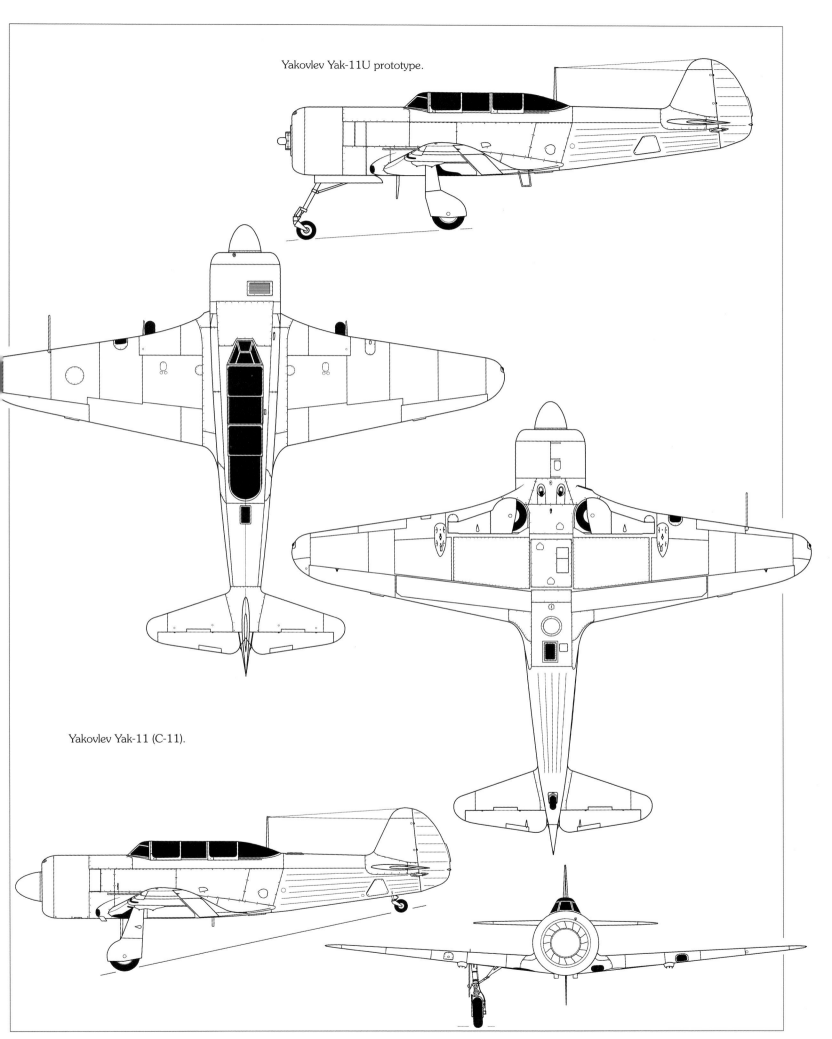

Yakovlev Yak-11U prototype.

Yakovlev Yak-11 (C-11).

179

1946-1950

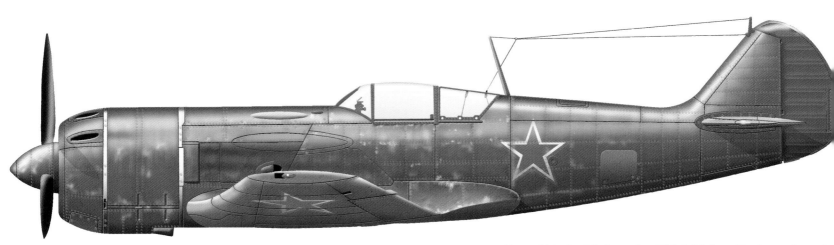

Lavochkin La-11 from the 911th Fighter Regiment based at Ust-Kut. When they were transferred by air from the factory where they were made to their base, four La-11s were painted red in order to make finding them easier in the case of an emergency landing in snow-covered regions.

GLOSSARY

(J. Marmain)

LAVOCHKIN

«Object 130», or La-130
(January 1946)

The very first «real» prototype for the La-9 was «Object 130», or La-130. In spite of a family resemblance with the La-7, there was in fact very little of the earlier aircraft. It was made entirely of metal with stressed skin to save weight. Its laminar profile wing was built around a main and an auxiliary spar. It was made up of a central section and two outer sections, with a 6° dihedral. There were Frise ailerons and the hydraulic balance tabs were covered with «Elektron».

The cross-section frame of the engine compartment on the monocoque fuselage was wider because the duct feeding air into the two-stage supercharger was installed in the upper leading edge of the engine cowling. The cooling air for the ASh-82FN (10 ft 3 in diameter ViSH-105V-4 propeller) was regulated by a set of adjustable frontal flaps controlled by the pilot, and by side flaps. Exhaust was evacuated by means of two separate outlets, on either side of the cowling below the cannon, through two sets of six pipes coming out through the side flaps. The oil radiator was placed in a redesigned (compared with the La-7) ventral duct.

The tail surfaces were enlarged. The tail fin was integrated into the structure of the fuselage. The two horizontal surfaces had a symmetrical profile and were fixed at an incidence of 1° (1.5° on the La-9). All the moving surfaces on the tail were balanced and fabric-covered.

The weight saved enabled five self-sealing tanks to be installed in the wings with a total capacity of 371 gallons. The oil tank contained 14 gallons. Armament comprised four synchronised NS-23 cannon installed on welded steel tube mountings. They were fired electro-pneumatically and the pilot had the choice of firing the upper pair or the lower pair or all four together. PBP (V) sights were installed under the windshield.

There was more room in the cockpit: it was more comfortable, better ventilated and sealed than the La-7 (the inside temperature was considered «bearable»). The canopy was moulded from a single piece and could be discarded in flight. On board the pilot had a better set of instruments, including among others an RSI-6 transmitter, an RSI-6M receiver, an RPKO-10M HF/DF gyro-compass and a SCh-3M IFF. Oxygen was contained in a gallon bottle. A Fairchild «Type 6» camera gun was incorporated in the leading edge of the right wing on a level with the undercarriage leg which itself was totally retractable. The single member main undercarriage legs had wheels with brakes and 600 x 200-mm tyres (300x120-mm for the tail wheel).

The «130» at Factory N°21 was completed in January 1946 and the following month it was transferred to Factory N°31 where thirty test flights were carried out by A.A. Popov up to May. The NII VVS received it on

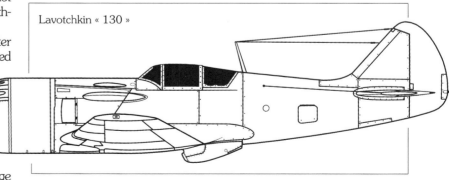

Above and below.
Two views of the «130» or La-130, the prototype for the La-9 series, during its State trials in May 1946 on the Chkalovskaya airfield.

(J. Marmain)

9 June for the State trials at the hands of A.G. Kubishkin and V.I. Alexeyenko.

Serious faults were found which affected the plane's handling, stability and armament. On 8 July the «130» returned to Factory N°21 where trials were resumed on 25 July. OKB-301 needed six weeks to carry out a series of modifications (armament, increased sweep on the leading edge of the wing central section), and change the engine. On 10 October, the prototype returned to the NII VVS and passed its State trials satisfactorily. But the final report highlighted the fact that the «130» was not equipped for night flying, nor was it equipped with an automatic pilot, and that in terms of overall performance, it was not particularly better than the Yak-3. On the other hand, compared with the La-7, it could fly in bad weather, it had a much longer range and the pilot had a better field of vision. The model was put into production in August 1946 with the designation La-9.

Lavotchkin « 130 »

Technical Specifications

Wingspan: 32 ft. 4 in.	**Length:** 28 ft. 5 1/2 in.	**Max. Take-off Weight:** 7 535 lb (8 087 lb overloaded.)
Weight Empty: 5 797 lb.		**Service Ceiling:** 35 640 ft.
Max. Speed: 431 mph. at 20 625 ft.		**Range:** 1 084 miles at 3 300 ft.

LAVOCHKIN

«Object 130R» or La-130R
unfinished prototype (Spring 1946)

Technical Specifications

Wingspan: 32 ft. 4 in.	Max. Take-off Weight: 7 895 lb.
Length: 28 ft. 11 in.	Total weight of fuel: 1 232 lb.
Wing Area: 189.644 sq. ft.	Max. Speed: 518 mph. at 2 640 ft.
Weight Empty:	Service Ceiling: Range:

In the spring of 1946, Lavochkin and Alexeyev tried one last time to fit an RD-1KhZ rocket-motor into a fighter. Two machines were ordered based on the prototype forerunner of the La-9, the entirely metal «130». The new model, designated «Object 130» (or La-130R depending on the sources), did not have any wing tanks. The centre fuselage tank was replaced by a stainless steel tank holding 473 lb of nitric acid; another holding 638 lb of kerosene was placed behind the standard ASh-83FN, for which a special oil radiator had been designed and installed in the front of the engine cowling with a frontal cooling intake. Finally a little 121-lb tank of kerosene was set into the wing central section, to be used for the RD-1KhZ positioned with all its accessories in the redesigned rear of the fuselage. All the piping for the nitric acid was covered with stainless steel and the enlarged tail surfaces were covered with «Elektron». The ASh-83FN was moved forward by nearly 7 inches in order to re-establish the CG to within sufficiently acceptable limits. The tail wheel was

reinforced to match the weight increase in the rear section of the plane. Armament comprised two synchronised NS-23 cannon with 180 shells.

During the two preceding years, the RD-1 and R-1KhZ rocket-motor trials using prototypes from different manufacturers only gave meagre results in terms of reliability (a number of ignition defects, poisonous fumes infiltrating into the cockpit, airframe corrosion, etc.) and performance under operational conditions. As a result the authorities, who were attracted by the very much more promising generation of turbo-jet engines, put an end to the scheduled rocket-motor, ramjet and pulse-jet programmes. The first prototype of the «130R» was thus not finished (its airframe was completed in 1947, but the engines were never fitted) and the second one was cancelled. All trials with stand-by engines were finally abandoned for good in 1948, at least where aircraft propulsion was concerned.

YAKOVLEV

Yak-3/VK-107A Prototype (Factory
N°292, version with metal wings)
(March 1946)

Technical Specifications

Wingspan: 30 ft. 4 in.	Max. Take-off Weight: 6 729 lb.
Length: 28 ft.	Max. Speed: 435 mph. at 19 635 ft.
Wing Area: 159.830 sq. ft.	Service Ceiling: 35 904 ft.
Weight Empty: 5 304 lb.	Range: 440 to 627 miles

At the beginning of 1946, after Factory N°31 had built 30 production examples of the all-metal Yak-3/VK-107A for evaluations (and a further eight in 1946), Factory N°292 was in turn engaged in this programme, as required by the GKO in its decision of 29 December 1944, but without making the same modifications. It retained the airframes of Serial N° 01-01, 03-01, 04-01 and made the following changes in March 1946: the wings, undercarriage doors, tail surfaces were made of metal; the aileron trim was completely re-designed; the landing gear system and the fuselage structure and sealing were reinforced; the ventilation of the cockpit was modified; an armoured windshield with flat panes was fitted (on serial N° 01-01 and 03-01 only). The VK-107A engine which had passed its «100 hours» on the bench certification, was equipped with radiators (OP-700 for the oil and OP-554U for the glycol) with filters in the air intakes, a cooling system for the spark plugs and the exhaust (like on the 1945 Yak-9U), a reinforced ventral duct and a protected distribution tank. The armament comprised a B-20M axial canon and two B-20S cannon for Serial N° 03-01 and 04-01 (all with 100 rounds), two B-20S can-

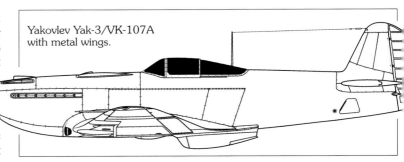

Yakovlev Yak-3/VK-107A
with metal wings.

non under the engine cowling for Serial N°01-01 (120 rounds each). The mountings for the B-20S cannon were reinforced. There was also an RSI-6 radio without antenna mast (or with mast, depending on the sources).

With these changes and despite an increase in the take-off weight (like the machines made by Factory N°31 these prototypes were simply referenced as Yak-3/VK-107As), the performance was very close to what the GKO was after: 435 mph at 19 635 ft instead of 437 mph. Its range was 627 miles at optimal combat speed. Flight characteristics remained unchanged compared to the standard Yak-3. The VVS were satisfied with the rigidity of the wing despite slight twisting of the skin near the wing roots when diving at more than 406 mph. But once again the VK-107A was not reliable. Some of its components were of poor quality; the cooling was still just as bad and the distribution tank turned

(RART)

One of the three VK-107A-powered Yak-3s with metal wings built by Factory N°292 during its factory trials in the spring of 1945.

out to be too small to regulate fuel consumption adequately. Serial N° 04-01's armament was not satisfactory and the on-board equipment only allowed for day-time missions. The lack of an artificial horizon, a DF/IFF receiver, a landing light and ultra-violet lighting for the cockpit, all limited the operational capabilities of the plane and the range of the radio was only 68 miles instead of 75 miles as required.

The factory trials were followed by the State's at the NII VVS at the hands of Proshakov, Khomalov, Antipov and a few others. They reported a considerable number of defects during the 44 flights made with 01-01, the 42 with 03-01 and the 37 with 04-01. The main ones were: power plant vibration; oil overheating in all circumstances and oil pressure dropping over 13 200 ft. Fuel distribution was irregular and the canon mounting was not strong enough. At the end of May, the three prototypes were delivered to LII where some rectifications were carried out (firing trials were not com-

pleted). Only serial N° 01-01 returned to the NII VVS on 26 June to undergo a new series of tests from 5 to 30 July. The 17 flights it made were for engine and armament reliability. At the end, the report turned the model down since it did not meet post-war military requirements and because there were still too many defects.

However, it recommended that a further 30 machines be produced for trials so that the defects could be rectified before perhaps starting a production series. A directive from the Ministers' Cabinet issued on 20 August 1946 increased this order to 75 «Yak-3/VK-107As with metal wings and three cannon» and included the correction of all the reported defects but requiring that the order be fulfilled by Factory N°31; it underlined the fact that the military authorities were not satisfied with Factory N°292's three prototypes and that bigger-calibre cannon could not be installed. In the end, the order was cancelled and the programme stopped once and for all.

LAVOCHKIN

«Object 120» project with mixed power plants (PVRD) or La-120PVRD (March 1946)
«Object 164» Prototype (or La-126PVRD or La-7/2PVRD-430, or La-7S) (June 1946)
La-7PPVRD Prototype (Spring or summer 1946)

The ramjet specialist, M.M. Bondariuk, presented his RD-430 model (or PVRD 430, the figure «430» indicating the diameter of the frontal cross section of the ramjet in millimetres) with 374 lb of static thrust in 1944. In March 1946, the Lavochkin OKB studied an experimental project based on the «Object 120» model (or La-120PVRD) equipped with two of these ramjets. This project was not followed up because in the end the «126» model was chosen powered by an ASh-82FN engine, armed with four 23-mm cannon with 200 rounds each (one of the forerunners of the La-9 series).

The «126» was modified so that it could be equipped with two RD-430 ramjets under the wings. Each was attached by means of four fixation points on the second rib of each wing section; the whole arrangement was faired to reduce drag as much as possible. The elevator spars were strengthened. The equipment for controlling the two RD-430s was installed in the cockpit and in place of the two cannon normally fitted under the engine cowling. A pressure gauge for the ramjets was fitted above the left-hand RD-430 on the upper wing surface so as to be visible from the cockpit.

Re-designated «Object 164» (or La-126PVRD or La-7/2PVRD-430) by the Lavochkin OKB, and the La-7S by the military authorities, this prototype carried out its factory tests between 26 June and 4 September 1946 at the hands of A.V. Davidov (29 flights) and A.A. Popov (five flights) for a total time of 12 hours and 30 minutes. The RD-430s were ignited 110 times at heights of 660 ft, 1 650 ft, 3 300 ft, 6 600 ft, 9 900 ft and 15 840 ft without any particular problems, except that on twenty occasions they refused to start through ignition and fuel pump malfunctions, and on one occasion because of the throttle blocking.

The maximum speeds recorded were 414 mph at 4 075 ft and 433 mph at 7 722 ft, i.e. 65 mph and 68 mph faster than when the two RD-430s were not working. In fact the increased speed was only 38 mph and 40 mph faster at the same altitudes as a standard La-9. Davidov noted that with more streamlined ramjet fairings and a more efficient consumption regulator, the «164» could fly 62 mph faster than an La-9 at 16 500 ft (50 mph at 6 600 ft). Moreover he thought that its flying characteristics were not very different

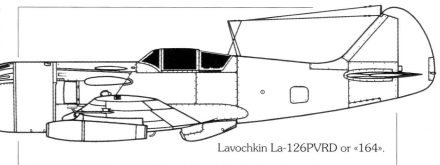

Lavochkin La-126PVRD or «164».

The «164» (or La-126PVRD) prototype during its trials. The ramjets were attached to the main spar of the wing. Note the front part painted red, which then continued with a stripe of the same colour up to the elevators. (J. Marmain)

from the La-9's but that the take-off distance was very long (330 to 412 ft longer).

Although the RD-430s were perfectly reliable operationally, needed less preparation time before take-off, used the same fuel as the main engine and could be shut down and started up again in flight without any hitches, it was nevertheless true that they generated a lot of drag and that their endurance was limited and that, anyway, the military authorities were already banking on turbojet propulsion units.

At the same time, another prototype based on the La-7 was fitted with two D-12 pulsejets (200 Kn thrust). It was re-designated La-7PPVRD, but nothing else is known about this machine.

Technical Specifications

Wingspan: 32 ft. 4 in.
Length: 28 ft. 5 in.
Wing Area: 189.321 sq. ft.
Weight Empty: 5 962 lb.
Max. Take-off Weight: 7 205 lb.
Range: 518 miles without RDs, 456 miles with RDs

Max. Speed: 412 mph.
at 0`ft without RDs*, 421 mph 0ft
with RDs.*
365 mph at 7 722 ft without RDs,
414 mph at 4 075 ft
and 433 mph at 7 722 with RDs
Service Ceiling:

(J. Marmain)

YAKOVLEV

One of the first examples of the Yak-9P
with a metal wing produced in 1946. Note
the absence of glazed window on the back
of the fuselage, because the machine was
not equipped with a radio compass.

Yak-9P/VK-107A Prototypes and short production run
(metal wing version) (June and October 1946)
Yak-9P/VK-107A (all-metal version) (October 1946)

Although it had already been used by the Yakovlev OKB, the «P» suffix was employed again in 1946 for a new variant derived from the Yak-9U/VK-107A fighter: the Yak-9P/VK-107A (the «P» suffix was officially approved but did not have any particular meaning in this case since it only represented a indexation sequence for the OKB, in the same way as the «L» and «Yu» had been before (see below). It was developed in response to a request from the MAP (ex-NKAP) dated 17 June 1946 for an all-metal version of the Yak-9 with M-107A engine. At the time the Soviet authorities were more concerned about the quality of aircraft, their finish and their lifespan - the very opposite of the wartime notion of «quantity» production. Thus with the end of the war, the ideas of strength, aerodynamic quality, engine and armament reliability and more sophisticated equipment became more important. With this in mind, there was no longer any question of building «mixed construction» airframes: «all-metal» construction became the standard.

The Yakovlev OKB first presented two Yak-9P/VK-107A (serial N° 01-03 and 01-04) prototypes with all-metal wings and a partly plywood-cov-

Technical Specifications

Wingspan: 32 ft. 1 in.	**Max. Speed:** 420 mph. at 18 810
Length: 28 ft. 3 in.	(412 mph at 16 500 ft).
Wing Area: 184.585 sq. ft.	**Service Ceiling:** 36 300 ft (34 650 ft).
Weight Empty: 5 704 lb (5 927 lb).	**Range:** 368 miles (706 to 750 miles).
Max. Take-off Weight: 7 099 lb (7 370 lb.)	The figures in brackets concern Yak-9P serial N° 03-92.

ered fuselage for evaluation. Apart from their new wings, they differed from Yak-9U serial N° 39-083 (see Yak-9UTI) from Factory N°166 for a variety of reasons: the ailerons were covered with metal; their balance was increased and their trim line was improved; modifications were made to the flap kinematics; the armour protecting the pilot (windshield, seat, rear glazing) was improved, and filters were fitted in the power plant air intakes. The armament was that of the Yak-9U (one axial ShVAK canon and two engine mounted UBSs). The two prototypes were tested from 28 June to 23 July 1946, making 51 and 57 flights respectively at the hands of Y.A. Antipov and V.I. Ivanov. In terms of performance and flight behaviour, they were scarcely different from the Yak-9Us except that they could take 8G when pulling out of a dive, after reaching a speed of 450 mph. The final report noted 21 defects to be attended to and recommended that 30 machines be produced for service evaluation after these had been rectified. Three weapon combinations on a «universal» mounting were suggested: one 20, 23 or 37-mm axial canon with respectively 120, 80 or 30 rounds, and two 20-mm cannon under the engine cowling (with a total of 240 rounds); or one 45-mm axial canon with 30 rounds and two 20-mm cannon (240 rounds); or one 57-mm axial canon (20 rounds) and one 20-mm canon with 120 rounds.

The report was approved at the cabinet meeting, but only on 20 August 1946, and required that Serial N°01-04 be presented for trials on 1 August with its complete equipment as requested by the VVS. Serial N° 01-03 had to be ready on 1 December 1946 without any defects and fitted with bigger tanks to take 770 to 1 100 lb of fuel. Serial N° 01-04 was tested from 9 to 17 August 1946 with a set of modern on-board instruments, including an RPKO-10M radio-compass, a STSh-3/IFF, an FS-155 light, an Anschutz artificial horizon, a PAU-22 camera gun and ultra-violet lighting in the cockpit. It underwent a

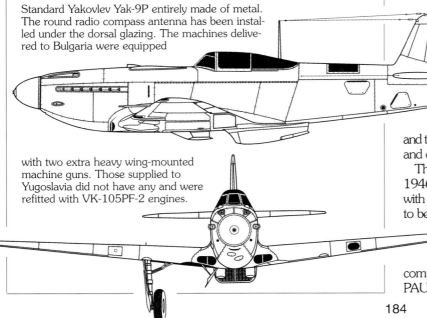

Standard Yakovlev Yak-9P entirely made of metal. The round radio compass antenna has been installed under the dorsal glazing. The machines delivered to Bulgaria were equipped with two extra heavy wing-mounted machine guns. Those supplied to Yugoslavia did not have any and were refitted with VK-105PF-2 engines.

184

further series of tests at the NII VVS from 23 March 1947 with tanks containing 1 100 lb of fuel, two BS-20S cannon instead of the UBSs and a universal mounting enabling a BS-20M, an NS-37, N-37 or N-45 axial canon to be installed with respectively 115, 75, 28 or 25 rounds (in the end the 57-mm canon was not chosen). These trials were carried out until 23 July 1947 and showed that all the various armament combinations could be applied to the production series; that the range was of the order of 625 miles thanks to the 140 gallons the aircraft could carry; and that the increase in the total weight caused by the various weapons carried and the extra fuel capacity only affected the flight characteristics slightly. Series production of the Yak-9P was warmly recommended but it was not started because the military authorities were already expressing an interest in the results obtained from the new generation of jet-powered aircraft.

A further 39 Yak-9Ps were however built by Factory N°153 in 1946 of which 29 were similar to the two prototypes (Serial N° 01-01 to 01-29) and ten were all-metal (Serial N° 01-30 to 01-39). All of them were powered, armed and equipped like the Yak-9Us. Serial N° 01-10 to 01-39 were put through very detailed operational evaluations from 4 October 1946 to 4 February 1947 which covered operational parameters just as much as maintenance, drawing up the manuals and the stocks of spare parts required. The 29 pilots assigned to this programme were from three regiments in the 246.IAD; they noted that the aircraft's handling was excellent, that acrobatic and dog-fight figures presented no particular problems up to 23 100 ft (above that, the machine «could not be used operationally») but that the finish was not perfect, that maintenance was difficult and that although the engine worked properly it was «cooled too much» when it reached the lower in-flight temperature ranges. The standard armament did not satisfy the VVS's demands and one axial canon with 20 rounds and two 20-mm cannon (240 rounds) were requested for the mass-production series. On-board equipment only allowed for day-time and good weather flying; so the equipment fitted in Serial N° 01-04 was what was required.

In spite of a few secondary defects, the report on the evaluations was approved by the ministerial cabinet on 17 September 1947, recommending that the engine's maximum rpm be brought down to 3 000 instead of 3 200 rpm so that it would continue to be reliable, and that the in-board equipment be the same as that tested on the Serial N° 01-04 prototype. As a result in the end 772 all-metal examples were built until December 1947 (the halt to the production was only called on 25 March 1948) for a total of 801 Yak-9Ps including the 29 of mixed construction.

In July 1947 the all-metal Yak-9P/VK-107A Serial N° 03-92 was built and fitted out exactly according to all the officially approved demands and with two extra wing tanks bringing total fuel capacity to 140 gallons (the standard Yak-9s only carried 94 gallons). Moreover the UBS cannon were replaced by B-20S cannon and all the armament combinations could be installed. This machine was evaluated from 12 October to 9 December 1947 and satisfied all the VVS's demands, including range which in this case was of the order of 706 to 750 miles at cruising speed. The increase in weight and the moving of the CG backwards reduced its handling quality and its vertical manoeuvrability and its stability. At the end of the year, another example was tested with a ViSH-107R reversible propeller designed by S.C. Bas-Dubov using a ViSH-107LO as a base. This enabled the landing run to be reduced (742 instead of 1 815 ft) and the brakes to be used fully without risking nosing- or rolling-over.

The Yak-9P was the last piston-engined fighter designed by the Yakovlev OKB. Albania, Poland, China, Hungary and Yugoslavia received contingents, but the VK-107A's lack of reliability and spare parts forced these countries (particularly Yugoslavia) to resort to «cannibalisation» by replacing them with M-105PF-2 engines (taken from Yak-3s) to enable the Yak-9s to remain in service longer. Many of them were transformed into two-seat trainers.

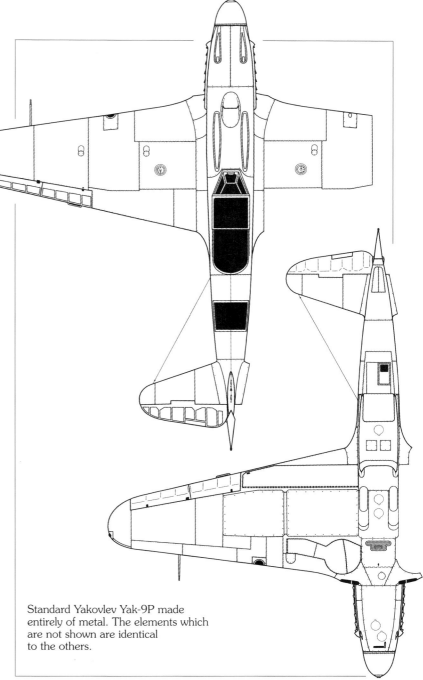

Standard Yakovlev Yak-9P made entirely of metal. The elements which are not shown are identical to the others.

(J. Marmain)

(J. Marmain)

Right, from top to bottom.
This Yak-9P with metal wings is preserved at the Monino Museum.

This entirely metal Yak-9P was captured by the Americans in North Korea. It was brought to the USA by boat, where it was painted white and tested at the Wright-Patterson base. Note the large dorsal glazing covering the radio compass antenna.

LAVOCHKIN

La-7UTI/PuVRD or UTI-La-7/PuVRD Prototypes (Summer 1946)

The anniversary of the VVS took place on 18 August. The crowd was invited to admire the aircraft flying around the skies over Tushino and in particular the latest types produced by the Soviet aircraft industry. In 1946 the military authorities had planned for a number of «jet-powered» aircraft (see below) to fly over the airfield. With this in mind and as a result of the first positive results obtained with the La-7PuVRD, the authorities ordered three La-7UTI (two-seat fighter trainers) airframes to be converted to the same standards. These machines were indeed adapted to take D-10 pulsejets but no sources mention how they were installed and if the aircraft underwent trials of any kind. It is known however that they did not take part in the air display on 18 August 1946. No particular designation was attributed to them but the rare documents which do refer to them call them the La-7UTI/PuVRD or UTI-La-7/PuVRD. No figures or other details.

LAVOCHKIN

La-9 «Type 48» (August 1946)

Following the favourable reports from the NII VVS test pilots, production of the «130» prototype was started at Factory N°21 with the designation La-9 «Type 48». The model carried 189 gallons of fuel in five self-sealing tanks and the oil tank could carry 15 gallons (in general the power plant leaked so much that the pilots actually had only about 11 gallons).

The first four examples left the factory in August 1946 but they were only accepted into the VVS in December. At the beginning of 1947, the first thirty La-9s were transferred to the airfield at Tiopli, near Moscow to undergo a programme of evaluations. The defects which were reported were gradually corrected in the course of production (until 1948). 197 modifications were made. It was only in May 1947 that the La-9s, serial N° 48210410 and 425 were put through a series of operational trials at the hands of the pilots A.G. Terentiev and K.F. Volintsev who confirmed the previous results, except for the range which was greater than that of the «130» (1 221 miles at optimum speed with an endurance of five hours, 662 miles and an endurance of 3 hours 21 minutes at 268 mph). Certain examples from the first production batches only had three NS-23 or NR-23 cannon, the lower left-hand canon being omitted although its port was not faired over.

In 1948, an La-9 tested an automatic APSN gear selector for the centrifugal supercharger as part of the development of the La-11. In 1949, another La-9 tried out more modern instruments, including an alarm warning the pilot of high «G» levels. Between 1946 and 1948, a total of 1 559 fighters (1549 according to different sources) came off the production lines - 15 in 1946, 840 in 1947 and 704 in 1948.

Technical Specifications

Wingspan: 32 ft. 4 in. **Length:** 28 ft. 5 in. **Wing Area:** 189.321 sq. ft. **Weight Empty:** 5 803 lb. **Max. Speed:** 431 mph. at 20 625 ft. **Max. Take-off Weight:** 7 535 lb (8 087 lb overweight). **Service Ceiling:** 35 640 ft. **Range:** 1 221 miles at 3 300 ft.

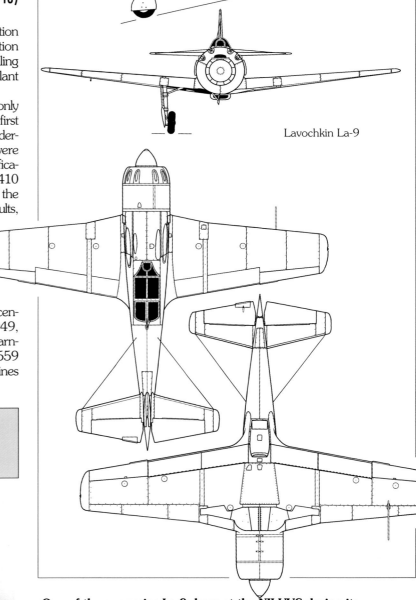

Lavochkin La-9

One of the pre-series La-9, here at the NII VVS during its evaluations. The plane is not equipped with a radio compass (the absence of round antenna behind the pilot's seat). *(J. Marmain)*

(J. Marmain)

(J. Marmain)

A production series La-9, entirely made of metal and armed with four 23-mm cannon (some only had three). The wing had a laminar profile and the round antenna for the radio compass is in the rear part of the cockpit. The badge painted on the cowling is that of Factory N°99.

An La-9 built by Factory N°99 (no badge on the cowling), here being evaluated at the NII VVS before being delivered to the military authorities.

MIKOYAN-GUREVICH

Mig-13
(End of 1946)

At the end of 1946, the A-VMF (the Soviet Navy Air Force) ordered sixteen I-250s re-designated as MiG-13s. They differed from the prototype I-250 (N-2) by their propellers with strange sabre-shaped blades (which were subsequently replaced with a more conventional AV-5B), by the increased fuel and glycol capacity and by its even greater tail fin. It was also equipped with an RSI-4 receiver-transmitter radio with antenna mast mounted at an angle and leaning forward on the windshield frame. The factory tests took place in July 1947 and I.M. Sukhomlin carried out the State tri-

Technical Specifications

Wingspan: 31 ft. 4 in.
Length: 27 ft.
Wing Area: 161.445 sq. ft.
Weight Empty: 6 661 lb.
Max. Take-off Weight: 8 648 lb.

Range: 1 136 miles (without VRDK). The performances of the MiG-13 were never measured, but most of the documents report that they were similar to the I-250 prototypes.

als at the NII VVS from 9 October 1947 to 8 April 1948 aboard MiG-13 serial N° 3810102 (Factory N°381, second machine from the first series). These machines were delivered to the units of the Baltic and Northern Fleets. They were not used very much but remained in service until 1950.

Note: Some sources mention the fact that a total of fifty examples for the MiG-13 production series during the period from end of 1946 to beginning of 1947 were armed with either a 20-mm axial canon and two 12.7-mm heavy machine guns, or three heavy weapons, or four 20-mm cannon. But these weapon combinations seem to be fanciful. It would also appear that one example was tried out fitted with a duct for the air supply divided into two, each conduit starting on either side of the fuselage.

Two views of a MiG-13, similar to the I-250 (N-2) prototype but with an even more slender tail fin and an antenna mast installed at an angle on the windshield frame. The MiG-13s served with the Soviet Navy Air Force but were not used very much until 1950.

(J. Marmain)

The La-9V prototype (a single-seat La-9 transformed into a two-seater) during its trials in May 1947. (J. Marmain)

LAVOCHKIN

La-9V Prototype and La-9UTI «Type 49» series, or UTI-La-9 (and ULa-9) (January 1947 and April 1948)

At the same time as the La-9 single-seat fighter, OKB-301 brought out a two-seat pilot training version designated La-9V. A second cockpit was positioned behind the original one, both fitted with dual controls and an intercom. The canopy was lengthened and comprised two sliding parts which could be discarded in flight. In order to simplify production, the tail wheel was fixed. The number of fuel tanks was reduced to three (833 lb). Armament consisted of only one synchronised NS-23 canon and 100 rounds. For centring reasons, the ventral oil radiator was moved under the nose. The model was equipped for night flying but also for target towing and photographic reconnaissance missions with a camera for taking vertical photographs.

The La-9V prototype (a single-seat La-9 transformed into a two-seater at Gorki) carried out eight test flights in January 1947. On 2 June it was transferred to the NII VVS for the State trials, at the hands of the pilot I.M. Dziuba, under the supervision of the Chief Engineer and pilot V.I. Alexeyenko. A lot of defects were reported but the two men did not think that they were important enough to fail the model in its State trials. The report also noted that the handling, the general flight characteristics and the technical parameters were satisfactory, and that the model could join the training schools and the VVS's operational regiments for training.

The second La-9V (considered as a prototype). The oil radiator has been moved under the nose on this model to re-establish the CG. (J. Marmain)

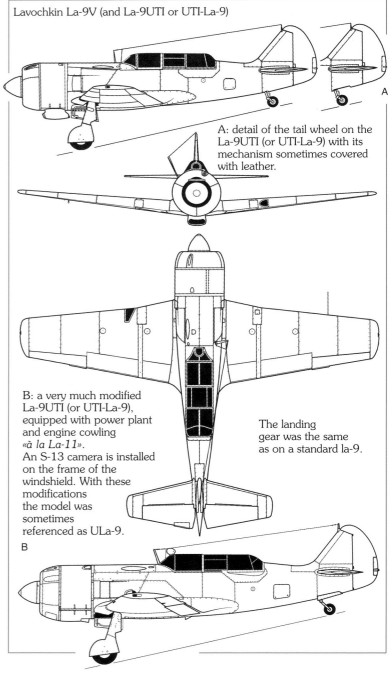

Lavochkin La-9V (and La-9UTI or UTI-La-9)

A: detail of the tail wheel on the La-9UTI (or UTI-La-9) with its mechanism sometimes covered with leather.

B: a very much modified La-9UTI (or UTI-La-9), equipped with power plant and engine cowling «à la La-11». An S-13 camera is installed on the frame of the windshield. With these modifications the model was sometimes referenced as ULa-9.

The landing gear was the same as on a standard la-9.

Series production started at Factory N°99 at Ulan-Ude in April 1948. A short while later, Serial N°49990609 was transferred to the NII VVS for conformity trials which caused it to be returned to OKB-301 where a series of modifications were carried out. Thus the NS-23 canon was replaced by a heavy synchronised UBS machine gun, the ASP-3 sights replaced the original ASP-1N, and new navigation and night-time flying search lights were installed as was an La-11-style windshield (see below). This modified La-9V went through its State trials, and the authorities ordered production to start, re-designating the aircraft as La-9UTI «Type 49» (often called UTI-La-9). Factory N°99 brought out 265 examples with an NS-23 canon or a UBS machine gun. Some of them were subsequently given another power-plant, like the La-11 (the oil radiator housed in the lower port of the engine cowling) and were sometimes designated as ULa-9 (1951).

Top to left at right.
La-9 serial N°49990609 modified as an La-9UTI (sometimes designated UTI-LA-9) with a UBS machine gun in place of the 23-mm canon. A camera gun was installed on the windshield frame. *(J. Marmain)*

A production series La-9UTI (or UTI-La-9) without its camera gun installed. The engine cowling has not been painted. *(J. Marmain)*

An La-9UTI re-engined «à la La-11» and re-designated ULa-9 (with a deeper cowling incorporating the oil radiator).

Technical Specifications

Wingspan: 32 ft. 4 in.	**Max. Take-off Weight:** 7 227 lb.
Length: 28 ft. 5 1/2 in.	**Max. Speed:** 411 mph. at 20 460 ft.
Wing Area: 189.321 sq. ft.	**Service Ceiling:** 36 712 ft.
Weight Empty: 5 618 lb.	**Range:** 596 miles at 3 300.

LAVOCHKIN

«Object 132» (or La-132) Project and «Object 132M» (or La-132M) Project (during 1946)

In 1946, the Lavochkin OKB returned to settle in Factory N°301 at Khimki (Moscow) where it started to work on jet-powered machines. This did not prevent it from continuing its experiments with stand-by motors or improving the La-9 model. Its first attempt concerned «Object 132» (or La-132) which was planned to have a 2 100 bhp (at take-off) ASh-93 engine enabling it to reach the speed of 459 mph at 24 750 ft. But it was not certified and the OKB had to replace it with an ASh-82FM fitted with larger-diameter cylinders, a fuel pump with an improved output and a three-stage supercharger (compared to the ASh-82FN). The prototype turned out to be very stable and at the third levelling out altitude (24 240 ft) it reached 445 mph. Unfortunately getting the power plant and the propeller to work correctly was problematic. The ASh-82FM was not mass-produced and the La-132 programme was shelved.

At the same time, a «back-up» project was also developed, designated «132M» (or La-132M) powered by an ASh-82M. But following the results of the «132», this project was also abandoned.

Technical Specifications

Wingspan: 32 ft. 4 in.
Length: 28 ft. 5 1/2 in.
Wing Area:
Weight Empty:
Max. Take-off Weight: 7 876 lb.
Max. Speed: 462 mph. at 21 450 ft (132), 456 mph at 16 500 ft (132M).
Service Ceiling: 39 600 ft (132), 37 950 ft (132M).
Range: 750 miles (132), 625 miles (132M).

The «32» prototype was in fact the «132» prototype (or La-132) photographed on the Chkalovskaya airfield. *(J. Marmain)*

LAVOCHKIN

«Object 138» and «Object 138D» Prototypes, or La-138 and La-138D (and sometimes La-9PVRD) (February 1947)

Technical Specifications

Wingspan: 32 ft. 4 in.	**Max. Speed:** 368 mph. at 0ft without VRD,
Length: 28 ft. 5 1/2 in.	412 mph at 0ft with VRD,
Wing Area: 189.321 sq. ft.	412 mph at 21 120 ft without VRD,
Weight Empty: 1 940 lb.	475 mph at 19 800 ft with VRD.
Max. Take-off Weight:	**Service Ceiling: Range:**
2 356 lb.	687 miles with VRD.

Before the programmes using stand-by engines were abandoned in 1948, the Lavochkin OKB was ordered to test the Bondariuk VRD-430 ramjets using a «130» (or La-130). Naturally the defects reported when the «164» was tested had to be rectified and the fuel capacity increased.

Two new prototypes were built using an La-9/ASh-82FN and tested in February 1947: «Object 138» and «Object 138D» (or La-138 and La-138D, or sometimes even La-138PVRD for both of them). OKB 301 had started its studies at the end of 1946 following a SovMIN resolution issued during the year, asking for speeds of 406 mph at sea-level and 475 mph at 19 800 ft. with the ramjets working (respectively 368 and 412 mph without the ramjets). The range had to be 687 miles at 3 300 ft.

Little is known about the design of these two machines except that the VRD-430s were installed using three faired fixation points under the wing on the second rib of each section, and that the planes were only armed with three 23-mm cannon (325 rounds), the fourth canon being eliminated in order to provide space for certain test equipment for the ramjets. As for the rest they were equipped in the same way as the «164».

The «138» carried out 20 flight tests whereas the «138D» made 38 flights. But apparently the programme did not go off as well as for the «164» because the VRD-430s were only satisfactory up to 9 900 feet and 19 tests were interrupted because they worked badly. Only ten flights

Lavochkin «138».

enabled the characteristics to be evaluated properly and the performances of the stand-by propulsion units gave an increase in speed of 70 mph, but only for 10 minutes. In fact the real speed difference when compared to a standard La-9 was only 37 mph and the disadvantages were always the same: there was a very clear reduction in speed when the VRD-430 ramjets were not used, the endurance was too short and there were a number of ignition problems. The authorities decided to stop the test programme, officially «until the VDR-430s were really ready». In fact the military authorities were no longer banking on anything else except the turbojet to power their combat aircraft.

A poor shot of the «138» flying over Tushino during the annual VVS parade. (J. Marmain)

The «138» prototype (La-138) in the process of being built and fitted out with its two VRD-430 ramjets. (J. Marmain)

LAVOCHKIN

«Object 134», or La-134 (or La-9M) Prototypes, «Object 134D» or La-134D and the La-11 «Type 51» series (May, June and August 1947)

The «134» prototype, or La-124, during its trails at Chkalovskaya in the summer of 1947. It gave rise to the La-11.

In May 1947, the test pilot A.G. Kotchetkov took off aboard «Object 134», or La-134 (or La-9M) (the three designations are all to be found in the relevant documents). It was a modified La-9 used as a prototype for the new all-metal La-11 escort fighter programme. It was only armed with three synchronised NS-23 cannon with 225 rounds, but its undercarriage was reinforced because of the increased weight caused by various modifications, including moving the oil radiator to the lower part of the ASh-82FN engine for centring reasons (which gave the cowling a tubby look) and increasing oil capacity. Fuel capacity was 183 gallons. OKB-301 studied the design for this machine for six months and the 18 factory test flights, for a total time of 12 hours and 13 minutes were used to determine flight parameters: speeds at different levelling-off altitudes, rate of climb, range at nominal engine speeds, and endurance, etc. The «134» was fitted with an AFA-IM camera (for vertical shots), navi-

The «134» during a test flight in 1947 to calculate its range.

The «134» without its wingtip tanks during trials at Chkalovskaya in the summer of 1947.

Lavochkin La-11.

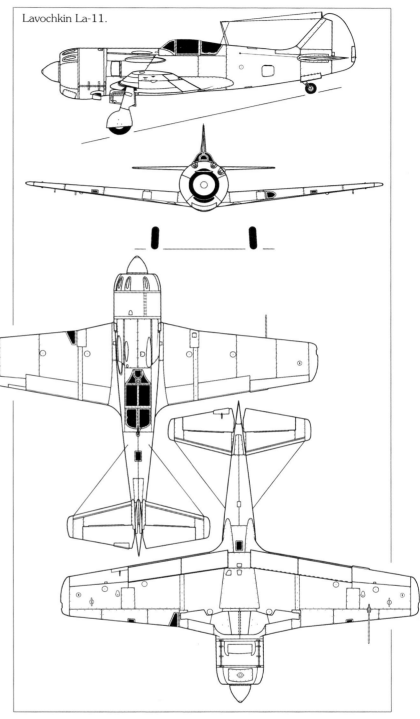

The «134D» or La-134 D prototype with two faired tanks on the wing tips.

gation lights, temperature gauge for the cylinders, a «Fairchild» camera gun (subsequently it was replaced by a Soviet-designed S-13, installed in the leading edge of the right-hand wing or on the windshield frame of the La-11s), a more comfortable seat and «toilet» installations for the pilot on long-range missions.

The «134» was transferred to the NII VVS at Tchkalovskaya on 18 June 1947 where five days later it was joined by the second prototype designated «Object 134D», or La-134D. This differed from the «134» by its fuel capacity which was increased to 244 gallons thanks to two extra tanks fitted in the wing tips and two faired tanks fixed to the tips giving a total extra capacity of 81 gallons. The two prototypes undertook a series of joint evaluation tests at the hands of A.G. Terentyev (134) and I.V. Timofeyev (134D). Some 111 defects «to be rectified urgently» were reported including re-centring the CG 2% further forward and improving the balance on the control surfaces to give better handling. The two prototypes carried out 71 test flights for a total flight time of 59 hours 13 minutes, including two long-range flights. The reports concluded that the «134» was better than the «130», but that an automatic pilot, a radar altimeter and a variety of other «modern» instruments would have to be installed.

After approving the trials evaluation report from the NII VVS on 22 August 1947, the SovMIN ordered production to begin under the designation La-11 «Type 51». The extra tanks on the wing tips were forgotten (the «134D» did not undergo any particular tests to determine the advantages or disadvantages of this particular arrangement, except to record a range of 2 031 miles at 3 300 ft) and the ejection system for the canopy was improved slightly (no test was made during the evaluation of the two prototypes, but Factory N°21 tested the system on an La-9 in 1946 then on an La-11 in 1947).

Just in 1948, some 210 modifications of various kinds were car-

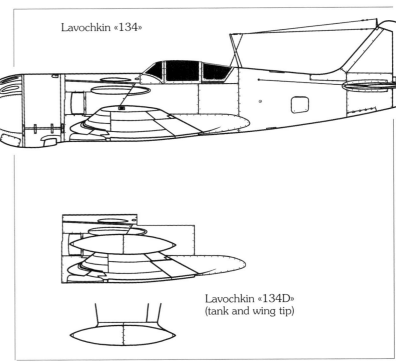

Lavochkin «134»

Lavochkin «134D»
(tank and wing tip)

ried out in the course of production. The La-11s were delivered to the Fighter Regiments of the VVS, but also to the pilot training schools and Navy Air Force units. The La-11 was built up to 1951: 100 in 1947, 650 in 1948, 150 in 1949 (production was interrupted that year), 150 in 1950 and 182 in 1951, for a total of 1 232 machines. In the summer of 1951, Factory N°81 carried out some tests with an La-11 armed with RS-82 rockets but these were not followed up. The NII VVS tested one machine with an ASh-82T, designed for the Ilyushin Il-14 transport plane.

An La-11 during its evaluation at Chkalovskaya in 1947.
(H. Leonard)

Right. **The La-11 preserved outside the Monino Museum. Its split flaps are set at 15°.**

In winter, the La-11 could be fitted with skis which were jettisoned just after take-off (they can be seen just in front of the wheels). Note the half-moon opening under the propeller for cooling the oil radiator.

(J. Marmain)

(J. Marmain)

An La-11, the last Lavochkin piston-engined fighter. Some took part in the first phases of the Korean War.

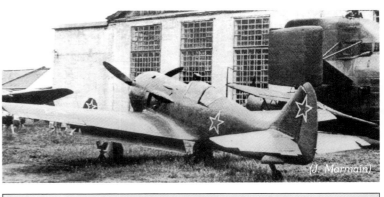

(J. Marmain)

Technical Specifications

Wingspan: 32 ft. 4 in. (33 ft. 11 in for the «134D») **Length:** 28 ft. 5 1/2 in.
Wing Area: 189.321 sq. ft.
Weight Empty: 6 094 lb.
Max. Take-off Weight: 8 206 lb. (8 791 lb overweight)

Max. Speed: 421 mph. at 20 460 ft, 422 mph («134D»)
Service Ceiling: 33 825 ft, 33 000ft («134D»)
Range: 1 584 miles, 2031 miles («134D»)
The figures apply to the «134» and the La-11.

LAVOCHKIN

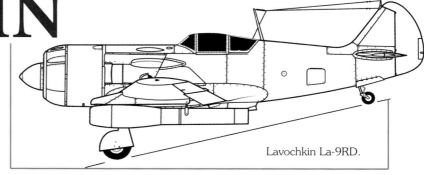

Lavochkin La-9RD.

La-9RD, or La-9/2D-13 Prototype, or La-9PVRD (July 1947)

By modifying and improving the casing, the diffusers and the rocker valves on his D-10 pulsejet, V.N. Tchelomeyi produced his D-13 design which was bench tested in July 1947. Two of them were attached under the modified wings (reinforced structure and slightly increased wing surface) of the La-9/ASh-82FN serial N° 48210509 from Factory N°21 which was renamed, strangely, La-9RD (perhaps because some documents designated Tchelomeyi's pulsejets as RD-10 and RD-13), or La-9/2D-13, sometimes La-9PuVRD. The «crazy» fuel consumption of the two D-13s which were fed fuel at very high pressure made the engineers increase the capacity of the fuel tanks. Earlier, in May 1947, the authorities had asked for a dozen La-9s to be brought up to the same standards and equipped with the same pulse jets in order to take part in the VVS anniversary in August. They were tested in the summer. Two of their cannon, their ammunition and the armour on the pilot's seat were removed in order to lighten the airframe and to provide the necessary space for the various D-13 test instruments, but also to re-establish the CG as far forward as possible. The Trials for the La-9RD were carried out at the beginning of August 1947 mainly to test the reliability of the D-13s and how well they worked. The machine took part in the VVS anniversary together with 12 other examples (see Note) by flying over the airfield at Tushino at 330 feet with a deafening roar. In November, the La-9RD was handed over to the NII VVS which had to carry out more intensive and thorough tests. The machine made 10 flights between 21 November 1947 and 13 January 1948. During the 4 hours and 11 minutes total flying time, the D-13s were ignited for 27 minutes. The results were not as brilliant as those obtained with the D-10s. The increase in speed was 79 mph at 8 580 ft, but this in fact was only 44 mph faster than the standard La-9 because the drag caused by the D-13s when not in use caused the speed to drop by 35 mph. In comparison with the ramjets, the trials revealed that the frontal drag of the D-13s was very much greater between 306 mph and 381 mph. Finally the deafening noise they made greatly disturbed both the pilots and those who could hear them on the ground. The final report on the trials concluded that the «pulsejets could not be used operationally». Take-off and initial acceleration were considered too long and slow, horizontal and vertical manoeuvrability was bad, the fuel consumption for the D-13s was «astronomical» and the extra speed when weighed against all these disadvantages was considered low. The programme was abandoned, all the more easily as all the builders were already engaged in jet-powered aircraft development.

(J. Marmain)

(J. Marmain)

(J. Marmain)

NB.: Concerning the number of La-9RDs, the sources do not agree. Some state that 12 were made, other only give nine. Only some of them do not include the original machine in these figures.

Technical Specifications

Wingspan: 32 ft. 4 in. **Length:** 28 ft. 5 1/2 in. **Wing Area:** 190.720 sq. ft. **Weight Empty:** 6 930 lb. **Max. Take-off Weight:** 8 393 lb.	**Max. Speed:** 341 mph. at 8 580 ft without the D-13s, 421 mph at 8 580 ft with the D-13s. **Service Ceiling: Range:**

Above, from top to bottom. **The La-9RD without its two pulse-jets. The faired attachment pylons can easily be seen under the wing.**

Two views of the La-9RD in the winter of 1947/1948. Its pulse-jets are attached under the wing by means of faired pylons.

LAVOCHKIN

Photographic reconnaissance La-11 (During 1950)

During 1950, the NII VVS tested a photographic reconnaissance variant of the La-11 equipped with an AFA-BA-40 mobile camera. The trials were conclusive, so much so that a hundred La-11s were converted to the same standards. They could carry two extra tanks underwing, but in this case they were clearly underpowered. To rectify this lack of power, Shvetsov, the engine designer and builder,

tried to boost an ASh-82FN so that it would develop 2 000 bhp. But this was doomed to failure because in order to obtain power of this sort, the engine's technology had to be entirely redesigned. As a result, the whole thing was abandoned. It had the same dimensions as the La-11. No figures for the performances.

EXCEPTIONS

This chapter deals only with jet-powered aircraft which were versions of models already mentioned in articles contained in the Encyclopaedia. In no way is this a way of misappropriating the object of this book.

CONTENTS

YAKOVLEV

Yak-7R/2DM-4S/D-1A

Technical specifications

Wingspan: 33 ft.
Length: 32 ft. 5 in.
Wing Area: 184.585 sq. ft.

Weight Empty: 3 410 lb.
Max. Take-off Weight: 6 402 lb.
Max. Speed: 500 mph.

In 1942, Yakovlev had his team study a project for a jet fighter within the experimental programmes on this type of propulsion. But unlike the other builders who were engaged in this venture, he did away with the normal engine and planned for two ramjets and a rocket motor. The study was based on the Yak-7A whose airframe was extensively modified in order to save time. Indeed only three elements were kept: the wings, the undercarriage and the tail. The absence of the normal engine and all its equipment and cooling system enabled the team to design a completely different fuselage which was in the shape of an «airfoil section» with a slight kink caused by the cockpit. The cone-shaped nose housed almost all the on-board equipment and two UBK machine guns with their ammunition (200 rounds per gun). It was followed by single-seat cockpit with a sliding canopy, positioned well forward of the wing leading edge in order to give the pilot excellent vision, except to the rear. Two kerosene tanks and one containing comburent (nitric acid) were fitted behind the cockpit to supply the D-1A-1 100 Dushkin-Shtokolov rocket-motor installed in the tail. Its exhaust nozzle stuck out beyond the tail surfaces. As a result the tailplane was

positioned higher up; the whole tail was 1 3/4 in slenderer and the new fuselage was 4 ft 4 in longer than the Yak-7A. The wings housed the four tanks used by the two DM-4S Merkulov ramjets. The ramjets were fitted into two cylindrical nacelles and hung under the wings. The tail wheel made entirely of metal because of the heat from the rocket-motor nozzle.

In practice the 2 420-lb thrust (10.78kN) from the rocket-motor was used to propel the aircraft during the take-off and climb phases of the flight so as to activate the ramjets and obtain their initial velocity. At the required height, the two DM-4Ss took over and the D-1A-1-100 was only used for interception and combat. The estimates included a speed of 500 mph at 26 400 ft, this height being reached in 80 seconds. Referenced as the Yak-7R/2DM-4S/D-1A, the project was finished on 27 August 1942. Unfortunately because the DM-4S ramjets were not mass-produced (this started only in 1944) and because the D-1A-1-100 was difficult to get to function properly (it was also tested on the Berezniak and Isayev «BI» programmes) the project could not be followed up further. Moreover in the end, Yakovlev thought that this type of propulsion unit limited the aircraft's range and operational use because of the huge fuel consumption of the two DM-4Ss (44 lb of kerosene per minute each) and the D-1A-1-100. The study subsequently served as a working basis when Yakovlev designed the Yak-3RD. (see below)

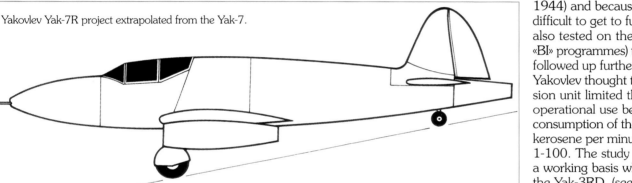

Yakovlev Yak-7R project extrapolated from the Yak-7.

GUDKOV-LIULKA
LAVOCHKIN

LaGG-3RTD-1
(or LaGG-3RD-1) Project (April 1943)

At the beginning of 1943, the engine designer A.M. Liulka was working relentlessly on the development of a turbojet within Bolkhovitinov's design team but under very difficult conditions. The idea was not just to develop a power plant which was destined to a great future, but also to try and save the Berezniak and Isayev «BI» programme, the first pure «jet» fighter tested in the USSR and whose Dushkin-Shtolokov D-1A-1-100 rocket-motor was very delicate to handle and prepare. The facilities available to Liulka did not allow him to pursue the development of his ideas. He then met M.I. Gudkov who was Chief-Designer at Factory N° 301, who had just finished his first fighter (the GU-1, see below) and shared the same opinions as him. Together the two men decided to propose the «very first true jet-powered fighter project».

They used a LaGG-3 airframe as a base; Gudkov knew it well; they cut

away all the front part of the fuselage which housed the M-105 and re-designed another one, very sloping this time, and able to house the Liulka RTD-1 (RD subsequently) turbojet with 880-lb thrust. Air was sucked into the turbojet through a large opening at the front, fed to the combustion chamber where the fuel was burned, causing the thrust which was evacuated through the exhaust nozzle. According to the plans which have been used up to this day, this came out under the aircraft's belly either at a level half way along the width of the wings or quite some distance further aft. All the front part was covered with metal panels, as was the underneath of the fuselage up to the tail wheel. Two guns were housed under the upper part of the engine cowling. The wing was re-designed. It was built around two main spars and one auxiliary spar onto which the ailerons and the split flaps were attached. The leading edge sweep on the central section was more pro-

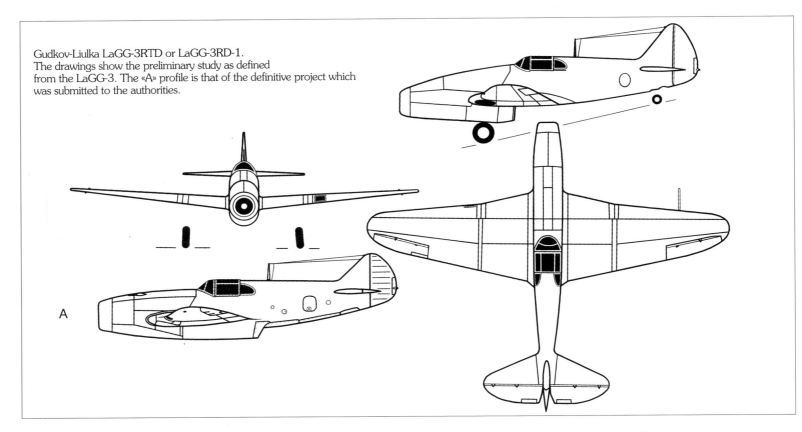

Gudkov-Liulka LaGG-3RTD or LaGG-3RD-1.
The drawings show the preliminary study as defined
from the LaGG-3. The «A» profile is that of the definitive project which
was submitted to the authorities.

A

nounced than on the outer sections. The undercarriage was that of the LaGG-3, as was the cockpit and all the rear part of the fuselage including the tail.

In order not to go through official channels and get caught up in the NKAP's red tape, Gudkov presented his project, the LaGG-3RTD-1 (also referenced as LaGG-3RD-1, the «RTD» having been re-designated RD-1 in the meantime) in April 1943, directly to his boss, A.I. Shakurin and to G.M. Malenkov, the secretary to the Soviet Communist Party Central Committee in charge of supervising the aircraft industry, without going through A.S. Yakovlev who was putting a lot of pressure on Gudkov at the time and who was Shakurin's deputy and responsible for the experimental aircraft sector.

The answer was not slow in coming, for on 27 April, the project was examined by a commission of experts from Principal Directorate N°7 of the NKAP responsible for experimental aircraft engine construction. The official conclusion was «six of one and half a dozen of the other». As it stood, the project was of no real interest since it was based on a classic fighter airframe. On the other hand, its jet power was deemed interesting. But the authorities considered that «building the airframe and the turbojet, which was not sufficiently developed, was premature». In this context, the Liulka-Gudkov association had no reason to be and the project was abandoned. No figures are known except for the length (39 ft 9 in), the wingspan (34 ft 7 in), the span of the tail (12 ft) and the track (11 ft 6 in).

YAKOVLEV ★

Yak-Jumo Prototypes (or Yak-3 Jumo, or Yak-15, or Yak-15-RD10, or Yak-RD) (October and December 1945) and Yak-17-RD-10 (or Yak-RD10) (September 1946)

The Russians first learnt of the existence of German rocket-motor-and turbojet-powered planes in 1943. A year later they were faced with a *fait-accompli*: the British had them, the Americans were testing them. In the USSR, apart from the «BI» rocket-motor programme which turned out to be complex to develop, no aircraft powered in the same way actually existed. Stalin told off all the heads of the aircraft industry and in February 1945, the builders were sent for and at the Kremlin, Stalin ordered them to pull out all the stops and develop jet-powered planes. Only A.M. Liulka succeeded in making any headway in developing his axial-flow turbojet; but it was a long way from being operational. As a result, Stalin recommended that the Junkers Jumo 004B and BMW 003A engines discovered in Germany be copied and mass-produced in Russia (they were, under the designations RD-10 and RD-20 respectively). In the Kremlin, Stalin asked Yakovlev to develop such a fighter as quickly as possible, a request confirmed in a directive dated 15 April 1945 by the State Defence Committee ordering the OKB at Factory N°115 to study, build and

submit for «trials», a fighter powered by a «Jumo 004» turbojet. While Sukhoi was engaged in designing a twin-engined jet aircraft copied off the Messerschmitt Me-262 and Mikoyan, Gurevich and Lavochkin were studying totally new single-jet and twin-jet powered aircraft designs, Yakovlev decided on the fastest solution possible: he thought that the Yak-3 was a good modern airframe, suitable for conversion to jet power; the pilots would not find the cockpit too unfamiliar and that as a result, they would feel safer and less suspicious of the new type of propulsion.

Referred to as the Yak-Jumo (or Yak-3-Jumo), the programme was entrusted to E.G. Adler assisted by Shekter. They kept the Yak-3/V-107A design, cut off the front part of the fuselage housing the piston engine and kept the cockpit, the tail, the undercarriage and most of the wings. Drawing up the plans started in May 1945. A 1 980-lb-thrust Jumo 004B jet was literally hooked up under the nose (Liulka and Gudkov had already used this type of configuration in 1942 on an LaGG-3 airframe (see above) installed on a mounting made of weld-

(J. Marmain)

(J. Marmain)

(J. Marmain)

(J. Marmain)

From top to bottom, and left to right.
Two views of the Jak-Jumo or Yak-3-Jumo, the first fighter prototype powered by a turbojet designed by the Yakovlev OKB, photographed in front of Factory N°115 buildings at Moscow.

Two views of the Yak-17-RD10 prototype with its unusual undercarriage. It was the second jet fighter designed by the Yakovlev OKB, photographed here during its trials. The model was not chosen in spite of a better performance than the Yak-3-Jumo which gave rise to the Yak-15.

ed steel tubes with rubber shock absorbers; the assembly was attached to the rest of the fuselage by an appropriately sloping structure. The axis of the «Jumo» was inclined 4°30' upwards and the exhaust nozzle was situated under the belly of the fuselage just ahead of the wing trailing edge. All the front of the Yak-3-Jumo was covered in chrome alloy plates (KhGSA).

The wing spars were reinforced and curved to fit over the turbojet. Two fuel tanks were set in the central wing section, between the spars, with a third one lodged above the «Jumo». The canopy was more streamlined with a windshield moulded from a single piece and a rearward-sliding canopy. The tail surfaces were slightly bigger. The planned armament comprised a ShVAK canon and a UBS under the upper part of the nose, then two B-20s, finally two Ns-23s with 60 rounds each but these were not installed on the prototype which appeared in October 1945 to carry out its first taxiing trials and a few short regulation «flea jumps» at the hands of M.I. Ivanov. Because of the exhaust under the belly of the fuselage, the metal skin was not quite long enough and, in particular, nobody had thought of the rubber tail wheel which was directly in the line of the exhaust nozzle and the hot gases.

Before undertaking a test flight of any length, the machine was sent back to the factory to undergo the necessary modifications and to have a retracting all-steel tail wheel. Then it was transferred to the TsAGI to go through a series of wind tunnel tests, with and without the turbojet operating until February 1948. After a new series of ground tests a few minor changes were carried out and the turbojet was replaced by a new Jumo 004B.

The first flight took place on 24 April 1946 with M.I. Ivanov at the controls, just three hours after the turbojet-powered MiG-3 prototype's first flight. Meanwhile, the Yak-Jumo was re-designated Yak-15 (according to the documents, the second prototype was also referred to as the Yak-15-RD10 or Yak-RD). To everybody's surprise, the tests went ahead without any major incident except that the steel panels covering the underside of the fuselage had to be attended to because of the damage caused by the burning hot turbojet exhaust gases. The prototype took part in the VVS anniversary at Tushino on 18 August 1946 in company with the MiG-9. Stalin ordered 12 examples to be built so that they could take part in the parade commemorating the anniversary of the «October Revolution» (in fact on 7 November), eighty days later. At the same time mass-production was ordered at Factory

N°31 at Tbilissi, well before all the trials were completed at the NII VVS. From December 1946 to April 1947, Serial N°31002 and 31005 armed with a NS-23 canon underwent a test programme for fighter training aircraft with G.A. Seyedov and A.G. Prochakov. The acrobatic trials turned out to be just as easy to do as for the Yak-3. But in terms of handling and stability, the Yak-15 did not satisfy the NII VVS's demands for a variety of reasons: the hardness of the joystick varied depending on engine speed; the wings were relatively thick for this type of power plant; the speed had to be limited to Mach 0.68; and the recommended maximum speed not to be exceeded was 437 mph at 10 395 feet. In spite of all that, the first pre-production series Yak-15s were delivered in September 1946 (October according to different sources). In all 280 examples were produced.

Before this, a second programme had been developed and a prototype built, which appeared on 3 September 1946 with the same armament. Designated Yak-17-RD-10 or Yak-RD, or Yak-RD10 according to the documents, it had an entirely new tail with a larger surface area; it had a laminar flow wing; the canopy was redesigned with a shorter end section; the landing gear consisted of two single-members with a wheel lever, which retracted backwards on either side of the RD-10 turbojet nozzle, twisting round to lodge in the wing near the fuselage. The whole of the front sloped downwards and was fatter; fuel capacity was increased to 160 gallons (1 298 lb). The prototype was tested on 20 September 1946, but although it was slightly faster, the Yak-Jumo was chosen in preference for mass-production because its design was thought to be better for converting the pilots to «jet» power, despite a report recommending the production of a two-seat version with tricycle undercarriage.

NB.: Two types appeared in the specialised Russian press. One shows the LaGG-3RTD with its very sloping engine cowling and the turbojet nozzle under the belly, directly below the windshield. The other is better finished with the turbojet incorporated into the front of the fuselage which slopes less, with its nozzle beyond the level of the wing trailing edge. The first seems to be a preliminary study whereas the other is no doubt the project presented to Shakurin and to Malenkov, since all the lower part of the fuselage is covered with metal panels to protect the structure from the bad effects of the burning gases.

Technical specifications

Wingspan: 30 ft. 4 in.	**Range:** 312 miles.*
Length: 28 ft. 8 1/2 in.	*These figures concern the Yak-*
Wing Area: 159.830 sq. ft.	*Jumo/Yak-15.*
Weight Empty: 4 367 lb.	**estimates based on the theoretical*
Max. Take-off Weight: 5 654 lb.	*speed of the turbo-jet, i.e. 8 700 rpm.*
Max. Speed: 500 mph. at 16 500 ft.	*In fact, the Jumo 004B never exceeded*
Service Ceiling: 45 210 ft.*	*6 000 rpm during the trials.*

ABBREVIATIONS and INITIALS

AIR FORCE

A Aviation
AA Air Army
AD Air Division
ADD Long Range Aviation (**ADD** until 1944 then 18th Air Army)
AK Air Corps
AO Air formation
AON Special Bomber Army
AP Air Regiment
AShPO Primary Training School
Aviabrigada Air Brigade (or aviation brigade)
Aviazveno Svyazi Liaison flight or formation
A-VMF Navy Air Force
A VDV Soviet Airborne Troops Aviation
BAB Air Bomber Brigade
BAD Air Bomber Division
BAK Bomber Air Corps
BAO Air Maintenance Battalion
BAP Air Bomber Regiment
BBAP Short-range Air Bomber Regiment
ShAD Air Assault Division
ShAK Air Assault Corps
ShAP Air Ground Attack Regiment
ShF Black Sea Fleet
DA Strategic (long-range) Aviation
DBA Strategic Bomber (long-range) Aviation
DBAD Strategic (long-range) Bomber Division
DBAP Strategic (long-range) Bomber Regiment
DD Long-range Support Aviation
DRAP Long-range Air Reconnaissance Regiment
Devyatka Name used for a formation composed of three x three planes (Zvenos)
Diviziya Air Division (four to six regiments)
DVK "Heavy Bomber division" (the idea is "air cruisers")
EON Special Combat Flight (notion of "special tasks)
EVK heavy bomber squadrons (idea of "air cruisers")
Eskadrilya Squadron
F Navy Air Force before VMF
FA Front line aviation (tactical aviation) the so-called "front", or "Military District Aviation"
Flotiliya Flotilla, generally a small regional aviation unit.
GvIAD (or **GIAD**) Fighter Air Division of the Guard
GvIAP (or **GIAP**) Fighter Air Regiment of the Guard
GvShAD (or **GShAD**) Air Assault Division of the Guard
Gv (or **G**) Guard (of the… + initials)
Istrebityel Fighter
IA Air Fighter squadron or fighter aviation
IAB Fighter Air Brigade
IAD Fighter Air Division
IAK Fighter Air Corps
IAK-PVO Fighter Air Corps assigned to defence (PVO)
IAP (National Defence) Fighter Air Regiment
IA-PVO (National Defence) Fighter Squadron
IAP-PVO Fighter Air Regiment
KAF Squadron attached to an Army Corps
KAO Air Corps
KAZ Air Corps (smaller than KAO)
KBF Baltic Fleet (Red Flag)
KVF Red Air Fleet
LBE Light Bomber Squadron
LShE Light Assault Squadron
LNBAP Light Night Bomber Air Regiment
LUK Leningrad Training Centre
MA Soviet Navy Air Force (before VMF)
MRAP Air Reconnaissance Regiment
MTAD Torpedo and mine-laying air division
MTAP Torpedo and mine-laying air division
NBAP (or **NSBAP**) Night Bomber Air Regiment
O suffix for "independent"
OAE Independent Navy Squadron
OAG Special Air Group
OShAE (or **OShAE**) Independent Air Assault Group
ODAP Independent Reconnaissance Air Regiment
ODVA Special Orient Army (Siberia)
OIAE Independent Fighter Squadron
OIAO Independent Fighter Formation (or unit?)
OKA Independent Air Army (Red Flag)
OLBAE Independent Light Bomber Squadron
OMAG Independent Naval Air Group
OMIAO Navy Air Force Independent Fighter Formation (or unit?)
OMRAO Independent Navy Air Force Reconnaissance Formation (or unit?)
OMRAP Independent Navy Reconnaissance Air Regiment
ORAE Independent Reconnaissance Squadron
ORAO Independent Reconnaissance Formation (or unit?)
ORAP Independent Reconnaissance Air Regiment
ORGAO Independent Seaplane Reconnaissance Formation (or unit?)
OTA Independent Heavy Bomber Formation (or unit?)
PAD Dive-bomber Air Division
PBAP Dive-bomber Air Regiment
Polk Regiment
PVO Air forces assigned to the defence of national territory
RAB Reserve Air Brigade
RAG Reserve Air Group (of the Stavka - Supreme Command Headquarters
RAP Reconnaissance Air Regiment
RKKVF Peasants' and Workers' Military Air Fleet
RVGK Supreme Command of the Reserves (VVS) or Reserves of the Supreme High Command
RVZ Air Maintenance (or reparation) unit
SAB Mixed Air Division
SAK Mixed Air Corps
SAP Mixed Air Regiment
SBAP Rapid Bomber Air Regiment (or rapid bombing air regiment)
SF North Sea Fleet
SVGK (Stavka) Supreme Command (Headquarters)
TAD Air Transport Division
TAP Air Transport Regiment
TBAP Heavy Bomber Regiment
TBE Heavy Bomber Squadron
TShF see **ShF**
TOF (or **ToF**) Pacific Fleet
TsARB (or **TSARB**) Central Air Maintenance (or repairs) Base
UVOFLOT Military Administration for the Air Fleet
UVVS name of the VVS before 1924 - Air Ministry
UVVS RKKA Supreme Administration of the Workers' and Peasants' (RKKA) Soviet Air Forces (UVVS)
VA Air Army
VAU Second Level Training School
VShL Military Pilot Training School
VShML Military Pilot Training School for the Navy (or the Navy air force)
VGK VVS Headquarters
VMF see A-VMF-VMF Soviet Union Naval Forces
VMS Naval Military Forces
VVF Military Air Forces
VVS Soviet Air Forces
VVS ShF Black Sea Air Forces (of the Red Flag)
VVS KBF Baltic Fleet Air Forces (of the Red Flag)
VVS RKKA or **VVA KA** Soviet Air Forces (VVS) of the Red Army of the Workers and the Peasants
VVS SF Soviet Air Forces of the North Sea Fleet (of the Red Flag)
VVS SSSR name of the Soviet Air Forces in 1924
VVS TOF (or ToF) Soviet Air Forces of the Pacific Fleet (of the Red Flag)
VVS VMF Soviet Air Forces (VVS) of the Navy (VMF), or Navy Air Force
Zveno Air Patrol (usually three planes)

INSTITUTIONS AND DESIGN TEAM ABBREVIATIONS

TsAGI Central Aero-hydrodynamic Institute
TsKB Central Construction (or Design) Office
TsKB Aviatresta Central Construction (or Design) Office State Trust
TsIAM Central Institute for Research into aircraft Engines
VIAM Scientific Research Institute for aeronautical materials
TTT Tactical and Technical Specifications
AGO Aviation and Hydrodynamics Department
AGOS Experimental Construction Department for Aircraft and seaplanes of the TsAGI
AN SSSR URSS Academy of Sciences
ANTK Scientific and Technical Aviation Complex
Aviavnito Technical and Scientific Research Organisation for all the Union, or Avia tion Department of Vnito (or Anito)
BNK New Construction (or designs) Office
BNT NKAP Office for New technologies
ShKO Drawings and Plans Department assigned to production lines
EOLID Service, In-flight and Streamlining Tests Department at the TsAGI
GAZ State aeronautical production factory
GDL Laboratory for Gas Dynamics
GIRD Study Group for jet engines (or group for the study of jet propulsion)
GIRT State Institute for Jet Engine Techniques (or Technology)
GosNII GVF State Institute for Scientific Research for the civilian air fleet
GosNII VVS State Institute for Scientific Research of the Soviet Air Forces, Ministry of Defence
GosSibNIA Institute for Scientific Aeronautical Research for the State of Siberia
GROSS Institute for Experimental Civilian Aeronautical Construction
IAM Institute for the Construction of Aero-Engines
IIKVF Institute for Engineers of the Red Air Fleet
IMTU Imperial Technical School in Moscow (in the Tsar's days)
KAI Kazan Institute of Aviation
KB Construction (or design) team
KhAI Kharkov Aviation Institute
KOSOS Experimental Aeronautical Construction Department; or Design Section of the TsAGI Experimental Construction Division
LIG Leningrad Institute of the Civilian Air Fleet (GVF)
LII In-flight Research Institute
LII GKAP In-flight Research and Trial Institute for the State Committee of the Aircraft Industry.
LK Leningrad Kombinat
MAI Moscow Aviation Institute
MAT Moscow School for Aeronautical Technology
MOTS Moscow Aero-technical School for the Special Services
MVTU Moscow Higher Technical School
NAMI Institute for Scientific Studies on Engines
NIAI Leningrad Institute for Research in Aeronautical Sciences
NIIAP VVS Science Institute for Aeronautical Instrument Trials
NIIAV VVS Science Institute for Aircraft Armament Trials
NII VVS Soviet Air Force Institute for In-flight Trials
NIPAV (AK) Scientific Trial Polygon for Aircraft Armament
OAM Aircraft Engine Department
OKB Design team (or experimental construction team)
OKB MS d° but for the Navy
OKO Experimental study section
OMOS Experimental Aeronautical Construction Section for the Navy air force.
OOK Special Construction (or design) Dept.
OOM Aircraft Engine Section
OOS Experimental Aircraft Construction Dept.
OPO Experimental Department
OSK Special Construction Section (or Dept.)
OSS Experimental Aircraft Construction Department - or Land-based Aircraft Section
Ostekhbyuro Special Technical Bureau for Military Inventions
OTB Special technical Bureau (Charaga)
RNII Scientific Research Institute for Diesel Engines (merger of GIRD and GDL in 1933)
SibNIA Siberian Institute for Aeronautical Research – the Siberian branch of the TsAGI
SKB Design (or studies) bureau assigned to the production in a factory
SNII Scientific Institute for Military and Civilian Aircraft Trials
SOK Special design (or construction) section
SOS Experimental Construction Section (or sector)
STO Special Technical Bureau (charaga)
UNIADI Ukrainian Institute for Scientific Research on Diesel Engines at Kharkov
UNII DVS Ukrainian Institute for Scientific Research on Internal Combustion Engines
UVI Military Invention Directorate
VVA Jukovsky Academy of the Soviet Air Force
VVIA D° but at Leningrad
ZOK TsAGI (and GVF) Prototype Production Factory

POLITICAL ABBREVIATIONS

Amtorg Organisation looking after USA imports
Aviasovyet Unified Aviation Council
Aviatrest State Union for the Aircraft Industry, or State Union for the Aviation Industry in the Supreme Administration of the Metallurgical Industry
Aviatrust Vnito Aviation Department, scientific and technical research organisation for the whole Union
CC VPK (b) Communist Party Central Committee
DOSAAF Association of Volunteers in support of the Army, Air Force and the Navy.
GKAP State Aircraft Industry Committee
GKAT State Aircraft Equipment Committee
GKO State Defence Committee (Ministry)
GlavkoAvia Supreme Aviation Administration - aircraft construction (or *Glavkoavia*)
Gkavvozdukhflot Supreme Air Force Board (Administration Council)
GU General Directorate (used as a suffix or Prefix added to another set of initials)
GUAP Supreme Directorate of the Aircraft Industry
Glavaviaprom The same as GUAP
Glavkoavia Supreme Combined Board (Administration Council) of aircraft production factories
Glavsevmorput Administration for the Northern Sea Routes
GUGVF Supreme Administration for the Civilian Air Fleet
GURKKVVF Supreme Administration of the Workers' and Peasants' Air Fleet
Glavvozdukhflot The same as GURKKVVF
GUSMP Supreme Administration of the Navy
GUVP Supreme Administration of Military Industry
GUVVSSA (GU-VVS) Supreme Directorate of Soviet Air Forces
GVF Civilian Air Fleet
KO Defence Committee (or council)
KOMTA Heavy Aviation Committee (from construction to…)
MAP Ministry of the Aircraft Industry
NKAP (or **NKAT**) State (or People's) Commissariat (or Ministry) for the aircraft Industry
Narkomat Oborony People's Commissariat (or Ministry) for Defence
Narkomaviaprom the same as NKAP (abbreviation)
NKEP State (or People's) Commissariat (or Ministry) for the Radio Industry
NKOP State (or People's) Commissariat (or Ministry) for the Defence Industry, or Main People's Board (Administration Council) of the Commissariat for Armament Production
NKTP State (or People's) Commissariat (or Ministry) for Heavy Industry
NKVD State (or People's) Commissariat (or Ministry) for Internal Affairs, or Ministry of the Interior
NKVM State (or People's) Commissariat (or Ministry) for Military and Naval Affairs
NKTVVS Scientific and Technical Committee
NTO-VSNKh Scientific and Technical Department of the Supreme Council for National Economy
OGPU Special Government Administration or Secret Police
Osoaviakhim Association for help to the Aircraft and Chemical Industries, or Association for the Promotion of the Aircraft and Chemical Industries
OVI War Inventions Department of the RKKA
RKKA Workers' and Peasants' Red Army
RKKVF (RKKVVF) Workers' and Peasants' Military Air Fleet (before becoming the VVS)
RVS Revolutionary Military Council
SNK (SovNarKom) People's Commissaries' Council (or Cabinet)
Stavka VGK Army Supreme Command
VAO State Trust for the Aircraft Industry and Unified Aeronautical Organisations
VKP (b) Communist Party Aircraft Construction Department
VNOS Aerial Observation Communication and Information Service
VSNkh Supreme Council for the National Economy

ARMAMENT ABBREVIATIONS

ShKas Aircraft machine gun
ShVAK Large-calibre aircraft canon
FAB Aircraft bomb (fragmentation)
FOTAB flares
FT Request coming from the front (turret)
RS Jet propelled missile (or rocket)
RSB Bomber radio
RSI Fighter radio
UBS Universal synchronised Beresine (machine gun)
UBT Universal Beresine for turret (machine gun)
VISh variable pitch propeller
AMTs aluminium-magnesium alloy
KPD efficiency coefficient
Ezkiznyi sketch

MANUFACTURER'S INITIALS OR ABBREVIATIONS

AIR A. I. Rykov (Yakovlev)
ANT A.N. Tupolev
BITCh B. I. Tcheranovski
BOK Byuro osobykh konstruktsky (design or construction office-team)
Sh V.D. Shavrov
K K. A. Kalinine
NV V. V. Nikitine
OKA 0. K. Antonov (Oleg Konstantinovitch)
RAF A. N. Rafaelyants
SAM S.A. Moskaleyev
Ya (or **Yak**) A.S. Yakovlev
ZIG Zavod imeni Golstmana
GAZ or **Zavod N°89** Aviation Factory N°89

ABBREVIATIONS (1940)

Ar A.A. Archangelski
Be G. M. Beriev
Yer Yermolayev
Gr P.D. Grushin
Gu Gudkov
Il S.V. Ilyushin
La Lavochkin
LaG Lavochkin-Gorbunov
LaGG Lavochkin-Gudkov-Gorbunov
MiG Mikoyan-Gurevich
Mya, VM V.M. Myassichtchev
Pe V. M. Petlyakov
Po N. N. Polikarpov
Su Sukhoi
Ta V.K. Taïrov
Tch V. Tchetverikov
Tu A.N. Tupolev
Yak A.S. Yakovlev
M or **AM** A. Mikulin
ASh Shvetsov
DV Dobrinin
VK V. Klimov

ANNEXES

LAVOCHKIN

YEAR (month or period)	Makers	Engine	Designation	Status	Observations
1939 (spring)	RIJKOV-LAVOCHKIN-G-G	(I-22) (I-301)	M-105P	Preliminary study	With Rijkov, Project I-22 = the designation was never used
1940 (March)	LAVOCHKIN-G-G	I-301 N°01 (LAGG-1)	M-105P	Prototype	With Gorbunov and Gudkov, re-designated LaGG-1
1940 (November)	LAVOCHKIN-G-G	I-301 N°02 (LAGG-1)	M-105P	Prototype	With Gorbunov and Gudkov, re-designated LaGG-1
1940 (December)	LAVOCHKIN-G-G	LaGG-3/M-105P "Type 31"	M-105P	Series	(6 528 built in 66 production batches, all versions included)
1941 (December)	LAVOCHKIN	LaGG-3/M-82 (or LaG-3/M-82)	M-82	Prototype	L-82 programme, Prototype first La-5 series
During 1941	LAVOCHKIN-G-G	LaGG-3/M-105PA "Type 31"	M-105PA	Series	From the 4th to the 28th production batch
1942 (beginning)	LAVOCHKIN-G-G	LaGG-3-37 (and N°34 batch)	M-105PF	Small series	of 20 machines with ShK-37 axial canon and Batch N°34 with NS-37 37-mm axial canon
1942 (February)	LAVOCHKIN	"Sparka" (LaGG two-seater)	M-105P	Prototype	Built by Gorbunov according to the sources
1942 (February?)	LAVOCHKIN	LaGG UTI (two-seater)	M-105P	1 or 2 prototypes	Training, conversion some doubt whether it existed
1942 (June)	LAVOCHKIN	LaGG-3/M-105PF "Type 31"	M-105PF	Series	From the 29th to the 66th Batches
1942 (June)	LAVOCHKIN	La-5 (LaG-5 or LaGG-5) "Type 37"	M-82A	Production Series (Series)	
1942 (August)	LAVOCHKIN	LaGG-3/2VRD (LaGG-3PVRD)	M-105PF + two VRD-1s	Prototype	Mixed power plants, with two ramjets
1942 (November)	LAVOCHKIN	La-5F "Type 37"	M-82F	Series	
1942 (December)	LAVOCHKIN	(La-5FN)	M-82FN	Two prototypes	Without any specific designation, but La-5FN forerunners
1942 (end of the year)	LAVOCHKIN	La-5FNV	M-82FNV	Prototype	The M-82FNV was re-designated M-82FN for the series La-5FN forerunner
1943 (March)	LAVOCHKIN	La-5 "Double" "Type 39"	M-82FN	Prototype	La-5FN prototype
1943 (April)	LAVOCHKIN	La-5/M-71	M-71	Prototype	
1943 (spring)	LAVOCHKIN	La-5FN "Type 39"	M-82FN	Series	Wing spars made of wood
1943 (summer)	LAVOCHKIN	La-5F/2TK-3 or La-5TK	M-82/2TK-3	Prototype	
1943 (August)	LAVOCHKIN	La-5UTI (UTI-La-5, ULa-5)	M-82	Series	Two seat liaison, reconnaissance (UTI-La-5 and ULa-5 were conversion at the front)
1944 (January)	LAVOCHKIN	"120 N°01" (La-1120 N°1)	Ash-82FN	Prototype	"1944 standard" La-5, La-7 prototype 1944 ()
1944 (March)	LAVOCHKIN	"120 N°2" (La-120 N°2)	Ash-82FN	Prototype	"1944-standard", La-7 prototype
1944 (May)	LAVOCHKIN	"1944 Standard" La-5FN	M-82FN	Series	Wing spars made of metal
1944 (May)	LAVOCHKIN	La-7 (Type 45)	M-82FN	Series	6 158 built of which 368 with three B-20 cannon
1944 (July)	LAVOCHKIN	La-7TK (La-7/ASh-82FN-2TK-3)	Ash-82FN/2TK-3	Prototype	
1944 (summer)	LAVOCHKIN	La-7TK (La-7/ASh-82FN-2TK-3)	Ash-82FN/2TK-3	Pre-production series	10 aircraft built
1944 (summer)	LAVOCHKIN	La-7TK (La-7/ASh-71FN-2TK-3)	Ash-71FN/2TK-3	Prototype	La-7/M-71 or La-7Ash-71 according to the sources
1944 (autumn)	LAVOCHKIN	La-7UTI (Type 46)	Ash-82FN	Prototype	Two-seat trainer, liaison and reconnaissance aircraft
1944 (October)	LAVOCHKIN	La-7R-1	ASh-82FN + RD-1	Prototype	Mixed power plants
1944 (December)	LAVOCHKIN	La-7/ASh-83	ASh-82FN	Prototype	ex-La-120 N°2
1944 (end of the year)	LAVOCHKIN	La-7L	ASh-82FN	Prototype	Laminar wing
1944 (end of the year)	LAVOCHKIN	La-7 (with NS-23 cannon and UBS	ASh-82FH	Prototype	Weapons test bench: one NS-23 canon and one UBS-20 canon
1945 (beginning)	LAVOCHKIN	La-7/RD-2M-3V	M-82FN + RD-2M-3V	Project	Mixed power plants
1945 (January)	LAVOCHKIN	La-7R-2	ASh-FN + RD-1KhZ	Prototype	Mixed propulsion units
1945 (July)	LAVOCHKIN	"120R" (La-120R)	ASh-83 + RD-1KhZ	Prototype	One of the two La-120s with the RD-1KhZ rocket-motor
1945 (November)	LAVOCHKIN	La-7PuVRD (or La-7PVRD)	ASh-82FN + two D-10s	Prototype	or La-7D-10 of La-7/2D-10 mixed propulsion units (Tchelomeyi pulse-jets)
1945 (end of the year)	LAVOCHKIN	"126", or La-126	ASh-82FN	Prototype	Forerunner of the La-9 programme
1946 (January)	LAVOCHKIN	"130" (La-130)	ASh-82FN	Prototype	Prototype for the La-9 version
1946 (March)	LAVOCHKIN	"120" (PVRD), or La-120PRVD	ASh-82FN + VRD-430	Project	Project to modify the "120" prototype for mixed propulsion units
1946 (Spring)	LAVOCHKIN	La-7UTI (UTI-La-7)	ASh-82FN	Series	584 built
1946 (spring)	LAVOCHKIN	"130R" (La-130R)	ASh-83FN + RD-1KhZ	Unfinished prototype	Mixed power units
1946 (spring/summer)	LAVOCHKIN	La-7PPVRD	ASh-82FN + two D-12	Prototype	La-7 prototype with two D-12 pulse-jets
1946 (summer)	LAVOCHKIN	La-7UTI/PuVRD or La-7PuVRD	ASh-82FN + two D-10s	Three prototypes	With two Tchelomeyi D-10 pulse-jets
1946 (June)	LAVOCHKIN	La-126PVRD ("164" or La-7S)	Ash- + VRD-430	Prototype	La-126 prototype modified for mixed propulsion units
1946 (August)	LAVOCHKIN	La69 "Type 48"	Ash-82FN	Production series	1 569 built
During 1946	LAVOCHKIN	"132" (La-132)	ASh-82-FM	Prototype	La-9 production series prototype
During 1946	LAVOCHKIN	"132M" (La-132M)	ASh-82M	Project abandoned	
1947 (January)	LAVOCHKIN	La-9V	ASh-82FN	Prototype	Two-seat trainer, reconnaissance
1947 (February)	LAVOCHKIN	"138" (La-138)	ASh-82FN + VRD-430	Prototype	or La-130PVRD Mixed propulsion units
1947 (February)	LAVOCHKIN	"138D" (La-138D)	ASh-82FN + VRD-430	Prototype	or La-130PVRD Mixed propulsion units
1947 (April)	LAVOCHKIN	La-9UTI "Type 49" (and ULa-9?)	ASh-82FN	Series	265 built - Two seat trainer, reconnaissance (ULa-9 = conversion with "à la La-11" engine)
1947 (May)	LAVOCHKIN	"134" (La-134 or La-9M)	ASh-82FN	Prototype	La-11 prototype
1947 (June)	LAVOCHKIN	"134D" (La-134D)	ASh-82FN	Prototype	La-11 Prototype
1947 (July)	LAVOCHKIN	La-9RD (La-9PuVRD)	ASh-82FN + two D-13s	Prototype	or La-9/2D-13, mixed propulsion units
1947 (July-August)	LAVOCHKIN	La-9RD (La-9PuVRD)	ASh-82FN + two D-13	Short run	or La-9/2D-13 Mixed propulsion units 9 or 12 built depending on the sources
1947 (August)	LAVOCHKIN	La-11 "Type 51"	ASh-82FN	Series	1 232 built
During 1950	LAVOCHKIN	La-11 Photo reconnaissance	Ash-82FN	Conversions	100 examples converted
During 1951	LAVOCHKIN	ULa-9	ASh-82FN	Conversions	Conversion of the La-9UTI with engine installed as in the La-11

MiG

YEAR (month or period)	Makers	Engine	Designation	Status	Observations
1940 (March)	MIKOYAN-GUREVICH	I-200 N°01	AM-35A	Prototype	Programme «Kh», MiG-1 prototype
1940 (May)	MIKOYAN-GUREVICH	I-200 N°02	AM-35A	Prototype	Programme «Kh», MiG-1 prototype
1940 (June)	MIKOYAN-GUREVICH	I-200 N°03	AM-35A	Prototype	Programme «Kh», MiG-1 prototype
1940 (autumn)	MIKOYAN-GUREVICH	MiG-1	AM-35A	Series	100 machines
1940 (December)	MIKOYAN-GUREVICH	MiG-3	AM-35A	Series (production series)	After the 100th machine of the «Kh»/I-200 programme 3 119 built
1940 (end of year)	MIKOYAN-GUREVICH	I-200 N°2	AM-37	Prototype	I-200 N°2 refitted with an AM-37
1941 (May)	MIKOYAN-GUREVICH	MiG-3/AM-37 («Object 72», Mig-7)	AM-37	Prototype	
1941 (July)	MIKOYAN-GUREVICH	MiG-3/AM-38	AM-38	Conversions	18 conversions for an unknown period
1941 (July)	MIKOYAN-GUREVICH	Reconnaissance MiG-3	AM-35A	5 prototypes	
1941 (November)	MIKOYAN-GUREVICH	I-210 (MiG-3/M-82A, MiG-9)	M-82A	Five prototypes	«IKh» programme
During 1941	MIKOYAN-GUREVICH	«Object KhS» (Pressurised MiG-3)	AM-35A (?)	Project	Included pressurisation
During 1941	MIKOYAN-GUREVICH	MiG-3 SPB	AM-35A	Project	For Vakhmistrov's «Zveno» programme with a Pe-8 as mother-plane
1942 (beginning)	MIKOYAN-GUREVICH	I-210 (MiG-9)	M-82A	Pre-production series	10 built
1942 (August)	MIKOYAN-GUREVICH	I-230 (MiG-3U or D)	AM-35A	Prototype	
1943 (summer)	MIKOYAN-GUREVICH	I-231 (MiG-3DD or «2D»)	AM-39	Prototype	
1943 (June)	MIKOYAN-GUREVICH	I-220 N°01 (MIG-11)	AM-38F (then AM-39)	Prototype	High Altitudes
1943 (July)	MIKOYAN-GUREVICH	I-220 N°02 (MIG-11)	AM-39 (then AM-37)	Prototype	High Altitudes
1943 (August)	MIKOYAN-GUREVICH	I-211 (Ye) (MiG-9)	M-82F	Two prototypes	
1943 (August)	MIKOYAN-GUREVICH	I-211 (Ye) (MiG-9)	M-82F	Pre-production series	8 built
1943 (September)	MIKOYAN-GUREVICH	MiG-3	Six-blade propeller	AM-35A	Prototype
1943 (December)	MIKOYAN-GUREVICH	I-221 («2A» or MiG-7)	AM-39A/2TK-2B	Prototype	
During 1943	MIKOYAN-GUREVICH	«Light-weight» MiG-3	AM-35	Two prototypes	NII VVS programme
During 1943	MIKOYAN-GUREVICH	I-230 (MiG-3U or D)	AM-35A	Pre-production series	4 or 5 built according to the sources
1944 (March)	MIKOYAN-GUREVICH	«N»	VK-107R + VRDK	Preliminary study	Mixed Propulsion
1944 (April)	MIKOYAN-GUREVICH	I-222 («3A» or MiG-7)	AM-439B-1/TK-300B	Prototype	
1944 (April)	MIKOYAN-GUREVICH	I-240	AM-43	Project	doubts about its existence
1944 (June)	MIKOYAN-GUREVICH	I-225 N°01 («5A»)	AM-42B/TK-300B	Prototype	
1944 (September)	MIKOYAN-GUREVICH	I-224 (Mig-7)	AM-39B-1/TK-300B	Prototype	
1945 (February)	MIKOYAN-GUREVICH	I-250 (N-1)	VK-107R + VRDK	Prototype	Mixed propulsion units
1945 (March)	MIKOYAN-GUREVICH	I-225 N°02 («5A»)	AM-FB/TK-300B	Prototype	Mixed power plants
1945 (May)	MIKOYAN-GUREVICH	I-250 (N-2)	VK-107R + VRDK	Prototype	Mixed power plants
1945 (June)	MIKOYAN-GUREVICH	I-250 (N) or MiG-13	VK-107R + VRDK	10 pre-prod. machines built	Mixed power plants
1946 (end)	MIKOYAN-GUREVICH	MiG-13 (I-250)	VK-107R + VRDK	16 built	Mixed propulsion units - 50 built depending on the sources

POLIKARPOV

1939 (summer-autumn)	POLIKARPOV	"K"/I-200 (Object 61)	AM-35-2TK-1	Preliminary study	Taken up by MiG: Project "Kh"/I-200 = MiG-1 and MiG-3
1939 (summer-autumn)	POLIKARPOV	"K"/I-200 (Object 63)	AM-35-2TK-1	Preliminary study	Taken up by MiG: Project "Kh"/I-200 = MiG-1 and MiG-3
1940 (January-March)	POLIKARPPOV	I-185/M-90 ("Object 62")	M-90	Unfinished prototype	Wind tunnel models and airframe without engine
1940 (January-March)	POLIKARPOV	DIT-85	M-90	Project	Two-seat project (training)
During 1940	POLIKARPOV	ITP (1)	M-105P	Preliminary study	
During 1940	POLIKARPOV	ITP (2)	AM-37P	Preliminary study	
1941 (January)	POLIKARPOV	I-185/M-81 ("RM", 02)	M-81	Prototype	Former I-185/M-90 airframe with a different engine
1941 (April)	POLIKARPOV	I-185/M-71 (01)	M-71	Prototype	ex-I-185/M-81 with different engine
1941 (May)	POLIKARPOV	ITP (M-1)	M-107P, then PA	Prototype	
1941 (July)	POLIKARPOV	I-185/M-82A	M-82A	Prototype	Second airframe of Programme I-185
1941 (September)	POLIKARPOV	I-185/M-71 (2)	M-71	Prototype	Third airframe
1942 (June)	POLIKARPOV	I-186 (I-185/M-71 "standard")	M-71 P	prototype	
1942 (November)	POLIKARPOV	ITP-M-2	AM-37 then AM-39A	Prototype	Fitted with another engine
1943 (February)	POLIKARPOV	I-187/M-71	M-71	Project	
1943 (February)	POLIKARPOV	I-187/M-71F	M-71F	Project	
1943 (February)	POLIKARPOV	I-187/M-90	M-90	Project	
1943 (February)	POLIKARPOV	I-187/M-95	M-95	Project	
1943 (March)	POLIKARPOV	VP (K)	AM-39A-TK-300B	Study	
1943 (end of the year)	POLIKARPOV	I-185/VP	M-71-TK-3	Study	
1943 (end of the year)	POLIKARPOV	I-185/VP	AM-39B-TK-300B	Study	
1943 (end of the year)	POLIKARPOV	Without any designation	?	Study	Twin-boom, pusher engine
During 1943	POLIKARPOV	I-185 Mixed power plants	(M-82 A +)	Two studies	Mixed propulsion units (pulse-jet, VRDK or turbojet?)

SUKHOI

1939 (March)	SUKHOI	I-135/M-105P-2TK-2	M-105P-2TK-2	Preliminary study	With two superchargers
1939 (July)	SUKHOI	I-135/M-105P-2TK-2	M-105P-2TK-2	Preliminary study	With two superchargers
1939 (October)	SUKHOI	Bell P-39 Type	M-120UV	Preliminary study	Without designation, engine in the centre of fuselage
1939 (October)	SUKHOI	Pressurised Bell P-39 Type	M-120UV	Preliminary study	With pressurisation system
1940 (May)	SUKHOI	I-135.1 (Su-1, I-330)	M-105P-2TK-2	Prototype	
1940 (July)	SUKHOI	I-135/M-90-2TK-2	M-90-2TK-2	Preliminary study	
1940 (July)	SUKHOI	I-135/M-120-2TK-2	M-120-2TK-2	Preliminary study	
1942 (February)	SUKHOI	Without designation	M-71	Unfinished prototype	Based on the Su-6/M-71F ground attack plane
1942 (May)	SUKHOI	I-135.2 (Su-3, I-360)	M-105P-2TK-2	Prototype	
1942 (end of the year)	SUKHOI	Su-7	M-71F-2TK-3	Prototype	
1943 (February)	SUKHOI	Su-6GK	M-71-ZTK-3	Preliminary project	Based on the Su-6 pressurised for high altitudes
1944 (February)	SUKHOI	Without any designation	M-107 + VRDK	Preliminary study	Mixed power plants
1944 (March)	SUKHOI	Su-5 (I-107)	VK-107A + VRDK	Preliminary Study	Mixed power plants
1944 (July)	SUKHOI	Without any designation	?	Study	With pressurisation for high altitudes
1944 (end of the year)	SUKHOI	Su-7R	M-82 FNV + RD-1KhZ	Prototype	Ex-Su-7 with M-82FN engine with a rocket-motor as well (mixed propulsion)
1945 (April)	SUKHOI	Su-5 N°1 (I-107)	VK-107R + VRDK	Prototype	Mixed power units
During 1945	SUKHOI	Su-5 N°2 (I-107)	VK-107A + VRDK	Prototype	Mixed propulsion units, for wind tunnel testing

YAKOVLEV

YEAR (month or period)	Makers	Engine	Designation	Status	Observations
1939 (December)	YAKOVLEV	I.26.1	M-105P	Prototype	1st Prototype Yak-1 series
1940 (March)	YAKOVLEV	I-26 (Yak-1)	M-105P	Pre-production series	11 examples built
1940 (April)	YAKOVLEV	I.26.1	M-105P	Prototype	2nd Prototype Yak-1 series
1940 (June)	YAKOVLEV	UTI-26.1	M-105P	Prototype	Two-seat trainer
1940 (July)	YAKOVLEV	I-28 ("1941 Yak-5, I-26V, I-28V)	M-105PD	Prototype	High altitude
1940 (September)	YAKOVLEV	UTI-26.2	M-105P	Prototype	Two-seat trainer. Modified for mixed power plant trials
1940 (September)	YAKOVLEV	I-26.3	M-105P	3rd Prototype	Yak-1 series
1940 (September)	YAKOVLEV	Yak-1/M-105P	M-105P	Production Series	
1941 (April)	YAKOVLEV	Yak-7UTI	M-105PA	Production series	186 with retractable undercarriage
1941 (April)	YAKOVLEV	I-30.1 (1941 Yak-3, I-26U)	M-105PD, then P, then PF	Prototype	
1941 (May)	YAKOVLEV	I-30.2 "Double" (1941 Yak-3)	M-105PD, then P	prototype	
1941 (August)	YAKOVLEV	Yak-7R (Yak-7UTI)	M-105P	Two prototypes	2 Yak-7UTIs transformed for photographic reconnaissance
1941 (September)	YAKOVLEV	Yak-7/M-105P	M-105P	Series	63 machines including prototype
1941 (September)	YAKOVLEV	Yak-7/M-105PA	M-105PA	Prototype	
1941 (November)	YAKOVLEV	Yak-7/M-105PA	M-105PA	Series	From 36th production batch
1941 (November)	YAKOVLEV	Yak-1/M-105PA "Winter Version"	M-105PA	Series	830 machines with skis
1941 (autumn)	YAKOVLEV	Yak-1/M-105PA	M-105PA	Series	
1941 (December)	YAKOVLEV	Yak-7/M-82A	M-82A	Prototype	
1942 (beginning)	YAKOVLEV	UTI-26PVRD (UTI-26.2/2DM-4S)	M-105P + two DM-4S	Prototype	UTI-26.2 Prototype with two DM-4S ramjets (also referred to as UTI-26.2/2DM-4S)
1942 (January)	YAKOVLEV	Yak-7A	M-105PA	Series 2	77 built
1942 (February)	YAKOVLEV	Yak-7V/M-105PA-2	M-105PA	Series	510 built with fixed undercarriage (M-105PA and PF engines)
1942 (March)	YAKOVLEV	"Light-weight" Yak-1/M*105PA	M-105PA	10 prototypes	
1942 (April)	YAKOVLEV	Yak-7B/M-105PA	M-105PA	Series	261 built
1942 (April)	YAKOVLEV	Yak-7-37	M-105PA	Prototype	Based on Yak-7 with axial 37-mm canon
1942 (May)	YAKOVLEV	Yak-7/M-105PF	M-105PF	Prototype	Prototype of the Yak-7B series
1942 (June)	YAKOVLEV	Yak-7D	M-105PA	Prototype	Fighter and long-range reconnaissance, Yak-9 forerunner, used for production of Yak-7DI prototype
1942 (June)	YAKOVLEV	Yak-7D	M-105PF	Prototype	Fighter and long-range reconnaissance Prototype for the Yak-9 family
1942 (July)	YAKOVLEV	Yak-1/M-105PF	M-105PF	Series	
1942 (July)	YAKOVLEV	Yak-1 "19-47" and "35-60" (Yak-1b	M-105PA	Prototype	Prototypes of the Yak-1b version
1942 (August)	YAKOVLEV	Yak-7-37	M-105PA	Short-run	Based on Yak-7 with 37-mm axial canon 212 built
1942 (August)	YAKOVLEV	Yak-7B (and Yak-7B/MPVO)	M-105PF	Series	5 120 built (including Yak-7B/MPVO With the rear fuselage frames cut down)
1942 (August)	YAKOVLEV	Yak-7R (Yak-7R/2DM-4S/D-1A)	2 x DM-4S + D-1A	Project	No standard engine but two ramjets and one rocket-motor
1942 (September)	YAKOVLEV	Yak-1b/M-105PF	M-105PF	Series	3 803 built
1942 (September)	YAKOVLEV	"Light-weight" Yak-2/M-105PF	M-105PF	20 prototypes	
1942 (September)	YAKOVLEV	Yak-7PD	M-105PD	Prototype	Plus 10 ordered for evaluation but not built
1942 (October)	YAKOVLEV	Yak-9	M-105PF	Series	459 built
1942 (October)	YAKOVLEV	Yak-9/M-106-1sk	M-106-1sk	Prototype	
1942 (December)	YAKOVLEV	Yak-1/M-106-1sk	M-106-1sk	Two prototypes	Serial N°50-85 and 1-111
1943 (and during 1944)	YAKOVLEV	Yak-1b/MPVO (Yak-1/M-105/MPVO)	M-105PF	Series	385 built for the PVO defence units
During 1943	YAKOVLEV	Yak-7V/M-105PF	M-105PF	Series	See Yak-7V/M-105PA
1943 (January)	YAKOVLEV	Yak-9/M-107A	M-107A	Prototype	
1943 (January)	YAKOVLEV	Yak-9T (Yak-9-37)	M-105PF	Series	2 748 built with 37-mm axial canon
1943 (January)	YAKOVLEV	Yak-9D	M-105PF	Series	3 058 built for long-range escort
1943 (January)	YAKOVLEV	Yak-2/M-106-1sk	M-106-1sk	Prototype	3rd prototype (serial N° 32-99)
1943 (February)	YAKOVLEV	Yak-1/M-106-1sk	M-106-1sk	Short run	47 built but only 19 accepted by the VVS
1943 (February)	YAKOVLEV	Yak-9VRDK	M-105REN + VRDK	Mixed propulsion project	
1943 (February)	YAKOVLEV	Yak-1M/M-106-1sk	M-106-1sk	Prototype	1st prototype for Yak-3 series
1943 (March)	YAKOVLEV	Yak-1/m-105PF	M-105PF	Prototype	Yak-3/M-106-1sk prototype refitted with an M-105PF
1943 (April)	YAKOVLEV	Yak-9PD/M-105PD	M-105PD	Five prototypes	Based on Yak-9D
1943 (April)	YAKOVLEV	Yak-9P	M-105PF	Prototype	First use of this designation
1943 (August)	YAKOVLEV	Yak-9PV/M-106PV (Yak-9/M-106PV)	M-105PD then 105PV	Prototype	Yak-9PD with another engine
1943 (September)	YAKOVLEV	Yak-1M/M-105 PF-2 "Double"	M-105PF	Prototype	2nd prototype Yak-3 version
1943 (September)	YAKOVLEV	Yak-9R (based on Yak-9)	M-105PF	Prototype	Fighter and reconnaissance, numerous conversions (no figures available) based on Yak-9
1943 (September)	YAKOVLEV	Yak-9R (based on Yak-9D)	M-105PF	Short run	Fighter and reco. - 35 built (officially) based on Yak-9D
1943 (October)	YAKOVLEV	Yak-9TK	M-105PF	Prototype	Basis for on Yak-9T
1943 (October)	YAKOVLEV	Yak-7B/M-105PF (Yak-7R)	M-105PF	Series	350 built for photographic reconnaissance
1943 (November)	YAKOVLEV	Yak-9U/M-105PF-2	M-105PF-2	Prototype	1944-model Yak-9
1943 (December)	YAKOVLEV	Yak-9U/M-107A	M-107A	Prototype	
During 1943	YAKOVLEV	Yak-7GK (1st serial N° 08-05)	M-105PF	Prototype	Yak-7B base with rear decking
During 1943	YAKOVLEV	Yak-7B/M-105PF Fuselage section frame reduced	M-105PF	Series	Rear decking cut down, all-round visibility canopy
During 1943	YAKOVLEV	Yak-1M/M-107A	M-107A	Prototype	Yak-1M/M-105PF with another engine
1944 (January)	YAKOVLEV	YAK-9K (Yak-9-45)	M-105PF	Short-run	54 built with 45-mm axial canon
1944 (January)	YAKOVLEV	Yak-3/VK-107A and "Double"	K-107A	Two prototypes	
1944 (March)	YAKOVLEV	Yak-7PVRD (Yak-7B/2DM-4S)	M-105PF + 2 x DM-4S	Prototype	A Yak-7B/M-105PF with rear decking fitted With 2 DM-4S ramjets
1944 (March)	YAKOVLEV	Yak-9B (Yak-9L)	VK-105PF	Series	109 built with bomb bay
1944 (March)	YAKOVLEV	Yak-3/VK-105PF	VK-105PF	Short run	51 built
1944 (April)	YAKOVLEV	Yak-9U/VK-105PF-2	VK-105PF-2	Short run	The first Yak-9U of the programme with VK-107A were equipped with VK-105PF-2s
1944 (April)	YAKOVLEV	Yak-9U/VK-107A	VK-107A	Series	3 941 built (including those with M-105PF-2 engines)
1944 (April)	YAKOVLEV	Yak-3PD/M-105PV	VK-105PV	Preliminary study	
1944 (April)	YAKOVLEV	Yak-9PD/M-106PV (Yak-9PV)	M-106PV	Prototype	
1944 (April)	YAKOVLEV	Yak-9PD/M-105PV (Yak-9PV)	M-106PV	Short run	30 built, based on Yak-9U
1944 (April)	YAKOVLEV	Yak-9DD (or Yak-9Yu)	VK-105PF	Series	399 built for long-range escort
1944 (May)	YAKOVLEV	YAK-9M/VK-105PF (and PVO)	VK-105PF	Series	4 239 built with a VK-105PF and PF-2, including PVO versions (but number unknown)
1944 (May)	YAKOVLEV	Yak-3/VK-105PF-2	VK-105PF-2	Series	4 797 built (including the various prototypes and versions)
1944 (July)	YAKOVLEV	Yak-9/VK-105PF-2 "Kourierski"	VK-105PF-2	Prototype	VIP liaisons
1944 (August)	YAKOVLEV	Yak-7L	M-105PF	Prototype	Laminar wing

YEAR (month or period)	Makers	Engine	Designation	Status	Observations
1944 (September)	YAKOVLEV	Yak-3PD/M-105PV, or Yaak-3PV	VK-105PV	Prototype	High altitude
1944 (October)	YAKOVLEV	Yak-9M/VK-105PF-2 (and PVO)	VK-105PF-2	Series	See Yak-9M/VK-105PF
1944 (October)	YAKOVLEV	Yak-3/VK-108 (1st prototype)	VK-108	Prototype	1st prototype
1944 (December)	YAKOVLEV	Yak-3RD	VK-105PF-2 + RD-1KhZ	Prototype	Mixed power plants
During 1944	YAKOVLEV	Yak-7GK (2nd)	M-105PF	Prototype	Based on Yak-7B with rear decking
1945 (January)	YAKOVLEV	Yak-3/VK-107A and "Double"	VK-107A	Two prototypes	N°01 and the "Double"
1945 (January)	YAKOVLEV	Yak-3PD/VK-105PD	VK-105PD	Prototype	High altitude
1945 (January)	YAKOVLEV	Yak-3T (or Yak-T-37)	VK-105PF-2	Prototype	Anti-tank Fighter with a 37-mm axial canon
1945 (January)	YAKOVLEV	Yak-3K (or Yak-3K/T-45)	VK-105PF-2	Prototype	Yak-3T tested with a 45-mm axial canon from doubtful source
1945 (February)	YAKOVLEV	Yak-9UT	VK-107A	Series	282 built 23-mm (37-mm on prototype) axial canon
1945 (March)	YAKOVLEV	Yak-3P	VK-105P	Series	596 built
1945 (April)	YAKOVLEV	"All-metal" Yak-3/VK-107A	VK-107A	Short run	Factory N°31 One prototype and 48 machines built between 1945 and 1946
1945 (April)	YAKOVLEV	Yak-3U	ASh-82FN	Prototype	Forerunner of the Yak-U, or Yak-11
1945 (August)	YAKOVLEV	Yak-9V	VK-105PF-2	Series	416 built + 377 conversions of Yak-9M into Yak-9V
1945 (May)	YAKOVLEV	Yak-9S	VK-105PF	Two prototypes	
1945 (June)	YAKOVLEV	Yak-3PD/VK-105PV or Yak-3PV	VK-105PV	Prototype	Ex-Yak-3PD/VK-105PD fitted with another engine
1945 (June)	YAKOVLEV	Yak-9UV	VK-107A	Prototype	Training, liaison and reconnaissance two-seater
1945 (August)	YAKOVLEV	Yak-3/VK-108 (2nd Prototype)	VK-108	Prototype	2nd Prototype
1945 (October)	YAKOVLEV	Yak-Jumo (or Yak-3-Jumo, or Yak-15)	Jumo 004B	Prototype	Single turbojet, programme Yak-15 prototype
1945 (December)	YAKOVLEV	Yak-RD (or Yak-RD-10)	RD-10	Prototype	Single-turbojet - Prototype for the Yak-15
1945 (end of the year)	YAKOVLEV	Yak-3UTI (or Yak-UTI)	ASh-21	Prototype	Forerunner of the Yak-11
1946 (March)	YAKOVLEV	Yak-3/VK-107A with metal wings	VK-107A	Three prototypes	Factory N°292
1946 (June)	YAKOVLEV	Yak-9P/VK-107A with metal wings	VK-107A	Two prototypes	Serial N° 01-03 and 01-04
1946 (September)	YAKOVLEV	Yak-17-RD10 (or YakRD-10)	RD-10 prototype Single turbojet	Prototype	For the Yak-15 programme
1946 (October)	YAKOVLEV	Yak-9P/VK-107A with metal wings	VK-107A	Pre-production series	29 built with metal wings
1946 (October)	YAKOVLEV	"All-metal" Yak-9P/VK-107A	VK-107A	Series	772 built entirely made of metal of which 10 were from the pre-production series
1946 (autumn)	YAKOVLEV	Yak-11 (and C-11)	ASh-21	Series	3 859 built, plus 707 C-11s in Czechoslovakia
1947 (October)	YAKOVLEV	Yak-9P/VK-107A Serial N° 03-92	VK-107A	Prototype	With two extra wing tanks and new on-board equipment
During 1951	YAKOVLEV	Yak-11U (and C-11U)	ASh-21	Short run	With tricycle undercarriage, designated C-11U in Czechoslovakia

FROM ABRAMOVICH TO TsAGI

YEAR (month or period)	Makers	Engine	Designation	Status	Observations
1943 (March)	ABRAMOVICH	S-1VRDK-1	M-82 + VRDK	Study	Mixed power plant study without propeller
1944 (summer)	ABRAMOVICH (La)	La-5VRDK	? + VRDK	Study	Mixed propulsion units Study by Abramovich at the TsAGI
1939 (August)	BELAYEV	"EOI/PBI"	M-106	Project	With "PBI", twin-boom and twin-tail
1939 (summer)	BELAYEV	"370" (1st Programme)	M-105	Preliminary study	Engine and propeller in the centre of the fuselage
1941 (during the year)	BELAYEV	"370" (2nd programme)	M-105/2TK-2	Unfinished prototype (?)	Twin-boom and Twin-tail, could have been the "EOI/PBI"
1939 (September)	BISNOVAT (TsAGI)	IS-TsAGI	M-105	1st Project	
1940 (January)	BISNOVAT (TsAGI)	IS-TsAGI	M-105	2nd Project	
1940 (autumn)	BISNOVAT	SK-2	M-105	Prototype	With experimental SK-1 mention
1940 (autumn)	BOROVKOV-FLOROV	"Object N°10"	M-71 + a DM	Preliminary project	Biplane with a ramjet in the tail
1940 (autumn)	BOROVKOV-FLOROV	"Object N°10"	M-71 + two DMs	Preliminary project	Biplane with two ramjets in the tail
1940 (end of the year)	BOROVKOV-FLOROV	"D" (IS-207)	M-71 + two DM-12		Twin-boom and twin-tail project, pusher engine
1942 (beginning)	GORBUNOV	LaG-5	M-82A	Prototype	Based on LaGG-3
1942 (beginning)	GORBUNOV	"Light-weight" LaGG-3	M-105PF	Prototype	Two production batches, N°23 and N°42
1943 (April)	GORBUNOV	"G-43" or "Gorbunov-43" (LaGG-3)	M-105PF	Prototype	Based on LaGG-3
1943 (May)	GORBUNOV	"105-1"	M-105PF	Prototype	Basis for LaGG-3
1944 (February)	GORBUNOV	"105-2" or LaGG-3 "Double"	M-105PF-2	Prototype	Basis for LaGG-3
1940 (September)	GUDKOV	Gu-1	Gu-37UV	Project	Prototype in 1943
1941 (August)	GUDKOV	K-37 (LaGG-3K-37) or Gu-37	M-105P	Three prototypes	Based on LaGG-3 with 37-mm axial canon
1941 (September)	GUDKOV	Gu-82	M-82	Prototype (s)	Based on LaGG-3 A second prototype has been mentioned sometimes
1943 (June)	GUDKOV	Gu-1	AM-37UV	Prototype	With central engine
1943 (June)	GUDKOV	Gu-2	AM-37UV	Project	With central engine
1943 (April)	GUDKOV-LIULKA (Lavochkin)	LaGG-3RTD-1 or LaGG-3RD-1	M-105 + RDT-1	Project	With standard engine and turbojet
1943 (July)	ILYUSHIN	Il-2i (or Il-2iB)	AM-38F	Prototype	Based on two-seat Il-2M "Shturmovik"
1944 (May)	ILYUSHIN	Il-1 (or Il-AM-42)	AM-42	Prototype	Based on the Il-2 Shturmovik
1944 (December)	KOROLEV (Lavochkin)	La-5Vi	ASh-82FNV/2TK-3 + 3 x RD-1	Study	Mixed power plants
1944 (December)	KOROLEV (Lavochkin)	La-5Vi	ASh-82FNV/2TK-3 + 1 x RD-1	Study	Mixed power plants
1944 (December)	KOROLEV (Lavochkin)	La-5Vi	ASh-82FNV/2TK-3 + 1 x RD-3	Study	Mixed power plants
1939 (summer)	KOCHERIGIN	OKB-3 (OSh-3/M-81-2TK-2)	M-81-2TK-2	Preliminary Study	
During 1941	KOTCHERIGIN	Without designation	M-300	Study	
During 1941	KOTCHERIGIN	Without designation	M-105P	Study	
During 1941	KOTCHERIGIN	Without designation	M-107P	Study	
During 1943	KOTCHERIGIN	Without any designation	AM-30	High-altitude project	
During 1939 and until 1941	KOZLOV	"EI" or "EOI" M-107	Unfinished	Prototype	Programme started in 1939
1940 (end of the year)	MOJAROVSKI-VENEVIDOV	BCh-MV "Kombain"	AM-38	Project	With Archangelski (Ground-attack with interceptor possibilities), Yak-2 trials photo, system KABB
During 1939	PASHININ	I-21 (IP-21)	M-107	Preliminary Study	
1940 (May)	PASHININ	I-21 (IP-21)	M-105P	Prototype	
1940 (October)	PASHININ	I-21.2 (IP-21)	M-105P	Prototype	
1941 (January)	PASHININ	I-21.3 (IP-21)	M-105P	Prototype	
During 1943	PELENBERG (MiG)	Without any designation	? VTOL	Study	
During 1943	SUKHANOV	"Koltseplan"	M-82A	Study VTOL	
1944 (Spring)	SOKOLOV (MAI)	Without any designation		Study	Pilot accommodated lying down
1941 (December)	TOMASHEVICH	"110" ("Object 110", or I-110)	M-107P	Prototype	
1943 (October)	TsAGI	Without designation	AM-39F + VRDK	Two studies	

202

CHRONOLOGICAL LIST OF ALL AIRCRAFT

Year (month or period)	Makers	Designation	Engine	Status	Observations
1939 (spring)	RIJKOV-LAVOCHKIN-G-G	(I-22) (I-301)	M-105P	Preliminary study	With Rijkov, Project I-22 = the designation was never used
1939 (March)	SUKHOI	I-135/M-105P-2TK-2	M-105P-2TK-2	Preliminary study	With two superchargers
1939 (July)	SUKHOI	I-135/M-105P-2TK-2	M-105P-2TK-2	Preliminary study	With two superchargers
1939 (August)	BELAYEV	"EOI/PBI"	M-106	Project	With "PBI", twin-boom and twin-tail
1939 (summer)	KOCHERIGIN	OKB-3 (OSh-3/M-81-2TK-2)	M-81-2TK-2	Preliminary Study	
1939 (summer)	BELAYEV	"370" (1st Programme)	M-105	preliminary study	Engine and propeller in the centre of the fuselage
1939 (summer-autumn)	POLIKARPOV	"K"/I-200 (Object 61)	AM-35-2TK-1	Preliminary study	Taken up by MiG: Project "Kh"/I-200 = MiG-1 and MiG-3
1939 (summer-autumn)	POLIKARPOV	"K"/I-200 (Object 63)	AM-35-2TK-1	Preliminary study	Taken up by MiG: Project "Kh"/I-200 = MiG-1 and MiG-3
1939 (September)	BISNOVAT (TsAGI)	IS-TsAGI	M-105	1st Project	
1939 (October)	SUKHOI	Bell P-39 Type	M-120UV	Preliminary study	Without designation, engine in the centre of fuselage
1939 (October)	SUKHOI	Pressurised Bell P-39 Type	M-120UV	Preliminary study	With pressurisation system
1939 (December)	YAKOVLEV	I.26.1	M-105P	Prototype	1st Prototype - Yak-1 series
During 1939	PASHININ	I-21 (IP-21)	M-107	Preliminary Study	
1940 (January)	BISNOVAT (TsAGI)	IS-TsAGI	M-105	2nd Project	
1940 (January-March)	POLIKARPPOV	I-185/M-90 ("Object 62")	M-90	Unfinished prototype	Wind tunnel models and airframe without engine
1940 (January-March)	POLIKARPOV	DIT-85	M-90		Two-seat project (training)
1940 (March)	LAVOCHKIN-G-G	I-301 N°01 (LAGG-1)	M-105P	Prototype	With Gorbunov and Gudkov, re-designated LaGG-1
1940 (March)	YAKOVLEV	I-26 (Yak-1)	M-105P	Pre-production series	11 examples built
1940 (March)	MIKOYAN-GUREVICH	I-200 N°01	AM-35A	Prototype	Programme "Kh", MiG-1 prototype
1940 (April)	YAKOVLEV	I.26.1	M-105P	Prototype	2nd Prototype Yak-1 series
1940 (May)	SUKHOI	I-135.1 (Su-1, I-330)	M-105P-2TK-2	Prototype	
1940 (May)	PASHININ	I-21 (IP-21)	M-105P	Prototype	
1940 (May)	MIKOYAN-GUREVICH	I-200 N°02	AM-35A	Prototype	Programme "Kh", MiG-1 prototype
1940 (June)	MIKOYAN-GUREVICH	I-200 N°03	AM-35A	Prototype	Programme "Kh", MiG-1 prototype
1940 (June)	YAKOVLEV	UTI-26.1	M-105P	Prototype	Two-seat trainer
1940 (July)	YAKOVLEV	I-28 ("1941 Yak-5, I-26V, I-28V)	M-105PD	Prototype	High altitude
1940 (July)	SUKHOI	I-135/M-90-2TK-2	M-90-2TK-2	Preliminary study	
1940 (July)	SUKHOI	I-135/M-120-2TK-2	M-120-2TK-2	Preliminary study	
1940 (September)	YAKOVLEV	UTI-26.2	M-105P	Prototype	Two-seat trainer - Modified for mixed power plant trials
1940 (September)	YAKOVLEV	I-26.3	M-105P	3rd Prototype	Yak-1 series
1940 (September)	YAKOVLEV	Yak-1/M-105P	M-105P	Production Series	
1940 (September)	GUDKOV	Gu-1	Gu-37UV	Project	Prototype in 1943
1940 (October)	PASHININ	I-21.2 (IP-21)	M-105P	Prototype	
1940 (November)	LAVOCHKIN-G-G	I-301 N° 02 (LaGG-1)	M-105P	Prototype	With Gorbunov and Gudkov, re-designated LaGG-1
1940 (autumn)	BOROVKOV-FLOROV	"Object N°10"	M-71 + a DM	Preliminary project	Biplane with a ramjet in the tail
1940 (autumn)	BOROVKOV-FLOROV	"Object N°10"	M-71 + two DMs	Preliminary project	Biplane with two ramjets in the tail
1940 (autumn)	BISNOVET	SK-2	M-105	Prototype	With experimental SK-1 (reference)
1940 (autumn)	MIKOTAN-GUREVICH	MiG-1	AM-35A	Series	100 machines
1940 (December)	MIKOYAN-GUREVICH	MiG-3	AM-35A	Series (production series)	After the 100th machine of the "Kh"/1-200 programme - 3 119 built
1940 (December)	LAVOCHKIN-G-G	LaGG-3/M-105P "Type 31"	M-105P	Series	(6 528 built in 66 production batches, all versions included)
1940 (during)	POLIKARPOV	ITP (1)	M-105P	Preliminary study	
1940 (during)	POLIKARPOV	ITP (1)	M-378P	Preliminary study	
1940 (end of the year)	BOROVKOV-FLOROV	"D" (IS-207)	M-71 + two DM-12		Twin-boom and twin-tail project, pusher engine
1940 (end of the year)	MOJAROVSKI-VENEVIDOV	BCh-MV "Kombain"	AM-38	Project with Archangelski	(Ground-attack with interceptor possibilities), Yak-2 trials photo, system KABB
1940 (end of year)	MIKOYAN-GUREVICH	I-200 N°2	AM-37	Prototype	I-200 N°2 refitted with an AM-37
1941 (January)	PASHININ	I-21.3 (IP-21)	M-105P	Prototype	
1941 (January)	POLIKARPOV	I-185/M-81 ("RM", 02)	M-81	Prototype	former I-185/M-90 airframe with a different engine
1941 (April)	POLIKARPOV	I-185/M-71		Prototype	Ex-I-185/M-81 with different engine
1941 (April)	YAKOVLEV	Yak-7UTI	M-105PA	Production series	186 with retractable undercarriage

Year (month or period)	Makers	Designation	Engine	Status	Observations
1941 (April)	YAKOVLEV	I-30.1 (1941 Yak-3, I-26U)	M-105PD, then P, then PF	Prototype	
1941 (May)	YAKOVLEV	I-30.2 "Double" (1941 Yak-3)	M-105PD,	Then P prototype	
1941 (May)	POLIKARPOV	ITP (M-1)	M-107P, then PA	Prototype	
1941 (May)	MIKOYAN-GUREVICH	MiG-3/AM-37 ("Object 72", Mig-7)	AM-37	Prototype	
1941 (July)	MIKOYAN-GUREVICH	MiG-3/AM-38	AM-38	conversions	18 conversions for an unknown period
1941 (July)	POLIKARPOV	I-185/M-82A	M-82A	Prototype	Second airframe of Programme I-185
1941 (July)	MIKOYAN-GUREVICH	Reconnaissance MiG-3	AM-35A	5 prototypes	
1941 (August)	GUDKOV	K-37 (LaGG-3K-37) or Gu-37	M-105P	Three prototypes	Based on LaGG-3 with 37-mm axial canon
1941 (August)	YAKOVLEV	Yak-7R (Yak-7UTI)	M-105P	Two prototypes	Two Yak-7UTIs transformed for photographic reconnaissance
1941 (September)	GUDKOV	Gu-82	M-82	Prototype (s)	Based on LaGG-3 - A second prototype has been mentioned sometimes
1941 (September)	POLIKARPOV	I-185/M-71 (2)	M-71	Prototype	Third airframe
1941 (September)	YAKOVLEV	Yak-7/M-105P	M-105P	Series	63 machines including prototype
1941 (September)	YAKOVLEV	Yak-7/M-105PA	M-105PA	Prototype	
1941 (November)	YAKOVLEV	Yak-7/M-105PA	M-105PA	Series	From 36th production batch
1941 (November)	YAKOVLEV	Yak-1/M-105PA "Winter Version"	M-105PA	Series	830 machines with skis
1941 (November)	MIKOYAN-GUREVICH	I-210 (MiG-3/M-82A, MiG-9)	M-82A	Five prototypes	"IKh" programme
1941 (autumn)	YAKOVLEV	Yak-1/M-105PA	M-105PA	Series	
1941 (December)	TOMASHEVICH	"110" ("Object 110", or I-110)	M-107P	Prototype	
1941 (December)	LAVOCHKIN	LaGG-3/M-82 (or LaG-3/M-82)	M-82		Prototype - L-82 programme, Prototype first La-5 series
1941 (December)	YAKOVLEV	Yak-7/M-82A	M-82A	Prototype	
1941 (during the year)	BELAYEV	"370" (2nd programme)	M-105/2TK-2	Unfinished prototype (?)	Twin-boom and Twin-tail, could have been the "EOI/PBI"
During 1941	LAVOCHKIN-G-G	LaGG-3/M-105PA "Type 31"	M-105PA	Series	From the 4th to the 28th production batch
During 1941	KOTCHERIGIN	Without designation	M-300	Study	
During 1941	KOTCHERIGIN	Without designation	M-105P	Study	
During 1941	KOTCHERIGIN	Without designation	M-107P	Study	
During 1941	MIKOYAN-GUREVICH	"Object KhS" (Pressurised MiG-3)	AM-35A (?)	Project	Included pressurisation
During 1941	MIKOYAN-GUREVICH	MiG-3 SPB	AM-35A	Project	for Vakhmistrov's "Zveno" programme with a Pe-8 as mother-plane
1942 (beginning)	MIKOYAN-GUREVICH	I-210 (MiG-9)	M-82A	Pre-production series	10 built
1942 (beginning)	GORBUNOV	"Light-weight" LaGG-3	M-105PF	Prototype	Two production batches, N°23 and N°42
1942 (beginning)	GORBUNOV	LaG-5	M-82A	Prototype	Based on LaGG-3
1942 (beginning)	LAVOCHKIN	LaGG-3-37 (and N°34 batch)	M-105PF	Small series	of 20 machines with ShK-37 axial canon and Batch N°34 with NS-37 37-mm axial canon
1942 (beginning)	YAKOVLEV	UTI-26PVRD (UTI-26.2/2DM-4S)	M-105P + two DM-4S	Prototype	UTI-26.2 Prototype with two DM-4S ramjets (also referred to as UTI-26.2/2DM-4S)
1942 (January)	YAKOVLEV	Yak-7A	M-105PA	Series	277 built
1942 (February)	YAKOVLEV	Yak-7V/M-105PA	M-105PA	Series	510 built with fixed undercarriage (M-105PA and PF engines)
1942 (February)	LAVOCHKIN	"Sparka" (LaGG two-seater)	M-105P	Prototype	Built by Gorbunov according to the sources
1942 (February?)	LAVOCHKIN	LaGGG UTI (two-seater)	M-105P	1 or 2 prototypes	Training, conversion some doubt whether it existed
1942 (February)	SUKHOI	Without designation	M-71	Unfinished prototype	Based on the Su-6/M-71F ground attack plane
1942 (March)	YAKOVLEV	"Light-weight" Yak-1/M"105PA	M-105PA	10 prototypes	
1942 (April)	YAKOVLEV	Yak-7B/M-105PA	Series	261 built	
1942 (April)	YAKOVLEV	Yak-7-37	M-105PA	Prototype	Based on Yak-7 with axial 37-mm canon
1942 (May)	SUKHOI	I-135.2 (Su-3, I-360)	M-105P-2TK-2	Prototype	
1942 (May)	YAKOVLEV	Yak-7/M-105PF	M-105PF	Prototype	Prototype of the Yak-7B series
1942 (June)	LAVOCHKIN	LaGG-3/M-105PF "Type 31"	M-105PF	Series	From the 29th to the 66th Batch
1942 (June)	LAVOCHKIN	La-5 (LaG-5 or LaGG-5) "Type 37"	M-82A	Production Series	(Series)
1942 (June)	POLIKARPOV	I-186 (I-185/M-71 "standard")	M-71	Prototype	
1942 (June)	YAKOVLEV	Yak-7D	M-105PA	Prototype	Fighter and long-range reconnaissance, Yak-9 forerunner, used for production of Yak-7DI prototype
1942 (June)	YAKOVLEV	Yak-7D	M-105PF	Prototype	Fighter and long-range reco. Prototype for the Yak-9 family
1942 (July)	YAKOVLEV	Yak-1/M-105PF	M-105PF	Series	

Year (month or period)	Makers	Designation	Engine	Status	Observations
1942 (July)	YAKOVLEV	Yak-1 "19-47" and "35-60" (Yak-1b	M-105PA	Prototype	Prototypes of the Yak-1b version
1942 (August)	YAKOVLEV	Yak-7-37	M-105PA	Short-run	Based on Yak-7 with 37-mm axial canon 212 built
1942 (August)	YAKOVLEV	Yak-7B (and Yak-7B/MPVO)	M-105PF	Series	5 120 built (including Yak-7B/MPVO with the rear fuselage frames cut down)
1942 (August)	LAVOCHKIN	LaGG-3/2VRD (LaGG-3PVRD)	M-105PF + two VRD-1s	Prototype	Mixed power plants, with two ramjets
1942 (August)	MIKOYAN-GUREVICH	I-230 (MiG-3U of D)	AM-35A	Prototype	
1942 (August)	YAKOVLEV	Yak-7R (Yak-7R/2DM-4S/D-1A)	2 x DM-4S + D-1A	Project	No standard engine but two ramjets and one rocket-motor
1942 (September)	YAKOVLEV	Yak-1b/M-105PF	M-105PF	Series	3 803 built
1942 (September)	YAKOVLEV	"light-weight" Yak-2/M-105PF	M-105PF	20 prototypes	
1942 (September)	YAKOVLEV	Yak-7PD	M-105PD	Prototype	Plus 10 ordered for evaluation but not built
1942 (October)	YAKOVLEV	Yak-9	M-105PF	Series	459 built
1942 (October)	YAKOVLEV	Yak-9/M-106-1sk	M-106-1sk	Prototype	
1942 (November)	LAVOCHKIN	La-5F "Type 37"	M-82F	Series	
1942 (November)	POLIKARPOV	ITP-M-2	AM-37 then AM-39A	Prototype	Fitted with another engine
1942 (December)	LAVOCHKIN	(La-5FN)	M-82FN	Two prototypes	Without any specific designation, but La-5FN forerunners
1942 (December)	YAKOVLEV	Yak-1/M-106-1sk	M-106-1sk	Two prototypes	Serial N°50-85 and 1-111
1942 (end of the year)	LAVOCHKIN	La-5FNV	M-82FNV	Prototype	The M-82FNV was re-designated M-82FN for the series La-5FN forerunner
1942 (end of the year)	SUKHOI	Su-7	M-71F-2TK-3	Prototype	
1943 (and during 1944)	YAKOVLEV	Yak-1b/MPVO (Yak-1/M-105/MPVO)	M-105PF	Series	385 built for the PVO defence units
During 1943	YAKOVLEV	Yak-7V/M-105PF	M-105PF	Series	See yak-7V/M-105PA
1943 (January)	YAKOVLEV	Yak-9/M-107A	M-107A	Prototype	
1943 (January)	YAKOVLEV	Yak-9T (Yak-9-37)	M-105PF	Series	2 748 built with 37-mm axial canon
1943 (January)	YAKOVLEV	Yak-9D	M-105PF	Series	3 058 built for long-range escort
1943 (January)	YAKOVLEV	Yak-2/M-106-1sk	M-106-1sk	Prototype	3rd prototype (serial N° 32-99)
1943 (Jan. or Feb.)	SUKHOI	Without any designation	M-30B + two ramjets	Mixed prop. project	
1943 (February)	YAKOVLEV	Yak-1/M-106-1sk	M-106-1sk	Short run	47 built but only 19 accepted by the VVS
1943 (February)	YAKOVLEV	Yak-9VRDK	M-105REN + VRDK	Mixed prop. project	
1943 (February)	SUKHOI	Su-6GK	M-71-ZTK-3	Preliminary project	Based on the Su-6 pressurised for high altitudes
1943 (February)	POLIKARPOV	I-187/M-71	M-71	Project	
1943 (February)	POLIKARPOV	I-187/M-71F	M-71F	Project	
1943 (February)	POLIKARPOV	I-187/M-90	M-90	Project	
1943 (February)	POLIKARPOV	I-187/M-95	M-95	Project	
1943 (February)	YAKOVLEV	Yak-1M/M-106-1sk	M-106-1sk	Prototype	1st prototype for Yak-3 series
1943 (March)	YAKOVLEV	Yak-1/m-105PF	M-105PF	Prototype	Yak-3/M-106-1sk prototype refitted with an M-105PF
1943 (March)	LAVOCHKIN	La-5 "Double" "Type 39"	M-82FN	Prototype	La-5FN prototype
1943 (March)	ABRAMOVICH	S-1VRDK-1	M-82 + VRDK	Mixed power plant study	Without propeller
1943 (March)	POLIKARPOV	VP (K)	AM-39A-TK-300B	Unfinished prototype	
1943 (March)	POLIKARPOV	VP (K)	AM-39A-TK-300B	Study	
1943 (June)	GUDKOV	Gu-1	AM-37UV	Prototype	With central engine
1943 (June)	GUDKOV	Gu-2	AM-37UV	Project	With central engine
1943 (April)	GUDKOV-LIULKA (Lavochkin)	LaGG-3RTD-1 or LaGG-3RD-1	M-105 + RDT-1	Project	With standard engine and turbojet
1943 (April)	YAKOVLEV	Yak-9PD/M-105PD	M-105PD	Five prototypes	Based on Yak-9D
1943 (April)	YAKOVLEV	Yak-9P	M-105PF	Prototype	First use of this designation
1943 (April)	GORBUNOV	"G-43" or "Gorbunov-43" (LaGG-3)	M-105PF	Prototype	Based on LaGG-3
1943 (April)	LAVOCHKIN	La-5/M-71	M-71	Prototype	
1943 (May)	GORBUNOV	"105-1"	M-105PF	Prototype	Basis for LaGG-3
1943 (spring)	LAVOCHKIN	La-5FN "Type 39"	M-82FN	Series	Wing spars made of wood
1943 (summer)	MIKOYAN-GUREVICH	I-231 (MiG-3DD or "2D")	AM-39	Prototype	
1943 (summer)	LAVOCHKIN	La-5F/2TK-3 or La-5TK	M-82/2TK-3	Prototype	

Year (month or period)	Makers	Designation	Engine	Status	Observations
1943 (June)	MIKOYAN-GUREVICH	I-220 N°01 (MIG-11)	AM-38F (then AM-39)	Prototype	High Altitudes
1943 (July)	MIKOYAN-GUREVICH	I-220 N°02 (MIG-11)	AM-39 (then AM-37)	Prototype	High Altitudes
1943 (July)	ILYUSHIN	Il-2i (or Il-2iB)	AM-38F	Prototype	Based on two-seat Il-2M "Shturmovik"
1943 (August)	MIKOYAN-GUREVICH	I-211 (Ye) (MiG-9)	M-82F	Two prototypes	
1943 (August)	MIKOYAN-GUREVICH	I-211 (Ye) (MiG-9)	M-82F	Pre-production series	8 built
1943 (August)	LAVOCHKIN	La-5UTI (UTI-La-5, ULa-5)	M-82	Series	Two seat liaison, reconnaissance (UTI-La-5 and ULa-5 were conversion at the front)
1943 (August)	YAKOVLEV	Yak-9PV/M-106PV	M-105PD then 105PV	Prototype	Yak-9PD with another engine (Yak-9/M-106PV)
1943 (September)	YAKOVLEV	Yak-1M/M-105 PF-2 "Double"	M-105PF	Prototype	2nd prototype Yak-3 version
1943 (September)	YAKOVLEV	Yak-9R (based on Yak-9)	M-105PF	Prototype	Fighter and reconnaissance, numerous conversions (no figures available) based on Yak-9
1943 (September)	YAKOVLEV	Yak-9R (based on Yak-9D)	M-105PF	Short run	Fighter and reconnaissance - 35 built (officially), based on Yak-9D
1943 (September)	MIKOYAN-GUREVICH	MiG-3 Six-blade propeller	AM-35A	Prototype	
1943 (October)	YAKOVLEV	Yak-9TK	M-105PF	Prototype	Based on Yak-9T
1943 (October)	TsAGI	without designation	AM-39F + VRDK	Two studies	
1943 (October)	YAKOVLEV	Yak-7B/M-105PF (Yak-7R)	M-105PF	Series	350 built for photographic reconnaissance
1943 (November)	YAKOVLEV	Yak-9U/M-105PF-2	M-105PF-2	Prototype	1944-model Yak-9
1943 (Nov.-Dec.)	LAVOCHKIN	La-7 "206"	M-82FN	Prototype	Prototype forerunner of La-7
1943 (December)	YAKOVLEV	Yak-9U/M-107A	M-107A	Prototype	
1943 (December)	MIKOYAN-GUREVICH	I-221 ("2A" or MiG-7)	AM-39A/2TK-2B	Prototype	
During 1943	MIKOYAN-GUREVICH	"Light-weight" MiG-3	AM-35	Two prototypes	NII VVS programme
During 1943	YAKOVLEV	Yak-7GK (1st serial N° 08-05)	M-105PF	Prototype	Yak-7B base with rear decking
During 1943	YAKOVLEV	Yak-7B/M-105PF Fuselage section frame reduced	M-105PF	Series	Rear decking cut down, all-round visibility canopy
During 1943	POLIKARPOV	I-185	Mixed pwr plants (M-82 +)	Two studies	Mixed propulsion units (pulse-jet, VRDK or turbojet?)
During 1943	KOCHERIGIN	Without any designation	AM-30	High-altitude project	
During 1943	PELENBERG (MiG)	Without any designation	? VTOL	Study	
During 1943	SUKHANOV	"Koltseplan"	M-82A	Study	VTOL
During 1943	YAKOVLEV	Yak-1M/M-107A	M-107A	Prototype	Yak-1M/M-105PF with another engine
During 1943	MIKOYAN-GUREVICH	I-230 (MiG-3U or D)	AM-35A	Pre-production series	4 or 5 built according to the sources
1943 (end of the year)	POLIKARPOV	I-185/VP	M-71-TK-3	Study	
1943 (end of the year)	POLIKARPOV	I-185/VP	AM-39B-TK-300B	Study	
1943 (end of the year)	POLIKARPOV	Without any designation	?		Twin-boom, pusher engine
1944 (January)	LAVOCHKIN	"120 N°01" (La-1120 N°1)	Ash-82FN	Prototype	"1944 standard" La-5, La-7 prototype 1944 ()
1944 (January)	YAKOVLEV	YAK-9K (Yak-9-45)	M-105PF	Short-run	54 built with 45-mm axial canon
1944 (January)	YAKOVLEV	Yak-3/VK-107A and "Double"	VK-107A	Two prototypes	
1944 (February)	SUKHOI	Without any designation	M-107 + VRDK	Preliminary study	Mixed power plants
1944 (February)	GORBUNOV	"105-2" or LaGG-3 "Double"	M-105PF-2	Prototype	Based on LaGG-3
1944 (spring)	SOKOLOV (MAI)	Without any designation		Study	Pilot accommodated lying down
1944 (March)	MIKOYAN-GUREVICH "N"	VK-107R + VRDK		Preliminary study	Mixed Propulsion
1944 (March)	LAVOCHKIN	"120 N°2" (La-120 N°2)	Ash-82FN	Prototype	"1944-standard", La-7 prototype
1944 (March)	SUKHOI	Su-5 (I-107)	VK-107A + VRDK	Preliminary Study	Mixed power plants
1944 (March)	YAKOVLEV	Yak-7PVRD (Yak-7B/2DM-4S)	M-105PF + 2 x DM-4S	Prototype	A Yak-7B/M-105PF with rear decking fitted with two DM-4S ramjets
1944 (March)	YAKOVLEV	Yak-9B (Yak-9L)	VK-105PF	Series	109 built with bomb bay
1944 (March)	YAKOVLEV	Yak-3/VK-105PF	VK-105PF	Short run	51 built
1944 (April)	YAKOVLEV	Yak-9U/VK-105PF-2	VK-105PF-2	Short run	The first Yak-9U of the programme with VK-107A were equipped with VK-105PF-2s
1944 (April)	YAKOVLEV	Yak-9U/VK-107A	VK-107A	Series	3 941 built (including those with M-105PF-2 engines)
1944 (April)	YAKOVLEV	Yak-3PD/M-105PV	VK-105PV	Preliminary study	
1944 (April)	YAKOVLEV	Yak-9PD/M-106PV (Yak-9PV)	M-106PV	Prototype	
1944 (April)	YAKOVLEV	Yak-9PD/M-105PV (Yak-9PV)	M-106PV	Short run	30 built, based on Yak-9U
1944 (April)	YAKOVLEV	Yak-9DD (or Yak-9Yu)	VK-105PF	Series	399 built for long-range escort

Year (month or period)	Makers	Designation	Engine	Status	Observations
1944 (April)	MIKOYAN-GUREVICH	I-222 ("3A" or MiG-7)	AM-439B-1/TK-300B	Prototype	
1944 (April)	MIKOYAN-GUREVICH	I-240	AM-43	Project	Doubts about its existence
1944 (May)	YAKOVLEV	YAK-9M/VK-105PF (and PVO)	VK-105PF	Series	4 239 built with a VK-105PF and PF-2, including PVO versions (but number unknown)
1944 (May)	YAKOVLEV	Yak-3/VK-105PF-2	VK-105PF-2	Series	4 797 built (including the various prototypes and versions)
1944 (May)	ILYUSHIN	Il-1 (or Il-AM-42)	AM-42	Prototype	Based on the Il-2 Shturmovik
1944 (May)	LAVOCHKIN	"1944 Standard" La-5FN	M-82FN	Series	Wing spars made of metal
1944 (May)	LAVOCHKIN	La-7 (Type 45)	Ash-82FN	Series	6 158 built of which 368 with three B-20 cannon
1944 (June)	MIKOYAN-GUREVICH	I-225 N°01 ("5A")	AM-42B/TK-300B	Prototype	
1944 (July)	YAKOVLEV	Yak-9/VK-105PF-2 "Kourierski"	VK-105PF-2	Prototype	VIP liaisons
1944 (July)	SUKHOI	Without any designation		Study	With pressurisation for high altitudes
1944 (July)	LAVOCHKIN	La-7TK (La-7/ASh-82FN-2TK-3)	Ash-82FN/2TK-3	Prototype	
1944 (summer)	LAVOCHKIN	La-7TK (La-7/ASh-82FN-2TK-3)	Ash-82FN/2TK-3	Pre-production series	10 aircraft built
1944 (summer)	LAVOCHKIN	La-7TK (La-7/ASh-71FN-2TK-3)	Ash-71FN/2TK-3	Prototype	La-7/M-71 or La-7Ash-71 according to the sources
1944 (summer)	ABRAMOVICH (La)	La-5VRDK	? + VRDK	Study	Mixed propulsion units - Study by Abramovich at the TsAGI
1944 (August)	YAKOVLEV	Yak-7L	M-105PF	Prototype	Laminar wing
1944 (autumn)	LAVOCHKIN	La-7UTI (Type 46)	Ash-82FN	Prototype	Two-seat trainer, liaison and reconnaissance airraft
1944 (September)	MIKOYAN-GUREVICH	I-224 (Mig-7)	AM-39B-1/TK-300B	Prototype	
1944 (September)	YAKOVLEV	Yak-3PD/M-105PV, or Yaak-3PV	VK-105PV	Prototype	High altitude
1944 (October)	YAKOVLEV	Yak-9M/VK-105PF-2 (and PVO)	VK-105PF-2	Series	See Yak-9M/VK-105PF
1944 (October)	YAKOVLEV	Yak-3/VK-108 (1st prototype)	VK-108	Prototype	1st prototype
1944 (October)	LAVOCHKIN	La-7R-1	ASh-82FN + RD-1	Prototype	Mixed power plants
1944 (December)	LAVOCHKIN	La-7/ASh-83		Prototype	Ex-La-120 N°2
1944 (December)	YAKOVLEV	Yak-3RD	VK-105PF-2 + RD-1KhZ	Prototype	Mixed power plants
1944 (December)	KOROLEV (Lavochkin)	La-5Vi	ASh-82FNV/2TK-3 + 3 x RD-1	Study	Mixed power plants
1944 (December)	KOROLEV (Lavochkin)	La-5Vi	ASh-82FNV/2TK-3 + 1 x RD-1	Study	Mixed power plants
1944 (December)	KOROLEV (Lavochkin)	La-5Vi	ASh-82FNV/2TK-3 + 1 x RD-3	Study	Mixed power plants
During 1944	YAKOVLEV	Yak-7GK (2°)	M-105PF	Prototype	Based on Yak-7B with rear decking
1944 (end of the year)	LAVOCHKIN	La-7L	ASh-82FN	Prototype	Laminar wing
1944 (end of the year)	SUKHOI	Su-7R	M-82 FNV + RD-1KhZ	Prototype	Ex-Su-7 with M-82FN engine + a rocket-motor as well (mixed propulsion)
1944 (end of the year)	LAVOCHKIN	La-7 (with NS-23 cannon and UBS	ASh-82FH	Prototype	Weapons test bench: one NS-23 canon and one UBS-20 canon
1945 (beginning)	LAVOCHKIN	La-7/RD-2M-3V	M-82FN + RD-2M-3V	Project	Mixed power plants
1945 (January)	LAVOCHKIN	La-7R-2	ASh-FN + RD-1KhZ	Prototype	Mixed propulsion units
1945 (January)	YAKOVLEV	Yak-3/VK-107A and "Double"	VK-107A	Two prototypes	N°01 and the "Double"
1945 (January)	YAKOVLEV	Yak-3PD/VK-105PD	VK-105PD	Prototype	High altitude
1945 (January)	YAKOVLEV	Yak-3T (or Yak-T-37)	VK-105PF-2	Prototype	Anti-tank Fighter with a 37-mm axial canon
1945 (January)	YAKOVLEV	Yak-3K (or Yak-3K/T-45)	VK-105PF-2	Prototype	Yak-3T tested with a 45-mm axial canon from doubtful source
1945 (February)	YAKOVLEV	Yak-9UT	VK-107A	Series	282 built, 23-mm (37-mm on prototype) axial canon
1945 (February)	MIKOYAN-GUREVICH	I-250 (N-1)	VK-107R + VRDK	Prototype	Mixed propulsion units
1945 (March)	MIKOYAN-GUREVICH	I-225 N°02 ("5A")	AM-FB/TK-300B	Prototype	Mixed power plants
1945 (March)	YAKOVLEV	Yak-3P	VK-105P	Series	596 built
1945 (April)	SUKHOI	Su-5 N°1 (I-107)	VK-107R + VRDK	Prototype	Mixed power units
1945 (1945)	YAKOVLEV	"All-metal" Yak-3/VK-107A	VK-107A	Short run	Factory N°31. 1 prototype and 48 machines built between 1945-46
1945 (April)	YAKOVLEV	Yak-3U	ASh-82FN	Prototype	Forerunner of the Yak-U, or Yak-11
1945 (August)	YAKOVLEV	Yak-9V	VK-105PF-2	Series	416 built + 377 conversions of Yak-9M into Yak-9V
1945 (May)	YAKOVLEV	Yak-9S	VK-105PF	Two prototypes	
1945 (May)	MIKOYAN-GUREVICH	I-250 (N-2)	VK-107R + VRDK	Prototype	Mixed power plants
1945 (June)	MIKOYAN-GUREVICH	I-250 (N) or MiG-13	VK-107R + VRDK		10 pre-production series machines built Mixed power plants
1945 (June)	YAKOVLEV	Yak-3PD/VK-105PV or Yak-3PV	VK-105PV	Prototype	ex-Yak-3PD/VK-105PD fitted with another engine
1945 (June)	YAKOVLEV	Yak-9UV	VK-107A	Prototype	Training, liaison and reconnaissance two-seater
1945 (July)	LAVOCHKIN	"120R" (La-120R)	ASh-83 + RD-1KhZ	Prototype	One of the two La-120s with the RD-1KhZ rocket-motor

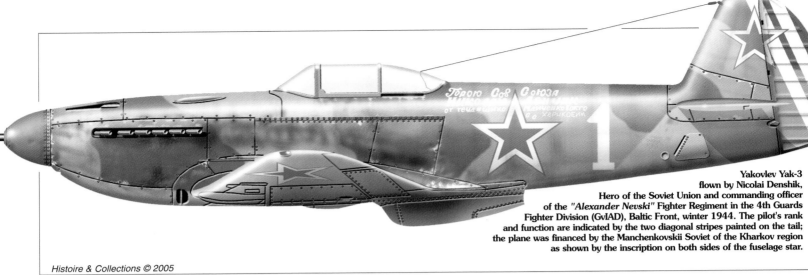

Yakovlev Yak-3
flown by Nicolai Denshik,
Hero of the Soviet Union and commanding officer
of the *"Alexander Nevski"* Fighter Regiment in the 4th Guards
Fighter Division (GvIAD), Baltic Front, winter 1944. The pilot's rank
and function are indicated by the two diagonal stripes painted on the tail;
the plane was financed by the Manchenkovskii Soviet of the Kharkov region
as shown by the inscription on both sides of the fuselage star.

Histoire & Collections © 2005

Year (month or period)	Makers	Designation	Engine	Status	Observations
1945 (August)	YAKOVLEV	Yak-3/VK-108 (2nd Prototype)	VK-108	Prototype	2nd Prototype
1945 (October)	YAKOVLEV	Yak-Jumo (or Yak-3-Jumo, or Yak-15)	Jumo 004B	Prototype	Single turbojet, programme Yak-15 prototype
1945 (November)	LAVOCHKIN	La-7PuVRD (or La-7PVRD)	ASh-82FN + two D-10s	Prototype	or La-7D-10 of La-7/2D-10 mixed propulsion units (Tchelomeyi pulse-jets)
1945 (December)	YAKOVLEV	Yak-RD (or Yak-RD-10)	RD-10	Prototype	Single-turbojet - Prototype for the Yak-15
1945 (end of the year)	LAVOCHKIN	"126", or La-126	ASh-82FN	Prototype	Forerunner of the La-9 programme
1945 (end of the year)	YAKOVLEV	Yak-3UTI (or Yak-UTI)	ASh-21	Prototype	Forerunner of the Yak-11
During 1945	SUKHOI	Su-5 N°2 (I-107)	VK-107A + VRDK	Prototype	Mixed propulsion units, for wind tunnel testing
1946 (January)	LAVOCHKIN	"130" (La-130)	ASh-82FN	Prototype P	Prototype for the La-9 version
1946 (March)	YAKOVLEV	Yak-3/VK-107A with metal wings	VK-107A	Three prototypes	Factory N°292
1946 (March)	LAVOCHKIN	"120" (PVRD), or La-120PRVD	ASh-82FN + VRD-430	Project	Project to modify the "120" prototype for mixed propulsion units
1946 (Spring)	LAVOCHKIN	La-7UTI (UTI-La-7)	ASh-82FN	Series	584 built
1946 (spring)	LAVOCHKIN	"130R" (La-130R)	ASh-83FN + RD-1KhZ	Unfinished prototype	Mixed power units
1946 (spring/summer)	LAVOCHKIN	La-7PPVRD	ASh-82FN + two D-12	Prototype	La-7 prototype with two D-12 pulse-jets
1946 (summer)	LAVOCHKIN	La-7UTI/PuVRD or La-7PuVRD	ASh-82FN + two D-10s	Three prototypes	With two Tchelomeyi D-10 pulse-jets
1946 (June)	LAVOCHKIN	La-126PVRD ("164" or La-7S)	Ash- + VRD-430	Prototype	La-126 prototype modified for mixed propulsion units
1946 (June)	YAKOVLEV	Yak-9P/VK-107A with metal wings	VK-107A	Two prototypes	Serial N° 01-03 and 01-04
1946 (August)	LAVOCHKIN	La69 "Type 48"	Ash-82FN	Production series	1569 built
1946 (September)	YAKOVLEV	Yak-17-RD10 (or YakRD-10)	RD-10 prototype	Single turbojet	Prototype for the Yak-15 programme
1946 (October)	YAKOVLEV	Yak-9P/VK-107A with metal wings	VK-107A	Pre-production series	29 built with metal wings
1946 (October)	YAKOVLEV	"All-metal" Yak-9P/VK-107A	VK-107A	Series	772 built entirely made of metal of which 10 were from the pre-prod. series
1946 (autumn)	YAKOVLEV	Yak-11 (and C-11)	Ash-21	Series	3 859 built, plus 707 C-11s in Czechoslovakia
During 1946	LAVOCHKIN	"132" (La-132)	ASh-82-FM	Prototype	La-9 production series prototype
During 1946	LAVOCHKIN	"132M" (La-132M)	ASh-82M	Project abandoned	
1946 (end)	MIKOYAN-GUREVICH	MiG-13 (I-250)	VK-107R + VRDK	16 built	Mixed propulsion units 50 built depending on the sources
1947 (January)	LAVOCHKIN	La-9V	ASh-82FN	Prototype	Two-seat trainer, reconnaissance
1947 (February)	LAVOCHKIN	"138" (La-138)	ASh-82FN + VRD-430		or La-130PVRD Mixed propulsion units
1947 (February)	LAVOCHKIN	"138D" (La-138D)	ASh-82FN + VRD-430	Prototype	or La-130PVRD Mixed propulsion units
1947 (April)	LAVOCHKIN	La-9UTI "Type 49" (and ULa-9?)	ASh-82FN	Series	265 built - Two seat trainer, reconnaissance (ULa-9 = conversion with " La-11" engine)
1947 (May)	LAVOCHKIN	"134" (La-134 or La-9M)	ASh-82FN	Prototype	La-11 prototype
1947 (June)	LAVOCHKIN	"134D" (La-134D)	ASh-82FN	Prototype	La-11 Prototype
1947 (July)	LAVOCHKIN	La-9RD (La-9PuVRD)	ASh-82FN + two D-13s	Prototype	or La-9/2D-13, mixed propulsion units
1947 (July-August)	LAVOCHKIN	La-9RD (La-9PuVRD)	ASh-82FN + two D-13	Short run	or La-9/2D-13. Mixed propulsion units (9 or 12 built depend. on the sources)
1947 (August)	LAVOCHKIN	La-11 "Type 51"	ASh-82FN	Series	1 232 built
1947 (October)	YAKOVLEV	Yak-9P/VK-107A Serial N° 03-92	VK-107A	Prototype	With two extra wing tanks and new on-board equipment
During 1950	LAVOCHKIN	La-11 - Photo reconnaissance	Ash-82FN	Conversions	100 examples converted
During 1951	YAKOVLEV	Yak-11U (and C-11U)	ASh-21	Short run	With tricycle undercarriage, designated C-11U in Czechoslovakia
During 1951	LAVOCHKIN	ULa-9	ASh-82FN	Conversions	Conversion of the La-9UTI with engine installed as in the La-11